Essays of an Americanist.

I. Ethnologic and Archaeologic.

II. Mythology and folk lore.

III. Graphic systems and literature.

IV. Linguistic

Daniel G. Brinton

Alpha Editions

This edition published in 2019

ISBN : 9789353974695

Design and Setting By
Alpha Editions
email - alphaedis@gmail.com

As per information held with us this book is in Public Domain.
This book is a reproduction of an important historical work. Alpha Editions uses the best technology to reproduce historical work in the same manner it was first published to preserve its original nature. Any marks or number seen are left intentionally to preserve its true form.

Essays of an Americanist.

I. Ethnologic and Archæologic.
II. Mythology and Folk Lore.
III. Graphic Systems and Literature.
IV. Linguistic.

BY

DANIEL G. BRINTON, A. M., M. D.,

PROFESSOR OF AMERICAN ARCHÆOLOGY AND LINGUISTICS IN THE UNIVERSITY OF PENNSYLVANIA, PRESIDENT OF THE NUMISMATIC AND ANTIQUARIAN SOCIETY OF PHILADELPHIA, PRESIDENT OF THE AMERICAN FOLK-LORE SOCIETY, MEMBER OF THE AMERICAN ANTIQUARIAN SOCIETY, THE AMERICAN PHILOSOPHICAL SOCIETY, THE SOCIÉTÈ ROYALE DES ANTIQUAIRES DU NORD, THE SOCIÉTÈ AMÉRICAINE DE FRANCE, THE BERLINER ANTHROPOLOGISCHE GESELLSCHAFT, THE REAL ACADEMIA DE HISTORIA, MADRID, ETC., ETC.

PHILADELPHIA:
PORTER & COATES.
1890.

PREFACE.

THE word "Essays" appears on the title of this book in the sense in which old Montaigne employed it—attempts, endeavors. The articles which make up the volume have been collected from many scattered sources, to which I have from time to time contributed them, for the definite purpose of endeavoring to vindicate certain opinions about debated subjects concerning the ancient population of the American continent.

In a number of points, as for example in the antiquity of man upon this continent, in the specific distinction of an American race, in the generic similarity of its languages, in recognizing its mythology as often abstract and symbolic, in the phonetic character of some of its graphic methods, in believing that its tribes possessed considerable poetic feeling, in maintaining the absolute autochthony of their culture—in these and in many other points referred to in the following pages I am at variance with most modern anthropologists; and these essays are to show more fully and connectedly than could their separate publication, what are my grounds for such opinions.

There is a prevailing tendency among ethnologists of to-day to underrate the psychology of savage life. This error arises partly from an unwillingness to go beyond merely physical investigations, partly from judging of the ancient condition of a tribe by that of its modern and degenerate representatives, partly from inability to speak its tongue and to gain the real sense of its expressions, partly from preconceived theories as to what a savage might be expected to know and feel. As against this error I have essayed to show that among very rude tribes we find sentiments of a high character, proving a mental nature of excellent capacity in certain directions.

Several of the Essays have not previously appeared in print, and others have been substantially re-written, so as to bring them up to the latest researches in their special fields. Nevertheless, the reader will find a certain amount of repetition in several of them, a defect which I hope is compensated by the greater clearness which this repetition gives to the special subject discussed.

Philadelphia, February, 1890.

CONTENTS.

	PAGE
PREFACE	iii, iv
TABLE OF CONTENTS	v-xii

PART I.

ETHNOLOGIC AND ARCHÆOLOGIC.

INTRODUCTORY 17–19

A REVIEW OF THE DATA FOR THE STUDY OF THE PRE-HISTORIC CHRONOLOGY OF AMERICA 20–47
Classification of Data. I. *Legendary:* of northern tribes; of Peruvians, Mexicans and Mayas; limited range. II. *Monumental:* pueblos of New Mexico; stone and brick structures of Mexico, Central America and Peru; ruins of Tiahuanaco; artificial shell heaps; the *sambaquis* of Brazil. III. *Industrial:* palæolithic implements; early polished stone implements; dissemination of cultivated food plants. IV. *Linguistic:* multitude and extension of linguistic stocks; tenacity of linguistic form; similarities of internal form; study of internal form. V. *Physical:* racial classifications; traits of the American type; permanence of the type. VI. *Geologic:* date of the glacial epochs in North and South America; the earliest Americans immigrants; lines of migrations. Importance of archæological studies.

CONTENTS.

ON PALÆOLITHS, AMERICAN AND OTHER 48–55

The cutting instrument as the standard of culture; the three "Ages" of Stone, Bronze and Iron; subdivisions of the Age of Stone into Palæolithic and Neolithic; a true "Palæolith"; subdivision of the Palæolithic period into the epochs of "simple" and "compound" implements; palæolithic finds along the Delaware river; the glacial period in America; earliest appearance of man in America.

ON THE ALLEGED MONGOLIAN AFFINITIES OF THE AMERICAN RACE 56–66

A practical question; Cuvier's triple division of the human species; alleged Mongolian affinities in language; supposed affinities in culture; imagined physical resemblances, as color, cranial analogies, the oblique or "Mongoloid" eye, etc. Insufficiency of all these.

THE PROBABLE NATIONALITY OF THE "MOUND-BUILDERS." . 67–82

Who were the "Mound-builders"? Known tribes as constructors of mounds, the Iroquois, Algonkins, Cherokees and Chahta-Muskoki family. Descriptions from De Soto's expedition; from Huguenots in Florida; from French writers on Louisiana; great size of the southern mounds; probable builders of Ohio mounds.

THE TOLTECS AND THEIR FABULOUS EMPIRE 83–100

Statement of the question; the current opinion; the adverse opinion; Tula as an historic site; the Serpent-Hill; the Aztec legends about Tula; date of the desertion of Tula; meaning of the name Tula or Tollan; the mythical cyclus of Tula; birth of Huitzilopochtli; myth of Quetzalcoatl at Tula; his subjects, the Toltecs; purely fabulous narratives concerning them.

CONTENTS. vii

PART II.

MYTHOLOGY AND FOLK-LORE.

INTRODUCTORY 101–103

THE SACRED NAMES IN QUICHE MYTHOLOGY 104–129
The Quiches of Guatemala, and their relationship; sources of information. Their Sacred Book, the *Popul Vuh;* its opening words; The name Hun-Ahpu-Vuch, the God of Light; Hun-Ahpu-Utiu; Nim-ak, the Great Hog; Nim-tzyiz; Tepeu; Gucumatz; Qux-cho and Qux-palo; Ah-raxa-lak and Ah-raxa-sel; Xpiyacoc and Xmucane, the primal pair; Cakulha; Huracan and Cabrakan; Chirakan, the god of the Storm and the Earthquake; Xbalanque and his journey to Xibalba, or the Descent into Hell.

THE HERO-GOD OF THE ALGONKINS AS A CHEAT AND LIAR . 130–134
Micmac story of Gluskap, the Liar; the Cree god, the Deceiver; Michabo and his tricks; psychological significance of such stories.

THE JOURNEY OF THE SOUL 135–147
General belief in a soul; Egyptian theory of its fate; it sinks and rises with the sun; invocation to Osiris; symbols of the river, the boat, the dog, and the sacred numbers; recurrence of these symbols in Greek, Vedantic and Norse beliefs; the Aztec account of the soul's journey to Paradise. Origin of these symbolic narratives from the apparent daily course of the Sun.

THE SACRED SYMBOLS IN AMERICA 148–162
The four symbols of the Ta Ki, the Triskeles, the Svastika and the Cross; the prevalence of the Triskeles in the Old World; the meaning of the Ta Ki in Chinese philosophy; the Yin and Yang; the Svastika; origin illustrated from

American picture-writing; the Copan stone; the earth-plain; the wheel-cross; winter-counts and year cycles; time-wheels and sun-motions; the Four Ages and Tree of Life.

THE FOLK-LORE OF YUCATAN 163–180

Mental activity of the Mayas; the diviners; the "field mass"; invocation to the rain-gods; fire-worship; prognostics; transformations of sorcerers; nagualism; a Maya witch story; the Balams; the Man of the Woods; stories of dwarfs and imps; female deceivers; fabulous birds and snakes.

FOLK-LORE OF THE MODERN LENAPE 181–192

Source of information; reminiscences of the tribe; Messianic hopes; relics of the Stone Age; methods of hunting and fishing; utensils, boats and houses; the native games; the sweat-lodge; their canticos, and the derivation of the term; medical knowledge; cure for rattlesnake bites; native trephining; position of the Lenâpé as "grandfathers"; wampum belts; totemic divisions; peculiarities of the dialect; Lenâpé grammar.

PART III.

GRAPHIC SYSTEMS AND LITERATURE.

INTRODUCTORY 193–194

THE PHONETIC ELEMENTS IN THE GRAPHIC SYSTEMS OF THE
    MAYAS AND MEXICANS 195–212

Material for the study; were the native hieroglyphs phonetic? Character and arrangement of phonetic symbols; the failure of Landa's alphabet; phonetic signs in Maya MSS.; hieroglyph of the firmament; phonetic terminals; signs of cardinal points; Mexican phonetic elements; principle of the rebus; examples; the ikonomatic system.

CONTENTS.   ix

THE IKONOMATIC METHOD OF PHONETIC WRITING 213–229
  Thought-Writing and Sound-Writing; the ikonomatic
  method explained; illustrations from Egyptian inscriptions;
  from the canting arms in heraldry; from the Mexican picture-
  writing; values of position and colors; determinatives and
  ideograms in Aztec MSS.; further illustrations from Maya
  hieroglyphs; Chipeway pictography.

THE WRITING AND RECORDS OF THE ANCIENT MAYAS . . 230–254
  1. Introductory—Phoneticism in Maya and Aztec writing.
  2. Discriptions by Spanish writers; by Peter Martyr; by Las
  Casas; by Alonso Ponce; by Lizana; by Aguilar; by Buena
  Ventura; by Cogolludo; by Soto-Mayor; by Landa; fac-
  simile of Landa's alphabet; critiques on it; conclusions. 3.
  References from native sources; Maya words for "writing,"
  "book," "calendar," etc.; a prophecy of Ahkul Chel translated. 4. The existing Codices; the Dresden Codex; the Codex Peresianus; the Codex Troano; the Codex Cortesianus;
  the mural paintings and inscriptions.

THE BOOKS OF CHILAN BALAM 255–273
  High civilization of ancient Mayas; destruction of their literature; modern Books of Chilan Balam; signification of this
  name; contents of the Books; specimen of the prophecies;
  linguistic value; opinion of Pio Perez; length of the Maya
  year-cycles; hieroglyphs of the months and days; the 13
  ahau katuns; medical contents of the books.

ON THE "STONE OF THE GIANTS." 274–283
  Location of the Stone near Orizaba; its figures; refer to a
  date in February, 1502; translation of the hieroglyphs, and
  identification of the date as that of the death of the Emperor
  Ahuitzotzin; the stone a sepulchral tablet.

NATIVE AMERICAN POETRY 284–304
  Nature of poetry; principle of repetition; Eskimo nith-

CONTENTS.

songs; other Eskimo songs; a Pawnee song; Kioway love songs; a Chipeway serenade; Aztec love songs; war-songs of the Otomis; of the Aztecs; of the Qquichuas; prophetic chants of the Mayas. Faculty of poetry universal.

PART IV

LINGUISTIC.

INTRODUCTORY 305-307

AMERICAN LANGUAGES, AND WHY WE SHOULD STUDY THEM. 308-327
Indian geographic names; language a guide to ethnology; reveals the growth of arts and the psychologic processes of a people; illustration from the Lenâpé tongue; structure of language best studied in savage tongues; rank of American tongues; characteristic traits; pronominal forms; idea of personality; polysynthesis; incorporation; holophrasis; origin of these; lucidity of American tongues; their vocabularies; power of expressing abstract ideas; conclusion.

WILHELM VON HUMBOLDT'S RESEARCHES IN AMERICAN LANGUAGES 328-348
What led Humboldt toward the American tongues; progress of his studies; fundamental doctrine of his philosophy of language; his theory of the evolution of languages; opinion on American languages; his criterion of the relative perfection of languages; not abundance of forms, nor verbal richness; American tongues not degenerations; Humboldt's classification of languages; psychological origin of Incorporation in language; its shortcomings; in simple sentences; in compound sentences; absence of true formal elements; the nature of the American verb.

SOME CHARACTERISTICS OF AMERICAN LANGUAGES 349-389
Study of the human species on the geographic system; have

American languages any common trait? Duponceau's theory of polysynthesis; Humboldt on Polysynthesis and Incorporation; Francis Lieber on Holophrasis; Prof. Steinthal on the incorporative plan; Lucien Adam's criticism of it; Prof. Müller's inadequate statement; Major Powell's omission to consider it; definitions of polysynthesis, incorporation and holophrasis; illustrations; critical application of the theory to the Othomi language; to the Bri-bri language; to the Tupi-Guarani dialects; to the Mutsun; conclusions; addendum; critique by M. Adam on this essay.

THE EARLIEST FORM OF HUMAN SPEECH AS REVEALED BY AMERICAN TONGUES 390–409

The *Homo alalus* or speechless man, a romance; linguistic stocks; the phonetic elements significant; examples; but not of same significance in different stocks; notion of *self* and *other;* pronouns a late development; alternating consonants and permutable vowels; examples; phoneticism inadequate; difficulties thus created; counter-sense in language; notion of Being and Not-Being; incorporation; sentence-words; no dependent clauses; no tenses; no adjectives; no numerals; notion of Animate and Inanimate; classificatory particles; primitive man a *visuaire.*

THE CONCEPTION OF LOVE IN SOME AMERICAN LANGUAGES. 410–432

Significance of love-words; various origins. I. Algonkin love-words; various senses; highest forms. II. Nahuatl love-words; poverty of the tongue; made up by terminations; words for friendship. III. Maya love-words; singular derivations; the Huasteca dialect; the Cakchiquel dialect; comparisons. IV. Qquichua love-words; abundant; various meanings. V. Tupi-Guarani love-words; meaning of. Conclusions.

THE LINEAL MEASURES OF THE SEMI-CIVILIZED NATIONS OF
    MEXICO AND CENTRAL AMERICA 433–451
  Metrical standards a criterion of progress; those of the
  Mayas; of the Cakchiquels; of the Mexicans or Aztecs; of
  the Mound-Builders of Ohio. Conclusions.

THE CURIOUS HOAX OF THE TAENSA LANGUAGE 452–467
  How it began; the deception exposed; absurdities of the invention; a wonderful calendar; a yet more wonderful marriage-song; a second Psalmanazar; rejoinder of the editor; reply to that; final verdict.

INDEX OF AUTHORS AND AUTHORITIES 469–474
INDEX OF SUBJECTS 475–489

PART I.

ETHNOLOGIC AND ARCHÆOLOGIC.

INTRODUCTORY.

EVER since America was discovered, the question about it which has excited the most general interest has been, Whence came its inhabitants? The inquiry, Who are the American Indians? has been the theme of many a ponderous folio and labored dissertation, with answers nearly as various as the number of debaters.

Few or none of them have reflected on the unphilosophical character of the inquiry as thus crudely put. Take a precisely analogous question, and this will be apparent—Whence came the African Negroes? All will reply—From Africa, of course. Originally? Yes, originally; they constitute the African or Negro sub-species of Man.

The answer in the case of the American Indians is entirely parallel—their origin is American; the racial type was created and fixed on the American continent; they constitute as true and distinct a sub-species as do the African or the White Race.

Each of the great continental areas moulded the plastic, primitive man into a conformation of body and mind peculiar to itself, in some special harmony with its own geographic features, thus producing a race or sub-species, subtly correlated in a thousand ways to its environment, but never forfeiting its claim to humanity, never failing in its parallel and progressive development with all other varieties of the species.

America was no exception to this rule, and it is time to dismiss as trivial all attempts to connect the American race genealogically with any other, or to trace the typical culture of this continent to the historic forms of the Old World. My early studies inclined me to these opinions, and they have been constantly strengthened by further research. Yet they are not popularly accepted; the very latest writer of competence on the pre-history of America says, "It is now generally held that the earliest population (of the continent) was intruded upon by other races, coming either from Asia or from the Pacific Islands, from whom were descended the various tribes which have occupied the soil down to the present time."*

It is true that this opinion is that generally held, and for this reason I have selected for reprinting some articles intended to show that it is utterly fallacious—devoid of any respectable foundation.

The first two papers treat of the archæologic material, and its value for ascertaining the pre-historic life of the American race; the third, on its pretended affinities to Asiatic

---

* Prof. H. W. Haynes, in *The Narrative and Critical History of America*, p. 329. Edited by Justin Winsor. Boston, 1889.

peoples. These are followed by two papers respectively on the Toltecs and Mound Builders, setting aright, I hope, the position of these semi-mythical shapes in the culture-history of North America, maintaining that for neither do we have to call in as explanation migrations from Asia, Europe, Oceanica or Africa, as has so often been attempted.

A REVIEW OF THE DATA FOR THE STUDY OF THE PRE-HISTORIC CHRONOLOGY OF AMERICA.*

EARLY in this century the doubt was expressed by Alexander von Humboldt † whether it is philosophical to inquire into the origin of any of the human races or subspecies. Although he expressed this doubt with particular reference to the American race, I believe I am right in assuming that the hesitancy he felt in pushing inquiry so far should now diminish in view of new methods of research and a wider range of observations. We may not, in fact we shall not, be able to trace the American or any other subspecies directly back to its origin in place or time; but by reviewing all the data which have been offered in solution of such a problem, we may preceptibly narrow the question, and also estimate the relative value of the means proposed. It is to such a review, applied to the American race, that I now invite your attention.

The data upon which theories of the antiquity, the genealogy and the affinities of this race have been constructed are varied. For convenience of treatment I shall class them under six heads. They are :

---

* This paper was my address as vice-president of the American Association for the Advancement of Science, before the Section of Anthropology, at the meeting in 1887. I have added the foot notes, and revised the text.

† *Vues des Cordillères, et Monumens des Peuples Indigènes de l'Amérique.* Introduction.

I. *Legendary*, including the traditions of the native tribes and their own statements of their history.

II. *Monumental*, where we have to do with those structures whose age or character seems to throw light on the question.

III. *Industrial*, under which heading we may inquire as to the origin of both the useful and the decorative arts in the New World.

IV. *Linguistic*, broaching the immense and important questions as to the diversity and affinities of languages.

V. *Physical*, which takes into consideration the anatomic and morphologic peculiarities of the American race; and finally,

VI. *Geologic*, where its position in the geologic horizons is to be determined, and the influence upon it of the physical geography of the continent.

Legendary. Turning to the first of these, the legendary data, I confess to a feeling of surprise that learned scholars should still hold to the opinion that the native tribes, even some of the most savage of them, retain to this day traditions which they had brought from their supposed Asiatic homes. Thus the missionaries, Bishop Henry Faraud and the Abbé Emile Petitot, both entirely familiar with the Cree and the Athapaskan languages and lore, insist that the myths and legends of these tribes bear such strong resemblances to the Semitic traditions that both must have had a common origin.* No one can deny the resemblance;

---

* See F. Michel, *Dix-huit Ans chez les Sauvages. Voyages et Missions de Mgr. Henry Faraud* (Paris, 1866), and Emile Petitot, *Monographie des Dènè-Dindjié?* (Paris, 1876).

but the scientific student of mythology discovers such identities too frequently, and at points too remote, to ask any other explanation for them than the common nature of the human mind.

The question has been often raised how long a savage tribe, ignorant of writing, is likely to retain the memory of past deeds. From a great many examples in America and elsewhere, it is probable that the lapse of five generations, or say two centuries, completely obliterates all recollection of historic occurrences. Of course, there are certain events of continuous influence which may be retained in memory longer—for example, the federation of prominent tribes; and perhaps a genealogy may run back farther. My friend, Dr. Franz Boas, informs me that some tribes on Vancouver's Island pretend to preserve their genealogies for twelve or fifteen generations back; but he adds that the remoter names are clearly of mythical purport.

It appears obvious that all efforts to establish a pre-historic chronology by means of the legends of savage tribes, are and must be vain.

The case is not much better with those semi-civilized American nations, the Mayas and Nahuas, who possessed a partially phonetic alphabet, or with the Quichuas, who preserved their records by the ingenious device of the quipu. Manco Capac, the alleged founder of the Peruvian state, floats before us as a vague and mythical figure, though he is placed in time not earlier than the date when Leif, the son of Erik, anchored his war-ship on the Nova Scotian coast.*

---

* Professor Gustav Storm has rendered it probable that the Vineland of the Northmen was not further south than Nova Scotia. See his *Studies on the Vineland Voyages*, in *Mems. de la Société Royale des Antiquaires du Nord.*, 1888.

LEGENDARY DATA.

Historians are agreed that the long lists of Incas in the pages of Montesinos, extending about two thousand years anterior to the Conquest, are spurious, due to the imagination or the easy credulity of that writer.

The annals of Mexico fare no better before the fire of criticism. It is extremely doubtful that their earliest reminiscences refer to any event outside the narrow valley parcelled out between the petty states of Tenochtitlan, Tezcuco, and Tlacopan.* The only fact that bears out the long and mysterious journey from the land of the Seven Caves, Chicomoztoc, in the distant northwest, by the great water, is that the learned and indefatigable Buschmann has conclusively shown that the four languages of Sonora and all the dialects of the Shoshonian family reveal marks of continued and deep impressions of the Nahuatl tongue.† But the chronicles of Mexico proper contain no fixed date prior to that of the founding of the city of Tenochtitlan, in the year 1325 of our era.

I am aware that there are still some writers who maintain that both the Mexican and the Maya astronomic cycles assume a commencement for their records centuries, even thousands of years, before the beginning of our era. These opinions, however, have not obtained the assent of other students. We are too ignorant both of the astronomy and the methods of writing of these nations to admit such claims; and the facts advanced are capable of quite other interpretation.

---

* Such was the opinion of the late José Fernando Ramirez, one of the most acute and learned of Mexican antiquaries. See his words in Orozco y Berra's Introduction to the *Cronica* of Tezozomoc, p. 213 (Mexico, 1878).

† *Die Spuren der Aztekischen Sprache in Nördlichen Mexiko*, etc. (Berlin, 1859.)

It is, on the whole, rare for the American tribes to declare themselves autochthonous. The Mayas, on the peninsula of Yucatan, stated that their earliest ancestors came there from beyond the seas, some from the far east, others from the west. So the Toltecs, under Quetzalcoatl, were fabled to have entered Mexico from beyond the Eastern Ocean. The Creeks and Choctaws pointed to the west, the Algonkins generally to the east, as their primal home.* These legends are chiefly mythical, not much truer than those of other tribes who claimed to have climbed up from some under-world. Sifting them all, we shall find in them little to enlighten us as to the pre-historic chronology of the tribes, though they may furnish interesting vistas in comparative mythology.

That in which we may expect the legends of tribes to be of most avail is their later history, the record of their wars, migrations and social development within a few generations. The spirit of the uncivilized man is, however, very careless of the past. We have means of testing the exactness of such traditions in some instances, and the result is rarely such as to inspire confidence in verbal records. Those of you who were present at the last meeting will remember how diversely two able students of Iroquois tradition estimated its value. Even when remarkable events are not forgotten, the dates of their occurrence are generally vague. The inference, therefore, is that very few data, dependent on legendary evidence alone, can be accepted.

---

* I would refer the reader who cares to pursue this branch of the subject to my analysis of these stories in *The Myths of the New World* (second ed., New York, 1876), and *American Hero-Myths* (Philadelphia, 1882).

Monumental. When we turn to the monumental data, to the architecture and structural relics of the ancient Americans, we naturally think first of the imposing stone-built fortresses of Peru, the massive pyramids and temples of Yucatan and Mexico, and the vast brick-piles of the Pueblo Indians.

It is doubtful if any of these notable monuments supply pre-historic dates of excessive antiquity. The pueblos, both those now occupied and the vastly greater number whose ruins lie scattered over the valleys and mesas of New Mexico and Arizona, were constructed by the ancestors of the tribes who still inhabit that region, and this at no distant day. Though we cannot assign exact dates to the development of this peculiar civilization, there are abundant reasons, drawn from language, physical geography and the character of the architecture, to include all these structures within the period since the commencement of our era.*

There is every reason to suppose that the same is true of all the stone and brick edifices of Mexico and Central America. The majority of them were occupied at the period of the Conquest; others were in process of building; and of others the record of the date of their construction was clearly in memory and was not distant. Thus, the famous temple of Huitzilopochtli at Tenochtitlan, and the spacious palace —or, if you prefer the word, "communal house"—of the ruler of Tezcuco, had been completed within the lifetime of many who met the Spaniards. To be sure, even then there were once famous cities fallen to ruin and sunk to oblivion

---

* The results of the recent "Hemenway South-western Exploring Expedition" do not in the least invalidate this statement.

in the tropical forests. Such was Palenque, which could not have failed to attract the attention of Cortes had it been inhabited. Such also was T'Ho, on the site of the present city of Mérida, Yucatan, where the earliest explorers found lofty stone mounds and temples covered with a forest as heavy as the primitive growth around it.* But tradition and the present condition of such of these old cities as have been examined, unite in the probability that they do not antedate the Conquest more than a few centuries.

In the opinion of some observers, the enigmatical ruins on the plain of Tiahuanaco, a few leagues from the shore of Lake Titicaca, in Peru, carry us far, very far, beyond any such modern date. "Even the memory of their builders," says one of the more recent visitors to these marvellous relics, General Bartolomé Mitre, "even their memory was lost thousands of years before the discovery of America."†

Such a statement is neither more nor less than a confession of ignorance. We have not discovered the period nor the people concerned in the ruins of Tiahuanaco. It must be remembered that they are not the remains of a populous city, but merely the foundations and beginnings of some vast religious edifice which was left incomplete, probably owing to the death of the projector or to unforeseen difficulties. If this is borne in mind, much of the obscurity about the origin, the purpose and the position of these structures will be removed. They do not justify a claim to an age of

---

* A brief but most interesting description of these monuments is preserved in a letter to the Emperor Charles V. by the Friar Lorenzo de Bienvenida, written from Yucatan in 1548.

† *Las Ruinas de Tiahuanaco.* Por Bartolomé Mitre. (Buenos Ayres, 1879.)

thousands of years before the Conquest; hundreds will suffice. Nor is it necessary to assent to the opinion advanced by General Mitre, and supported by some other archæologists, that the most ancient monuments in America are those of most perfect construction, and, therefore, that in this continent there has been, in civilization, not progress but failure, not advance but retrogression.

The uncertainty which rests over the age of the structures at Tiahuanaco is scarcely greater than that which still shrouds the origin of the mounds and earthworks of the Ohio and Upper Mississippi valleys. Yet I venture to say that the opinion is steadily gaining ground that these interesting memorials of vanished nations are not older than the mediæval period of European history. The condition of the arts which they reveal indicates a date that we must place among the more recent in American chronology. The simple fact that tobacco and maize were cultivated plants is evidence enough for this.*

There is, however, a class of monuments of much greater antiquity than any I have mentioned. These are the artificial shell-heaps which are found along the shores of both oceans and of many rivers in both North and South America. They correspond to the kitchen-middens of European archæology.

In several parts of the continent they have been examined by competent observers and the question of their date approximately ascertained. I need not say this differs widely,

---

* This assertion was attacked by Dr. C. C. Abbott, in an address before the American Association in 1888 (*Proceedings*, Vol. XXXVII, p. 308). But if we assume the mediæval period of European history to have begun with the fall of the Western Empire, I do not retire from my position.

for these refuse heaps of ancient villages or stations were of course begun at wide intervals.

Long ago I called attention to the singular size and antiquity of those I found in Florida and along the Tennessee River;* and the later researches of Professor Jeffries Wyman would, in his opinion, measure the age of some of the former by tens of thousands of years.†

Further to the south, in Costa Rica, Dr. Earl Flint has examined the extensive artificial shell deposits which are found along the shores of that republic. They are many feet in height, covered by a dense forest of primeval appearance, and are undoubtedly of human origin.

In Brazil such shell-heaps are called *sambaquis*, and they are of frequent occurrence along the bays and inlets of the coast. Some of them are of extraordinary dimensions, rising occasionally to more than a hundred feet in height. The lower layers have been consolidated into a firm, stony breccia of shells and bones, while the surface stratum, from six to ten feet thick, is composed of sand and vegetable loam supporting a growth of the largest trees. Yet even the lowest layers of this breccia, or shell-conglomerate, yield tokens of human industry, as stone axes, flint arrow-heads, chisels, and fragments of very rude pottery, as well as human bones, sometimes split to extract the marrow. The shells are by no means all of modern type. Many are of

---

* D. G. Brinton, *The Floridian Peninsula, its Literary History, Indian Tribes and Antiquities*, p. 177-181 (Philadelphia, 1859). The shell-heaps along the Tennessee River 1 described in the *Annual Report of the Smithsonian Institution*, for 1866, p. 356.

† His accounts were principally in the Fourth and Seventh *Reports of the Peabody Museum*.

species now wholly extinct, or extinct in the locality. This fact alone carries us back to an antiquity which probably should be counted by thousands of years before our era.

At that remote period not only did a fishing and hunting race dwell along the Brazilian coast, but this race was fairly advanced on the path to culture; it was acquainted with pottery, with compound implements, and with the polishing of stone. We further know that this race was not that which occupied the land when the whites discovered it; for the human skulls disinterred from the sambaquis are, craniologically, almost diametrically opposite those of the Botocudos and the Tupis. Yet if we can trust the researches of Dr. Lund in the caverns of Brazil, the oldest skulls in these deposits, found in immediate connection with the bones of extinct mammalia, belonged to the ancestors of these tribes. Markedly dolichocephalic, they present an entire contrast to the brachycephalic type from the sambaquis.*

This class of monuments, therefore, supply us data which prove man's existence in America in what some call the "diluvial," others the "quaternary," and others again the "pleistocene" epoch—that characterized by the presence of some extinct species.

Industrial. Let us now turn to the industrial activity of the American race, and see whether it will furnish us other data concerning the pre-historic life of the New World. We may reasonably look in this direction for aid, since it is now universally conceded that at no time did man spring into being fully armed and equipped for the struggle for exist-

---

* See the *Verhandlungen der Berliner Gesellschaft für Anthropologie*, 1886, 1887, 1888.

ence, but everywhere followed the same path of painful effort from absolute ignorance and utter feebleness to knowledge and power. At first, his only weapons or tools were such as he possessed in common with the anthropoid apes: to wit, an unshapen stone and a broken stick. Little by little, he learned to fit his stone to his hand and to chip it to an edge, and with this he could sharpen the end of his stick, thus providing himself with a spear and an axe.

It was long before he learned to shape and adjust the stone to the end of the stick, and to hurl this by means of a cord attached to a second and elastic stick—in other words, a bow; still longer before he discovered the art of fashioning clay into vessels and of polishing and boring stones. These simple arts are landmarks in the progress of the race: the latter divides the history of culture into the palæolithic or rough stone period, and the neolithic or polished stone period; while the shaping of a stone for attachment to a handle or shaft marks the difference between the epoch of compound implements and the earlier epoch of simple implements, both included in the older or palæolithic age.*
With these principles as guides, we may ask how far back on this scale do the industrial relics in America carry us?

I have spoken of the great antiquity of some of the American shell-heaps, how they carry us back to the diluvial epoch, and that of numerous extinct species. Yet it is generally true that in the oldest hitherto examined in Bra-

---

* I have brought out the distinction between the epoch of simple implements and that of compound implements in an article which is reprinted in this collection. The expressions "early" and "late" applied to these epochs do not refer to absolute periods of time, but are relative to the progress of individual civilizations.

zil, Guiana, Costa Rica and Florida, fragments of pottery, of polished stone, and compound implements, occur even in the lowest strata.* Venerable though they are, they supply no date older than what in Europe we should call the neolithic period. The arrow-heads which have been exhumed from the loess of the ancient lake-beds of Nebraska, the net-sinkers and celts which have been recovered from the auriferous gravels of California, prove by their form and finish that the tribes who fashioned them had already taken long strides beyond the culture of the earlier palæolithic age. The same is true, though in a less degree, of the chipped stones and bones which Ameghino exhumed from the lacrustine deposits of the Pampas, although he proves that these relics were the products of tribes contemporary with the extinct glyptodon and mylodon, as well as the fossil horse and dog. In the very oldest station which he examined, there appears to have been found a quartz arrow-head; yet he argues that this station dated from the pliocene division of the tertiary, long anterior to the austral glacial epoch.† This leaves another such open conflict between geology and the history of culture, as Professor Rau has already pointed out as existing in Californian archæology.

There is, however, one station in America which has furnished an ample line of specimens, and among them not

---

* Exceptions are some of the Floridian shell-heaps and a limited number elsewhere.

† Florentino Ameghino, *La Antiguedad del Hombre en el Plata*, Tomo II, p. 434, *et al.* (Buenos Ayres, 1881.) The bow and arrow, being a compound implement, nowhere belonged to the earliest stage of human culture. See also H. W. Haynes' article, "The Bow and Arrow unknown to Palæolithic Man." in *Proceedings of Boston Soc. Nat. History*, Vol. XXIII.

one, so far as I know, indicating a knowledge of compound implements. This is that of the "Trenton gravels," New Jersey. There we appear to be in face of a stage of culture as primitive as that of the stations of Chelles and St. Acheul in France, absolutely without pottery, without polished stone, without compound implements.*

Assuming that these post-glacial gravels about Trenton supply one of the earliest authentic starting points in the history of culture on this continent, the later developments of industry will furnish a number of other data. This first date was long before the extinction of the native American horse, the elephant, the mammoth, and other animals important to early man. There is nothing unlikely therefore in the reported discoveries of his pointed flints or his bones in place along with the remains of these quadrupeds.

Not only the form but the material of implements supplies us data. If man in his earliest stage was, as some maintain, quite migratory, it is certain that he did not carry his stone implements with him, nor did he obtain by barter or capture those of other tribes. All the oldest implements are manufactured from the rocks of the locality. When, therefore, we find a weapon of a material not obtainable in the vicinity, we have a sure indication that it belongs to a period of development considerably later than the earliest. When the obsidian of the Yellowstone Park is found in Ohio, when the black slate of Vancouver's Island is exhumed in Delaware, it is obvious we must assume for such extensive transits a very noticeable æsthetic and commercial development.

---

* Dr. C. C. Abbott, the discoverer and principal explorer of these gravels, reported his discoveries in numerous papers, and especially in his work *Primitive Industry*, chap. xxxii.

I can but touch in the lightest manner on the data offered by the vast realm of industrial activity. The return it offers is abundant, but the harvesting delicate. In the dissemination of certain kinds of arts, certain inventions, certain decorative designs and æsthetic conceptions from one tribe to another, we have a most valuable means of tracing the pre-historic intercourse of nations: but we must sedulously discriminate such borrowing from the synchronous and similar development of independent culture under like conditions.

In one department of industry we shall be largely free from this danger, that is, in the extension of agriculture. One of America's ablest ethnologists, Dr. Charles Pickering, as the result of a lifetime devoted to his science, finally settled upon the extension of cultivated plants as the safest guide in the labyrinth of pre-historic migrations. Its value is easily seen in America when we reflect that the two tropical plants, maize and tobacco, extended their area in most remote times from their limited local habitat about the Isthmus of Tehuantepec to the north as far as the St. Lawrence river and to the south quite to the Archipelago of Chiloe. Their presence is easily traced by the stone or earthen-ware implements required for their use. How many ages it must have required for these plants to have thus extended their domain, amid hostile and savage tribes, through five thousand miles of space! The squash, the bean, the potato and the mandioca, are native food-plants offering in a less degree similar material for tracing ancient commerce and migration. Humboldt and others have claimed as much for the banana (*Musa paradisiaca*), but the recent researches of Dr. Karl von den Steinen have removed that valued fruit from the list of native American plants. Both species of banana (*M. paradisiaca* and *M. sapientium*) were undoubtedly introduced into the New World after the discovery.* Indeed, summing up the reply to an inquiry which has often been addressed to the industrial evolution of the indigenes of our continent, I should say that they did not borrow a single art or invention nor a single cultivated plant from any part of the Old World previous to the arrival of Columbus. What they had was their own, developed from their own soil, the outgrowth of their own lives and needs.

Linguistic. This individuality of the race is still more strongly expressed in their languages. You are all aware that it is upon linguistic data almost exclusively that American ethnology has been and must be based. The study of the native tongues becomes therefore of transcendent importance in the pre-historic chronology of the Continent. But to obtain its best results, this study must be conducted in a much more thorough manner than has hitherto been the custom.

In America we are confronted with an astonishing multiplicity of linguistic stocks. They have been placed at about eighty in North and one hundred in South America. It is stated that there are that many radically diverse in elements and structure. To appreciate the vista in time that this fact opens to our thoughts, we must recognize the tenacity of life manifested by these tongues. Some of them have scores of dialects, spoken by tribes wandering over the

---

* *Expedition durch Central-Brasilien*, pp. 310–314 (Leipzig, 1886).

THE NUMEROUS NATIVE DIALECTS.

widest areas. Take the Athapascan or Tinné, for example, found in its greatest purity amid the tribes who dwell on the Arctic sea, and along the Mackenzie river, in British America, but which is also the tongue of the Apaches who carried it almost to the valley of Mexico. The Algonkin was spoken from Hudson Bay to the Savannah river and from Newfoundland to the Rocky Mountains. The Guarani of the Rio de la Plata underlies dialects which were current as far north as Florida.

How, then, in spite of such tenacity of American languages, have so many stocks come into existence? This was the question which my predecessor in this chair last year undertook to answer. His suggestions appear to me extremely valuable, and only in one point do I widely differ from him, and that is, in the length of time required for these numerous tongues to originate, to sever into dialects and to be carried to distant regions.* According to the able linguist, Dr. Stoll, the difference which is presented between the Cakchiquel and Maya dialects could not have arisen in less than two thousand years;† and any one who has carefully compared the earliest grammars of an American tongue with its present condition will acknowledge that the changes are surprisingly few. To me the exceeding diversity of languages in America and the many dialects into which these have split, are cogent proofs of the vast antiquity of the race, an antiquity stretching back tens of thousands of years.

---

* The reference is to Mr. Horatio Hale's Address "On the Origin of Language and the Antiquity of Speaking Man." See *Proc. of the Am. Assoc. for the Adv. of Science*, vol. xxxv., p. 239, sq.

† *Ethnographie der Republik Guatemala*, p. 157 (Zurich, 1884)

Nothing less can explain these multitudinous forms of speech.

Underlying all these varied forms of expression, however, I think future investigation will demonstrate some curious identities of internal form, traits almost or entirely peculiar to American languages, and never quite absent from any of them.

Such was the opinion of the two earliest philosophical investigators of these tongues, P. S. Duponceau and Wilhelm von Humboldt. They called these traits *polysynthesis* and *incorporation*, and it was proposed to apply the term *incorporative* as a distinguishing adjective to all American languages. Of late years this opinion has been earnestly combatted by M. Lucien Adam and others; but my own studies have led me to adopt the views of the older analysts against these modern critics. I do not think that the student can compare any two stocks on the continent without being impressed with the resemblance of their expression of the relations of Being, through the incorporative plan.

Along with this identity of plan, there coëxists the utmost independence of expression. An American language is usually perfectly transparent. Nothing is easier than to reduce it to its ultimate elements, its fundamental radicals. These are few in numbers and interjectional in character. The Athapascan, the Algonkin, whose wide extension I have referred to, have been reduced to half a dozen particles or sounds expressive of the simplest conceptions.* Upon these, by combination, repetition, imitation and other such processes, the astonishing structure of the tongue has been

---

* See Howse, *Grammar of the Cree Language*, p. 143, sqq.

erected, every portion of it displaying the mechanism of its origin. It is this transparency which renders these tongues so attractive to the philosophic student of human expression, and so valuable to him who would obtain from them the record of the progress of the nation.

A thorough study of such a language would embrace its material, its formal and its psychologic contents. Its material elements include the peculiarities of its vocabulary: for example, its numerals and the system they indicate, its words for weights and measures, for color and direction, for relations of consanguinity and affinity, for articles of use and ornament, for social and domestic conditions, and the like.

Few studies of American languages go beyond this material or lexicographic limit; but in truth these are merely the externalities of a tongue, and have nothing to do with linguistic science proper. This concerns itself with the forms of the language, with the relation of parts of speech to each other and to the sentence, and with the historical development of the grammatical categories. Beyond this, again, is the determination of the psychical character of the tribe through the forms instinctively adopted for the expression of its thoughts, and reciprocally the reaction exerted by these forms on the later intellectual growth of those who were taught them as their only means of articulate expression.

These are data of the highest value in the study of prehistoric time; but so far as America is concerned, I could name very few scholars who have pursued this promising line of research.

Physical. Much more attention has been paid to the physical than the linguistic data of the native Americans, but it may freely be said, with not more satisfactory results. This failure is partly owing to the preconceived notions which still govern the study of ethnology. Linnæus offered the cautious division of the human species into races named from the five great geographical areas it inhabited ; Blumenbach pointed out that this roughly corresponded with the division into five colors, the white, black, yellow, brown and red races, occupying respectively Europe, Africa, Asia, Polynesia and America. Unfortunately, Cuvier chose to simplify this scheme, by merging the brown and red races, the Polynesian or Malayan and the American, into the yellow or Mongolian. The latest writers of the French school, and I am sorry to add various Americans, servilely follow this groundless rejection of the older scheme, and speak of Malayans and Americans alike as Mongolians or Mongoloids. Neither in language nor ethnic anatomy is there any more resemblance than between whites and Mongolians.

It is gratifying to see that the more accurate German investigators decidedly reject the blunder of Cuvier, and declare that the American race is as independent as any other of those named. Thus Dr. Paul Ehrenreich, who has lately published an admirable monograph on the Botocudos of Brazil, a tribe often quoted for its so-called "Mongoloid" aspect, declares that any such assertion must be contradicted in positive terms. Both in osteology and anatomy, in formation of the hair and shape of the skull, the differences are marked, permanent and radical.

What is true of the Botocudos is not less so of the other

American tribes which are claimed to present Mongolian traits. Such assertions are based on the superficial observations of travellers, most of whom do not know the first principles of ethnic anatomy. This is sufficiently shown by the importance they attach to the oblique eye, a slight malformation of the skin of scarcely any weight.*

The anatomy and physiology of the various American tribes present, indeed, great diversity, and yet, beneath it all is a really remarkable fixedness of type. We observe this diversity in the shape of the skull, which may be, as among the Botocudos, strictly dolichocephalic, while the Araucanians are brachycephalic ; the nasal index varies more than in the extremest members of the white race ; the tint of the skin may be a dark brown with an under-color of red, or of so light a hue that a blush is easily perceptible. The beard is usually absent, but D'Orbigny visited a tribe who wore it full and long.† The height varies from an average of six feet four inches for adult males in Patagonia to less than five feet among the Warraus of Guiana ; and so it is with all the other traits of the race. There is not one which is not subject to extensive variation.

On the other hand, these variations are not greater than can be adduced in various members of the white or black race. In spite of them all, there is a wonderful family likeness among tribes of American origin. No observer well acquainted with the type would err in taking it for another. Darwin says that the Fuegians so closely resemble the Bo-

---

* This question is discussed in more detail in the next essay.

† *L'Homme Americain*, Tome 1, p. 126. The tribe is the Guarayos, an offshoot of the Guaranis.

tocudos that they seem members of the same tribe. I have seen Arawacks from Guiana who in the northwest would have passed for Sioux.

In spite of the total dissimilarity of climate and other physical surroundings, the tribes of the tropics differ no more from those near the Arctic circle than they do among themselves. This is a striking lesson how independent of environment are the essential characteristics of a race, and it is a sweeping refutation of those theories which make such characteristics dependent upon external agencies.

A still more remarkable fact has been demonstrated by Professor J. Kollmann of Bâle: to wit, that the essential physical identity of the American race is as extended in time as it is in space. This accurate student has analyzed the cranioscopic formulas of the most ancient American skulls, those from the alleged tertiary deposits of the Pampas, those from the caverns of Lagoa Santa in Brazil, that obtained from Rock Bluff, Illinois, the celebrated Calaveras skull from California, and one from Pontemelo in Buenos Ayres of geologic antiquity. His results are most interesting. These very ancient remains prove that in all important craniologic indicia the earliest Americans, those who were contemporaries of the fossil horse and other long since extinct quadrupeds, possessed the same racial character as the natives of the present day, with similar skulls and a like physiognomy.* We reach therefore the momentous conclusion that the American race throughout the whole continent, and from its earliest appearance in time, is and has been *one*, as distinct in type as any other race, and from its isolation

---

* *Zeitschrift für Ethnologie*, 1884, p. 181.

probably the purest of all in its racial traits. This is a fact of the first order in establishing its prehistoric chronology.

Geologic. I have left the geologic data to the last, as it is these which carry us with reasonable safety to the remotest periods. No one who examines the evidence will now deny that man lived in both North and South America during and after the glacial epochs, and that he was the contemporary of many species of animals now extinct. As you are aware, the attempt has several times been made to fix the date for the final retrocession of the glaciers of North America. The estimates have varied from about 12,000 years ago up to 50,000, with a majority in favor of about 35,000 years.

There have also been various discoveries which are said to place the human species in America previous to the appearance of the glaciers. Some remains of man's industry or of his skeleton have been reported from interglacial, others from tertiary deposits.* Unfortunately, these finds have not always been sufficient, or not of a character to convince the archæologist. I have before adverted to the impossibility, for instance, of an archæologist accepting the discovery of a finely-polished stone implement in a tertiary gravel, except as an intrusive deposit. It is a violent anachronism, which is without a parallel in other countries. Even the discovery of a compound implement, as a stemmed arrow-

---

* Since this address was delivered Mr. H. T. Cresson has reported the finding of chipped implements made of argillite in a deposit of mid-glacial age on the banks of the Delaware River—*Proc. Boston Soc. Nat. Hist.* vol. xxiv; and portions of two skeletons completely converted into limonite have been exhibited at the Academy of Natural Sciences, Philadelphia, from a deposit in Florida, *below* one containing the remains of the extinct giant bison.

head, in strata of tertiary date, is, with our present knowledge, quite out of the question.

Although there are well recognized signs of glacial action in South America, it is not certain that the glacial epoch coincided in time in the two continents. That there was a reasonable approximation is probable from the appearance of later deposits. We may suppose therefore that the habitable area of the New World was notably less at that period, and that the existing tribes were confined to a much narrower space. This would force them into closer relations, and tend powerfully to the production of that uniformity of type to which I have before referred.

We might also expect to discover in the tropical regions of America more frequent evidence of the primitive Americans than in either temperate zone. This has not been the case, probably because the geologic deposits of the tropics have been less investigated. Throughout the West Indies there is an entire absence of palæolithic remains. Those islands were first peopled by tribes in the polished stone stage of culture. In the valley of Mexico human remains have been disinterred from a volcanic deposit of supposed tertiary age, and you have all heard of those human footprints which Dr. Earl Flint has unearthed in Nicaragua. These are found under layers of compact volcanac tufas, separated by strata of sand and vegetable loam. There can be no doubt of their human origin or of their great antiquity; but no geologist need be informed of the difficulty of assigning an age to volcanic strata, especially in a tropical country, subject to earthquakes, subsidence and floods.*

---

* I have discussed this fully in a paper in the *Proceedings* of the Amer. Philosoph. Soc. for 1887, entitled "On an Ancient Human Footprint from Nicaragua."

It would not be in accordance with my present purpose to examine the numerous alleged finds of human remains in the strata of the tertiary and quaternary. All such furnish data for the pre-historic chronology of America, and should be carefully scrutinized by him who would obtain further light upon that chronology. I must hasten to some other considerations which touch the remote events to which I am now alluding.

Since a comparison of the fauna of South America and Africa, and a survey of the sea-bottom between those continents, have dispelled the dream of the ancient Atlantis, and relegated that land connection at least to the eocene period of the tertiary, no one can suppose the American man to have migrated from Africa or southwestern Europe. For other and equally solid reasons, no immigration of Polynesians can be assumed. Yet zoölogists, perfectly willing to derive man from an anthropoid, and polygenists to the utmost, hesitate to consider man an autochthon in the New World. There is too wide a gap between the highest monkeys and the human species in this continent.* Discoveries of fossil apes might bridge this, but none such has been reported.

If we accept the theory that man as a species spread from one primal centre, and in the higher plasticity of his early life separated into well defined races, which became unalterably fixed not much later than the close of the glacial epoch —and this theory appears to be that now most agreeable to anthropologists—then the earliest Americans made their ad-

---

* Man must have descended from the catarrhine division of the anthropoids, none of which occur in the New World. See Darwin, *The Descent of Man*, p. 153.

vent on this continent as immigrants. This is our first fact in their pre-historic chronology ; but before we can assign it an accurate position on the scale of geologic time, we must await more complete discoveries than we now have at our command.

We must also wait until our friends the geologists have come to some better understanding among themselves as to what took place in the pleistocene age. You have heard me talking freely about the glacial epoch and its extension in America ; but geologists are by no means of one mind as to this extension, and a respectable minority of them, led by Sir J. William Dawson, deny the existence or even possibility of any continental glacier. What others point out as a terminal moraine they explain to be "nothing but the southern limit of the ice-drift of a period of submergence."*

It is clear that when we speak about the migration of the Americans at a time when the polar half of each continent was either covered with a glacier thousands of feet thick, or submerged to that depth beneath an arctic sea, we have to do with geographical conditions totally unlike those of to-day. I call attention to this obvious fact because it has not been obvious to all writers.

In your archæological reading you will rarely come across a prettier piece of theoretical history than Mr. Lewis A. Morgan's description of the gradual peopling of the two Americas by tracing the lines of easiest subsistence. He begins at the fishy rivers of the northwest coast, and follows the original colony which he assumes landed at that point,

---

* Address at the British Association for the Adv. of Science, 1887.

all the way to Patagonia and Florida.* But how baseless becomes this vision when we consider the geography of America as it is shown by geology to have been at a period contemporary with the earliest remains of man! We know to a certainty that the human race had already spread far and wide over both its continental areas before Mr. Morgan's lines of easiest nutrition had come into existence.

Properly employed, a study of those geologic features of a country which determine its geography will prove of vast advantage in ascertaining the events of pre-historic time. These features undoubtedly fixed the lines of migration and of early commerce. Man in his wanderings has always been guided by the course of rivers, the trend of mountain chains, the direction of ocean currents, the position of deserts, passes and swamps. The railroad of to-day follows the trail of the primitive man, and the rivers have ever been the natural highways of nations. The theories of Morgan therefore remain true as theories; only in their application he fell into an error which was natural enough to the science of twenty years ago. Perhaps when twenty years more shall have elapsed, the post-tertiary geology of our continent will have been so clearly defined that the geography of its different epochs will be known sufficiently to trace these lines of migration at the various epochs of man's residence in the western world, from his first arrival.

I have now set before you, in a superficial manner it is true, the various sources from which we may derive aid in establishing the pre-historic chronology of America. I have

---

* His article, which was first printed in the *North American Review*, 1870, may be found in Beach's *Indian Miscellany*, p. 158 (Albany, 1877).

also endeavored, to a limited extent, to express myself as to the relative value of these sources. None of them can be neglected, and it will be only from an exhaustive study of them all that we can expect to solve the numerous knotty problems, and lift the veil which hangs so darkly on all that concerns the existence of the American race before the sixteenth century.

We are merely beginning the enormous labor which is before us; we have yet to discover the methods by which we can analyze fruitfully the facts we already know. But I look forward with the utmost confidence to a rich return from such investigations. The day is coming, and that rapidly, when the pre-historic life of man in both the New and the Old World will be revealed to us in a thousand unexpected details. We have but to turn backward about thirty years to reach a time when the science of pre-historic archæology was unknown, and its early gropings were jeered at as absurdities. Already it has established for itself a position in the first rank of the sciences which have to do with the highest of problems. It has cast a light upon the pathway of the human race from the time that man first deserved his name down to the commencement of recorded history. Its conquests are but beginning. Year by year masses of new facts are brought to knowledge from unexpected quarters, current errors are corrected, and novel methods of exploration devised.

As Americans by adoption, it should be our first interest and duty to study the Americans by race, in both their present and past development. The task is long and the opportunity is fleeting. A century more, and the anthropologist will scarcely find a native of pure blood ; the tribes and languages of to-day will have been extinguished or corrupted. Nor will the archæologist be in better case. Every day the progress of civilization, ruthless of the monuments of barbarism, is destroying the feeble vestiges of the ancient race ; mounds are levelled, embankments disappear, the stones of temples are built into factories, the holy places desecrated. We have assembled here to aid in recovering something from this wreck of a race and its monuments : let me urge upon you all the need of prompt action and earnest work, inasmuch as the opportunities we enjoy will never again present themselves in such fulness.

ON PALÆOLITHS, AMERICAN AND OTHER.*

THERE has been much talk in scientific circles lately about Palæoliths, and much misunderstanding about them. Let me try to explain in a few words what they are, what they tell, and what mistakes people make about them.

Since man first appeared on this planet, his history has been a slow progress from the most rudimentary arts up to those which he now possesses. We know this, because in a given locality those remains of his art which are found undisturbed in strata geologically the oldest are always the rudest. The exceptions to this rule are in appearance only, as for instance when a given locality was not occupied by men until they had already acquired considerable knowledge of arts, or when a cultivated nation was overrun by a barbarous one.

The general line of advance I have indicated shows, wherever we can trace it, many similarities—similarities not necessarily dependent on an ancient intercourse, but simply because primitive man felt everywhere the same wants, and satisfied them in pretty much the same manner.

---

* The subject of an address before the American Association for the Advancement of Science in 1888, with revision.

He felt the need of defence and attack, and everywhere a stick and a stone offered themselves as the handiest and most effective weapons; he used both wherever he was, and adapted them to like shapes.

In casting about for some standard wherewith to measure the long progress from this simple beginning to the present day, antiquaries have hit upon a very excellent one—the choice of a material employed at any given epoch for obtaining a cutting edge—for manufacturing *l'instrument tranchant*. Man conquers nature as he does his enemy—by cutting her down. The world at present uses iron, or its next product steel, for that purpose; before it came into vogue many nations employed bronze; but in the earliest periods of man's history, and to-day in some savage tribes, stone was the substance almost exclusively wrought for this purpose. These distinctions divide the progress of man into the three great periods; the Age of Iron, the Age of Bronze, and the Age of Stone.

Do not make the mistake of supposing that the remains of human art reveal this sequence in every locality; I have already hinted that this is not the case. And do not make that other mistake of supposing that all three are found in chronologic sequence over the whole world. On the contrary, they are synchronous even to-day, as there are now tribes in Brazil in the Age of Stone and nations in Asia in the Age of Bronze. The word "Age" in this connection does not mean a definite period of time, but a recognized condition of art.

In Western Europe, however, where these terms originated, the three Ages were chronologic. Previous to about two thousand years before the Christian era, all the nations in that region employed stone exclusively to manufacture their cutting implements; later, bronze was preferred for the same purpose; and still later, iron. I say "preferred," for do not imagine that the implement of stone or of bronze was straightway discarded when the better material was learned. We know that stone battle-axes were used in Ireland and Germany down to the tenth century, and bronze was employed by Romans and Egyptians long after they became acquainted with iron.

Each of these three Ages has various subdivisions. Those of the Age of Stone are particularly important. They are two, based upon the manner in which the stone was brought to an edge. All the specimens in geologically the oldest deposits have been brought to an edge by a process of chipping off small pieces, so as to produce a sharp line or crest on a part or the whole of the border of the stone. This artificial process leaves such peculiar traces that a practiced eye cannnot confound it with any accidental chipping which natural means effect.

The later deposits of the Age of Stone show that the early workmen had acquired another manner of dressing their material; they rubbed one stone against another, thus grinding it down to a sharp polished edge.

These two methods give the names to the two periods of the Age of Stone, the Period of Chipped Stone and the Period of Polished Stone. Do not suppose, however, that the workmen in polished stone forgot the art of chipping stone. On the contrary, they continued it side by side with their new learning, and you will find on the sites of their workshops plenty of stone implements in form and technical production like the chipped implements of the older period.

We know that the polished or ground-stone implements came into use later than the earliest chipped implements, for in the oldest beds the latter are found exclusively. Hence the time when they were used exclusively is called the older stone implement period or the Palæolithic period; while, the time when both chipped and polished stones were used, metals were yet unknown, is named the newer stone implement period, or the Neolithic period. A true "Palæolith" is a typical chipped stone implement, the position of which when found leads us to believe that it was manufactured in the older of these periods.

We are not entirely dependent on its position to decide its antiquity. The kind of stone it is, the amount of weather-wearing or *patine* it shows, certain characteristics of shape and size, the indication that the chipping was done in a peculiar manner, all these aid the skilled observer in pronouncing definitely as to whether it is a true Palæolith.

Nor is position always a guarantee of antiquity. A genuine Palæolith may have been washed into newer strata, or be exposed by natural agencies on the surface of the ground, and in such cases it may not be possible to distinguish it from the products of Neolithic industry. A recent product of art may have sunk or been buried in an ancient stratum, and thus become what is termed an "intrusive deposit."

The Palæolithic period itself is advantageously subdivided further into two Epochs, an earlier one in which men made "simple" implements only, and a later one in which they manufactured "compound" implements as well. I was the first to point out this distinction, and as I have found it really useful, and as others have also expressed to me the value which it has been to them in this line of research, I will explain it further.* A "compound" implement is one composed of several parts adapted to each other, as the bow and the arrow, the spear with its shaft and blade, or the axe with its head and helve and the means of fastening the one to the other. These were not early acquisitions. During long ages man contented himself with such tools or weapons as he could frame of a single piece of wood or stone, simply holding it in his hand. When he found he could increase its effectiveness by fitting it to a handle, the discovery marked an era in his culture.

He may indeed in his rudest ages have lashed a stone to the end of his club, or have inserted a spall of flint in the split end of a stick; but these are not compound implements in the proper sense of the term. The expression means an art-product which clearly shows that it was but one part of a mechanical apparatus. The arrow-head with its stem, barbs and body, the stone axe with its grooves or drilled perforation for the handle, are incomplete in themselves, they disclose a preconceived plan for the adjustment of parts which man in his earliest and rudest condition does not seem to have possessed. The most ancient strata in which the remains of human art have been found, either in Europe or America, yield "simple" implements only; "compound" implements are a conquest of his inventive faculty at a later date.

---

* The earliest publication I made on this subject was in an article on Pre-historic Archæology, contributed to *The Iconographic Encyclopædia* (Vol. II, p. 28, Philadelphia, 1886).

So far as America is concerned it is probable that the oldest remains of man yet discovered on the northern continent have been those exhumed in the valley of the Delaware River, in the states of Pennsylvania, New Jersey and Delaware. According to the most careful geological observers that large deposit of gravel covering about five thousand acres on both banks of the river below Trenton is a postglacial deposit not less than twelve or fifteen thousand years old. Imbedded in this at various depths a large number of true palaeoliths have been discovered by Dr. C. C. Abbott, Professor F. A. Putnam, myself and others. Every one of them so far as I am aware belongs to the class of "simple" implements, not an arrowhead nor grooved axe nor stemmed scraper having been reported.

Another deposit of gravel further down the Delaware River is much older: The best authorities in such matters believe that it was deposited, not after the recession of the great glacier which once covered Canada and the northern portion of the United States, but while that tremendous phenomen was at its height, and when all the streams of the central United States were periodically choked with vast masses of ice and snow. In this, which is called the Columbian gravel, chipped stone implements have been found by Mr. Cresson, all of the "simple" variety, and at such depths as to preclude the theory of an intrusive deposit. These discoveries carry the age of the appearance of man in the Delaware valley back to a date which is possibly over a hundred thousand years ago.

The great glacier left its mass of boulders, pebbles and broken stone, which it pushed before it, or carried with it, in a long line of so-called "moraines," extending, roughly speaking, from New York to St. Louis. In this mass, at its edges where the great wash from the melting ice poured down, palaeoliths have been found in undisturbed position, proving that also there man had struggled with the inclemency of the ice-age, and, poorly provided as he was, had come out victorious. Here too all the implements he left are of the "simple" type, indicating at once the vast antiquity of the period and the presence of a race substantially the same as that to the east at the same date.

No tribe has been known to history which was confined to the knowledge of "simple" implements, or which manufactured stone implements exclusively in the Palæolithic forms. Wherever, therefore, these are found without the admixture of artificially ground or polished stones we may be sure we face the remains of a time whose antiquity cannot be measured by any chronology applied to the historic records of humanity.

This enables us in a measure to define the limits of the region known to the human race at this, its earliest epoch ; with our present deficient knowledge we can do so only partially and by exclusion. It is safe to state that in Europe Palæolithic man did not occupy the central alpine area of Switzerland and its surroundings, nor the plains of Russia, nor any part of the Scandinavian peninsula, Scotland, Ireland, nor Iceland. In North America he had no habitations north of the forty-first parallel of latitude except perhaps close to the shores of the two great oceans ;* it is not prob-

---

* A possible exception may have been along the line of the Mississippi River, where a palæolithic workshop appears to have been discovered above St. Paul, by Miss Babbitt.

able that his foot pressed the soil of any of the West Indian Islands ; but when the great Austral Glacier was in its recession depositing the fertile loam of the pampas of Buenos Ayres human beings with their rude Palæoliths were following up the retreating line of ice, as in the Northern Hemisphere. Ages uncounted and uncountable have passed since then, but man has left indestructible evidences that even in that early morn of his existence he had explored and conquered that continent which a late generation has chosen to call "the New World."

ON THE ALLEGED MONGOLIAN AFFINITIES OF THE AMERICAN RACE.*

WERE the question I am about to discuss one of merely theoretical bearings, I should not approach it; but the widespread belief that the American tribes are genealogically connected with the Mongolians is constantly directing and coloring the studies of many Americanists, very much as did at one time the belief that the red men are the present representatives of the ten lost tribes of Israel. It is practically worth while, therefore, to examine the grounds on which the American race is classed by these anthropologists as a branch of the Mongolian, and to inquire whether the ancient culture of America betrayed any positive signs of Mongolian influence.

You will permit me to avoid the discussion as to what constitutes races in anthropology. To me they are zoölogical sub-species, marked by fixed and correlated characteristics, impressed so firmly that they have suffered no appreciable alteration within the historic period either through time or environment. In this sense, Blumenbach, in the last century, recognized five races, corresponding to the five great land-areas of the globe, and to their characteristic faunal and

---

* This Paper was read before the American Association for the Advancement of Science, at its meeting in Cleveland, 1888.

floral centres. This division was an eminently scientific one, and still remains the most in accord with anatomical and linguistic reasearch. About twenty years after the appearance of Blumenbach's work, however, the eminent naturalist Cuvier published his great work on "The Animal Kingdom," in which he rejected Blumenbach's classification, and proposed one dividing the human species into three races,—the white or Caucasian, the black or Ethiopian, and the yellow or Mongolian. In the latter he included the Malays and the American Indians.

This triple division has been very popular in France, and to some extent in other countries. It is not, and it was not in its inception, a scientific deduction from observed facts, but was a sort of *a priori* hypothesis based on the physiological theories of Bichat, and at a later day derived support from the philosophic dreams of Auguste Comte. Bichat, for instance, had recognized three fundamental physiological systems in man—the vegetative or visceral, the osso-muscular, and the cerebro-spinal. The anthropologists, in turn, considered it a happy thought to divide the human species into three races, each of which should show the predominance of one or other of these systems. Thus the black race was to show the predominance of the vegetative system; the yellow race, the osso-muscular system; the white race, the nervous system.* As Bichat had not discovered any more physiological systems, so there could be no more human races on the earth: and thus the sacred triplets of the Comtian philosophy could be vindicated.

How little value attaches to any such generalizations you

---

* See Foley, *Des Trois Grandes Races Humaines*, Paris, 1881.

will readily perceive, and you will be prepared, with me, to dismiss them all, and to turn to the facts of the case, inquiring whether there are any traits of the red race which justify their being callled "Mongolian" or "Mongoloid."

Such affinities have been asserted to exist in language, in culture, and in physical peculiarities, and I shall take these up *seriatim* for examination.

First, as to language.

The great Mongolian stock is divided into the southern branch, speaking monosyllabic, isolating languages, and the northern branch, whose dialects are polysyllabic and aggluttinating. The latter are sometimes called Turanian or Ural-Altaic; and as they are geographically contiguous to the Eskimo, and almost to the Athabascans, we might reasonably expect the linguistic kinship, if any exists, to be shown in this branch of Mongol speech. Is such the case? Not in the least. To prove it, I think it enough to quote the positive statement of the best European authority on the Ural-Altaic languages, Dr. Heinrich Winkler. He emphatically says, that, in the present state of linguistic science, not only is there no connection apparent between any Ural-Altaic and any American language, but that such connection is shown to be highly improbable. The evidence is all the other way.*

I need not, therefore, delay over this part of my subject, but will proceed to inquire whether there are any American affinities to the monosyllabic, isolating languages of Asia.

---

* *Uralaltaische Völker und Sprachen*, p. 167. I do not think that the verbal coincidences pointed out by Petitot in his *Monographie des Déné Dindjé*, and by Platzmann in his *Amerikanisch-Asiatische Etymologien*, merit serious consideration.

RELATIONSHIP OF LANGUAGES.

There is one prominent example, which has often been put forward, of a supposed monosyllabic American language ; and its relationship to the Chinese has frequently been asserted—a relationship, it has been said, extending both to its vocabulary and its grammar. This is the Otomi, spoken in and near the valley of Mexico. It requires, however, but a brief analysis of the Otomi to see that it is not a monosyllabic language in the linguistic sense, and that in its sentence-building it is incorporative and polysynthetic, like the great majority of American tongues, and totally unlike the Chinese. I may refer to my own published study of the Otomi, and to that of the Count de Charencey, as proving what I say. *

Some have thought that the Maya of Yucatan has in its vocabulary a certain number of Chinese elements; but all these can readily be explained on the doctrine of coincidences. The Mexican antiquary Mendoza has marshalled far more coincidences of like character and equal worth to show that the Nahuatl is an Aryan dialect descended from the Sanscrit. † In fine, any, even the remotest, linguistic connection between American and Mongolian languages has yet to be shown ; and any linguist who considers the radically diverse genius of the two groups of tongues will not expect to find such relationship.

I shall not detain you long with arguments touching sup-

---

* Brinton, in *Proceedings of the American Philosophical Society*, for 1885 ; Charencey, *Mélanges de Philologie et Paléographie Américaine*, p 80 (Paris, 1883). See also a later Essay in this volume.

† This example of misdirected erudition may be seen in the *Anales del Museo Nacional de Mexico*. Tomo I.

posed Mongolian elements of culture in ancient America. Any one at all intimately conversant with the progress of American archæology in the last twenty years must see how rapidly has grown the conviction that American culture was homebred, to the manor born: that it was wholly indigenous and had borrowed nothing—nothing, from either Europe, Asia, or Africa. The peculiarities of native American culture are typical, and extend throughout the continent. Mr. Lewis Morgan was perfectly right in the general outline of his theory to this effect, though, like all persons enamored of a theory, he carried it too far.

This typical, racial American culture is as far as possible, in spirit and form, from the Mongolian. Compare the rich theology of Mexico or Peru with the barren myths of China. The theory of governments, the method of house-construction, the position of woman, the art of war,* are all equally diverse, equally un-Mongolian. It is useless to bring up single art-products or devices, such as the calendar, and lay stress on certain similarities. The doctrine of the parallelism of human development explains far more satisfactorily all these coincidences. The sooner that Americanists generally, and especially those in Europe, recognize the absolute autochthony of native American culture, the more valuable will their studies become.

It is no longer in season to quote the opinions of Alexander von Humboldt and his contemporaries on this subject,

---

* Prof. Morse has also poined out to me that the Mongolian arrow-release—one of the most characteristic of all releases—has been nowhere found on the American continent. This is an important fact, proving that neither as hunters nor conquerors did any stray Mongols leave a mark on American culture

as I see is done in some recent works. The science of archæology has virtually come into being since they wrote, and we now know that the development of human culture is governed by laws with which they were unacquainted. Civilization sprang up in certain centres in both continents, widely remote from each other; but, as the conditions of its origin were everywhere the same, its early products were much alike.

It is evident from what I have said, that the asserted Mongolian or Mongoloid connection of the American race finds no support either from linguistics or the history of culture. If anywhere, it must be in physical resemblances. In fact, it has been mainly from these that the arguments have been drawn. Let us examine them.

Cuvier, who, as I have said, is responsible for the confusion of the American with the Mongolian race, based his racial scheme on the color of the skin, and included the American within the limits of the yellow race. Cuvier had seen very few pure Mongolians, and perhaps no pure-blooded Americans; otherwise he would not have maintained that the hue of the latter is yellow. Certainly it is not. You may call it reddish, or coppery, or cinnamon, or burnt sugar, but you cannot call it yellow. Some individuals or small tribes may approach the peculiar dusky olive of the Chinaman, but so do some of the European peoples of Aryan descent; and there are not wanting anthropologists who maintain that the Aryans are also Mongoloid. The one position is just as defensible as the other on the ground of color.

Several of the most prominent classifications of mankind

are based upon the character of the hair; the three great divisions being, as you know, into the straight, the curly, and the woolly haired varieties. These external features of the hair depend upon the form of the individual hairs as seen in cross-section. The nearer this approaches a circle, the straighter is the hair. It is true that both Mongolians and Americans belong to the straight haired varieties; but of the two, the American has the straighter hair, that whose cross-section comes nearer to a perfect circle. So that by all the rules of terminology and logic, if we are to call either branch a variation from the other, we should say that the Mongol is a variety of the American race, and call it "Americanoid," instead of *vice versa*.

The color of the hair of the two races is, moreover, distinctly different. Although superficially both seem black, yet, observed carefully by reflected light, it is seen that the ground-tone of the Mongolian is bluish, while that of the American is reddish.

Of positive cranial characteristics of the red race, I call attention to the interparietal bone (the *os Incæ*), which is found in its extreme development in the American, in its greatest rarity among the Mongolians; also to the form of the glabella, found most prominent in American crania, least prominent in Altaic or northern Mongoloid crania; and the peculiar American characteristics of the occipital bone, flattened externally, and internally presenting in nearly forty per cent. of cases the "Aymarian depression," as it has been termed, instead of the internal occipital protuberance.*

---

* Hovelacque et Hervé, *Anthropologie*, pp. 231, 234, 236; and on the Inca bone, see Dr. Washington Matthews in the *American Anthropologist*, vol. II., p. 337.

The shape of the skull has been made another ground of race-distinction; and, although we have learned of late years that its value was greatly over-estimated by the earlier craniologists, we have also learned that in the average, and throughout large numbers of peoples, it is a very persistent characteristic, and one potently indicative of descent or relationship. Now, of all the peoples of the world, the Mongols, especially the Turanian branch, are the most brachycephalic; they have the roundest heads; and it is in a high degree noteworthy that precisely the American nation dwelling nearest to these, having undoubted contact with them for unnumbered generations, are long-headed, or dolichocephalic, in a marked degree. I mean the Eskimo, and I cannot but be surprised that such an eminent anthropologist as Virchow,* in spite of this anatomical fact, and in defiance of the linguistic evidence, should have repeated the assertion that the Eskimo are of Mongolian descent.

Throughout the American continent generally, the natives were not markedly brachycephalic. This was abundantly illustrated more than twenty years ago by the late Prof. James Aitkins Meigs, in his "Observations on the Cranial Forms of the American Aborigines." They certainly, in this respect, show no greater Mongoloid affinities than do their white successors on the soil of the United States.

If color, hair, and crania are thus shown to present such feeble similarities, what is it that has given rise to a notion of the Mongoloid origin of the American Indian? Is it the so-called Mongolian eye, the oblique eye, with a seeming

---

* In *Verhandlungen der Berliner Anthrop. Gesellschaft*, 1881-82.

droop at its inner canthus? Yes, a good deal has been made of this by certain writers, especially by travellers who are not anatomists. The distinguished ethnologist Topinard says the Chinese are very often found without it, and I can confirm this opinion by those I have seen in this country. It is, indeed, a slight deformity, affecting the skin of the eyebrow only, and is not at all infrequent in the white race. Surgeons know it under the name *epicanthus*, and, as with us it is considered a disfigurement, it is usually removed in infancy by a slight operation. In a few American tribes it is rather prevalent, but in most of the pure Indians I have seen, no trace of it was visible. It certainly does not rank as a racial characteristic.*

The nasal index has been recommended by some anatomists as one of the most persistent and trustworthy of racial indications. The Mongolian origin of the red race derives faint support from this quarter. From the measurements given in the last edition of Topinard's work † the Mongolian index is 80, while that of the Eskimo and tribes of the United States and Canada, as far as observed, is 70, that of the average Parisian of to-day being 69 (omitting fractions). According to this test, the American is much closer to the white than to the yellow race.

Most of the writers (for instance, Avé-Lallemant, St. Hilaire, Peschel, and Virchow) who have argued for the

---

* Dr. Franz Boas, whose accurate studies of the Indians of the Northwest coast are well known, informs me that he has rarely or never noted the oblique eye among them. Yet precisely on that coast we should look for it, if the Mongolian theory has any foundation. Dr. Ranke's recent studies have proved the oblique eye to be merely an arrest of development.

† *Elements d' Anthropologie*, p. 1003.

Mongoloid character of the Americans, have quoted some one tribe which, it is asserted, shows marked Chinese traits. This has especially been said of the natives of three localities,—the Eskimo, the tribes of the North Pacific coast, and the Botocudos of Brazil. So far as the last-mentioned are concerned, the Botocudos, any such similarity has been categorically denied by the latest and most scientific traveller who has visited them, Dr. Paul Ehrenreich. It is enough if I refer you to his paper in the *Zeitschrift für Ethnologie* for 1887, where he dismisses, I should say once for all, the notion of any such resemblance existing. I have already pointed out that the Eskimo are totally un-Mongolian in cranial shape, in nasal index, and in linguistic character. They do possess in some instances a general physiognomical similarity, and this is all; and this is not worth much, as against the dissimilarities mentioned. The same is true of the differences and similarities of some tribes of the north-west coast. In estimating the value of resemblances observed in this part of our continent, we should remember that we have sufficient evidence to believe that for many generations some slight intercourse has been going on between the adjacent mainlands and islands of the two continents in the regions of their nearest proximity. The same train of events led to a blending of the negro and the white races along the shores of the Red Sea; but any one who recognizes the distinction of races at all—and I am aware that certain eccentric anthropologists do not—will not, on that account, claim that the white race is negroid. With just as little reason, it seems to me, has it been argued that the native Americans as a race are Mongoloid.*

An acute philosopical writer has stated that the superficial observer is apt to be impressed with the similarities of objects; while the profounder student finds his attention more profitably attracted to their differences. By this maxim we may explain this theory of the affinities of the American race as well as many another which has been broached.

---

* When this paper appeared in *Science* (September 14th, 1888), it led to a reply from Dr. H. F. C. Ten Kate, of Leyden, who had published various studies endeavoring to prove the Mongoloid character of the American race. His arguments, however, were merely a repetition of those which I believe I have refuted in the above article, and for that reason 1 do not include the discussion.

THE PROBABLE NATIONALITY OF THE "MOUND-BUILDERS."

[The following Essay is reprinted without alteration. It appeared in the *American Antiquarian* for October, 1881, aud has certain degree of historic value as illustrating the progress of archæologic study in the United States. It is, I believe, the first reasoned argument that the constructors of the mounds of the Ohio Valley were the ancestors of tribes known and resident not remote from the sites of these ancient works. Though this opinion has not yet been fully accepted, the tendency of later studies is unquestionably in its favor.]

THE question, Who were the Mound-builders? is one that still remains open in American archæology. Among the most recent expressions of opinion I may quote Prof. John T. Short, who thinks that one or two thousand years may have elapsed since they deserted the Ohio valley, and probably eight hundred since they finally retired from the Gulf coast.* Mr. J. P. MacLean continues to believe them to have been somehow related to the "Toltecs." † Dr. J. W. Foster, making a tremendous leap, connects them with a tribe "who, in times far remote, flourished in Brazil," and adds : "a broad chasm is to be spanned before we can link

---

* *The North Americans of Antiquity*, p. 106, (1880.)
† *The Mound Builders*, chap. xii, (Cinn., 1879.)

the Mound-builders to the North American Indians. They were essentially different in their form of government, their habits and their daily pursuits. The latter were never known to erect structures which should survive the lapse of a generation."*

On the other hand, we have the recent utterance of so able an ethnologist as Major J. W. Powell to the effect that, "With regard to the mounds so widely scattered between the two oceans, it may be said that mound-building tribes were known in the early history of discovery of this continent, and that the vestiges of art discovered do not excel in any respect the arts of the Indian tribes known to history. There is, therefore, no reason for us to search for an extralimital origin through lost tribes for the arts discovered in the mounds of North America." †

Between opinions so discrepant the student in archæology may well be at a loss, and it will therefore be worth while to inquire just how far the tribes who inhabited the Mississippi valley and the Atlantic slope at the time of the discovery were accustomed to heap up mounds, excavate trenches, or in other ways leave upon the soil permanent marks of their occupancy.

Beginning with the warlike northern invaders, the Iroquois, it clearly appears that they were accustomed to construct burial mounds. Colden states that the corpse was placed in a large round hole and that "they then raise the Earth in a round Hill over it."‡ Further particulars are

---
* *Pre-Historic Races of the United States of America*, pp. 388, 347, (Chicago, 1873.)
† *Transactions of the Anthropological Society of Washington*, D. C., p. 116, (1881.(
‡ *History of the Five Nations*, Introduction, p. 16 (London, 1750).

given by Lafitau : the grave was lined with bark, and the body roofed in with bark and branches in the shape of an arch, which was then covered with earth and stones so as to form an *agger* or *tumulus*.* In these instances the mound was erected over a single corpse ; but it was also the custom among the Hurons and Iroquois, as we are informed by Charlevoix, to collect the bones of their dead every ten years, and inter them in one mass together. † The slain in a battle were also collected into one place and a large mound heaped over them, as is stated by Mr. Paul Kane,‡ and that such was an ancient custom of the Iroquois tribes, is further shown by a tradition handed down from the last century, according to which the Iroquois believed that the Ohio mounds were the memorials of a war which in ancient times they waged with the Cherokees. || Mr. E. G. Squier, who carefully examined many of the earthworks in the country of the ancient Iroquois, was inclined at first to suppose the remains he found there were parts of "a system of defence extending from the source of the Allegheny and Susquehanna in New York, diagonally accross the country through central and northern Ohio to the Wabash," and hence drew the inference that "the pressure of hostilities [upon the mound-builders] was from the north-east."§ This opinion has been repeated by some recent writers ; but Mr. Squier

---

* *Meurs des Sauvages Américains comparés aux Meurs du Premiers Temps*, chap. xiii.

† *Journal Historique*, p. 377.

‡ *Wanderings of an Artist among the Indians of North America*, p. 3 (London, 1859).

| H. R. Schoolcraft, *Notes on the Iroquois*, pp. 162, 163, compare pp. 66, 67.

¶ Squier and Davis, *Ancient Monuments of the Mississippi Valley*, p. 44.

himself substantially retracted it in a later work, and reached the conviction that whatever ancient remains there are in Western New York and Pennsylvania are to be attributed to the later Indian tribes and not to the Mound-builders.*

The neighbors of the Iroquois, the various Algonkin tribes, were occasionally constructors of mounds. In comparatively recent times we have a description of a "victory mound" raised by the Chippeways after a successful encounter with the Sioux. The women and children threw up the adjacent surface soil into a heap about five feet high and eight or ten feet in diameter, upon which a pole was erected, and to it tufts of grass were hung, one for each scalp taken.†

Robert Beverly, in his *History of Virginia*, first published in 1705, describes some curious constructions by the tribes there located. He tells us that they erected "pyramids and columns" of stone, which they painted and decorated with wampum, and paid them a sort of worship. They also constructed stone altars on which to offer sacrifices. ‡ This adoration of stones and masses of rocks—or rather of the genius which was supposed to reside in them—prevailed also in Massachussetts and other Algonkin localities, and easily led to erecting such piles.‖

Another occasion for mound building among the Virginian Indians was to celebrate or make a memorial of a solemn

---

* *Aboriginal Monuments of the State of New York*, p. 11.

† Mr. S. Taylor, *American Journal of Science*, vol. xliv, p. 22.

‡ *History of Virginia*, book ii, chap. iii, ch. viii.

‖ See a well-prepared article on this subject by Prof. Finch, in the *American Journal of Science*, vol. vii, p. 153.

treaty. On such an occasion they performed the time honored ceremony of "burying the hatchet," a tomahawk being literally put in the ground, "and they raise a pile of stones over it, as the Jews did over the body of Absalom."*

I am not aware of any evidence that the Cherokees were mound-builders : but they appreciated the conveniences of such structures, and in one of their villages William Bartram found their council house situated on a large mound. He adds: "But it may be proper to observe that this mount on which the rotunda stands is of a much ancienter date than the building, and perhaps was raised for another purpose."† Lieutenant Timberlake is about our best early authority on the Cherokees, and I believe he nowhere mentions that they built upon mounds of artificial construction. Adair, however, states that they were accustomed to heap up and add to piles of loose stones in memory of a departed chief, or as monuments of important events.‡

The tribes who inhabited what we now call the Gulf States, embracing the region between the eastern border of Texas and the Atlantic Ocean south of the Savannah River, belonged, with few and small exceptions, to the great Chahta-Muskokee family, embracing the tribes known as Choctaws, Chikasaws, Muskokees or Creeks, Seminoles, Allibamons, Natchez and others. The languages of all these have numerous and unmistakable affinities, the Choctaw or Chahta presenting probably the most archaic form. It is among them, if anywhere within our limits, that we

---

* *History of Virginia*, bk. iii, chap vii.
† *Travels*, p. 367 (Dublin, 1793).
‡ *History of the North American Indians*, p. 184. See note at end of this Essay.

must look for the descendants of the mysterious "Moundbuilders." No other tribes can approach them in claims for this distinction. Their own traditions, it is true, do not point to a migration from the north, but from the west; nor do they contain any reference to the construction of the great works in question; but these people seem to have been a building race, and to have reared tumuli not contemptible in comparison even with the mightiest of the Ohio Valley.

The first explorer who has left us an account of his journey in this region was Cabeza de Vaca, who accompanied the exposition of Pamfilo de Narvaez in 1527. He, however, kept close to the coast for fear of losing his way, and saw for the most part only the inferior fishing tribes. These he describes as generally in a miserable condition. Their huts were of mats erected on piles of oyster shells (the shell heaps now so frequent along the southern coast). Yet he mentions that in one part, which I judge to be somewhere in Louisiana, the natives were accustomed to erect their dwellings on steep hills and around their base *to dig a ditch*, as a means of defence.*

Our next authorities are very important. They are the narrators of Captain Hernando de Soto's famous and ill starred expedition. Of this we have the brief account of Biedma, the longer story of "the gentleman of Elvas," a Portuguese soldier of fortune, intelligent and clear-headed, and the poetical and brilliant composition of Garcilasso de la

---

* *Relatione que fece Alvaro Nurez, detto Capo di Vacca*, **Ramusio**, *Viaggi*, tom. iii, fol. 317, 323 (Venice, 1556.)

Vega. In all of these we find the southern tribes described as constructing artificial mounds, using earthworks for defence, excavating ditches and canals, etc. I quote the following passage in illustration:

"The town and the house of the Cacique Ossachile are like those of the other caciques in Florida. * * * The Indians try to place their villages on elevated sites; but inasmuch as in Florida there are not many sites of this kind where they can conveniently build, they erect elevations themselves in the following manner: They select the spot and carry there a quantity of earth which they form into a kind of platform two or three pikes in height, the summit of which is large enough to give room for twelve, fifteen or twenty houses, to lodge the cacique and his attendants. At the foot of this elevation they mark out a square place according to the size of the village, around which the leading men have their houses. * * * To ascend the elevation they have a straight passage way from bottom to top, fifteen or twenty feet wide. Here steps are made by massive beams, and others are planted firmly in the ground to serve as walls. On all other sides of the platform, the sides are cut steep."*

Later on La Vega describes the village of Capaha:

"This village is situated on a small hill, and it has about five hundred good houses, surrounded with a ditch ten or twelve cubits (brazas) deep, and a width of fifty paces in most places, in others forty. The ditch is filled with water from a canal which has been cut from the town to Chicagua.

---

*La Vega, *Historia de la Florida*, Lib. ii, cap. xxii.

The canal is three leagues in length, at least a pike in depth, and so wide that two large boats could easily ascend or descend it, side by side. The ditch which is filled with water from this canal surrounds the town except in one spot, which is closed by heavy beams planted in the earth."*

Biedma remarks in one passage, speaking of the provinces of Ycasqui and Pacaha: "The caciques of this region were accustomed to erect near the house where they lived very high mounds (*tertres très-elevées*), and there were some who placed their houses on the top of these mounds."†

I cannot state precisely where these provinces and towns were situated; the successful tracing of De Soto's journey has never yet been accomplished, but remains as an interesting problem for future antiquaries to solve. One thing I think is certain; that until he crossed the Mississippi he at no time was outside the limits of the wide spread Chahta-Muskokee tribes. The proper names preserved, and the courses and distances given, both confirm this opinion. We find them therefore in his time accustomed to erect lofty mounds, terraces and platforms, and to protect their villages by extensive circumvallations. I shall proceed to inquire whether such statements are supported by later writers.

Our next authorities in point of time are the French Huguenots, who undertook to make a settlement on the St. John River near where St. Augustine now stands in Florida. The short and sad history of this colony is familiar to all.

---

* Ibid, Lib. vi, cap. vi. See for other examples from this work: Lib. ii, cap. xxx, Lib. iv, cap. xi, Lib. v, cap. iii, etc.

† *Relation de ce qui arriva pendant le Voyage du Capitaine Soto*, p. 88 (Ed. Ternaux Compans).

The colonists have, however, left us some interesting descriptions of the aborigines. In the neighborhood of St. Augustine these belonged to the Timuquana tribe, specimens of whose language have been preserved to us, but which, according to the careful analysis recently published by Mr. A. S. Gatschet,* has no relationship with the Chahta-Muskokee, nor, for that matter, with any other known tongue. Throughout the rest of the peninsula a Muskokee dialect probably prevailed.

The "Portuguese gentleman" tells us that at the very spot where De Soto landed, generally supposed to be somewhere about Tampa Bay, at a town called Ucita, the house of the chief "stood near the shore upon a very high mound made by hand for strength." Such mounds are also spoken of by the Huguenot explorers. They served as the site of the chieftain's house in the villages, and from them led a broad, smooth road through the village to the water.† These descriptions correspond closely to those of the remains which the botanists, John and William Bartram, discovered and reported about a century ago.

It would also appear that the natives of the peninsula erected mounds over their dead, as memorials. Thus the artist Le Moyne de Morgues, writes: "Defuncto aliquo rege ejus proviciæ, magna solemnitate sepelitur, et ejus tumulo crater, e quo bibere solebat, imponitur, defixis circum ipsum tumulum multis sagittis."‡ The picture he gives of the "tumulus" does not represent it as more than three or four

---

* *Proceedings* of the American Philosophical Society, 1879-1880.
† *Histoire Notable de la Floride*, pp. 138, 164, etc.
‡ *Brevis Narratio*, in De Bry, *Peregrinationes in Americam*, Pars. ii, Tab. xl, (1591.)

feet in height; so that if this was intended as an accurate representation, the structure scarcely rises to the dignity of a mound.

After the destruction of the Huguenot colony in 1565, the Spanish priests at once went to work to plant their missions. The Jesuit fathers established themselves at various points south of the Savannah River, but their narratives, which have been preserved in full in a historic work of great rarity, describe the natives as broken up into small clans, waging constant wars, leading vagrant lives, and without fixed habitations.* Of these same tribes, however, Richard Blomes, an English traveler, who visited them about a century later, says that they erected piles or pyramids of stones, on the occasion of a successful conflict, or when they founded a new village, for the purpose of keeping the fact in long remembrance.† About the same time another English traveler, by name Bristock, claimed to have visited the interior of the country and to have found in "Apalacha" a half-civilized nation, who constructed stone walls and had a developed sun worship; but in a discussion of the authenticity of his alleged narrative I have elsewhere shown that it cannot be relied upon, and is largely a fabrication.‡ A correct estimate of the constructive powers of the Creeks is given by the botanist, William Bartram, who visited them twice in the latter half of the last century. He found they had "chunk yards" surrounded by low walls of earth, at

---

* Alcazar, *Chrono-Historia de la Compania de Jesus en la Provincia de Toledo*, Tom. ii, Dec. iii, cap. vi, (Madrid, 1710.)

† *The Present State of His Majestie's Isles and Territories in America*, p. 156, (London, 1667.)

‡ *The Floridian Peninsula*, p. 95, sqq. (Phila. 1859.)

one end of which, sometimes on a moderate artificial elevation, was the chief's dwelling and at the other end the public council house.* His descriptions resemble so closely those in La Vega that evidently the latter was describing the same objects on a larger scale—or from magnified reports.

Within the present century the Seminoles of Florida are said to have retained the custom of collecting the slain after a battle and interring them in one large mound. The writer on whose authority I state this, adds that he "observed on the road from St. Augustine to Tomaka, one mound which must have covered two acres of ground,"† but this must surely have been a communal burial mound.

Passing to the tribes nearer the Mississippi, most of them of Choctaw affiliation, we find considerable testimony in the French writers to their use of mounds. Thus M. de la Harpe says : " The cabins of the Yasous, Courous, Offogoula and Ouspie are dispersed over the country on mounds of earth made with their own hands."‡ The Natchez were mostly of Choctaw lineage. In one of their villages Dumont notes that the cabin of the chief was elevated on a mound.§ Father Le Petit, a missionary who labored among them, gives the particulars that the residence of the great chief or "Brother of the Sun," as he was called, was erected on a mound (*butte*) of earth carried for that purpose. When the chief died, the house was destroyed, and the same mound was not used as the site of the mansion of his successor, but

---

* Bartram MSS., in the Library of the Pennsylvania Historical Society.

† *Narrative of Occola Nikkanoche, Prince of Econchatti,*, by his Guardian, pp. 71-2, (London, 1841.)

‡ *Annals*, in Louisiana *Hist. Colls.*, p. 196.

§ *Memoires Historiques de la Louisiane,* Tome ii, p. 109.

was left vacant and a new one was constructed.* This interesting fact goes to explain the great number of mounds in some localities; and it also teaches us the important truth that we cannot form any correct estimate of the date when a mound-building tribe left a locality by counting the rings in trees, etc., because long before they departed, certain tumuli or earthworks may have been deserted and tabooed from superstitious notions, just as many were among the Natchez.

We have the size of the Natchez mounds given approximately by M. Le Page du Pratz. He observes that the one on which was the house of the Great Sun was "about eight feet high and twenty feet over on the surface."† He adds that their temple, in which the perpetual fire was kept burning, was on a mound about the same height.

The custom of communal burial has been adverted to. At the time of the discovery it appears to have prevailed in most of the tribes from the Great Lakes to the Gulf. The bones of each phratry or gens—the former, probably—were collected every eight or ten years and conveyed to the spot where they were to be finally interred. A mound was raised over them which gradually increased in size with each additional interment. The particulars of this method of burial have often been described, and it is enough that I refer to a few authorities in the note.‡ Indeed it has not

---

* *Letters Edifiantes et Curieuses*, Tome. i, p. 261.

† *History of Louisiana*, vol. ii, p. 188, (Eng. Trans, London, 1763.)

‡ Adair, *History of the North American Indians*, pp. 184, 185:—William Bartram, *Travels*, p. 561: Dumont, *Memoires Historiques de la Louisiane*, Tome i, pp. 246, 264, et al.: Bernard Romans, *Natural and Civil History of Florida*, pp. 88-90, (a good account.)

The *Relations des Jesuits* describe the custom among the Northern Indians.

been pretended that such mounds necessarily date back to a race anterior to that which occupied the soil at the advent of the white man.

I have not included in the above survey the important Dakota stock who once occupied an extended territory on the upper Mississippi and its affluents, and scattered clans of whom were resident on the Atlantic Coast in Virginia and Carolina. But, in fact, I have nowhere found that they erected earthworks of any pretentions whatever.

From what I have collected, therefore, it would appear that the only resident Indians at the time of the discovery who showed any evidence of mound-building comparable to that found in the Ohio valley were the Chahta-Muskokees. I believe that the evidence is sufficient to justify us in accepting this race as the constructors of all those extensive mounds, terraces, platforms, artificial lakes and circumvallations which are scattered over the Gulf States, Georgia and Florida. The earliest explorers distinctly state that such were used and constructed by these nations in the sixteenth century, and probably had been for many generations. Such too, is the opinion arrived at by Col. C. C. Jones, than whom no one is more competent to speak with authority on this point. Referring to the earthworks found in Georgia he writes: "We do not concur in the opinion so often expressed that the mound-builders were a race distinct from and superior in art, government, and religion, to the Southen Indians of the fifteenth and sixteenth centuries."

It is a Baconian rule which holds good in every department of science that the simplist explanation of a given fact or series of facts should always be accepted ; therefore if we can point out a well known race of Indians who, at the time of the discovery, raised mounds and other earthworks, not wholly dissimilar in character and not much inferior in size to those in the Ohio valley, and who resided not very far away from that region and directly in the line which the Mound Builders are believed by all to have followed in their emigration, then this rule constrains us to accept for the present this race as the most probable descendants of the Mound Tribes, and seek no further for Toltecs, Asiatics or Brazilians. All these conditions are filled by the Chahta tribes.*

It is true, as I have already said, that the traditions of their own origin do not point to the north but rather to the west or northwest; but in one of these traditions it is noticeable that they claim their origin to have been from a large artificial mound, the celebrated *Nanih Waiya*, the Sloping Hill, an immense pile in the valley of the Big Black River;† and it may be that this is a vague reminiscence of their remote migration from their majestic works in the north.

The size of the southern mounds is often worthy of the descendants of those who raised the vast piles in the northern valleys. Thus one in the Etowah Valley, Georgia, has a cubical capacity of 1,000,000, cubic feet.‡ The Messier Mound, near the Chatahoochee River, contains about 700,000 cubic feet.§ Wholly artificial mounds 50 to 70 feet in height,

---

* *Antiquities of the Southern Indians,* particularly the Georgian Tribes, p. 135, (New York, 1873.)

† For particulars of this see my *Myths of the New World,* pp. 241-2, (New York, 1876.)

‡ C. C. Jones. *Monumental Remains of Georgia,* p. 32.

§ Ibid. *Antiquities of the Southern Indians,* p. 169.

SIZE OF MOUNDS.

with base areas of about 200 by 400 feet, are by no means unusual in the river valleys of the Gulf States.

With these figures we may compare the dimensions of the northern mounds. The massive one near Miamisburg, Ohio, 68 feet high, has been calculated to contain 311,350 cubic feet—about half the size of the Messier Mound. At Clark's Works, Ohio, the embankments and mounds together contain about 3,000,000 cubic feet;* but as the embankment is three miles long, most of this is not in the mounds themselves. Greater than any of these is the truncated pyramid at Cahokia, Illinois, which has an altitude of 90 feet and a base area of 700 by 500 feet. It is, however, doubtful whether this is wholly an artificial construction. Professor Spencer Smith has shown that the once famous "big mound" of St. Louis was largely a natural formation; and he expresses the opinion that many of the mounds in Missouri and Illinois, popularly supposed to be artificial constructions, are wholly, or in great part, of geologic origin.† There is apparently therefore no such great difference between the earth structures of the Chahta tribes, and those left us by the more northern mound-builders, that we need suppose for the latter any material superiority in culture over the former when first they became known to the whites; nor is there any improbability in assuming that the Mound-builders of the Ohio were in fact the progenitors of the Chahta tribes, and were driven south probably about three or four hundred years before the discovery. Such is the conviction to which the above reasoning leads us.

---

*Squier & Davis, *Ancient Monuments of the Mississippi Valley*, p. 29.
† *Origin of the Big Mound of St. Louis*, a paper read before the St. Louis Academy of Science.

In the course of it, I have said nothing about the condition of the arts of the Mound-builders compared with that of the early southern Indians; nor have I spoken of their supposed peculiar religious beliefs which a recent writer thinks to point to "Toltec" connections;* nor have I discussed the comparative craniology of the Mound-builders, upon which some very remarkable hypotheses have been erected; nor do I think it worth while to do so, for in the present state of anthropologic science, all the facts of these kinds relating to the Mound-builders which we have as yet learned, can have no appreciable weight to the investigator.

---

*Thomas E. Pickett, *The Testimony of the Mounds: Considered with especial reference to the Pre-historic Archæology of Kentucky and the Adjoining States*, pp. 9, 28, (Maysville, 1876.)

[Investigations conducted since the above Essay was printed require some modifications in its statements. The researches of Professor Cyrus Thomas render it likely that the Cherokees were also Mound-builders, and that they occupied portions of Western Pennsylvania and Western Virginia less than two centuries ago. (See also my work *The Lenâpé and their Legends*, pp. 16-18. Philadelphia, 1885.) Probably the Ohio Valley Mound-builders were the ancestors of some of the Cherokees as well as of the Chahta-Muskoki tribes. Craniologic data from the Ohio mounds are still too vague to permit inferences from them.]

THE TOLTECS AND THEIR FABULOUS EMPIRE.

IN the first addition of my *Myths of the New World*,* published in 1868, I asserted that the story of the city of Tula and its inhabitants, the Toltecs, as currently related in ancient Mexican history, is a myth, and not history. This opinion I have since repeated in various publications,† but writers on pre-Columbian American civilization have been very unwilling to give up their Toltecs, and lately M. Charnay has composed a laborious monograph to defend them.‡

Let me state the question squarely.

The orthodox opinion is that the Toltecs, coming from the north (-west or -east), founded the city of Tula (about forty

---

* *Myths of the New World.* By D. G. Brinton, chap. vi. *passim.*

† Especially in *American Hero Myths, a study in the Native Religions of the Western Continent*, pp. 35, 64,82, etc. (Philadelphia, 1882.)

‡ M. Charnay, in his essay, *La Civilisation Toltèque*, published in the *Revue d' Ethnographie*, T.iv., p. 281, 1885, states his thesis as follows : " Je veux prouver l'existence du Toltèque que certains ont niée ; je veux prouver que les civilisations Américaines ne sont qu'une seule et même civilisation ; enfin, je veux prouver que cette civilisation est toltèque." I consider each of these statements an utter error. In his *Anciennes Villes du Nouveau Monde*, M. Charnay has gone so far as to give a map showing the migrations of the ancient Toltecs. As a translation of this work, with this map, has recently been published in this country, it appears to me the more needful that the baseless character of the Toltec legend be distinctly stated.

miles north of the present city of Mexico) in the sixth century, A. D.; that their State flourished for about five hundred years, until it numbered nearly four millions of inhabitants, and extended its sway from ocean to ocean over the whole of central Mexico;* that it reached a remarkably high stage of culture in the arts; that in the tenth or eleventh century it was almost totally destroyed by war and famine;† and that its fragments, escaping in separate colonies, carried the civilization of Tula to the south, to Tabasco (Palenque), Yucatan, Guatemala and Nicaragua. Quetzalcoatl, the last ruler of Tula, himself went to the south-east, and reappears in Yucatan as the culture-hero Cukulkan, the traditional founder of the Maya civilization.

This, I say, is the current opinion about the Toltecs. It is found in the works of Ixtlilxochitl, Veitia, Clavigero, Prescott, Brasseur de Bourbourg, Orozco y Berra, and scores of other reputable writers. The dispersion of the Toltecs has been offered as the easy solution of the origin of the civilization not only of Central America, but of New Mexico and the Mississippi valley.‡

---

* Ixtlilxochitl, in his *Relaciones Historicas* (in Lord Kingsborough's *Antiquities of Mexico*, Vol. ix., p. 333), says that during the reign of Topiltzin, last king of Tula, the Toltec sovereignty extended a thousand leagues from north to south and eight hundred from east to west; and in the wars that attended its downfall five million six hundred thousand persons were slain !!

† Sahagun (*Hist. de la Nueva España*, Lib. viii, cap. 5) places the destruction of Tula in the year 319 B. C.; Ixtlilxochitl (*Historia Chichimeca*, iii, cap. 4) brings it down to 969 A. D.; the *Codex Ramirez* (p. 25) to 1168; and so on. There is an equal variation about the date of founding the city.

‡ Since writing the above I have received from the Comte de Charencey a reprint of his article on *Xibalba*, in which he sets forth the theory of the late M. L. Angrand, that all ancient American civilization was due to two "currents" of Toltecs, the western, straight-headed Toltecs, who entered Anahuac by land from the

FABLED HISTORY OF TULA.   85

The opinion that I oppose to this, and which I hope to establish in this article, is as follows:

Tula was merely one of the towns built and occupied by that tribe of the Nahuas known as *Azteca* or *Mexica*, whose tribal god was Huitzilopochtli, and who finally settled at Mexico-Tenochtitlan (the present city of Mexico); its inhabitants were called Toltecs, but there was never any such distinct tribe or nationality; they were merely the ancestors of this branch of the Azteca, and when Tula was destroyed by civil and foreign wars, these survivors removed to the valley of Mexico and became merged with their kindred; they enjoyed no supremacy, either in power or in the arts; and the Toltec "empire" is a baseless fable. What gave them their singular fame in later legend was partly the tendency of the human mind to glorify the "good old times" and to merge ancestors into divinities, and especially the significance of the name Tula, "the Place of the Sun," leading to the confounding and identification of a half-forgotten legend with the ever-living light-and-darkness myth of the gods Quetzalcoatl and Tezcatlipoca.

To support this view, let us inquire what we know about Tula as an historic site.

Its location is on one of the great ancient trails leading from the north into the Valley of Mexico.* The ruins of

---

north-west, and the eastern, flat-headed Toltecs, who came by sea fom Florida. It is to criticise such vague theorizing that I have written this paper.

* Motolinia, in his *Historia de los Indios de Nueva España*, p. 5, calls the locality "el puerto llamado Tollan," the pass or gate called Tollan. Through it, he states, passed first the Colhua and later the Mexica, though he adds that some maintain these were the same people. In fact, Colhua is a form of a word which means "ancestors;" *colli*, forefather; *no-col-huan*, my forefathers; *Colhuacan*, "the place

the old town are upon an elevation about 100 feet in height, whose summit presents a level surface in the shape of an irregular triangle some 800 yards long, with a central width of 300 yards, the apex to the south-east, where the face of the hill is fortified by a rough stone wall.* It is a natural hill, overlooking a small muddy creek, called the *Rio de Tula*.† Yet this unpretending mound is the celebrated *Coatepetl*, Serpent-Mount, or Snake-Hill, famous in Nahuatl legend, and the central figure in all the wonderful stories about the Toltecs.‡ The remains of the artificial tumuli and

of the forefathers," where they lived. In Aztec picture-writing this is represented by a hill with a bent top, on the "ikonomatic" system, the verb *coloa*, meaning to bend, to stoop. Those Mexica who said the Colhua proceeded them at Tula, simply meant that their own ancestors dwelt there. The *Anales de Cuauhtitlan* (pp. 29, 33) distinctly states that what Toltecs survived the wars which drove them southward became merged in the Colhuas. As these wars largely arose from civil dissensions, the account no doubt is correct which states that others settled in Acolhuacan, on the eastern shore of the principal lake in the Valley of Mexico. The name means "Colhuacan by the water," and was the State of which the capital was Tezcoco.

* This description is taken from the map of the location in M. Charnay's *Anciennes Villes du Nouveau Monde*, p. 83. The measurements I have made from the map do not agree with those stated in the text of the book, but are, I take it, more accurate.

† Sometimes called the *Rio de Montezuma*, and also the *Tollanatl*, water of Tula. This stream plays a conspicuous part in the Quetzalcoatl myths. It appears to be the same as the river *Atoyac* (= flowing or spreading water, *atl*, *toyaua*), or *Xipacoyan* (= where precious stones are washed, from *xiuitl*, *paca*, *yan*), referred to by Sahagun, *Hist. de la Nueva España*, Lib. ix., cap. 29. In it were the celebrated "Baths of Quetzalcoatl," called *Atecpanamochco*, "the water in the tin palace," probably from being adorned with this metal (*Anales de Cuauhtitlan*).

‡ See the *Codex Ramirez*, p. 24. Why called Snake-Hill the legend says not. I need not recall how prominent an object is the serpent in Aztec mythology. The name is a compound of *coatl*, snake, and *tepetl*, hill or mountain, but which may also may mean town or city, as such were usually built on elevations. The form *Coatepec* is this word with the postposition *c*, and means "at the snake-hill," or, perhaps, "at Snake-town."

walls, which are abundantly scattered over the summit, show that, like the pueblos of New Mexico, they were built of large sun-baked bricks mingled with stones, rough or trimmed, and both walls and floors were laid in a firm cement, which was usually painted of different colors. Hence probably the name *Palpan*, "amid the colors," which tradition says was applied to these structures on the Coatepetl.* The stone-work, represented by a few broken fragments, appears equal, but not superior, to that of the Valley of Mexico. Both the free and the attached column occur, and figure-carving was known, as a few weather-beaten relics testify. The houses contained many rooms, on different levels, and the roofs were flat. They were no doubt mostly communal structures. At the foot of the Serpent-Hill is a level plain, but little above the river, on which is the modern village with its corn-fields.

These geographical particulars are necessary to understand the ancient legend, and with them in mind its real purport is evident.†

That legend is as follows: When the Azteca or Mexica

---

* Or to one of them. The name is preserved by Ixtlilxochitl, *Relaciones Historicas*, in Kingsborough, *Mexico*, Vol, ix., p. 326. Its derivation is from *palli*, a color (root *pa*), and the postposition *pan*. It is noteworthy that this legend states that Quetzalcoatl in his avatar as *Ce Acatl* was born in the Palpan, "House of Colors;" while the usual story was that he came from Tla-pallan, the place of colors. This indicates that the two accounts are versions of the same myth.

† There are two ancient Codices extant, giving in picture-writing the migrations of the Mexi. They have been repeatedly published in part or in whole, with varying degrees of accuracy. Orozco y Berra gives their bibliography in his *Historia Antigua de Mexico*, Tom. iii. p. 61, note. These Codices differ widely, and seem contradictory, but Orozco y Berra has reconciled them by the happy suggestion that they refer to sequent and not synchronous events. There is, however, yet much to do before their full meaning is ascertained.

—for these names were applied to the same tribe*—left their early home in Aztlan—which Ramirez locates in Lake Chalco in the Valley of Mexico, and Orozco y Berra in Lake Chapallan in Michoacan†—they pursued their course for some generations in harmony; but at a certain time, somewhere between the eighth and the eleventh century of our era, they fell out and separated. The legend refers to this as a dispute between the followers of the tribal god Huitzilopochtli and those of his sister Malinalxochitl. We may understand it to have been the separation of two "totems." The latter entered at once the Valley of Mexico, while the

---

* The name Aztlan is that of a place and Mexitl that of a person, and from these are derived *Aztecatl*, plural, *Azteca*, and *Mexicatl*, pl. *Mexica*. The Azteca are said to have left Aztlan under the guidance of Mexitl (*Codex Ramirez*). The radicals of both words have now become somewhat obscured in the Nahuatl. My own opinion is that Father Duran (*Hist. de Nueva España*, Tom. i, p. 19) was right in translating Aztlan as "the place of whiteness," *el lugar de blancura*, from the radical *iztac*, white. This may refer to the East, as the place of the dawn; but there is also a temptation to look upon Aztlan as a syncope of *a-izta-tlan*,—"by the salt water."

Mexicatl is a *nomen gentile* derived from *Mexitl*, which was another name for the tribal god or early leader Huitzilopochtli, as is positively stated by Torquemada (*Monarquia Indiana*, Lib. viii, cap xi). Sahagun explains Mexitl as a compound of *metl*, the maguey, and *citli*, which means " hare " and " grandmother " (*Hist. de Nueva España*, Lib. x. cap. 29). It is noteworthy that one of the names of Quetzalcoatl is *Meconetzin*, son of the maguey (Ixtilxochitl, *Rel. Hist.*, in Kingsborough, Vol. ix, p. 238). These two gods were originally brothers, though each had divers mythical ancestors.

† Orozco y Berra, *Historia Antigua de Mexico*, Tom. iii, cap. 4. But Albert Gallatin was the first to place Aztlan no further west than Michoacan (*Trans. American Ethnolog. Society*, Vol. ii, p. 202). Orozco thinks Aztlan was the small island called Mexcalla in Lake Chapallan, apparently because he thinks this name means "houses of the Mexi;" but it may also signify "where there is abundance of maguey leaves," this delicacy being called *mexcalli* in Nahuatl, and the terminal *a* signfying location or abundance. (See Sahagun, *Historia de Nueva España*, Lib. vii, cap. 9.) At present, one of the smaller species of maguey is called *mexcalli*.

followers of Huitzilopochtli passed on to the plain of Tula and settled on the Coatepetl. Here, says the narrative, they constructed houses of stones and of rushes, built a temple for the worship of Huitzilopochtli, set up his image and those of the fifteen divinities (gentes?) who were subject to him, and erected a large altar of sculptured stone and a court for their ball play.* The level ground at the foot of the hill they partly flooded by damming the river, and used the remainder for planting their crops. After an indeterminate time they abandoned Tula and the Coatepetl, driven out by civil strife and warlike neighbors, and journeyed southward into the Valley of Mexico, there to found the famous city of that name.

This is the simple narrative of Tulan, stripped of its contradictions, metaphors and confusion, as handed down by those highest authorities the Codex Ramirez, Tezozomoc and Father Duran.† It is a plain statement that Tula and its Snake-Hill were merely one of the stations of the Azteca in their migrations—an important station, indeed, with natural strength, and one that they fortified with care, where for some generations, probably, they maintained an inde-

---

* It is quite likely that the stone image figured by Charnay, *Anciennes Villes du Nouveau Monde*, p. 72, and the stone ring used in the *tlachtli*, ball play, which he figures, p. 73, are those refered to in the historic legend.

† The *Codex Ramirez*, p. 24, a most excellent authority, is quite clear. The picture-writing—which is really phonetic, or, as I have termed it, *ikonomatic*—represents the Coatepetl by the sign of a hill (*tepetl*) inclosing a serpent (*coatl*). Tezozomoc, in his *Cronica Mexicana*, cap. 2, presents a more detailed but more confused account. Duran, *Historia de las Indias de Nueva España*, cap. 3, is worthy of comparison. The artificial inundation of the plain to which the accounts refer probably means that a ditch or moat was constructed to protect the foot of the hill. Herrera says: "Cercaron de agua el cerro llamado Coatepec." *Decadas de Indias*, Dec. iii, Lib. ii, cap. 11.

pendent existence, and which the story-tellers of the tribe recalled with pride and exaggeration.

How long they occupied the site is uncertain.* Ixtlilxochitl gives a list of eight successive rulers of the "Toltecs," each of whom was computed to reign at least fifty-two years, or one cycle; but it is noteworthy that he states these rulers were not of "Toltec" blood, but imposed upon them by the "Chichimecs." This does not reflect creditably on the supposed singular cultivation of the Toltecs. Probably the warrior Aztecs subjected a number of neighboring tribes and imposed upon them rulers.†

If we accept the date given by the *Codex Ramirez* for the departure of the Aztecs from the Coatepetl—A. D. 1168—then it is quite possible that they might have controlled the site for a couple of centuries or longer, and that the number of successive chieftians named by Ixtlilxochitl should not be

---

* The *Annals of Cuauhtitlan*, a chronicle written in the Nahuatl language, gives 309 years from the founding to the destruction of Tula, but names a dynasty of only four rulers. Veitia puts the founding of Tula in the year 713 A. D. (*Historia de Nueva España*, cap. 23.) Let us suppose, with the laborious and critical Orozco y Berra (notes to the *Codex Ramirez*, p. 210) that the Mexi left Aztlan A. D., 648. These three dates would fit into a rational chronology, remembering that there is an acknowledged hiatus of a number of years about the eleventh and twelfth centuries in the Aztec records (Orozco y Berra, notes to *Codex Ramirez*, p. 213). The *Anales de Cuauhtitlan* dates the founding of Tula *after* that of Tlaxcallan, Huexotzinco and Cuauhtitlan (p. 29).

† As usual, Ixtlilxochitl contradicts himself in his lists of rulers. Those given in his *Historia Chichimeca* are by no means the same as those enumerated in his *Relaciones Historicas* (Kingsborough, *Mexico*, Vol. ix, contains all of Ixtitlxochitl's writings). Entirely different from both is the list in the *Anales de Cuauhtitlan*. How completely euhemeristic Ixtlilxochitl is in his interpretations of Mexican mythology is shown by his speaking of the two leading Nahuatl divinities Tezcatlipoca and Huitzilopochtli as "certain bold warriors" ("ciertos caballeros muy valerosos." *Relaciones Historicas*, in Kingsborough, Vol. ix, p. 326).

ar wrong. The destructive battles of which he speaks as preceding their departure—battles resulting in the slaughter of more than five million souls—we may regard as the grossly overstated account of some really desperate conflicts.

That the warriors of the Azteca, on leaving Tula, scattered over Mexico, Yucatan and Central America, is directly contrary to the assertion of the high authorities I have quoted, and also to most of the mythical descriptions of the event, which declare they were all, or nearly all, massacred.*

The above I claim to be the real history of Tula and its Serpent-Hill, of the Toltecs and their dynasty. Now comes the question, if we accept this view, how did this ancient town and its inhabitants come to have so wide a celebrity, not merely in the myths of the Nahuas of Mexico, but in the sacred stories of Yucatan and Guatemala as well—which was unquestionably the case?

To explain this, I must have recourse to some of those curious principles of language which have had such influence in building the fabric of mythology. In such inquiries we have more to do with words than with things, with names than with persons, with phrases than with facts.

First about these names, Tula, Tollan, Toltec—what do

---

* See the note to page 84. But it is not at all likely that Tula was absolutely deserted. On the contrary, Herrera asserts that *after* the foundation of Mexico and the adjacent cities (despues de la fundacion de Mexico i de toda la tierra) it reached its greatest celebrity for skilled workmen. *Decadas de Indias*, Dec. iii, Lib. ii, cap. 1. The general statement is that the sites on the Coatepetl and the adjacent meadows were unoccupied for a few years—the *Anales de Cuauhtitlan* says nine years—after the civil strife and massacre, and then were settled again. The *Historia de los Mexicanos por sus Pinturas*, cap. 11, says, "y ansi fueron muertos todos os de Tula, que no quedó ninguno."

they mean? They are evidently from the same root. What idea did it convey?

We are first struck with the fact that the Tula I have been describing was not the only one in the Nahuatl district of Mexico. There are other Tulas and Tollans, one near Ococingo, another, now San Pedro Tula, in the State of Mexico, one in Guerrero, San Antonio Tula in Potosi,* etc. The name must have been one of common import. Herrera, who spells it *Tulo*, by an error, is just as erroneous in his suggestion of a meaning. He says it means "place of the tuna," this being a term used for the prickly pear.† But *tuna* was not a Nahuatl word; it belongs to the dialect of Haiti, and was introduced into Mexico by the Spaniards. Therefore Herrera's derivation must be ruled out. Ixtlilxochitl pretends that the name Tollan was that of the first chieftain of the Toltecs, and that they were named after him; but elsewhere himself contradicts this assertion.‡ Most writers follow the *Codex Ramirez*, and maintain that Tollan—of which Tula is but an abbreviation—is from *tolin*, the Nahuatl word for rush, the kind of which they made mats, and means "the place of rushes," or where they grow.

The respectable authority of Buschmann is in favor of this derivation; but according to the analogy of the Nahuatl language, the "place of rushes" should be *Toltitlan* or *Tolinan*, and there are localities with these names.§

---

* See Buschmann, *Ueber die Aztekischen Ortsnamen*, ss. 682, 788. Orozco y Berra, *Geografía de las Lenguas de Mejico*, pp. 248, 255.

† *Historia de las Indias Occidentales*, Dec. iii, Lib. ii, cap. 11.

‡ *Relaciones Historicas*, in Kingsborough's *Mexico*, Vol. ix, p. 392. Compare his *Historia Chichimeca*.

§ Buschmann, *Ueber die Aztekischen Ortsnamen*, ss. 682, 797.

DERIVATION OF TULA.

Without doubt, I think, we must accept the derivation of Tollan given by Tezozomoc, in his *Cronica Mexicana*. This writer, thoroughly familiar with his native tongue, conveys to us its ancient form and real sense. Speaking of the early Aztecs, he says: "They arrived at the spot called Coatepec, on the borders of *Tonalan, the place of the sun.*"*

This name, Tonallan, is still not unusual in Mexico. Buschmann enumerates four villages so called, besides a mining town, *Tonatlan*,† "Place of the sun" is a literal rendering, and it would be equally accurate to translate it "sunny-spot," or "warm place," or "summer-place." There is nothing very peculiar or distinctive about these meanings. The warm, sunny plain at the foot of the Snake-Hill was called, naturally enough, Tonallan, syncopated to Tollan, and thus to Tula.‡

---

* *Cronica Mexicana*, cap. 1. " Partieron de alli y vinieron á la parte qne llaman Coatepec, términos de Tonalan, lugar del sol." In Nahuatl *tonallan* usnally means summer, snn-time. It is syncopated from *tonalli* and *tlan ;* the latter is the locative termination ; *tonalli* means warmth, *sunniness*, akin to *tonatiuh*, sun ; bnt it also means soul, spirit, especially when combined with the possessive pronouns, as *totonal*, our soul, onr immaterial essence. By a further syncope *tonallan* was reduced to Tollan or Tnllan, and by the elision of the terminal semi-vowel, this again became Tula. This name may therefore mean "the place of sonls," an accessory signification which doubtless had its inflnence on the growth of the myths concerning the locality.

It may be of some importance to note that Tula or Tollan was not at first the name of the town, but of the locality—that is, of the warm and fertile meadow-lands at the foot of the Coatepetl. The town was at first called Xocotitlan, the place of fruit, from *xocotl*, fruit, *ti*, connective, and *tlan*, locative ending. (See Sahagun, *Historia de Nueva España*, Lib. x, cap. 29, secs. 1 and 12.) This name was also applied to one of the quarters of the city of Mexico when conqnered by Cortes, as we learn from the same authority.

† Buschmann, *Ueber die Aztekischen Ortsnamen*, ss. 794, 797, (Berlin, 1852.)

‡ The verbal radical is *tona*, to warm (hazer calor, Molina, *Vocabulario de la Lengua Mexicana*, s. v.) ; from this root come many words signifying warmth, fer-

But the literal meaning of Tollan—"Place of the Sun"—brought it in later days into intimate connection with many a myth of light and of solar divinities, until this ancient Aztec pueblo became apotheosized, its inhabitants transformed into magicians and demigods, and the corn-fields of Tula stand forth as fruitful plains of Paradise.

In the historic fragments to which I have alluded there is scant reference to miraculous events, and the gods play no part in the sober chronicle. But in the mythical cyclus we are at once translated into the sphere of the supernal. The Snake-Hill Coatepetl becomes the Aztec Olympus. On it dwells the great goddess "Our Mother amid the Serpents," *Coatlan Tonan*,* otherwise called "The Serpent-skirted," *Coatlicue*, with her children, The Myriad Sages, the *Centzon Huitznahua*.† It was her duty to sweep the Snake-Hill

---

tility, abundance, the sun, the east, the summer, the day, and others expressing the soul, the vital principle, etc. Siméon, *Dict. de la Langue Nahuatl*, s. v. *tonalli*.) As in the Algonkin dialects the words for cold, night and death are from the same root, so in Nahuatl are those for warmth, day and life. (Comp. Duponceau, *Mémoire sur les Langues de l'Amérique du Nord*, p. 327, Paris, 1836.)

* *Coatlan, to-nan*, from *coatl*, serpent ; *tlan*, among ; *to-nan*, our mother. She was the goddess of flowers, and the florists paid her especial devotion (Sahagun, *Historia*, Lib. ii, cap. 22). A precinct of the city of Mexico was named after her, and also one of the edifices in the great temple of the city. Here captives were sacrificed to her and to the Huitznahua. (Ibid., Lib. ii. Appendix. See also Torquemada, *Monarquia Indiana*, Lib. x. cap. 12.)

† *Centzon Huitznahua*, "the Four Hundred Diviners with Thorns." Four hundred, however, in Nahuatl means any indeterminate large number, and hence is properly translated myriad, legion. *Nahuatl* means wise, skillful, a diviner, but is also the proper name of the Nahuatl-speaking tribes ; and as the Nahuas derived their word for south from *huitzli*, a thorn, the Huitznahua may mean "the southern Nahuas." Sahagun had this in his mind when he said the Huitznahua were goddesses who dwelt in the south (*Historia de Nueva España*, Lib. vii, cap. 5). The word is taken by Father Duran as the proper name of an individual, as we shall see in a later note.

BIRTH OF THE HERO-GOD.   95

every day, that it might be kept clean for her children. One day while thus engaged, a little bunch of feathers fell upon her, and she hid it under her robe. It was the descent of the spirit, the divine Annunciation. When the Myriad Sages saw that their mother was pregnant, they were enraged, and set about to kill her. But the unborn babe spake from her womb, and provided for her safety, until in due time he came forth armed with a blue javelin, his flesh painted blue, and with a blue shield. His left leg was thin and covered with the plumage of the humming-bird. Hence the name was given to him "On the left, a humming-bird," Huitzilopochtli.* Four times around the Serpent-Mountain did he drive the Myriad Sages, until nearly all had fallen dead before his dart, and the remainder fled far to the south. Then all the Mexica chose Huitzilopochtli for their god, and paid honors to the Serpent-Hill by Tula as his birthplace.†

---

* *Huitzilopochtli*, from *huitzilin*, humming-bird, *opochtli*, the left side or hand. This is the usual derivation ; but I am quite sure that it is an error arising from the ikonomatic representation of the name. The name of his brother, Huitznahna, indicates strongly that the prefix of both names is identical. This, I doubt not, is from *huitz-tlan*, the south ; *ilo*, is from *iloa*, to turn ; this gives us the meaning "the left hand turned toward the south." Orozco y Berra has pointed out that the Mexica regarded left-handed warriors as the more formidable (*Historia Antigua de Mexico*, Tom. i, p. 125). Along with this let it be remembered that the legend states that Huitzilopochtli was born in Tula, and insisted on leading the Mexica toward the south, the opposition to which by his brother led to the massacre and to the destruction of the town.

† This myth is recorded by Sahagun, *Historia de Nueva España*, Lib. iii, cap. 1, "On the Origin of the Gods." It is preserved with some curious variations in the *Historia de los Mexicanos por sus Pinturas*, cap. 11. When the gods created the sun they also formed four hundred men and five women for him to eat. At the death of the women their robes were preserved, and when the people carried these to the Coatepec, the five women came again into being. One of these was Coatlicue, an untouched virgin, who after four years of fasting placed a bunch of white feathers

An equally ancient and authentic myth makes Huitzilopochtli one of four brothers, born at one time of the uncreated, bi-sexual divinity, the God of our Life, Tonacatecutli, who looms dimly at the head of the Aztec Pantheon. His brothers were the black and white Tezcatlipoca and the fair-skinned, bearded Quetzalcoatl. Yet a third myth places the birthplace of Quetzalcoatl directly in Tula, and names his mother, Chimalman, a virgin, divinely impregnated, like Coatlicue, by the descending spirit of the Father of All.*

Tula was not only the birthplace, but the scene of the highest activity of all these greatest divinities of the ancient Nahuas. Around the Coatepetl and on the shores of the Tollanatl—"the Water of Tula"—as the stream is called which laves the base of the hill, the mighty struggles of the gods took place which form the themes of almost all Aztec mythology. Tulan itself is no longer the hamlet of rush houses at the foot of the Coatepec, surmounted by its pueblo of rough stone and baked brick; it is a glorious city, founded and governed by Quetzalcoatl himself, in his first avatar as Hueman, the strong-handed. "All its structures were

---

in her bosom, and forthwith became pregnant. She brought forth Huitzilopochtli completely armed, who at once destroyed the Huitznahua. Father Duran translates all of this into plain history. His account is that when the Aztecs had occupied Tollan for some time, and had fortified the hill and cultivated the plain, a dissension arose. One party, followers of Huitzilopochtli, desired to move on; the other, headed by a chieftain, Huitznahua, insisted on remaining. The former attacked the latter at night, massacred them, destroyed the water-dams and buildings, and marched away (*Historia de las Indias de Nueva España*, Tom. i, pp. 25, 26). According to several accounts, Huitznahua was the brother of Huitzilopochtli. See my *American Hero Myths*, p. 81.

* I have discussed both these accounts in my *American Hero Myths*, chap. iii., and need not repeat the authorities here.

stately and gracious, abounding in ornaments. The walls within were incrusted with precious stones or finished in beautiful stucco, presenting the appearance of a rich mosaic. Most wonderful of all was the temple of Quetzalcoatl, It had four chambers, one toward the east finished in pure gold, another toward the west lined with turquoise and emeralds, a third toward the south decorated with all manner of delicate sea-shells, and a fourth toward the north resplendent with red jasper and shells."* The descriptions of other buildings, equally wondrous, have been lovingly preserved by the ancient songs.† What a grief that our worthy friend, M. Charnay, digging away in 1880 on the Coatepec, at the head of a gang of forty-five men, as he tells us,‡ unearthed no sign of these ancient glories, in which, for one, he fully believed! But, alas! I fear that they are to be sought nowhere out of the golden realm of fancy and mythical dreaming.

Nor, in that happy age, was the land unworthy such a glorious city. Where now the neglected corn-patches sur-

---

* The most highly-colored descriptions of the mythical Tula are to be found in the third and tenth book of Sahagun's *Historia de Nueva España*, in the *Anales de Cuauhtitlan*, and in the various writings of Ixtlilxochitl. Later authors, such as Veitia, Torquemada, etc., have copied from these. Ixtlilxochitl speaks of the "legions of fables" about Tulan and Quetzalcoatl which even in his day were still current ("otras trescientas fabulas que auu todavia corren." *Relaciones Historicas*, in Kingsborough, *Mexico*, Vol. ix, p. 332).

† In the collection of *Ancient Nahuatl Poems*, which forms the seventh volume of my *Library of Aboriginal American Literature*, p. 104, I have printed the original text of one of the old songs recalling the glories of Tula, with its "house of beams" *huapalcalli*, and its "house of plumed serpents," *coatlaquetzalli*, attributed to Quetzalcoatl.

‡ *Les Anciennes Villes du Nouveau Monde*, p. 84 (Paris, 1885).

round the shabby huts of Tula, in the good old time "the crops of maize never failed, and each ear was as long as a man's arm; the cotton burst its pods, not white only, but spontaneously ready dyed to the hand in brilliant scarlet, green, blue and yellow; the gourds were so large that they could not be clasped in the arms; and birds of brilliant plumage nested on every tree!"

The subjects of Quetzalcoatl, the Toltecs, were not less marvelously qualified. They knew the virtues of plants and could read the forecast of the stars; they could trace the veins of metals in the mountains, and discern the deposits of precious stones by the fine vapor which they emit; they were orators, poets and magicians; so swift were they that they could at once be in the place they wished to reach; as artisans their skill was unmatched, and they were not subject to the attacks of disease.

The failure and end of all this goodly time came about by a battle of the gods, by a contest between Tezcatlipoca and Huitzilopochtli on the one hand, and Quetzalcoatl on the other. Quetzalcoatl refused to make the sacrifices of human beings as required by Huitzilopochtli, and the latter, with Tezcatlipoca, set about the destruction of Tula and its people. This was the chosen theme of the later Aztec bards. What the siege of Troy was to the Grecian poets, the fall of Tula was to the singers and story-tellers of Anahuac—an inexhaustible field for imagination, for glorification, for lamentation. It was placed in the remote past—according to Sahagun, perhaps the best authority, about the year 319 before Christ.* All arts and sci-

---

* *Historia de Nueva España*, Lib. viii, cap. 5.

ences, all knowledge and culture, were ascribed to this wonderful mythical people; and wherever the natives were asked concerning the origin of ancient and unknown structures, they would reply; "'The Toltecs built them.'"*

They fixedly believed that some day the immortal Quetzalcoatl would appear in another avatar, and would bring again to the fields of Mexico the exuberant fertility of Tula, the peace and happiness of his former reign, and that the departed glories of the past should surround anew the homes of his votaries.†

What I wish to point out in all this is the contrast between the dry and scanty historic narrative which shows Tula with its Snake-Hill to have been an early station of the Azteca, occupied in the eleventh and twelfth century by one of their clans, and the monstrous myth of the later priests and poets, which makes of it a birthplace and abode of the gods, and its inhabitants the semi-divine conquerors and civilizers of Mexico and Central America. For this latter fable there is not a vestige of solid foundation. The references to Tula and the Toltecs in the *Chronicles of the*

---

* Father Duran relates, "Even to this day, when I ask the Indians, 'Who created this pass in the mountains? Who opened this spring? Who discovered this cave? or, Who built this edifice?' they reply, 'The Toltecs, the disciples of Papa.'" *Historia de las Indias de Nueva España*, cap. 79. *Papa*, from *papachtic*, the bushy-haired was one of the names of Quetzalcoatl. But the earlier missionary, Father Motilinia, distinctly states that the Mexica invented their own arts, and owed nothing to any imaginary teachers, Toltecs or others. "Hay entre todos los Indios muchos oficios, y de todos dicen *que fueron inventores los Mexicanos.*" *Historia de los Indios de la Nueva España*, Tratado iii, cap. viii.

† Quetzalcoatl announced that his return should take place 5012 years after his final departure, as is mentioned by Ixtilxochitl (in Kingsborough, *Mexico*, Vol. ix, p. 332). This number has probably some mystic relation to the calendar.

Mayas and the *Annals of the Kakchiquels* are loans from the later mythology of the Nahuas. It is high time for this talk about the Toltecs as a mighty people, precursors of the Azteca, and their instructors in the arts of civilization, to disappear from the pages of history. The residents of ancient Tula, the Tolteca, were nothing more than a sept of the Nahuas themselves, the ancestors of those Mexica who built Tenochtitlan in 1325. This is stated as plainly as can be in the Aztec records, and should now be conceded by all. The mythical Tula, and all its rulers and inhabitants, are the baseless dreams of poetic fancy, which we principally owe to the Tezcucan poets.*

---

* *American Hero Myths*, p. 35. The only writer on ancient American history before me who has wholly rejected the Toltecs is, I believe, Albert Gallatin. In his able and critical study of the origin of American civilization (*Transactions of the American Ethnologcal Society*, Vol. i, p. 203) he dismissed them entirely from historical consideration with the words: "The tradition respecting the Toltecs ascends to so remote a date, and is so obscure and intermixed with mythological fables, that it is impossible to designate either the locality of their primitive abodes, the time when they first appeared in the vicinity of the Valley of Mexico, or whether they were preceded by nations speaking the same or different languages." Had this well-grounded skepticism gained the ears of writers since 1845, when it was published, we should have been saved a vast amount of rubbish which has been heaped up under the name of history.

Dr. Otto Stoll (*Guatemala ; Reisen und Schilderungen*, ss, 408, 409, Leipzig, 1886) has joined in rejecting the ethnic existence of the Toltecs. As in later Nahuatl the word *toltecatl* meant not only "resident of Tollan," but also "artificer" and "trader," Dr. Stoll thinks that the Central American legends which speak of "Toltecs" should be interpreted merely as referring to foreign mechanics or pedlers, and not to any particular nationality. I quite agree with this view.

PART II.

MYTHOLOGY AND FOLK-LORE.

INTRODUCTORY.

FASHIONS in the study of mythology come and go with something like the rapidity of change in costume feminine, subject to the autocracy of a Parisian man-modiste. Myths have been held in turn to be of some deep historical, or moral, or physical purport, and their content has been sought through psychologic or philologic analysis. Just now, all these methods are out of fashion. The newest theory is that myths generally mean nothing at all; that they are merely funny or fearsome stories and never were much more; and that at first they were not told of anybody in particular nor about anything in particular.

As for philologic analysis, it is accused of failures and contradictory results; the names which it makes its material are alleged not to have belonged to the original story; and their etymology casts no more light on the meaning or the source of the myth than if they were Smith or Brown.

According to this facile method, the secret of all mythology is an open one, because there is no secret at all. No painful preliminary study of language is necessary to the science, no laborious tracing of names through their various dialectic forms and phonetic changes to their first and original sense, for neither their earlier nor later sense is to the purpose.

This new method goes still further. Some former mythologists had supposed that even in the savage state man feels a sense of awe before the mighty forces of nature and the terrible mysteries of life; that joy in light and existence, dread of death and darkness, love of family and country, are emotions so intimate, so native to the soul, as nowhere to be absent—so potent as to find expressions in the highest imagative forms of thought and speech. Not so the latest teachers. They sneer at the possibility of such inspiration even in the divine legends of cultivated nations, and are ready to brand them all as but the later growths of "myths, cruel, puerile and obscene, like the fancies of the savage myth-makers from which they sprang."*

Like other fashions, this latest will also pass away, because it is a fashion only, and not grounded on the permanent, the verifiable facts of human nature. Etymology is as yet far from an exact science, and comparative mythologists in applying it have made many blunders: they have often erred in asserting historical connections where none existed; they have been slow in recognizing that primitive man works with very limited materials, both physical and mental, and as everywhere he has the same problems to solve, his physical and mental productions are necessarily

---
*Andrew Lang, *Custom and Myth*, p. 28.

very similar. These are objections, not against the method, but against the manner of its application.

Those who have studied savage races most intimately and with most unbiased minds have never found their religious fancies merely "puerile and obscene," as some writers suppose, but significant and didactic. Savage symbolism is rich and is expressed both in object and word ; and what appears cruelty, puerility or obscenity assumes a very different aspect when regarded from the correct, the native, point of view, with a full knowledge of the surroundings and the intentions of the myth-makers themselves.

In the sections which follow I have endeavored to illustrate these opinions by some studies from American mythology. I have chosen a series of unpromising names from the sacred books of the Quiches of Guatemala, and endeavored to ascertain their exact definition and original purport. I have taken up the most unfavorable aspect of the Algonkin hero-god, and shown how parallel it is to the tendencies of the human mind everywhere; in the Journey of the Soul, the striking analogies of Egyptian, Aryan and Aztec myth have been brought together and an explanation offered, which I believe will not be gainsaid by any competent student of Egyptian symbolism. The Sacred Symbols found in all continents are explained by a similar train of reasoning ; while the modern folk-lore of two tribes of semi-Christianized Indians of to-day reveals some relics of the ancient usages.

THE SACRED NAMES IN QUICHE MYTHOLOGY.*

Contents.—The Quiches of Guatemala, and their relationship—Their Sacred Book, the *Popol Vuh*—Its opening words—The name Hun-Ahpu-Vuch — Hun-Ahpu-Utiu — Nim-ak — Nim-tzyiz — Tepeu—Gucumatz—Qux-cho and Qux-palo—Ah-raxa-lak and Ah-raxa-sel—Xpiyacoc and Xmucane—Cakulha—Huracan—Chirakan—Xbalanque and his Journey to Xibalba.

OF the ancient races of America, those which approached the nearest to a civilized condition spoke related dialects of a tongue, which from its principal members has been called the "Maya-Quiche" linguistic stock. Even to-day, it is estimated that about half a million persons use these dialects. They are scattered over Yucatan, Guatemala and the adjacent territory, and one branch formerly occupied the hot lowlands on the Gulf of Mexico, north of Vera Cruz.

The so-called "metropolitan" dialects are those spoken relatively near the city of Guatemala, and include the Cakchiquel, the Quiche, the Pokonchi and the Tzutuhil. They are quite closely allied, and are mutually intelligible, resembling each other about as much as did in ancient Greece

---
* Revised extracts from an article read before the American Philosophical Society in 1881.

the Attic, Ionic and Doric dialects. These closely related members of the Maya-Quiche family will be referred to under the sub-title of the Quiche-Cakchiquel dialects.

The civilization of these people was such that they used various mnemonic signs, approaching our alphabet, to record and recall their mythology and history. Fragments, more or less complete, of these traditions have been preserved. The most notable of them is the National Legend of the Quiches of Guatemala, the so-called *Popol Vuh*. It was written at an unknown date in the Quiche dialect, by a native who was familiar with the ancient records. A Spanish translation of it was made early in the last century by a Spanish priest, Father Francisco Ximenez, and was first published at Vienna, 1857.* In 1861 the original text was printed in Paris, with a French translation by the Abbé Brasseur (de Bourbourg). This original covers about 175 octavo pages, and is therefore highly important as a linguistic as well as an archæologic monument.

Both these translations are open to censure. It needs but little study to see that they are both strongly colored by the views which the respective translators entertained of the purpose of the original. Ximenez thought it was principally a satire of the devil on Christianity, and a snare spread by him to entrap souls; Brasseur believed it to be a history of the ancient wars of the Quiches, and frequently carries his euhemerism so far as to distort the sense of the original.

What has added to the difficulty of correcting these erroneous impressions is the extreme paucity of material for

---

* *Las Historias del Origen de los Indios de esta Provincia de Guatemala.* Por el R. P. F. Francisco Ximenez.

studying the Quiche. A grammar written by Ximenez has indeed been published, but no dictionary is available, if we except a brief "Vocabulary of the Principal Roots" of these dialects by the same author, which is almost useless for critical purposes.

It is not surprising, therefore, that some writers have regarded this legend with suspicion, and have spoken of it as but little better than a late romance concocted by a shrewd native, who borrowed many of his incidents from Christian teachings. Such an opinion will pass away when the original is accurately translated. To one familiar with native American myths, this one bears undeniable marks of its aboriginal origin. Its frequent obscurities and inanities, its generally low and narrow range of thought and expression, its occasional loftiness of both, its strange metaphors, and the prominence of strictly heathen names and potencies, bring it into unmistakable relationship to the true native myth. This especially holds good of the first two-thirds of it, which are entirely mythological.

As a contribution to the study of this interesting monument, I shall undertake to analyze some of the proper names of the divinities which appear in its pages. The especial facilities that I have for doing so are furnished by two MS. Vocabularies of the Cakchiquel dialect, presented to the library of the American Philosophical Society by the Governor of Guatemala in 1836. One of these was written in 1651, by Father Thomas Coto, and was based on the previous work of Father Francisco Varea. It is Spanish-Cakchiquel only, and the final pages, together with a grammar and an essay on the native calendar, promised in a body of the work, are unfortunately missing. What remains, however, makes a folio volume of 972 double columned pages, and contains a mass of information about the language. The second MS. is a copy of the Cakchiquel-Spanish Vocabulary of Varea, made by Fray Francisco Ceron in 1699. It is a quarto of 493 pages. I have also in my possession copies of the *Compendio de Nombres en Lengua Cakchiquel*, by P. F. Pantaleon de Guzman (1704), and of the *Arte y Vocabulario de la Lengua Cakchiquel*, by the R. P. F. Benito de Villacañas, composed about 1580.

Father Coto observes that the natives loved to tell long stories, and to repeat chants, keeping time to them in their dances. These chants were called *nugum tzih*, garlands of words, from *tzih*, word, and *nug*, to fasten flowers into wreaths, to set in order a dance, to arrange the heads of a discourse, etc. As preserved to us in the *Popol Vuh*, the rhythmical form is mostly lost, but here and there one finds passages, retained intact by memory no doubt, where a distinct balance in diction, and an effort at harmony are noted.

The name *Popol Vuh* given to this work is that applied by the natives themselves. It is translated by Ximenez "libro del comun," by Brasseur "livre national." The word *popol* is applied to something held in common ownership by a number; thus food belonging to a number is *popol naim;* a task to be worked out by many, *popol zamah;* the native council where the elders met to discuss public affairs was *popol tzih*, the common speech or talk. The word *pop* means the mat or rug of woven rushes or bark on which the family or company sat, and from the community of interests thus typified, the word came to mean anything in common.

Vuh or *uuh* is in Quiche and Cakchiquel the word for *paper* and *book*. It is an original term in these and connected dialects, the Maya having *uooh,* a letter, writing; *uoch,* to write.

There is a school of writers who deprecate such researches as I am about to make. They are of opinion that the appellations of the native gods were derived from trivial or accidental circumstances, and had no recondite or symbolic meaning. In fact, this assertion has been made with reference to the very names which I am about to discuss.

I do not share this opinion. Many of the sacred names among the American tribes I feel sure had occult and metaphorical significance. This is proved by the profound researches of Cushing among the Zuñis; of Dorsey among the Dakotas; and others. But to reach this hidden purport, one must study all the ideas which the name connotes, especially those which are archaic.

I begin with the mysterious opening words of the *Popol Vuh*. They introduce us at once to the mighty and manifold divinity who is the source and cause of all things, and to the original couple, male and female, who in their persons and their powers typify the sexual and reproductive principles of organic life. These words are as follows:

"Here begins the record of what happened in old times in the land of the Quiches.

"Here will we begin and set forth the story of past time, the outset and starting point of all that took place in the city of Quiche, in the dwelling of the Quiche people.

"Here we shall bring to knowledge the explanation and the disclosure of the Disappearance and the Reappearance through the might

THE NAME HUN-AHPU-VUCH.   109

of the builders and creators, the bearers of children and the begetters of children, whose names are Hun-ahpu-vuch, Hun-ahpu-utiu, Zaki-nima-tzyiz, Tepeu, Gucumatz, u Qux-cho, u Qux-palo, Ah-raxa-lak, Ah-raxa-tzel.

"And along with these it is sung and related of the grandmother-grandfather, whose name is Xpiyacoc and Xmucane, the Concealer and Protector; two-fold grandmother and two-fold grandfather are they called in the legends of the Quiches."*

It will be here observed that the declaration of the attributes of the highest divinity sets forth distinctly sexual ideas, and, as was often the case in Grecian, Egyptian and Oriental mythology, this divinity is represented as embracing the powers and functions of both sexes in his own person; and it is curious that both here and in the second paragraph, the *female* attributes are named *first*.

First in the specific names of divinity given is *Hun-ahpu-vuch*. To derive any appropriate signification for this has baffled students of this mythology. *Hun* is the numeral *one*, but which also, as in most tongues, has the other meanings of first, foremost, self, unique, most prominent, "the one," etc. *Ah pu* is derived both by Ximenez and Brasseur from the prefix *ah*, which is used to signify knowledge or possession of, or control over, mastership or skill in, origin from or practice in that to which it is prefixed; and *ub*, or *pub*, the *sarbacana* or blowpipe, which these Indians used to employ as a weapon in war and the chase. *Ah pu*, therefore, they take to mean, He who uses the sarbacane, a

---

*See Dr. Otto Stoll, *Ethnographie der Republik Guatemala*, p. 118. I regret to differ from this able writer, whose studies of the Quiche und Cakchiquel are the most thorough yet made, and from whose version the above translation of the opening lines of the *Popol Vuh* is taken.

hunter. *Vuch*, the last member of this compound name, is understood by both to mean the opossum.

In accordance with these deriviations the name is translated "an opossum hunter."

Such a name bears little meaning in this relation; little relevancy to the nature and functions of deity; and if a more appropriate and not less plausible composition could be suggested, it would have intrinsic claims for adoption. There is such a composition, and it is this: The derivation of Ahpu from *ah-pub* is not only unnecessary but hardly defensible. In Cakchiquel the sarbacane is *pub*, but in Quiche the initial *p* is dropped, as can be seen in many passages of the *Popol Vuh*. The true composition of this word I take to be *ah-puz*, for *puz* has a signification associated with the mysteries of religion; it expressed the divine power which the native priests and prophets claimed to have received from the gods, and the essentially supernatural attributes of divinity itself. It was the word which at first the natives applied to the power of forgiving sins claimed by the Catholic missionaries; but as it was associated with so many heathen notions, the clergy decided to drop it altogether from religious language, and to leave it the meaning of necromancy and unholy power. Thus Coto gives it as the Cakchiquel word for *magic* or *necromancy*,*

---

* In his *MS. Dictionary* is the following entry:

"PODER: *vtziniçabal*, vel *vtzintaçibal;* deste nombre usa la *Cartilla* en el Credo para decir por obra del poder del Spirito Santo. Al poder que tienen los Sacerdotes de perdonar pecados y dar sacramentos, se llaman, o an llamado, *puz, naual*. Asi el Ph. Varea en su *Diccionario* y el Sancto Vico en la *Theologia Indorum* usa en muchas partes destos vocablos en este sentido. Ya no estan tan en uso, pues entienden por el nombre *poder* y *vtzintaçibal;* y son vocablos que antiguamente aplicaban a sus idolos, y oy se procura que vayan olbidando todo aquello con que se les puede hacer memoria dellos."

The word *puz* is used in various passages of the *Popol Vuh* to express the supernatural power of the gods and priests; but probably by the time that Ximenez wrote, it had, in the current dialect of his parish, lost its highest signification, and hence it did not suggest itself to him as the true derivation of the name I am discussing.

The third term, *Vuch* or *Vugh*, was chosen according to Ximenez because this animal is notoriously cunning, "*por su astucia.*" This may be correct, and we may have here a reminiscence of an animal myth. But the word has several other significations which should be considered. It was the name of a sacred dance; it expressed the trembling in the ague chill; the warmth of water; and the darkness which comes before the dawn.*

Of these various meanings one is tempted to take the last, and connect Hun-ahpu-vuch with the auroral gods, the forerunners of the light, like the "Kichigouai, those who make the day," of Algonkin mythology.

There is a curious passage in the *Popol Vuh* which is in support of such an opinion. It occurs at a certain period of the history of the mythical hero Hunahpu. The text reads:

"Are cut ta chi r'ab zakiric,	"And now it was about to become white,
"Chi zaktarin,	And the dawn came,
"U xecah ca xaquinuchic.	The day opened.
"Ama x-u ch'ux ri Vuch?	'Is the *Vuch* about to be?'

---

* Coto says, "*Vugh;* nota que esta mesmo nombre tiene un genero de baile en que con los pies dan bueltas a un palo; tambien significa el temblor de cuerpo que da con la terciana, o la misma cission; significa asi mesmo quando quiere ya amanescer aquel ponerse escuro el cielo; tambien quando suele estar el agua del rio o laguna, por antiparastassis, caliente, al tal calorsillo llaman *Vugh.*"

"Ve, x-cha ri mama.
"Ta chi xaquinic;
"Quate ta chi gekumar chic;
"Cahmul xaquin ri mama.

"Ca xaquin-Vuch," ca cha vinak vacamic.

Yes, answered the old man.
Then he spread apart his legs;
Again the darkness appeared;
Four times the old man spread his legs.
"Now the opossum (*Vuch*) spreads his legs," say the people yet (meaning that the day approaches).

As the same word *Vuch* meant both the opossum and the atmospheric change which in that climate precedes the dawn, the text may be translated either way, and the homophony would give rise to a double meaning of the name. This homophony contains, indeed, rich material for the development of an animal myth, identifying the *Vuch* with the God of Light, just as the similarity of the Algonkin *waubisch*, the dawn, and *waubos*, the rabbit, gave occasion to a whole cycle of curious myths in which the Great Hare or the Mighty Rabbit figures as the Creator of the world, the Day Maker, and the chief God of the widely spread Algonkin tribes.*

In the second name, *Hun-ahpu-utiu*, the last member *utiu* means the coyote, the native wolf, an animal which plays an important symbolic part in the cosmogonical myths of Californian, Mexican and Central American tribes. It ap-

---

* I have traced the growth of this myth in detail in *The Myths of the New World, a Treatise on the Symbolism and Mythology of the Red Race of America*, chap. vi, (New York, 1876.) Dr. Otto Stoll in his most recent discussion of the myth of Hunahpu does not urge the meaning "opossum hunter," and remarks that in the Pokonchi dialect *henahpo* means "moon-man," and "month," referring therefore to a night-god. *Ethnologie der Indianer Stämme von Guatemala*, p. 32, (Leyden 1889.)

pears generally to represent the night, and I would render the esoteric sense of the two names by "Master of the Night," and "Master of the Approaching Dawn."

The same concealed sense seems to lurk in the next name, *Zaki-nima-tzyiz*, literally, "The Great White Pisote," the pisote being the proboscidian known as *Nasua narica*, L.

These names are repeated in a later passage of the *Popol Vuh* (p. 20).

"Make known your name, Hun-ahpu-vuch, Hun-ahpu-utiu, twofold bearer of children, twofold begetter of children, Nim-ak, Nim-tzyiz, master of the emerald, etc.

The name *Nim-ak* is elsewhere given *Zaki-nim-ak*. The former means "Great Hog," the latter "White, Great Hog." Brasseur translates *ak* as wild boar (*sanglier*), but it is the common name for the native hog, without distinction of sex. In a later passage,* we are informed that it was the name of an old man with white hair, and that Zaki-nima-tzyiz was the name of an old woman, his wife, all bent and doubled up with age, but both beings of marvelous magic power. Thus we find here an almost unique example of the deification of the hog; for once, this useful animal, generally despised in mythology and anathematized in religion, is given the highest pedestal in the Pantheon.

Perhaps we should understand these and nearly all similar brute gods to be relics of a primitive form of totemic worship, such as was found in vigor among some of the northern tribes. Various other indications of this can be discovered among the branches of the Maya family. The

---
* *Popol Vuh*, p. 40.

Cakchiquels were called "the people of the bat" (*zoq'*), that animal being their national sign or token, and also the symbol of their god.* The *tucur* owl, *chan* or *cumatz* serpent, *balam* tiger, and *geh* deer, are other animals whose names are applied to prominent families or tribes in these nearly related myths.

The priests and rulers also assumed frequently the names of animals, and some pretended to be able to transform themselves into them at will. Thus it is said of Gucumatz Cotuha, fifth king of the Quiches, that he transformed himself into an eagle, into a tiger, into a serpent, and into coagulated blood.† In their dances and other sacred ceremonies they used hideous masks, carved, painted and ornamented to represent the heads of eagles, tigers, etc. These were called *coh*, as *cohbal ruvi cot*, the mask of an eagle; *cohbal ruvi balam*, the mask of a tiger, etc. In Maya the same word is found, *koh*, and in the Codex Troano, one of few original Maya manuscripts we have left, these masks are easily distinguished on the heads of many of the persons represented. Recent observers tell us that in the more remote parishes in Central America these brute-faced masks are still worn by the Indians who dance in accompanying the processions of the Church!‡ Even yet, every new-born child among the Quiches is solemnly named after some beast by the native "medicine man" before he is baptized by the padre.||

---
* *Ibid*. pp. 225, 249.
† *Ibid*. p. 314.
‡ *Die Indianer von Santa Catalina Istlavacan; ein Beitrag zur Culturgeschichte der Urbewohner Central Amerikas.* Von Dr. Karl Scherzer, p. 9 (Wien, 1856).
|| *Ibid*., p. 11.

This brings me to a name which has very curious meanings, to wit, *Tepeu*. It is the ordinary word in these dialects for lord, ruler, chief or king. Its form in Cakchiquel is *Tepex*, in Maya *Tepal*, and it is probably from the adjective root *tep*, filled up, supplied in abundance, satisfied. In Quiche and Cakchiquel it is used synonymously with *galel* or *gagal* and *ahau*, as a translation of Señor or Cacique. But it has another definite meaning, and that is, the disease *syphilis*; and what is not less curious, this meaning extends also in a measure to *gagal* and *ahau*.

This extraordinary collocation of ideas did not escape the notice of Ximenez, and he undertakes to explain it by suggestion that as syphilis arises from cohabitation with many different women, and this is a privilege only of the great and powerful, so the name came to be applied to the chiefs and nobles, and to their god.*

Of course, syphilis has no such origin; but if the Indians thought it had, and considered it a proof of extraordinary genetic power, it would be a plausible supposition that they applied this term to their divinity as being the type of the fecundating principle. But the original sense of the adjective *tep* does not seem to bear this out, and it would rather appear that the employment of the word as the name of the disease was a later and secondary sense. Such is the opinion of Father Coto, who says that the term was applied jestingly to those suffering from syphilitic sores, because, like a chieftain or a noble, they did no work, but had to sit still with their hands in their laps, as it were, waiting to get well.†

---

* *Escolios à las Historias del Origen de los Indios*, p. 157.

† To quote his words:

"BUBAS: *galel* vel *tepex*. * * Quando an pasado dicen *xin colah ahauarem*,

The same strange connection occurs in other American mythologies. Thus in the Aztec tongue *nanahuatl* means a person suffering from syphilis; it is also, in a myth preserved by Sahagun, the name of the Sun-God, and it is related of him that as a sacrifice, before becoming the sun, he threw into the sacrificial flames, not precious gifts, as the custom was, but the scabs from his sores.* So also Caracaracol, a prominent figure in Haytian mythology, is represented as suffering from sores or buboes.

The name *Gucumatz* is correctly stated by Ximenez to be capable of two derivations. The first takes it from *gugum*, a feather; *tin gugumah*, I embroider or cover with feathers. The second derivation is from *gug*, feather, and *cumatz*, the generic name for serpent. The first of these is that which the writer of the *Popol Vuh* preferred, as appears from his expression; "They are folded in the feathers (*gug*), the green ones; therefore their name is Gugumatz; very wise indeed are they" (p. 6). The brilliant plumage of the tropical birds was constantly used by these tribes as an ornament for their clothing and their idols, and the possession of many of these exquisite feathers was a matter of pride.

The names *u Qux cho*, *Qux palo*, mean "the Heart of the Lake, the Heart of the Sea." To them may be added *u Qux*

---

id est, ya an dejado su señoria, porque el que las tiene se esta sentado, sin hacer cosa, como si fuese señor ó señora.

"SEÑORA: *xogohau* ; Señoria, *xogohauarem*. * * Deste nombre *xogohau* vsan metaphoricamente para decir que una muger moza tiene bubas ; porque se esta sin hacer cosa, mano sobre mano, * * y quando a auado de la enfermedad, dicen, si es varon : *xucolah rahauarem achi rumal tepex*. *Tepex* es la enfermedad de bubas."

* Sahagun, *Historia de Nueva España*, Lib. vii, cap. 2. He translates *Nanahuatzih*, "el buboso," Comp. Boturini, *Idea de una Nueua Historia de la America*, pp. 37, 38.

cah, "the Heart of the Sky," and *u Qux uleu*, "the Heart of the Earth," found elsewhere in the *Popol Vuh*, and applied to divinity. The literal sense of the word heart was, however, not that which was intended; in those dialects this word had a much richer metaphorical meaning than in our tongue; in them it stood for all the psychical powers, the memory, will and reasoning faculties, the life, the spirit, the soul.*

It would be more correct, therefore, to render these names the "spirit" or "soul" of the lake, etc., than the "heart." They represent broadly the doctrine of "animism" as held by these people, and generally by man in his early stages of religious development. They indicate also a dimly understood sense of the unity of spirit or energy in the different manifestations of organic and inorganic existence.

This was not peculiar to the tribes under consideration. The heart was very generally looked upon, not only as the seat of life, but as the source of the feelings, intellect and passions, the very soul itself.† Hence, in sacrificing victims it was torn out and offered to the god as representing the immaterial part of the individual, that which survived the death of the body.

The two names *Ah-raxa-lak* and *Ah-raxa-sel* literally

---

* The MS. Dictionary of Coto says, s. v. Corazon: "Attribuenle todos los affectos de las potencias, memoria y entendimiento y voluntad, * * unde *ahgux*, el cuidadoso, entendido, memorioso * *; toman este nombre *gux* por el alma de la persona, y por el spirito vital de todo viviente, v. g. *xel ru gux Pedro*, murió Pedro, vel, salio el alma de Pedro, * * deste nombre *gux* se forma el verbo *tin gux lah*, por pensar, cuidar, imaginar."

† "De adonde," remarks Granados y Galvez, "viene que mis Otomites, de una misma manera llaman á la alma que al corazon, aplicandoles á entrambos la voz *muy*." *Tardes Americanas*, Tarde iv, p. 101. (Mexico, 1778.)

mean, "He of the green dish," "He of the green cup." Thus Ximenez gives them, and adds that forms of speech with *rax* signify things of beauty, fit for kings and lords, as are brightly colored cups and dishes.

Rax is the name of the colors blue and green, which it is said by many writers cannot be distinguished apart by these Indians; or at least that they have no word to express the difference. *Rax*, by extension, means new, strong, rough, violent, etc.* Coming immediately after the names "Soul of the Lake," "Soul of the Sea," it is possible that the "blue plate" is the azure surface of the tropical sea.

In the second paragraph I have quoted, the narrator introduces us to "the ancestress (*iyom*), the ancestor (*mamom*), by name Xpiyacoc, Xmucane." These were prominent figures in Quiche mythology; they were the embodiments of the paternal and maternal powers of organic life; they were invoked elsewhere in the *Popol Vuh* to favor the germination of seeds, and the creation of mankind; they are addressed as "ancestress of the sun, ancestress of the light." The old man, Xpiyacoc, is spoken of as the master of divination by the *tzite*, or sacred beans; the old woman, Xmucane, as she who could forecast days and seasons (*ahgih*); they were the parents of those mighty ones "whose name was Ahpu," masters of magic.† From this ancient couple, Ximenez tells us the native magicians and medicine men of his day claimed to draw their inspiration, and they were especially consulted touching the birth of infants, in which they were still called upon to assist in spite of the efforts of

---

* Ximenez, *Gramatica de la Lengua Quiche*, p. 17.
† *Popol Vuh*, pp. 18, 20, 23, 69, etc.

the padres. It is clear throughout that they represented mainly the peculiar functions of the two sexes.

Their names perhaps belonged to an archaic dialect, and the Quiches either could not or would not explain them. All that Ximenez says is that Xmucane means *tomb* or *grave*, deriving it from the verb *tin muk*, I bury.

In most or all of the languages of this stock the root *muk* or *muc* means to cover or cover up. In Maya the passive form of the verbal noun is *mucaan*, of which the *Diccionario de Motul** gives the translation "something covered or buried," the second meaning arising naturally from the custom of covering the dead body with earth, and indicated that the mortuary rites among them were by means of interment; as, indeed, we are definitely informed by Bishop Landa.† The feminine prefix and the terminal euphonic *e* give precisely *X-mucaan-e*, meaning "She who is covered up," or buried.

But while etymologically satisfactory, the appropriateness of this derivation is not at once apparent. Can it have reference to the seed covered by the soil, the child buried in the womb, the egg hidden in the nest, etc., and thus typify one of the principles or phases of reproduction? For there is no doubt, but that it is in the category of divinities presiding over reproduction this deity belongs. Not only is she called "primal mother of the sun and the light,"‡

---

* "Cosa que esta encubierta ó enterrada." The *Diccionario de Motul* is the most complete dictionary of the Maya ever made. It dates from about 1590 and has its name from the town of Motul, Yucatan, where it was written. The author is unknown. Only two copies of it are in existence, one, very carefully made, with numerous notes, by Dr. Berendt, is in my possession. It is a thick 4to of 1500 pages.

† *Relacian de las Cosas de Yucatan*, § XXXIII.

‡ " R'atit zih, r'atit zak," *Popol Vuh*, pp. 18, 20.

but it is she who cooks the pounded maize from which the first of men were formed.

Both names may be interpreted with appropriateness to the sphere and functions of their supposed powers, from radicals common to the Maya and Quiche dialects. *Xmucane* may be composed of the feminine prefix *x* (the same in sound and meaning as the English pronominal adjective *she* in such terms as *she-bear*, *she-cat*): and *mukanil*, vigor, force, power.

Xpiyacoc is not so easy of solution, but I believe it to be a derivative from the root *xib*, the male, whence *xipbil*, masculinity,* and *oc* or *ococ*, to enter, to accouple in the act of generation.†

We can readily see, with these meanings hidden in them, the subtler sense of which the natives had probably lost, that these names would be difficult of satisfactory explanation to the missionaries, and that they would be left by them as of undetermined origin.

The second fragment of Quiche mythology which I shall analyze is one that relates to the Gods of the Storm. These are introduced as the three manifestations of *Qux-cha*, the Soul of the Sky, and collectively "their name is Hurakan:"

"Cakulha Hurakan is the first; Chipi-cakulha is the second; the third is Raxa-cakulha; and these three are the Soul of the Sky."

Elsewhere we read:

---

* Especially the *membrum virile*, Pio Perez, *Diccionario de la Lengua Maya*, s. v.
† "Entrar, juntarse el macho con la hembra." Brasseur, *Vocabulaire Maya français*, s. v.

"Speak therefore our name, honor your mother, your father; call ye upon Hurakan, Chipi-cakulha, Raxa-cakulha, Soul of the Earth, Soul of the Sky, Creator, Maker, Her who brings forth, Him who begets; speak, call upon us, salute us."*

Cakulha (Cakchiquel, *cokolhay*) is the ordinary word for the lightning; Raxa-cakulha, is rendered by Coto as "the flash of the lightning" (*el resplandor del rayo*); Chipi-cakulha is stated by Brasseur to mean "le sillonnement de l'eclair;" *chip* is used to designate the latest, youngest or least of children, or fingers, etc., and the expression therefore is "the track of the lightning."

There remains the name Hurakan, and it is confessedly difficult. Brasseur says that no explanation of it can be found in the Quiche or Cakchiquel dictionaries, and that it must have been brought from the Antilles, where it was the name applied to the terrible tornado of the West Indian latitudes, and, borrowed from the Haytians by early navigators, has under the forms *ouragan*, *huracan*, *hurricane*, passed into European languages. I am convinced, however, that the word Hurakan belongs in its etymology to the Maya group of dialects, and must be analyzed by them.

One such etymology is indeed offered by Ximenez, but an absurd one. He supposed the word was compounded of *hun*, one; *ru* his; and *rakan*, foot, and translates it "of one foot." This has very properly been rejected,.

On collating the proper names in the *Popol Vuh* there are several of them which are evidently allied to Hurakan. Thus we have *Cabrakan*, who is represented as the god of the earthquake, he who shakes the solid earth in his might

---
* *Popol Vuh*, pp. 8, 14.

and topples over the lofty mountains. His name is the common word for earthquake in these dialects. Again, one of the titles of Xmucane is *Chirakan Xmucane.*

The terminal *rakan* in these names is a word used to express greatness in size, height or bigness. Many examples are found in Coto's *Vocabulario.**

For a person tall in stature he gives the expression *togam rakan;* for large in body, the Cakchiquel is *naht rakan*, and for gigantic, or a giant, *hu rakan.*

This idea of strength and might is of course very appropriate to the deity who presides over the appalling forces of the tropical thunder-storm, who flashes the lightning and hurls the thunderbolt.

It is also germane to the conception of the earthquake god. The first syllable, *cab*, means twice, or two, or second ; and apparently has reference to *hun*, one or first, in *hurakan.* As the thunderstorm was the most terrifying display of power, so next in order came the earthquake.

The name *Chirakan* as applied to Xmucane may have many meanings ; *chi* in all these dialects means primarily *mouth;* but it has a vast number of secondary meanings, as in all languages. Thus, according to Coto, it is currently

---

* I take the following entries from Coto's *MSS.:*

"LARGA COSA : Lo ordinario es poner *rakan* para significar la largura de palo, cordel, etc.

"GIGANTE : *hu rapah rakan chi vinak*, *hu chogah rakan chi vanak ;* este nombre se usa de todo animal que en su specie es mas alto que los otros. Mco. Pº Saz, serm. de circumsciss, dice del Gigante Golias : *tugotic rogoric rakan chiachi* Gigante Golias."

Ignorant, apparently, of this meaning, Dr Stoll continues in his latest work to interpret Hurakan "with one foot." *Die Ethnologie der Indianer Stämme von Guatemala*, p. 31, (Leiden, 1889.) The chapter on mythology is the least satisfactory in this important work.

THE DESCENT INTO HELL. 123

used to designate the mouth of a jar, the crater of a volcano, the eye of a needle, the door of a house, a window, a gate to a field, in fact, almost any opening whatever. I suspect that as here used as part of the name of the mythical mother of the race and the representation of the female principle, it is to be understood as referring to the *ostium vaginæ*, from which, as from an immeasurable *vagina gentium*, all animate life was believed to have drawn its existence.

If the derivation of Hurakan here presented is correct, we can hardly refuse to explain the word as it occurs elsewhere with the same meaning as an evidence of the early influence of the Maya race on other tribes. It would appear to have been through the Caribs that it was carried to the West India islands, where it was first heard by the European navigators. Thus the *Dictionaire Galibi* (Paris, 1743,) gives for "diable," *iroucan, jeroucan, hyorokan*, precisely as Coto gives the Cakchiquel equivalent of "diablo" as *hurakan*. This god was said by the Caribs to have torn the islands of the West Indian archipelago from the mainland, and to have heaped up the sand hills and bluffs along the shores.* As an associate or "captain" of the hurricane, they spoke of a huge bird who makes the winds, by name *Savàcon*, in the middle syllable of which it is possible we may recognize the bird *vaku*, which the Quiches spoke of as the messenger of Hurakan.

I now pass to the myth of the descent of the hero-god, Xbalanque, into the underworld, Xibalba, his victory over

---

* De la Borde, *Relation de l'origine, etc., des Caraibes*, p. 7. (Paris, 1674.)

the inhabitants, and triumphant return to the realm of light. The exploits of this demigod are the principal theme of the earlier portion of the *Popol Vuh*.

It was the vague similarity of this myth to the narrative of the descent of Christ into hell, and his ascent into heaven, to which we owe the earliest reference to these religious beliefs of the Guatemalan tribes; and it is a gratifying proof of their genuine antiquity that we have this reference. Our authority is the Bishop of Chiapas, Bartolome de las Casas, with other contemporary writers. The Bishop writes that the natives of Guatemala alleged that Xbalanque was born at Utlatlan, the ancient Quiche capital, and having governed it a certain time with success, went down to hell to fight the devils. Having conquered them, he returned to the upper world, but the Quiches refused to receive him, so he passed on into another province.*

As related in the *Popol Vuh*, the myth runs thus:

The divine pair, Xpiyacoc and Xmucane had as sons Hunhun-Ahpu and Vukub-Hun-Ahpu (Each-one-a-Magician and Seven-times-a-Magician). They were invited to visit Xibalba, the Underworld, by its lords, Hun-Came and Vukub-Came (One-Death and Seven-Deaths), and accepting the invitation, were treacherously murdered. The head of Hunhun-Ahpu was cut off and suspended on a tree. A maiden, by name Xquiq, (Blood,) passed that way, and looking at the tree, longed for its fruit; then the head of Hunhun-Ahpu cast forth spittle into the outstretched palm of

---

*Las Casas, *Historia Apologetica de las Indias Occidentales*, cap cxxiv (Madrid edition): P. F. Alonzo Fernandez, *Historia Ecclesiastica de Nvestros Tiempos*, p. 137 (Toledo, 1611).

THE STORY OF THE HERO GOD.

the maiden, and forthwith she became pregnant. Angered at her condition, her father set about to slay her, but she escaped to the upper world and there brought forth the twins Hun-Ahpu and Xbalanque. They grew in strength, and performed various deeds of prowess, which are related at length in the *Popol Vuh*, and were at last invited by the lords of the Underworld to visit them. It was the intention of the rulers of this dark land that the youths should meet the same fate as their father and uncle. But, prepared by warnings, and skilled in magic power, Xbalanque and his brother foiled the murderous designs of the lords of Xibalba; pretending to be burned, and their ashes cast into the river, they rose from its waves unharmed, and by a stratagem slew Hun-Came and Vukub-Came. Then the inhabitants of the Underworld were terrified and fled, and Hun-Ahpu and Xbalanque released the prisoners and restored to life those who had been slain. The latter rose to the sky to become its countless stars, while Hunhun-Ahpu and Vukub-Hun-Ahpu ascended to dwell the one in the sun, the other in the moon.

The portion of the legend which narrates the return of Xbalanque to the upper world, and what befell him there, as referred to in the myth preserved by Las Casas, is not preserved in the *Popol Vuh*.

The faint resemblance which the early missionaries noticed in this religious tradition to that of Christ would not lead any one who has at all closely studied mythology to assume that this is an echo of Christian teachings. Both in America and the Orient the myths of the hero god, born of a virgin, and that of the descent into Hades, are among the most common. Their explanation rests on the universality and prominence of the processes of nature which are typified under these narratives. It is unscientific to attempt to derive one from the other, and it is not less so to endeavor to invest them with the character of history, as has been done in this instance by the Abbé Brasseur and various other writers.

The Abbé maintained that Xibalba was the name of an ancient State in the valley of the Usumasinta in Tabasco, the capital of which was Palenque.* He inclined to the belief that the original form was *tzibalba*, which would mean *painted mole*, in the Tzendal dialect and might have reference to a custom of painting the face. This far-fetched derivation is unnecessary. The word *Xibalba*, (Cakchiquel *Xibalbay*, Maya *Xibalba*, *Xabalba*, or *Xubalba*) was the common term throughout the Maya stock of languages to denote the abode of the spirits of the dead, or Hades, which with them was held to be under the surface of the earth, and not, as the Mexicans often supposed, in the far north. Hence the Cakchiquels used as synonymous with it the expression "the centre or heart of the earth."†

After the conquest the word was and is in common use in Guatemalan dialects to mean *hell*, and in Maya for *the devil*. Cogolludo states that it was the original Maya term for the

---

* *Dissertation sur les Mythes de l'Antiquité Americane*, § 8 (Paris, 1861); see also his note to the *Popol Vuh*, p. 70.

† *Ch'u qux uleu*, "in its heart the earth." (Coto, *Dicc.* s. v.)

Coto adds that the ancient meaning of the word was a ghost or vision of a departed spirit—"antiguamente este nombre *Xibalbay* significaba el demonio, vel los diffuntos ó visiones que se les aperescian, y asi decian, y aun algunos ay que lo dicen oy *xuqutzii xibalbay ri cetzam chi nu vach*, se me apereció el diffunto."

THE NATIVE HADES.   127

Evil Spirit, and that it means "He who disappears, or vanishes."* He evidently derived it from the Maya verb, *xibil*, and I believe this derivation is correct; but the signification he gives is incomplete. The original sense of the word was "to melt," hence "to disappear." † This became connected with the idea of disappearance in death, and of ghosts and specters.

It is interesting to note how the mental processes of these secluded and semi-barbarous tribes led them to the same association of ideas which our greatest dramatist expresses in Hamlet's soliloquy:

"O, that this too, too solid flesh would melt,
Thaw, and resolve itself into a dew;"

and which Cicero records in the phrase *dissolutio naturæ*, in the sense of death.‡

The natural terror and fright with which death and ghosts are everywhere regarded, and especially, as Landa remarks, by this people, explain how this secondary meaning became predominant in the word. The termination *ba* means in the Guatemalan dialects, where, whence, whither, *bey*, a path or road; *Xibilbay* thus signifies, in the locative sense, "the place where they (*i. e.* the dead) disappear," the

---

* "El Demonio se llamaba *Xibilha*, que quiere decir el que se desparece ó deshauece." *Historia de Yucathan*, Lib. iv, cap. vii. Cogolludo had lived in Yucatan twenty-one years when he was making the final revision of his History, and was moderately well acquainted with the Maya tongue.

† The *Diccionario de Motul*, MS., gives:

"XIBIL, *xibi*, *xibic*: cundir como gota de aceita; esparcirse la comida en la digestion, y deshacerse la sal, nieve ó yelo, humo ó niebla. *Item*: desparecerse una vision ó fantasma. *Item*: temblar de miedo y espantarse."

‡ *De Legibus*, Lib. ii, cap. 2.

Hades, the Invisible Realm, which was supposed to be under the ground.

It was a common belief among many tribes in America, that their earliest ancestors emerged from a world which underlies this one on which we live, and in ancient Cakchiquel legend, the same or a similar notion seems to have prevailed.

The name of the hero-god *Xbalanque* is explained by the Abbé Brasseur as a compound of the diminutive prefix *x*, *balam*, a tiger, and the plural termination *que*.* Like so many of his derivations, this is quite incorrect. There is no plural termination *que*, either in the Quiche or in any related dialect; and the signification "tiger" (jaguar, *Felix unca* Lin. in Mexican *ocelotl*), which he assigns to the word *balam*, is only one of several which belong to it.

The name is compounded of the prefix, either feminine or diminutive, *x; balam*, or, as given by Guzman, *balan ;*† and *queh*, deer. This is the composition given by Ximenez, who translates it literally as "a diminutive form of tiger and deer."‡

The name *balam*, was also that of a class of warriors: of a congregation of priests or diviners; and of one of the inferior orders of deities. In composition it was applied to a spotted butterfly, as it is in our tongue to the "tiger-lily;" to the king-bee; to certain rapacious birds of prey, etc.

None of the significations concerns us here; but we do see our way when we learn that both *balam* and *queh* are names

---

* "Les petits Tigres," *Mythes de l'Antiquité Americane*, § viii, *Popol Vuh*, p. 34. note.

† *Compendio de Nombres en Lengua Cakchiquel*, MS.

‡ *Las Historias del Origen de los Indios*, p. 16.

THE DIVINITY OF LIGHT.

of days in the Quiche-Cakchiquel calendar. The former stood for the twelfth, the latter for the seventh in their week of twenty days.* Each of the days was sacred to a particular divinity, but owing to the inadequate material preserved for the study of the ancient calendars of Guatemala, we are much in the dark as to the relationship of these divinities.

Suffice it to say that the hero-god whose name is thus compounded of two signs in the calendar, who is born of a virgin, who performs many surprising feats of prowess on the earth, who descends into the world of darkness and sets free the sun, moon and stars to perform their daily and nightly journeys through the heavens, presents in these and other traits such numerous resemblances to the Divinity of Light, reappearing in so many American myths, the Daymaker of the northern hunting tribes, that I do not hesitate to identify the narrative of Xbalanque and his deeds as one of the presentations of this widespread, this well-nigh universal myth—guarding my words by the distinct statement, however, that the identity may be solely a psychological, not a historical one.

---

* Father Varea, in his *Calepino de la Lengua Cakchiquel, MS.*, gives the following entries:

"BALAM: el tigre, *zakbalam*, tigre pequeño de su naturelezo; *gana balam*, el grande, tambein sig^a un signo de los Indios. *Maceval gih P^o balam*, ó *Maria xbalam*. *Balam* se llama el echizero."

"*Queh:* el veuado. Sig^a un cierto dia; otras veces dos dias; otras veces es signo de trece, otras veces cinco ó seis dias á la queuta de los Indios: *xa hun queh væ gih*, ó, *cuy queh, voo queh, vahaki*, ó, *oxlahuh queh*.

THE HERO-GOD OF THE ALGONKINS AS A CHEAT AND LIAR.*

IN the pleasant volume which Mr. Charles G. Leland has written on the surviving aboriginal folk-lore of New England,† the chief divinity of the Micmacs and Penobscots appears under what seems at first the outrageously incongruous name of *Gluskap, the Liar!* This is the translation of the name as given by the Rev. S. T. Rand, late missionary among the Micmacs, and the best authority on that language. From a comparison of the radicals of the name in related dialects of the Algonkin stock, I should say that a more strictly literal rendering would be "word-breaker," or "deceiver with words." In the Penobscot dialect the word is divided thus,—*Glus-Gahbé*, where the component parts are more distinctly visible.‡

The explanation of this epithet, as quoted from native sources by Mr. Leland, is that he was called the liar because "when he left earth, like King Arthur, for fairy land, he promised to return, and has never done so."

It is true that the Algonkian Hero-God, like all the Amercan culture-heroes, Ioskeha, Quetzalcoatl, Zamna, Bochica,

---
* Published in the *American Antiquarian*, for May, 1885.
† *The Algonquin Legends of New England*, (Boston, 1884.)
‡ The Micmac word *kêlooskábáwe*, means "he is a cheat," probably one who cheats by lying. See Rand, *Micmac Dictionary*, s. v. A cheat.

Viracocha, and the rest, disappeared in some mysterious way, promising again to visit his people, and has long delayed his coming. But it was not for that reason that he was called the "deceiver in words." Had Mr. Leland made himself acquainted with Algonkin mythology in general, he would have found that this is but one of several, to our thinking, opprobrious names they applied to their highest divinity, their national hero, and the reputed saviour and benefactor of their race.

The Crees, living northwest of the Micmacs, call this divine personage, whom, as Father Lacombe tells us, they regard as "The principal deity and the founder of these nations," by the name *Wisakketjâk*, which means "the trickster," "the deceiver." * The Chipeways apply to him a similar term, *Nenaboj*, or as it is usually written, *Nanabojoo*, and *Nanaboshoo*, "the Cheat," perhaps allied to *Nanabanisi*, he is cheated.†

This is the same deity that reappears under the names *Manabozho*, *Michabo*, and *Messou*, among the Chipeway tribes; as *Napiw* among the Blackfeet; and as *Wetucks* among the New England Indians where he is mentioned by Roger Williams as "A man that wrought great miracles among them, with some kind of broken resemblance to the Sonne of God." ‡

---

*Dictionaire de la Langue des Cris, sub. voce *Wisakketjâk*. "Homme fabuleux des différeutes tribus du Nord, auquel elles attribuent une puissance surnaturelle, avec un grand nombre de ruses, de tours, et de folies. Il est regardé comme le principal génie et le fondateur de ces nations. Chez les Sauteux on l'appelle *Nenaboj*, chez les Pieds-Noirs, *Napiw*. *Wisakketjakow*, C'est un fourbe, un trompeur."

† Baraga, *Otchipwe Dictionary*.

‡ *Key into the language of America*, p. 24.

These appellations have various significations. The last mentioned is apparently from *ock* or *ogh*, father, with the prefix *wit*, which conveys the sense "in common" or "general." Hence it would be "the common father."

Michabo, constantly translated by writers "the Great Hare," as if derived from *michi*, great, and *wabos*, hare, is really a verbal form from *michi* and *wabi*, white, and should be translated, "the Great White One." The reference is to the white light of the dawn, he, like most of the other American hero-gods, being an impersonation of the light.

The name *Wisakketjâk*, though entirely Algonkin in aspect, offers serious etymological difficulties, so unmanageable indeed that one of the best authorities, M. Cuoq, abandons the attempt.* Its most apparent root is *wisak*, which conveys the sense of annoyance, hurt or bitterness, and the name would thus seem to be applied to one who causes these disagreeable sensations.

In all the pure and ancient Algonkin cosmogonical legends, this divinity creates the world by his magic powers, peoples it with game and animals, places man upon it, teaches his favorite people the arts of the chase, and gives them the corn and beans. His work is disturbed by enemies of various kinds, sometimes his own brothers, sometimes by a formidable serpent and his minions.

These myths, when analyzed through the proper names they contain, and compared with those of the better known mythologies of the old world, show plainly that their original purport was to recount, under metaphorical language, on the

---

* *Leixque de la Langue Algonquine*, p. 443. (Montreal, 1886.)

one hand the unceasing struggle of day with night, light with darkness, and on the other, that no less important conflict which is ever waging between the storm and sunshine, the winter and summer, the rain and the clear sky.

Writers whose knowledge of religions was confined to that of the Semitic race, as represented in our Bible, have maintained that the story of Michabo's battles with the serpent, who is certainly represented as a master of magic and subtlety, and hence dangerous to the human race, must have come from contact with the missionaries. A careful study of the myth will dispel all doubts on this point. Years ago, Mr. E. G. Squier showed that this legend was unquestionably of aboriginal source; but he failed to perceive its significance.* The serpent, typical of the sinuous lightning, symbolizes the storm, the rains and the water.

But to return to the class of names with which we began. The struggles of Michabo with these various powerful enemies I have just named, constitute the principal theme of the countless tales which are told of him by the native story-tellers, only a small part of which, and those much disfigured, came under the notice of Mr. Leland, among the long civilized eastern tribes. Mr. Schoolcraft frequently refers to these "innumerable tales of personal achievement, sagacity, endurance, miracle and trick which place him in almost every scene of deep interest which can be imagined."†
These words express the spirit of the greater number of these legends. Michabo does not conquer his enemies by brute

---

* See his article in *The American Review*, for 1848, entitled " Manabozho and the Great Serpent, an Algonquin legend."

† *Algic Researches*, Vol. I, p. 134.

force, nor by superior strength, but by craft and ruses, by transforming himself into unsuspected shapes, by cunning and strategy. He thus comes to be represented as the arch-deceiver; but in a good sense, as his enemies on whom he practices these wiles are also those of the human race, and he exercises his powers with a benevolent intention.

Thus it comes to pass that this highest divinity of these nations, their chief god and culture-hero, bears in familiar narrative the surprising titles, "the liar," "the cheat," and "the deceiver."

It would be an interesting literary and psychological study to compare this form of the Michabo myth with some in the old world, which closely resemble it in what artists call *motive*. I would name particularly the story of the "wily Ulysses" of the Greeks, the "transformations of Ebu Seid of Serug" and the like in Arabic, and the famous tale of Reynard the Fox in medieval literature. The same spirit breathes in all of them; all minister to the delight with which the mind contemplates mere physical strength beaten in the struggle with intelligence. They are all peans sung for the victory of mind over matter. In none of them is there much nicety about the means used to accomplish the ends. Deceit by word and action is the general resource of the heroes. They all act on the Italian maxim:

> "O per fortuna, o per ingano,
> Il vencer sempre e laudabil cosa."

THE JOURNEY OF THE SOUL.*

I AM about to invite your attention to one of the many curious results of comparative mythology. This science, which is still in its infancy, may be regarded by some of you, as it is by the world at large, as one of little practical importance, and quite remote from the interests of daily life and thought. But some of the results it attains are so startling, and throw such a singular light on various familiar customs and popular beliefs, that the time is not far off when it will be recognized as one of the most potent solvents in the crucible of intelligence.

The point to which I shall address myself to-night is the opinion entertained by three ancient nations, very wide apart in space, time and blood, concerning the journey of the soul when it leaves the body.

These nations are the ancient Egyptians, the ancient Aryans, and the Aztecs or Nahua of Central Mexico.

All these people believed, with equal faith, in the existence of a soul or spirit in man, and in its continuing life after the death of the body. How they came by this belief does not concern my present thesis; that they held it in unquestioning faith none can deny who has studied even superficially their surviving monuments. They supposed

---

* An address delivered at the annual meeting of the Numismatic and Antiquarian Society of Philadelphia, and published in its *Proceedings* for 1883.

this assumed after-life was continued under varying conditions in some other locality than this present world, and that it required a journey of some length for the disembodied spirit to reach its destined abode. It is the events which were supposed to take place on this journey, and the goals to which it led, that I am about to narrate. It will be seen that there are several curious similarities in the opinions of these widely diverse peoples, which can only be explained by the supposition that they based their theories of the soul's journey and goal on some analogy familiar to them all.

I begin with the Egyptian theory. It appears in its most complete form in the sepulchral records of the New Kingdom, after the long period of anarchy of the Shepherd Kings had passed, and when under the 18th, 19th and 20th dynasties, Egypt may be said to have risen to the very pinnacle of her greatness.

The collection of the sacred funerary texts into the famous ritual known as "The Book of the Dead," dates from this time. Many of its chapters are, indeed, very much older; but Egyptian religion, which was not stationary, but constantly progressive toward higher intellectual forms and purer ethical standards, can best be judged as it was in this period, that of the Theban dynasties of the New Kingdom. To assign a date, we may say in round numbers, two thousand years before the Christian era.

From that invaluable document, therefore, the "Book of the Dead," we learn what this ancient people expected to happen to the soul when it left the body. Of the millions of mummies which were zealously prepared in those ages, none was complete unless it had folded with it one or a number of chapters of this holy book, the formulas in which were safeguards and passwords to the spirit on its perilous journey.

The general statement is that the soul on leaving the corpse passes toward the West, where it descends into the divine inferior region called Amenti, over which presides Osiris, "chief of chiefs divine," who represents the Sun-god in his absence, in other words the sun at night, the sun which has sunk in the west and stays somewhere all night.

In this place of darkness the soul undergoes its various tests. The deeds done in the flesh, the words spoken in life, the thoughts of the heart, are brought up against it by different accusers, who appear in the form of monsters of the deep. As the sun has to combat the darkness of the night and to overcome it before it can again rise, so the soul has to combat the record of its sins, and conquer the frightful images which represent them. This was to be done in the Egyptian, as in almost all religions, by the power of magic formulas, in other words by prayers, and the invocation of holy names.

Having succeeded, the soul saw the nightly constellations and the heavenly stars, and reached the great celestial river, whose name was Nun. This was the self-created, primordial element. From its green depths all created things, even the gods themselves, took their origin. It is called in the texts, "father of all gods." From it rose Ra, the Sun-god, in his brightness. In its dark depths lies bound in chains of iron the serpent Refref, the symbol of evil, otherwise called Apap. But, though bound, this monster endeavors to seize each soul that crosses the river.

The fortunate soul repels the serpent by blows and incantations which destroy its power, but the unfortunate one is swallowed up and annihilated.

This danger passed, the soul reaches the farther strand, and rises from the waters, as Horus, who represents the sun at dawn, rises from the eastern waves. This is the purpose of all the rites and prayers—to have the soul, as the expression is, "rise at day" or "rise in the daytime." In other words, to rise as the sun and with the sun, or, to use again the constant formula of the "Book of the Dead," to "enter the boat of the Sun;" for the Sun was supposed to sail through celestial and translucent waters on its grand journey from horizon to zenith and zenith to horizon. Starting at dawn as the child Horus, son of the slain and lost Osiris, the orb of light became at midday the mighty Ra, and as evening approached, was transformed into Khep-Ra or Harmachis, again to become Osiris when it had sunk beneath the western verge.

So strict and absolute was the analogy supposed by the Egyptians to exist between the course of the sun and the destiny of the soul, that every soul was said to become Osiris at the moment of death, and in the copies of the "Book of the Dead," enclosed in a mummy, the proper name of the defunct is always preceded by the name "Osiris," as we might say "Osiris Rameses" or "Osiris Sesostris."

To illustrate further what I have said, I will translate a few passages from the most recent and correct version of the "Book of the Dead," that published at Paris a few months ago, and made by Prof. Paul Pierret, of the Egyptian Museum of the Louvre.

THE INVOCATION TO OSIRIS.

The following is an extract from the first chapter of this Ritual:

"O ye who open the roads! O ye who make smooth the paths to the souls in the abode of Osiris! Make smooth the paths, open the roads to Osiris Such-a-one that he may enter, by the aid of this chapter, into the abode of Osiris; that he may enter with zeal and emerge with joy; that this Osiris Such-a-one be not repulsed, nor miss his way, that he may enter as he wishes and leave when he wills. Let his words be made true and his orders executed in the abode of Osiris.

"This Osiris Such-a-one is journeying toward the west with good fortune. When weighed in the balance he is found to be without sin; of numerous mouths, none has condemned him; his soul stands erect before Osiris; out of his mouth when on earth no impurity proceeded."

(Here the soul speaks:)

"I place myself before the master of the gods; I reach the divine abode; I raise myself as a living god; I shine among the gods of heaven; I am become as one of you, O ye gods. I witness the progress of the holy stars. I cross the river Nun. I am not far removed from the fellowship of the gods. I eat of the food of the gods. I sit among them. I am invoked as a divine being; I hear the prayers offered to me; I enter the boat of the sun; my soul is not far from its lord. Hail to thee, Osiris! Grant that I sail joyously to the west, that I be received by the lords of the west; that they say to me, 'Adoration, adoration and peace be thine;' and that they prepare a place for me near to the chief of chiefs divine."

Through the rhetoric of this mystic rhapsody we see that

the soul goes to the abode of Osiris, is judged and tested as to its merits, and if approved crosses in safety the river Nun and becomes as one of the gods themselves; a companion of Osiris and Ra.

Such, in broad outline, was the orthodox Egyptian doctrine. There was a vast amount of accessory matter and mysticism added to this simple statement, but the foundation is always the same.

To one or two points I will call attention for later reference in this paper.

In the 13th Chapter of the "Book of the Dead," the defunct is supposed to repeat the following formula:

"I arrive as a hawk, I depart as a phenix. I am the God of the morning. I have finished the journey and worshipped the sun in the lower world. Heavily braided is the hair of Osiris. I am one of the dogs of Horus. I have finished the journey and worshipped Osiris."

The reference to the hair of Osiris and the transformation of the soul into a dog, are incidents to which I shall refer in another connection.

Another interesting fact is the frequent recurrence of the numbers four and eight in the Egyptian theories of the spiritual world. In the 16th Chapter of the "Book of the Dead," it is prescribed that four pictures as set forth should be painted on the sarcophagus, in order that the soul may pass through the four apertures of the sky. The chapter identifies these with the cardinal points from which blow the four winds. In chapter 17th, which is one of the oldest texts in the book, reference is made to the eight gods of Hermapolis; elsewhere the number is mentioned. This

THE ROAD TO HADES.

illustrates the easy transfer of the plan of terrestrial geography to that of the spiritual world.

Passing now to the mythology of the Aryan nations, we find that the three great cycles of its poetry, the Indian, the Greek, and the Norse, agree closely in their opinions of the destination of the soul.

After death, according to their belief, the soul descended into a world below the surface of the earth. The Greeks called it the realm of Hades, from the name of its ruler, otherwise known as Pluto. The latter name signifies the wealthy, because sooner or later all the children of men and all their possessions come under his power. The meaning of Hades is unknown, as its derivation from *æidos*, unseen, is now generally doubted by the best Greek scholars.

The entrance to this realm was supposed to be guarded by two dogs, the more famous of which, Cerberus in Greek, is in the Vedas spoken of by the same name, Carvara. The soul must pacify these dogs and pass them without injury if it would enjoy the delights that lay beyond. Within the gates stretched a broad desert through which flowed the river Acheron, which in later myths came to have various branches, the Styx, Lethe, Polyphegmon, etc. This was to be crossed in the boat of Charon, the silent ferryman, who spake no word but exacted of each ghost a toll.

The dark river crossed, the spirit appeared before the judges, and by them its future fate was decided. An adverse decision condemned it to wander lonely in the darkness, but a favorable verdict authorized its entrance into the happy fields of Elysium. This joyous abode was in the far west, in that land beyond the shining waters and the purple sunset sea, where the orb of light goes to rest himself at night. Its light is eternal, its joys perennial, its happiness perfect.

With little difference, this faith was shared by ancient Indians and ancient Norsemen. The latter often buried with the dead a canoe or boat, destined to convey the soul across the waves to the happy land beyond.

Even the ancient Kelt of Cornwall or Brittany had this same myth of the Islands of the Blessed, lying somewhere far out in the Western Sea. What to the Greek was the Garden of the Hesperides with its fruit of golden quinces, was to the Kelt the Isle of Avalon, with its orchards of apples.

Thither was conveyed the noble Arthur when slain on the field of Lyoness. He was borne away in a royal boat by the fairy women of the strand. There Ogier the Dane, worn by the wars of a hundred years, was carried by his divine godmother to be restored to youth and strength, and to return again to wield his battle-axe under the Oriflamme of France.

Wherever we turn, whether in the most ancient chants of the Vedas, in the graceful forms of the Greek religious fancy, in the gaunt and weird imaginings of the Norse poets, or in the complex but brilliant pictures of mediæval romance, we find the same distinct plan of this journey of the soul.

I pass now to the New World, almost to the antipodes of India, and take up the doctrines of the Aztecs. We have sufficiently ample accounts of their notions, preserved by various early writers, especially by Father Sahagun, who took down the words of the priests in their own tongue, and at a date when their knowledge was not dimmed or distorted by Christian teaching. Something may also be learned from Tezozomoc, a native chronicler, and others.

From these it appear that the Aztecs held that after death the souls of all people pass downward into the under-world, to the place called *Mictlan*. This is translated by the missionaries as "hell" or "inferno," but by derivation it means simply "the place of the slain," from an active verb meaning "to kill."

To explain this further, I add that in all primitive American tribes, there is no notion of natural death. No man "dies," he is always "killed." Death as a necessary incident in the course of nature is entirely unknown to them. When a person dies by disease, they suppose he has been killed by some sorcery, or some unknown venomous creature.

The journey to Mictlan was long and perilous. The soul first passed through a narrow defile between two mountains which touched each other, where it was liable to be crushed; it then reached a path by which lay in wait a serpent; next was a spot where a huge green lizard whose name was "The Flower of Heat," was concealed. After this, eight deserts stretched their wild wastes, and beyond these, eight steep hills reared their toilsome sides into the region of snow. Over their summits blew a wind so keen that it was called "The Wind of Knives." Much did the poor soul suffer, exposed to this bitter cold, unless many coats of cotton and other clothing were burnt upon his tomb for use at this lofty pass.

These hills descended, the shivering ghost reached the river called "By the Nine Waters." It was broad, and deep, and swift. Little chance had the soul of crossing its dark current, was the aid for this purpose forgotten during life, or by the mourners. This aid was a dog, of the species trained by the Aztecs and held in high esteem by them.

But the dog must be of a particular color; white would not answer, else he would say, when brought to the brink, "As for me, I am already washed." Black would fail as much, for the animal would say, "I am too black myself to help another wash." The only color was red, and for this reason great numbers of reddish curs were fostered by the Aztecs, and one was sacrificed at each funeral. Clinging to it, the soul crossed the river and reached the further brink in safety, being purged and cleansed in the transit of all that would make it unfit for the worlds beyond.

These worlds were threefold. One was called "The nine Abodes of the Dead," where the ordinary mass of mankind were said to go and forever abide. The second was paradise, Tlalocan, the dwelling-place of the Tlalocs, the gods of fertility and rain. It was full of roses and fruits. No pain was there, and no sorrow. Scorching heat and cold were alike unknown. Green fields, rippling brooks, balmy airs and perpetual joy, filled the immortal days of the happy souls in Tlalocan. Those who were destined for its elysian years were divinely designated by the diseases or accidents of which they died. These were of singular variety. All struck by lightning or wounded, the leprous, the gouty, the dropsical, and what at first sight seems curious, all those who died of the forms of venereal diseases, were believed to pass directly to this Paradise.

The third and highest reward was reserved for the brave who died upon the field of battle, or, as captives, perished by the malice of public enemies, and for women who died in childbirth. These went to the sun in the sky, and dwelt up in the bright heavens. After four years they returned to earth, and under the form of bright-plumaged singing birds rejoiced the hearts of men, and were again spectators of human life.

In this Aztec doctrine the ruler of the underworld is spoken of as *Mictlantecutli*, which the obtuse missionaries persistently render as the devil.

The name means simply "Lord of the Abode of the Slain," or of the dead. In several of myths he is brought into close relation with the Aztec national hero-god, Quetzalcoatl.

Like Osiris, Quetzalcoatl was said to be absent, to have gone away to the home of the sun, that home where the sun rests at night. More specifically, this was said to be under the earth, and it was spoken of as a place of delights, like Tlalocan. Its name was *Cincalco*, which means the House of Abundance; for no want, no dearth, no hunger and no suffering, were known there. With him dwelt the souls of his disciples and the Toltecs, his people, and at some day or other he and they would return to claim the land and to restore it to its pristine state of perfection.

The thoughts in these faiths which I have described are the same. In each of them the supposed history of the destiny of the soul follows that of the sun and the stars. In all of them the spirits are believed to descend into or under the surface of the earth, and then, after a certain lapse of time, some fortunate ones are released to rise like the orbs of light into the heavens above.

Striking analogies exist among them all. The river which in each flows through the underworld, is nothing else than the great world-stream which in the primitive geography of every nation is believed to surround the habitable land, and beyond which the sun sinks at night. To reach the abode of the sun in the west this river must be crossed.

The numbers 4 and 8 which occur in the Egyptian and Aztec geography of the underworld, are relics of the sacredness attached to the cardinal points.

The ruler of the realm of shadows is not a malevolent being. Osiris, Hades or Pluto, Mictlantecutli, Quetzalcoatl, all originally represented the sun in its absence, and none of them in any way corresponds to the mediæval or modern notion of the devil. As Osiris, who is unquestionably the departed Sun-god, was represented with heavy and braided hair, so his Aztec correlative was also named *Tzontemoc*, which means, he of the abundant falling hair. In each case the analogy was to the long slanting rays of the setting sun.

The role of the dog in these myths is a curious one. He appears as a guardian and preserver. Even Cerberus is good to the good soul. It has been argued by the eminent Sanscrit antiquary Rajendalala, in his late volume on the Indo-Aryans, that this is a reminiscence of an ancient custom of throwing the dead bodies to the dogs to be consumed, rather than have them decay. This to me is not a very satisfactory explanation, but I have none other to offer in its place, and I therefore merely call attention to this singular similarity of notions.

Though I have confined my comparison to these three

ancient nations, you would err widely if you imagine that it is for lack of material to extend it. I could easily summon numberless other analogies from classic, from Persian, from Turanian, from Semitic sources, to show that these notions were almost universal to the race of man.

They carried themselves into early Christian teachings, and to-day the wording of this ancient Sun-myth is repeated in most of the churches of Christendon. We have but to mention the "river of death" which is supposed to limit human life; we have but to look at the phraseology of the Nicene Symbol, where it is said that Christ "descended into hell (Hades)," and after three days rose from the dead and ascended into heaven, to see how persistently the old ideas have retained their sway over the religious sentiments and expressions of man.

THE SACRED SYMBOLS IN AMERICA.*

WHAT I am about to say is, to a certain degree, polemical. My intention is to combat the opinions of those writers who, like Dr. Hamy, M. Beauvois and many others,† assert that because certain well-known Oriental symbols, as the Ta Ki, the Triskeles, the Svastika and the Cross, are found among the American aborgines, they are evidence of Mongolian, Buddhistic, Christian or Aryan immigrations, previous to the discovery by Columbus ; and I shall also try to show that the position is erroneous of those who, like William H. Holmes, of the Bureau of Ethnology, maintain that "it is impossible to give a satisfactory explanation of the religious significance of the cross as a religious symbol in America."‡

In opposition to both these views I propose to show that the primary significance of all these widely extended sym-

---

* This paper was read before the American Philosophical Society in December, 1888, and was printed in its *Proceedings*.

† Dr. E. T. Hamy, *An Interpretation of one of the Copan Monuments*, in *Journal of the Anthropological Institute*, February 1887 ; also, *Revue d' Ethnographie*, 1886, p. 233 ; same author, *Le Svastika et la Roue Solaire en Amérique, Revue d' Ethnographie*, 1885, p. 22. E. Beauvois, in *Annales de Philosophie Chretienne*, 1877, and in various later publications. Ferraz de Macedo, *Essai Critique sur les Ages Prehistoriques de Bresil*, Lisbon, 1887, etc.

‡ See his article, " Art in Shell of the Ancient Americans," *Second Annual Report of the Bureau of Ethnology*, p. 270.

bols is quite clear; and that they can be shown to have arisen from certain fixed relations of man to his environment, the same everywhere, and hence suggesting the same graphic representations among tribes most divergent in location and race; and, therefore, that such symbols are of little value in tracing ethnic affinities or the currents of civilization; but of much import in investigating the expressions of the religious feelings.

Their wide prevalence in the Old World is familiar to all students. The three legs diverging from one centre, which is now the well-known arms of the Isle of Man, is the ancient *Triquetrum*, or, as Olshausen more properly terms it, the *Triskeles*,* seen on the oldest Sicilian coins and on those of Lycia, in Asia Minor, struck more than five hundred years before the beginning of our era. Yet, such is the persistence of symbolic forms, the traveler in the latter region still finds it recurring on the modern felt wraps used by the native inhabitants.† As a decorative motive, or perhaps with a deeper significance, it is repeatedly found on ancient Slavic and Teutonic vases, disinterred from mounds of the bronze age, or earlier, in Central and Northern Europe. Frequently the figure is simply that of three straight or curved lines springing from a central point and surrounded by a circle, as:

---

* See his article in *Zeitschrift für Ethnologie*, 1886, p. 223.
† Von Luchan, in *Zeitschrift für Ethnologie*, 1886, p. 301.

FIG. 1.   FIG. 2.

In the latter we have the precise form of the Chinese Ta Ki, a symbolic figure which plays a prominent part in the mystical writing, the divination and the decorative art of China.*

As it is this symbol which, according to Dr. Hamy, the distinguished ethnologist and Director of the Museum of the Trocadero, Paris, indicates the preaching of Buddhistic doctrines in America, it merits close attention.

The Ta Ki, expressed by the signs:

FIG. 3.

is properly translated, "The Great Uniter" (*ta*, great; *ki*, to join together, to make one, to unite); as in modern Chinese philosophy, expressed in Platonic language, the One is distinguished from the Many, and is regarded as the basis of the numerical system. But as the Chinese believe in the

---

* See Dumoutier, *Le Svastika et la Roue Solaire en Chine*, in *Revue d' Ethnologie*, 1885, pp. 333, *sq*.

CHINESE PHILOSOPHY.

mystic powers of numbers, and as that which reduces all multiplicy to unity naturally controls or is the summit of all things, therefore the Ta Ki expresses the completest and highest creative force.

In Chinese philosophy, the Universe is made up of opposites, heaven and earth, light and darkness, day and night, land and water, concave and convex, male and female, etc., the highest terms for which are *Yin* and *Yang*. These are held to be brought into fructifying union by Ta Ki. Abstractly, the latter would be regarded as the synthesis of the two universal antitheses which make up all phenomena.*

The symbolic representation of Yin and Yang is a circle divided by two arcs with opposite centres, while the symbol of Ta Ki adds a third arc from above uniting these two.

FIG. 4.   FIG. 5.

It is possible that these symbols are of late origin, devised to express the ideas above named. One Chinese scholar (Mr. S. Culin) tells me that it is doubtful if they occur earlier than the twelfth century, A. D., and that they were probably introduced for purposes of divination. In this case, I believe that they were introduced from the South, and that they originally had another and concrete significance, as I shall explain later.

---

* I am indebted for some of these explanations to Mr. K. Sungimoto, an intelligent Japanese gentleman, well acquainted with Chinese, late resident in Philadelphia.

Others consider these symbols as essentially Mongolian. The Ta Ki or Triskeles is to them the Mongolian, while the Svastika is the ethnic Aryan symbol. Such writers suspect Indo-European immigration where they discover the latter, Chinese immigration were they find the former emblem.

The Svastika, I need hardly say, is the hooked cross or gammated cross, usually represented as follows:

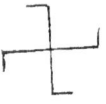

FIG. 6.

the four arms of equal length, the hook usually pointing from left to right. In this form it occurs in India and on very early (neolithic) Greco-Italic and Iberian remains. So much has been written upon the Svastika, however, that I need not enter upon its archæological distribution.

Its primary significance has been variously explained. Some have regarded it as a graphic representation of the lightning, others as of the two fire-sticks used in obtaining fire by friction, and so on.

Whatever its significance, we are safe in considering it a form of the Cross, and in its special form obtaining its symbolic or sacred association from this origin.

The widely-spread mystic purport of the Cross symbol has long been matter of comment. Undoubtedly in many parts of America the natives regarded it with reverence anterior to the arrival of Europeans; as in the Old World it was long a sacred symbol before it became the distinctive emblem of Christianity.

ORIGIN OF THE TA KI.

As in previous writings I have brought together the evidence of the veneration in which it was held in America, I shall not repeat the references here.

I believe we may go a step further and regard all three of these symbols, the Ta Ki or Triskeles, the Svastika, and the Cross as originally the same in signification, or, at least, closely allied in meaning. I believe, further, that this can be shown from the relics of ancient American art so clearly that no one, free from prejudice, and whose mind is open to conviction, will deny its correctness.

My theory is that all of the symbols are graphic representations of the movements of the sun with reference to the figure of the earth, as understood by primitive man everywhere, and hence that these symbols are found in various parts of the globe without necessarily implying any historic connections of the peoples using them.

This explanation of them is not entirely new. It has previously been partly suggested by Professors Worsaae and Virchow; but the demonstration I shall offer has not heretofore been submitted to the scientific world, and its material is novel.

Beginning with the Ta Ki, we find its primary elements in the symbolic picture-writing of the North American Indians. In that of the Ojibways, for example, we have the following three characters:

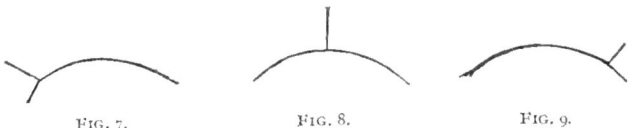

FIG. 7.   FIG. 8.   FIG. 9.

Of these, the Fig. 7 represents the sunrise; Fig. 9, sunset; Fig. 8, noonday. The last-mentioned is the full day at its height.* Where, in rock-writing or scratching on wood, the curve could not conveniently be used, straight lines would be adopted:

FIG. 10.

thus giving the ordinary form of the Triskeles. But the identical form of the Ta Ki is found in the calendar scroll attached to the Codex-Poinsett, an unpublished original Mexican MS., on agave paper, in the library of the American Philosophical Society. A line from this scroll is as follows:

FIG. 11.

Here each circle means a day, and those with the Triskeles, culminating days. †

---

* George Copway, *Traditional History of the Ojibway Nation*, p. 134. It will be noted that in the sign for sunrise the straight line meets the curve at its *left* extremity, and for sunset at its *right*. This results from the superstitious preference of facing the south rather than the north.

† The triplicate constitution of things is a prominent feature of the ancient Mexican philosophy, especially that of Tezcuco. The visible world was divided into three parts, the earth below, the heavens above, and man's abode between them. The whole was represented by a circle divided into three parts, the upper part painted blue, the lower brown, the centre white (See Duran, *Historia*, Lam. 15ᵃ, for an example). Each of these three parts was subdivided into three parts, so that when the Tezcucan king built a tower as a symbol of the universe, he called it "The Tower of Nine Stories" (see my *Ancient Nahuatl Poetry*, Introduction, p. 36).

THE COPAN STONE.

Another form of representing days is seen in the Vatican Mexican Codex, published in Kingsborough's *Mexico*, Vol. iii:

FIG. 12.

This is not far from the figure on the stone at Copan, described in Dr. Hamy's paper, where the design is as follows:

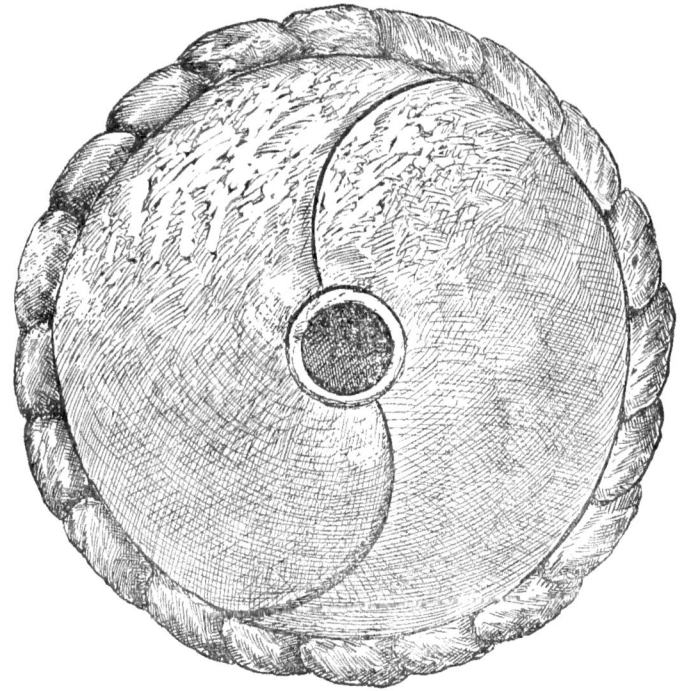

FIG. 13.

This does not resemble the Ta Ki, as Dr. Hamy supposes, but rather the Yin-Yang; yet differs from this in having a central circle (apparently a cup-shaped depression). This central circular figure, whether a boss or nave, or a cup-shaped pit, has been explained by Worsaae as a conventionalized form of the sun, and in this he is borne out by primitive American art, as we shall see. The twenty elevations which surround the stone, corresponding in number to the twenty days of the Maya month, indicate at once that we have here to do with a monument relating to the calendar.

Turning now to the development of this class of figures in primitive American art, I give first the simplest representations of the sun, such as those painted on buffalo skins by the Indians of the Plains, and scratched on the surface of rocks. The examples are selected from many of the kind published by Col. Garrick Mallery.*

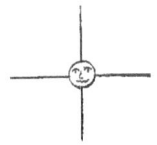

FIG. 14.

The design is merely a rude device of the human face, with four rays proceeding from it at right angles. These four rays represent, according to the unanimous interpretation of the Indians, the four directions defined by the appar-

---

* Mallery, *Pictography of the North American Indians*, in *Fourth Annual Report of the Bureau of Ethnology*, p. 239.

THE FOUR-SIDED EARTH-PLAIN.

ent motions of the sun, the East and West, the North and South. By these directions all travel and all alignments of buildings, corpses, etc., were defined ; and hence the earth was regarded as four-sided or four-cornered ; or, when it was expressed as a circle, in accordance with the appearance of the visible horizon, the four radia were drawn as impinging on its four sides:

FIG. 15.   FIG. 16.

Fig. 15 is a design on a vase from Maraja, Brazil, and is of common occurrence on the pottery of that region.* Fig. 16 represents the circle of the visible horizon, or the earth-plain, with the four winds rushing into it when summoned by a magician. It is a figure from the Meday Magic of the Ojibways.† Dr. Ferraz de Macedo has claimed that such devices as Fig. 16 "show Chinese or Egyptian inspiration."‡ It is certainly unnecessary to accept this alternative when both the origin and significance of the symbol are so plain in native American art.

When the symbol of the sun and the four directions was inscribed within the circle of the visible horizon, we obtain the figure representing the motions of the sun with reference to the earth, as in:

---

† Dr. Ferraz de Macedo, *Essai Critique sur les Ages Préhistorique de Brésil*, p. 38 (Lisbonne, 1887).

* *Captivity and Adventures of John Tanner*, pp. 359, 360.

‡ Op. cit., p. 38.

FIG. 17.

This is what German archæologists call the wheel-cross, *Radkreuz*, distinguished, as Worsaae pointed out, by the presence of the central boss, cup or nave, from the ring-cross, *Ringkreuz*, Fig. 18:

FIG. 18.   FIG. 19.

in which, also, the arms of the cross do not reach to the circumference of the wheel. Worsaae very justly laid much stress on the presence of the central boss or cup, and correctly explained it as indicative of the sun; but both he and Virchow, who followed him in this explanation, are, I think, in error in supposing that the circle or wheel represents the rolling sun, *die rollende Sonne*. My proof of this is that this same figure was a familiar symbol, with the signification stated, in tribes who did not know the mechanical device of the wheel, and could have had, therefore, no notion of such an analogy as the rolling wheel of the sun.*

---

* See Worsaae, *Danish Arts*, and Virchow, in various numbers of the *Zeitschrift für Ethnologie*. The ring-cross is a common figure in American symbolism and decorative art. It frequently occurs on the shields depicted in the Bologna Codex, and the two codices of the Vatican (Kingsborough's *Antiquities of Mexico*, Vols. ii.

THE NATIVE YEAR-COUNTS.

When applied to time, the symbol of the circle in primitive art referred to the return of the seasons, not to an idea of motion in space. This is very plainly seen both in art and language. In the year-counts or winter-counts of the American tribes, the years were very generally signified by circles arranged in rows or spirals. Fig. 20 shows the Dakota winter-count, as depicted on their buffalo robes.*

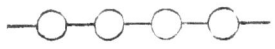

FIG. 20.

This count is to be read from right to left, because it is written from left to right, and hence the year last recorded is at the end of the line.

Precisely similar series of circles occur on the Aztec and Maya codices, with the same signification. Moreover, the year-cycles of both these nations were represented by a circle on the border of which the years were inscribed. In Maya this was called *uazlazon katun*, the turning about again, or revolution of the katuns.†

The Aztec figure of the year-cycle is so instructive that I give a sketch of its principal elements (Fig. 21), as portrayed in the atlas to Duran's History of Mexico.‡

---

and iii). Dr. Ferraz de Macedo says that the most common decorative design on both ancient and modern native Brazilian pottery is the ring-cross in the form of a double spiral, as in Fig. 19 (*Essai Critique sur les Ages Prehistorique de Bresil*, p. 40). A very similar form will be found in the Bologna Codex, pl. xviii, in Kingsborough's *Mexico*, Vol. ii.

* See Mallery, *Pictography of the North American Indians*, pp. 88, 89, 128, etc.
† This name is given in Landa, *Relacion de las Cosas de Yucatan*, p. 313.
‡ *Historia de la Nueva España*, Trat. III, cap. i.

FIG. 21.

In this remarkable figure we observe the development and primary signification of those world-wide symbols, the square, the cross, the wheel, the circle, and the svastika. The last-mentioned is seen in the elements of the broken circle, which are :

FIG. 22.

These, conventionalized into rectilinear figures for scratching on stone or wood, became:

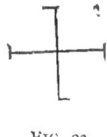

FIG. 23.

In the Mexican time-wheel, the years are to be read from right to left, as in the Dakota winter-counts; each of the quarter circles represents thirteen years; and these, also, are to be read from right to left, beginning with the top of the figure, which is the East, and proceeding to the North, South and West, as indicated.

The full analysis of this suggestive and authentic astronomical figure will reveal the secret of most of the rich symbolism and mythology of the American nations. It is easy to see how from it was derived the Nahuatl doctrine of the *nahua ollin*, or Four Motions of the Sun, with its accessories of the Four Ages of the world. The Tree of Life, so constantly recurring as a design in Maya and Mexican art, is but another outgrowth of the same symbolic expression for the same ideas.

That we find the same figurative symbolism in China, India, Lycia, Assyria and the valley of the Nile, and on ancient urns from Etruria, Iberia, Gallia, Sicilia and Scythia, needs not surprise us, and ought not to prompt us to assert any historic connection on this account between the early development of man in the New and Old World. The path of culture is narrow, especially in its early stages, and men everywhere have trodden unconsciously in each other's footsteps in advancing from the darkness of barbarism to the light of civilization.

THE FOLK-LORE OF YUCATAN.*

YUCATAN presents a strange spectacle to the ethnologist. The native race, which in nearly every other part of the American continent has disappeared before the white invaders or else become their acknowledged inferior, has there gained the upper hand. The native language has ousted the Spanish to that extent that whole villages of whites speak Maya only, and the fortunes of war in the last generation have sided so much with the native braves that they have regained undisputed possession of by far the larger part of the peninsula.

Is there to be recognized in this a revival of that inherent energy which prompted their ancestors to the construction of the most remarkable specimens of native architecture on the continent, and to the development of a ripe social and political fabric?

It can scarcely be doubted; but, however that may be, such considerations cannot fail to excite our interest in all that relates to a race of such plucky persistence.

As throwing a side-light on their mental constitution, their superstitions and folk-lore merit attention. I happen

---

* Printed originally in *The Folk-Lore Journal*, London, 1883.

to have some material on this which has never been published, and some more which has only appeared in mediums quite inaccessible even to diligent students. Of the former are a manuscript by the Licentiate Zetina of Tabasco, a native of Tihosuco, and some notes on the subject by Don Jose Maria Lopez, of Merida, and the late Dr. Carl Hermann Berendt; while of the latter a report by Don Bartholomé Granado de Baeza, *cura* of Yaxcabá, written in 1813, and an article of later date by the learned cura, Estanislao Carrillo, are particularly noteworthy.* From these sources I have gathered what I here present, arranging and studying the facts they give with the aid of several dictionaries of the tongue in my possession.

These Mayas, as the natives called themselves, were converted at the epoch of the conquest (about 1550) to Christianity in that summary way which the Spaniards delighted in. If they would not be baptized they were hanged or drowned; and, once baptized, they were flogged if they did not attend mass, and burned if they slid back to idol-worship. They were kept in the densest ignorance, for fear they should learn enough to doubt. Their alleged Christianity was therefore their ancient heathenism under a new name, and brought neither spiritual enlightenment nor intellectual progress. As a recent and able historian of

---

* *Informe del Señor Cura de Yaxcabà*, Don Bartolomé del Granado Baeza, in the *Registro Yucateco*, tomo i, pp. 165 *et seq.*

The Rev. Estanislao Carrillo was cura of Ticul, where he died in 1846. He was a zealous archæologist, and is frequently mentioned by Mr. Stephens in his travels in Yucatan. He is deservedly included in the *Manual de Biografia Yucateca* of Don Francisco de P. Sosa (Merida, 1866). His article on the subject of the text appeared in the *Registro Yucateco*, tomo iv. p. 103.

Yucatan has said, "the only difference was that the natives were changed from pagan idolaters to Christian idolaters."*

To this day the belief in sorcerers, witchcraft and magic is as strong as it ever was, and in various instances the very same rites are observed as those which we know from early authors obtained before the conquest.

The diviner is called *h'men*, a male personal form of the verb *men*, to understand, to do. He is one who knows, and who accomplishes. His main instrument is the *zaztun*, "the clear stone" (*zaz*, clear, transparent; *tun*, stone). This is a quartz crystal or other translucent stone, which has been duly sanctified by burning before it gum copal as an incense, and by the solemn recital of certain magic formulas in an archaic dialect passed down from the wise ancients. It is thus endowed with the power of reflecting the past and future, and the soothsayer gazes into its clear depths and sees where lost articles may be recovered, learns what is happening to the absent, and by whose witchery sickness and disaster have come upon those who call in his skill. There is scarcely a village in Yucatan without one of these wondrous stones.

The wise men have also great influence over the growing crops, and in this direction their chiefest power is exercised. By a strange mixture of Christian and pagan superstition, they are called in to celebrate the *misa milpera*, the "field mass" (*misa*, Spanish, "mass"; *milpera*, a word of Aztec derivation, from *milpa*, "cornfield"). In the native tongue

---

* "De idolatras paganos que eran, solo se ha conseguido que se conviertan en idolatras cristianos."—Apolinar Garcia y Garcia, *Historia de la Guerra de Castas en Yucatan*, Prologo, p. xxiv (Merida, 1865).

this is called the *tich*, which means the offering or sacrifice. It is a distinct survival of a rite mentioned by Diego de Landa, one of the earliest bishops of the diocese of Yucatan.*

The ceremony is as follows : On a sort of altar constructed of sticks of equal length the native priest places a fowl, and, having thrown on its beak some of the fermented liquor of the country, the *pitarrilla*, he kills it, and his assistants cook and serve it with certain maize cakes of large size and special preparation. When the feast is ready, the priest approaches the table, dips a branch of green leaves into a jar of *pitarrilla*, and asperges the four cardinal points, at the same time calling on the three persons of the Christian Trinity, and the sacred four of his own ancient religion, the *Pah ah tun*. These mysterious beings were before the conquest and to this day remain in the native belief the gods of rain, and hence of fertility. They are identical with the winds, and the four cardinal points from which they blow. To each is sacred a particular color, and in modern times each has been identified with a saint in the Catholic calendar. Thus Father Baeza tells us that the red Pahahtun is placed at the East, and is known as Saint Dominic ; to the North the white one, who is Saint Gabriel ; the black, toward the West, is Saint James ; the yellow is toward the South, and is a female, called in the Maya tongue *X'Kanleox*, "the yellow goddess," and bears the Christian name of Mary Magdalen.

The name *Pahahtun* is of difficult derivation, but it probably means "stone, or pillar, set up or erected," and this

---

* Landa, *Relacion de las Cosas de Yucatan*, pp. 208 *et seq*. The work of Landa was first printed at Paris in 1864.

tallies quite exactly with a long description of the ancient rites connected with the worship of these important divinities in the old times. There are some discrepancies in the colors assigned the different points of the compass, but this appears to have varied considerably among the Central American nations, though many of them united in having some such symbolism. A curious study of it has been made by the well-known archæologist, the Count de Charencey.*

The invocation to these four points of the compass in its modern form was fortunately obtained and preserved in the original tongue by that indefatigable student, the late Abbé Brosseur de Bourbourg, while on a visit to the plantation of Xcanchakan, in the interior of Yucatan.† The translation of it runs as follows :—

"At the rising of the Sun, Lord of the East, my word goes forth to the four corners of the heaven, to the four corners of the earth, in the name of God the Father, God the Son, and God the Holy Ghost.

"When the clouds rise in the east, when he comes who sets in order the thirteen forms of the clouds, the yellow lord of the hurricane, the hope of the lords to come, he who rules the preparation of the divine liquor, he who loves the guardian spirits of the fields, then I pray to him for his precious favor ; for I trust all in the hands of God the Father, God the Son, and God the Holy Ghost."

Such is an example of the strange mixture of heathen and

---

* Charencey, *Des Couleurs considérées comme Symboles des Points de l'Horizon chez les Peuples du Nouveau-Monde*, in the *Actes de la Société Philologique*, tome vi (Octobre 1876).

† *Chrestomathie de Litérature Maya*, p. 101, in the second volume of the *Etudes sur le Système Graphique et la Langue des Mayas* (Paris, 1870).

Christian superstition which has been the outcome of three centuries of so-called Christian instruction!

There still continue to be relics of an ancient form of fire-worship which once prevailed commonly throughout the peninsula. The missionaries refer to it as "the festival of fire,"* but the exact rites performed were so carefully concealed that we have no description of them. That they are not yet out of date is apparent from a copy of a native calendar for 1841-2, obtained by Mr. Stephens when in Yucatan. In it the days are marked as lucky or unlucky, and against certain ones such entries are made as "now the burner lights his fire," "the burner gives his fire scope," "the burner takes his fire," "the burner puts out his fire." This burner, *ah toc*, is the modern representative of the ancient priest of the fire, and we find a few obscure references to an important rite, the *tupp kak*, extinction of the fire, which was kept up long after the conquest, and probably is still celebrated in the remoter villages. The sacred fire in ancient Maya land is said to have been guarded by chosen virgins, and it appears in some way to have been identified with the force which gives life to the animal and vegetable world.

Another of the modern ceremonies which is imbued with the old notion, common to them as to all primitive people, of a soul with material wants, is that called "the feast of the food of the soul." Small cakes are made of the flesh of hens and pounded maize, and are baked in an underground oven. Of these as many are placed on the altar of the church as the person making the offering has deceased relatives for whose

---

* La fiesta de fuego, que hasta ahora en esta provincia se hacia."—Fr. Diego Lopez Cogolludo, *Historia de Yucatan*, tomo i, p. 483 (3d ed. Merida, 1867).

well-being he is solicitous. These cakes are called *hanal pixan*, "the food of the soul." Evidently they are intended to represent the nourishment destined for the soul on its journey through the shadowy lands of death.

Along with these there are many minor superstitions connected especially with the growth of crops and fruits. Thus it is widely believed that the fruit known as the white zapote (*Sapota achras*, in Maya, *choch*) will not ripen of itself. One must tap it lightly several times as it approaches maturity, repeating the formula :

> *Hoken, cheché ; ocen, takan :*
> Depart, greenness : enter, ripeness.

The owl is looked upon as an uncanny bird, presaging death or disease, if it alights on or even flies over a house. Another bird, the *cox*, a species of pheasant, is said to predict the approach of high northerly winds, when it calls loudly and frequently in the woods ; though this, according to one writer, is not so much a superstition as an observation of nature, and is usually correct.

A singular ceremony is at times performed to prevent the death of those who are sick. The dread being who in mediæval symbolism was represented by a skeleton, is known to the Mayas as *Yum Cimil*, Lord of Death. He is supposed to lurk around a house where a person is ill, ready to enter and carry off his life when opportunity offers. He is, however, willing to accept something in lieu thereof, and to bring about this result the natives perform the rite called *kex*, or "barter." They hang jars and nets containing food and drink on the trees around the house, repeating certain invocations, and they believe that often the Lord of Death will be satisfied with these, and thus allow the invalid to recover.

Those diviners to whom I have alluded are familiarly known as *Tat Ich*, Daddy Face, and *Tata Polin*, Daddy Head, a reference, I suspect, to a once familiar name of a chief divinity, *Kin ich*, the face (or eye) of the day, *i. e.* the Sun.

A power universally ascribed to these magicians is that of transforming themselves into beasts. Were it not for so many examples of delusions in enlightened lands, it would be difficult to explain the unquestioning belief which prevails on this subject throughout Central America. Father Baeza relates that one of these old sorcerers declared in a dying confession that he had repeatedly changed himself into various wild beasts. The English priest, Thomas Gage, who had a cure in Guatemala about 1630, tells with all seriousness a number of such instances. Even in our own days the learned Abbé Brasseur de Bourbourg is not entirely satisfied that animal magnetism, ventriloquism, and such trickery, can explain the mysteries of *nagualism*, as the Central American system of the black arts is termed. He is not certain that we ought to exclude the assistance of the invisible diabolic agencies ! *

The sacred books of the Quiches, a tribe living in Guatemala related to the Mayas, ascribe this power to one of their

---

* Thomas Gage, *A New Survey of the West Indies*, pp. 377 *et seq.* (London, 1699), The Abbé Brasseur is willing to consider these tales fictitious, "supposé qu'ils n'eussent eu, en realité, aucune communication avec les puissances du monde invisible," about which, however, he is evidently not altogether sure.—*Voyage sur l'Isthme de Tehuantepec*, p. 175 (Paris, 1862).

most celebrated kings. As an illustration the passage is worth quoting:

"Truly this Gucumatz became a wonderful king. Every seven days he ascended to the sky, and every seven days he followed the path to the abode of the dead ; every seven days he put on the nature of a serpent and he became truly a serpent ; every seven days he put on the nature of an eagle and again of a tiger, and he became truly an eagle and a tiger; every seven days also he put on the nature of coagulated blood, and then he was nothing else but coagulated blood."*

Men and women alike might possess this magic power. This is shown in a curious little native story heard by Dr. Berendt in the wilds of Yucatan from a Maya woman, who told it to prove the value of *salt* as a counter-charm to the machinations of these mysterious beings. The doctor wrote it down with scrupulous fidelity, and added a verbal translation. As it has never been published, and as it is at once an interesting bit of authentic folk-lore and a valuable example of the Maya language, I give it here in the original tongue with a literal, interlinear translation :—

A MAYA WITCH STORY.

Huntu hxib tsoocubel yetel huntul xchup ; ma tu yoheltah uaix
A   man   married   with   a   woman ; not did he know (her) as

uay.   Hunpe kin tu yalahti : "Huche capel mut tabb."   Tu
a witch.   One   day he said to her : "Mix   two measures (of) salt."   She

huchah paibe, ca tu katah : "Paax tial tech?"   Hunpel akab
mix'd (them) first, then she asked : "Why this (wishest) thou ?"   One   night

pixaan hxibe ca tu yilah u hokol u yatan. Ca tu chaah u mazcabe
woke the man and he saw go out his wife. Then he took his   axe

ca tu mucul thulbelah tu pach ti kax. Ca kuchioob ti chichan
and secretly followed behind (her) to the wood. When they arrived at a little

---

* *Popol Vuh, le Livre Sacré des Quiches*, p. 315 (Paris, 1864).

chakan, yan u zazil uh, ca tu mucuba hxib tu booy nohoch
meadow, there being a bright moon, then hid himself the man in the shade of a great
yaxche. Ca tu pucah u nok xchup tu pach, uaan xmabuc tu
seiba tree. Then threw her garments the woman behind (her), standing naked in the
tan uh: ca tu sipah u yothel, ca culhi chembac. Ca
face of the moon: then she stripped off her skin, and remained mere bones. Then
naci ti caan. Ca emi tucaten, ca tu yalahi: Zazaba
she rose to the sky. When she came down again, then she said to him: "Wouldst thou
xtac caan?" Hemac ma uchuc u nacal tucaten, tumen tu thootal
reach to the sky?" But not could she ascend again, because of the throwing
taab.
(of) salt.

To the Maya, the woods, the air, and the darkness are filled with mysterious beings who are ever ready to do him injury or service, but generally injury, as the greater number of these creations of his fancy are malevolent sprites.

Of those which are well disposed, the most familiar are the *Balams* (Maya, *Hbalamob*, masculine plural form of *balam*). This word is the common name of the American tiger, and as a title of distinction was applied to a class of priests and to kings. The modern notions of the Balams are revealed to us by the Licentiate Zetina of Tihosuco, in his manuscripts to which I have previously referred.

He tells us that these beings are supposed to be certain very ancient men who take charge of and guard the towns. One stands north of the town, a second south, a third east, and the fourth to the west. They are usually not visible during the day, and if one does see them it is a sign of approaching illness, which suggests that it is the disordered vision of some impending tropical fever which may occasionally lead to the belief in their apparition.

At night the Balams are awake and vigilant, and prevent many an accident from befalling the village, such as violent rains, tornadoes, and pestilential diseases. They summon each other by a loud, shrill whistle; and, though without wings, they fly through the air with the swiftness of a bird. Occasionally they have desperate conflicts with the evil powers who would assail the town. The signs of these nocturnal struggles are seen the next day in trees broken down and uprooted, the ground torn up, and large stones split and thrown around.

Another of their duties is to protect the cornfields or *milpas*. It seems probable, from comparing the authorities before me, that the Balams in this capacity are identical with the *Pa ahtuns*, whom I have referred to above, and that both are lineal descendants of those agricultural deities of the ancient Mayas, the *Chac* or *Bacab*, which are described by Bishop Landa and others. No Indian on the peninsula neglects to propitiate the Balam with a suitable offering at the time of corn-planting. Were he so negligent as to forget it, the crop would wither for lack of rain or otherwise be ruined.

An instance of this is told by Señor Zetina. An Indian near Tihosuco had paid no attention to the usual offering, perhaps being infected with evil modern skeptical views. His crop grew fairly; and as the ears were about ripening he visited his field to examine them. As he approached he saw with some dismay a tall man among the stalks with a large basket over his shoulders, in which he threw the ripening ears as fast as he could pluck them. The Indian saluted him hesitatingly. The stranger replied, "I am here gathering in that which I sent." Resting from his work, he drew from his pocket an immense cigar, and, taking out a flint and steel, began to strike a light. But the sparks he struck were flashes of lightning, and the sound of his blows was terrible thunderclaps which shook the very earth. The poor Indian fell to the ground unconscious with fright; and when he came to himself a hail-storm had destroyed his corn, and as soon as he reached home he himself was seized with a fever which nigh cost him his life.

The Balams are great smokers, and it is a general belief among the Indians that the shooting stars are nothing else than the stumps of the huge cigars thrown down the sky by these giant beings.

Sometimes they carry off children for purposes of their own. When Dr. Berendt was exploring the east coast of Yucatan he was told of such an occurrence on the Island of San Pedro, north of Belize. A little boy of four years wandered to some cacao bushes not more than fifty yards from the house, and there all trace of him was lost. There was no sign of wolf or tiger, no footprint of kidnapper. They sought him the whole day in vain, and then gave up the search, for they knew what had happened—the Balam had taken him!

The Balams have also the reputation of inculcating a respect for the proprieties of life. Zetina tells this story which he heard among his native friends: One day an Indian and his wife went to their corn-patch to gather ears. The man left the field to get some water, and his wife threw off the gown she wore lest it should be torn, and was naked. Suddenly she heard some one call to her in a loud voice, *Pixe avito, xnoh cizin*, which Zetina translates literally into Spanish, *Tapa ta culo, gran diablo!* At the same time she received two smart blows with a cane. She turned and beheld a tall man with a long beard, and a gown which reached to his feet. This was the Balam. He gave her two more smart blows on the part of the person to which he had referred, and then disappeared; but the marks of the four blows remained as long as she lived.

It is vain to attempt to pursuade the Indian that such notions are false and cannot be facts. He will not try to reason with you. He contents himself with a patient gesture and the despairing exclamation, *Bix ma hahal?* "How can it be otherwise than true?" (*Bix*, how, *ma*, not, *hahal*, true.)

These Balams are in fact the gods of the cardinal points and of the winds and rains which proceed from them, and are thus a survival of some of the central figures of the ancient mythology. The wind still holds its pre-eminence as a supernatural occurrence in the native mind. One day Dr. Berendt was traveling with some natives through the forests when the sound of a tropical tornado was heard approaching with its formidable roar through the trees. In awe-struck accents one of his guides said, "*He catal nohoch yikal nohoch tat:* Here comes the mighty wind of the Great Father." But it is only in an unguarded moment that in the presence of a white man the Indian betrays his beliefs, and no questioning could elicit further information. A hint is supplied by Señor Zetina. He mentions that the whistling of the wind is called, or attributed to, *tat acmo*, words which mean Father Strong-bird. This suggests many analogies from the mythologies of other races; for the notion of the primeval bird, at once lord of the winds and father of the race, is found in numerous American tribes, and is distinctly contained in the metaphors of the first chapter of Genesis.

The *balam*, as I have said, is esteemed a kindly and protective being; he is affectionately referred to as *yum balam*, Father Balam. He is said to have a human form, that of an old man with a long beard and ample flowing robes. But there are other gigantic spectres of terrible aspect and truculent humor. One of these is so tall that a man cannot reach his knees. He stalks into the towns at midnight, and planting his feet like a huge Colossus, one on each side of the roadway, he seizes some incautious passer-by and breaks his legs with his teeth, or conquers him with a sudden faintness. The name of this terror of late walkers is Giant Grab, *Ua ua pach*.

Another is the *Che Vinic*, the Man of the Woods, called by the Spanish population the Salonge. He is a huge fellow without bones or joints. For that reason if he lies down he cannot rise without extreme difficulty; hence he sleeps leaning against a tree. His feet are reversed, the heels in front, the toes behind. He is larger and stronger than a bull, and his color is red. In his long arms he carries a stick the size of a tree-trunk. He is on the watch for those who stray through the woods, and, if he can, will seize and devour them. But a ready-witted man has always a means of escape. All he has to do is to pluck a green branch from a tree, and waving it before him, begin a lively dance. This invariably throws the Wood Man into convulsions of mirth. He laughs and laughs until he falls to the ground, and once down, having no joints, he cannot rise, and the hunter can proceed leisurely on his journey. It is singular, says Dr. Berendt, how widely distributed is the belief in this strange fancy. It recurs in precisely the same form in Yucatan, in Peten, in Tabasco, around Palenque, etc.

Another ugly customer is the *Culcalkin*. This word means "the priest without a neck," and the hobgoblin so named is described as a being with head cut off even with the shoulders, who wanders around the villages at night, frightening men and children.

In contrast to the giants are the dwarfs and imps which are ready in their malicious ways to sour the pleasures of life. The most common of these are the *h'lox*, or more fully, *h'loxkatob*, which means "the strong clay images."* They are, indeed, believed to be the actual idols and figures in clay which are found about the old temples and tombs, and hence an Indian breaks these in pieces whenever he finds them, to the great detriment of archæological research. They only appear after sunset, and then in the shape of a child of three or four years, or sometimes not over a span in height, naked except wearing a large hat. They are swift of foot, and can run backwards as fast as forwards. Among other pranks, they throw stones at the dogs and cause them to howl. Their touch produces sickness, especially chills and fever. It is best, therefore, not to attempt to catch them.

Of similar malevolent disposition is the *Chan Pal*, Little Boy, who lurks in the woods and is alleged to bring the small-pox into the villages.

Others are merely teasing in character, and not positively

---

*The derivation of this word is from *kat*, which in the *Diccionario Maya-Español del Convento de Motul*, MS, of about 1580, is defined as "la tierra y barro de las olleras," but which Perez in his modern Maya dictionary translates "ollas ó figuras de barro"; *ob*, is the plural termination; *lox*, is strong, or the strength of anything; *h'* or *ah*, as it is often written, is the rough breathing which in Maya indicates the masculine gender.

harmful. Thus there is the *X bolon thoroch* who lives in the house with the family, and repeats at night the various sounds of domestic labor which have been made during the day. The word *thoroch* is applied to the sound caused by the native spindle revolving in its shaft; *bolon* is "nine," a number used to express the superlative degree in certain phrases; while the initial *X* shows that the imp is of the feminine gender. The name therefore signifies "the female imp who magnifies the sound of the spindle." Other such household imps are the *Bokol h'otoch*, Stir-the-House, who creeps under the floors and makes a noise like beating a cake to scare the inmates; the *Yancopek*, Pitcher-Imp, who crawls into jars and jugs; and the *Way cot*, Witch-bird, who lurks on or behind walls and drops stones on passers by.

The female sex is further represented in the Maya folklore by a personage who has a curious similarity to legendary ladies of the old world, sirens, mermaids, the Lorelei, and others. She is called *X tabai*, the (female) Deceiver. Her home is under shady bowers in the forests, and there the ardent hunter suddenly espies her, clothed, and combing with a large comb (*x ache*) her long and beautiful hair. As he approaches she turns and flees, but not with discouraging haste, rather in such a manner and with such backward glances as to invite pursuit. He soon overtakes her, but just as he clasps her beauteous form in his strong embrace, her body changes into a thorny bush, and her feet become claws like those of a wild fowl. Torn and bleeding he turns sadly homeward, and soon succumbs to an attack of fever with delirium.

Another very similar creature is *X Thoh Chaltun*, Miss

Pound-the-Stones. She slily waits around the villages, and when she sees some attractive youth she awakes his attention by tapping on the stones, or in default of these on an empty jar which she carries for the purpose. Does the foolish youth respond to the seductive invitation, she coyly moves to the woods, where the amorous pursuer meets like disappointment and a similar sad fate as the victim of the *X tabai*.

As may be supposed, many superstitions cling around the animal world. Each species of brute has its king, who rules and protects it. Even the timid native hare may thus assert its rights. An Indian told Dr. Berendt that once upon a time a hunter with two dogs followed a hare into a cave. There he found a large hole, leading under the earth. He descended, and came to the town of the hares. They seized him and his dogs, and brought him before the king, and it was no easy matter for him to get off by dint of protests and promises.

There are also tales of the Straw Bird or Phantom Bird, The hunter unexpectedly sees a handsome bird on a branch before him. He fires and misses. He repeats his shot in vain. After a while it falls of itself, and proves to be nothing but a colored feather. Then he knows that he has been fooled by the *Zohol chich*.

An object of much dread is the Black Tail, *Ekoneil*, an imaginary snake with a black, broad, and forked tail. He glides into houses at night where a nursing mother is asleep; and, covering her nostrils with his tail, sucks the milk from her breasts.

These are probably but a small portion of the superstitions

of the modern Mayas. They are too reticent to speak of these subjects other than by accident to the white man. He is quite certain either to ridicule or to reprove such confidences. But what is above collected is a moderately complete, and certainly, as far as it goes, an accurate notion of their folk-lore.

FOLK-LORE OF THE MODERN LENAPE.*

IN August 1886, and September 1887, I had many conversations with the Rev. Albert Seqaqknind Anthony, an educated Delaware Indian, then assistant missionary to the Six Nations, in Ontario, Canada. Our immediate business was the revision of the "Lenâpé-English Dictionary," which has since been published by the Historical Society of Pennsylvania; but in the intervals of that rather arduous and dry labor, we sought recreation in broader subjects of thought, and our discourse often fell on the ancient traditions, folk-lore, and customs of the Lenâpé, now fast disappearing.

Mr. Anthony was on his father's side a Delaware, or Lenâpé, of the Minsi tribe, while his grandmother was a Shawnee. He himself was born on the Ontario Reservation, and up to his thirteenth year spoke nothing but pure Lenâpé. His memory carries him back to the fourth decade of this century.

One of his earliest reminiscences was of the last surviving emigrant from the native home of his ancestors in Eastern Pennsylvania—a venerable squaw (*ochquèu*, woman, hen), supposed to be a hundred years old. At the time her parents left the mountains between the Lehigh and Susquehanna

---

* From the *Journal of American Folk-lore*, 1888.

rivers, she was "old enough to carry a pack"—twelve years, probably. This must have been about 1760, as after the French War (1755) the natives rapidly deserted that region.

I was surprised to find how correctly the old men of the tribe had preserved and handed down reminiscences of their former homes along the Delaware River. The flat marshy "Neck," south of Philadelphia, between the Delaware and Schuylkill rivers, was pointed out to me by Mr. Anthony (who had never seen it before) as the spot where the tribe preferred to gather the rushes with which they manufactures rugs and mats. He recognized various trees, not seen in Canada, by the descriptions he had heard of them.

Such narratives formed the themes of many a long tale by the winter fire in the olden time. Like most Indians, the Lenâpé are, or rather were—for, alas! the good old customs are nearly all gone—inexhaustible *raconteurs*. They had not only semi-historic traditions, but numberless fanciful tales of spirits and sprites, giants and dwarfs, with their kith and kin. Such tales were called *tomoacan*, which means "tales for leisure hours." They relate the deeds of potent necromancers, and their power over the *machtanha*, "those who are bewitched."

It greatly interested me to learn that several of these tales referred distinctly to the culture-hero of the tribe, that ancient man who taught them the arts of life, and on his disappearance—these heroes do not die—promised to return at some future day, and restore his favorite people to power and happiness. This Messianic hope was often the central idea in American native religions, as witness the worship of

Quetzalcoatl in Mexico, of Kukulcan in Yucatan, of Viracocha in Peru. Mr. Anthony assured me that it was perfectly familiar to the old Delawares, and added that in his opinion their very name, *Lenâpé*, conveys an esoteric meaning, to wit, "the man comes," with reference to the second advent of their culture-hero.* This is singular confirmation of the fragmentary myths collected by the Swedish engineer Lindstrom in 1650, and by the Moravian Bishop Ettwein about a century later. These I have collected in "The Lenâpé and their Legends" (Philadelphia, 1885), and have discussed the general subject at such length in my "American Hero-Myths" (Philadelphia, 1882) that the reader will probably be satisfied to escape further expansion of it here.

Only in traditions does the "Stone Age" survive among the Delawares. In Mr. Anthony's youth, the bow-and-arrow was still occasionally in use for hunting; but he had never seen employed arrow-points of stone. They were either of deer's horns or of sharpened bones. The name for the compound instrument "bow-and-arrow" is *manhtaht*, the first *a* being nasal; and from this word, Mr. Anthony states, is derived the name *Manhattan*, properly *manahah tank*, "the place where they gather the wood to make bows." The bow-string is *tschipan:* the arrow, *allunth*. The generic name for stone weapon is still familiar, *achsinhican*, and the word from which we derive "tomahawk," *t'mahican*, is strictly applied to a stone hatchet. War-clubs were of several varieties, called *apech'lit* and *mehittqueth*, which were different from an ordinary stick or cane, *alauwan*.

---

* The form from which he derives it is *lenni-peu*.

Though the war-whoop is heard no more, its name remains, *kowa'mo*, and tradition still recalls their ancient contests with the Iroquois, their cruel and hated enemies, to whom they applied the opprobrious epithet *mengwe* (that is, *glans penis*).

Hunting is scarcely worth the name any longer on the Canadian reservations. The debated question as to whether the Lenâpé knew the buffalo attracted me. Mr. Anthony assured me that they did. It was called *sisiliti*, which he explained as "the animal that drops its excrement when in motion," walking or running; though he added that another possible derivation is from *siselamen*, to butt against, from which comes *sisejahen*, to break in pieces by butting.

In former times a favorite method of hunting in the autumn was for a large number of hunters to form a line and drive the game before them. This was called *p'mochlapen*. This answered well for deer, but now little is left save the muskrat, *chuaskquis*, the ground-hog, *monachgen*, the white rabbit, *wapachtques*, the weasel, *mani'tohumisch*, and the little chipmunk, *pochqwapiith* (literally, "he sits upright on something"). For such small game, it is scarcely worth while running the risk of the bite of the blow-adder, *pethbotalwe*, and the much-feared "bloody-mouthed lizard," *mokdomus;* though I suspect both are more terrible in tale than in fact.

In fishing, they appear to have known not only the brush-net and the spear, but the hook-and-line as well. The line, *wendamakan*, was twisted from the strands of the wild hemp, *achhallap*, or of the milk-weed, *pichtokenna;* and the hook was armed with a bait, *awauchkon*, which might be *wecheeso*, the ground-worm, literally, "he who extends and retracts himself," or the *waukchelachees*, grasshopper, literally, "one that hops." This corresponds with what the old Swedish traveler, Peter Kalm, relates in the first half of the last century. He describes the native hooks as made of bone or of the spur of a fowl.

They still gather for food the *ptukquim*, walnut, literally, "round nut;" the *quinokquim*, butternut, literally, "oblong nut;" and various berries, as the *lechlochhilleth*, the red raspberry, literally, "the berry that falls to pieces."

Among utensils of ancient date and aboriginal invention seem to have been wooden dishes or bowls, *wollakanes*, made from the elm-tree, *wollakanahungi;* wooden mortars, in which corn was pounded, *laquachhakan;* and *peyind*, cups with handles. The art of pottery, which they once possessed, has been entirely lost.

Although now resident inland, they remember the manufacture and use of canoes, *amochol*. Some were of birch bark, *wiqua*, and were called *wiqua-amochol;* others were dug-outs, for which they preferred the American sycamore, distinctively named canoe-wood, *amochol-he*.

The ordinary word for house is still *wikwam*, wigwam, while a brush-hut is called *pimoakan*. I was particular to inquire if, as far as now known, the Lenâpé ever occupied communal houses, as did the Iroquois. Mr. Anthony assured me that this was never the custom of his nation, so far as any recollection or tradition goes. Every family had its own lodge. I called his attention to the discovery in ancient village sites in New Jersey of two or three fire-places in a row, and too close to belong to different lodges. This has been adduced by Dr. C. C. Abbott as evidence of communal dwellings. He replied that these were the sites of the village council-houses; he himself could remember some with two or three fires; but their only permanent occupants were the head chief with his wives and children.

Though most of the national games are no longer known to the rising generation, in my informant's boyhood they still figured conspicuously by the native firesides, where now "progressive euchre" and the like hold sway. One such was *qua'quallis*. In this a hollow bone is attached by a string to a pointed stick. The stick is held the hand, and the bone is thrown up by a rapid movement, and the game is to catch the bone, while in motion, on the pointed end of the stick. It was a gambling game, often played by adults.

A very popular sport was with a hoop, *tautmusq*, and spear or arrow, *allunth*. The players arranged themselves in two parallel lines, some forty feet apart, each one armed with a reed spear. A hoop was then rolled rapidly at an equal distance between the lines. Each player hurled his spear at it, the object being to stop the hoop by casting the spear within its rim. When stopped, the shaft must lie within the hoop, or the shot did not count.

A third game, occasionally seen, is *maumun'di*. This is played with twelve flat bones, usually those of a deer, and a bowl of wood, constructed for the purpose. One side of each bone is white; the other, colored. They are placed in the bowl, thrown into the air, and caught as they descend. Those with the white side uppermost are the winning pieces. Bets usually accompany this game, and it had, in the old days, a place in the native religious rites; probably as a means of telling fortunes.

THE SWEAT-LODGE AND CANTICOS. 187

The Delawares on the Ontario Reservation have long since been converted to Christianity, and there is little trace left of their former pagan practices. If they remain anywhere, it is in their medical rites. I inquired particularly if there are any remnants of the curious adoration of the sacred twelve stones, described by Zeisberger a century and a quarter ago. I found that the custom of the "sweat-lodge," a small hut built for taking sweat-baths, still prevails. The steam is generated by pouring water on hot stones. This is done by the "medicine-man," who is known as *quechksa'piet*. He brings in one stone after another, and pours water upon it until it ceases "to sing;" and invariably he uses precisely *twelve* stones.

Probably some of the more benighted still seek to insure the success of their crops by offering food to the *m'sink*. This is a false face, or mask, rudely cut from wood to represent the human visage, with a large mouth. The victuals are pushed into the mouth, and the genius is supposed to be thus fed.

Our word *cantico*, applied to a jollification, and by some etymologists, naturally enough, traced to the Latin *cantare*, in reality is derived from the Lenâpé *gentkehn*, to sing and dance at the same time. This was their most usual religious ceremony, and to this day *gendtoma* means "to begin religious services," either Christian or heathen; and *gendtowen* signifies "to be a worshipper." These dances were often connected with sacred feasts, toward which each participant contributed a portion of food. To express such a communal religious banquet they used the term *w'chindin*, and for inviting to one, *wingindin;* and they were clearly distinguished from an ordinary meal in common, an eating together, *tachquipuin* or *tachquipoagan*.

My informant fully believes that there is yet much medical knowledge held secretly by the old men and women. He has known persons bitten by the rattlesnake who were promptly and painlessly cured by a specific known to these native practitioners. It is from the vegetable *materia medica*, and is taken internally. They also have some surgical skill. It was interesting to learn that an operation similar to *trephining* has been practiced among the Lenâpé time out of mind for severe headaches. The scalp on or near the vertex is laid open by a crucial incision, and the bone is scraped. This perhaps explains those trepanned skulls which have been been disinterred in Peru and other parts of America.

The national legends have mostly faded out, but the Lenâpé perfectly remember that they are the "grandfather" of all the Algonkin tribes, and the fact is still recognized by the Chipeways and some others, whose orators employ the term *numoh'homus*, "my grandfather," in their formal addresses to the Lenâpé. The old men still relate with pride that, in the good old times, before any white man had landed on their shores, "the Lenâpé had a string of white wampum beads, *wapakeekq'*, which stretched from the Atlantic to the Pacific, and on this white road their envoys travelled from one great ocean to the other, safe from attack."

There are still a few among them who pretend to some knowledge of the art of reading the wampum belts. The beads themselves are called *keekq'*; a belt handed forth at a treaty is *nochkunduwoagan*, literally, "an answering;" and after the treaty has been ratified the belt is called *aptunwoagan*, the covenant.

The tribal and totemic divisions are barely remembered, and the ancient prohibitions about endogamous marriage have fallen completely into desuetude. Mr. Anthony's term for totem, or sub-tribe, is *w'aloch'ke;* as, *tulpenaloch'ke*, the Turtle totem. The name *Minsi*, he believes, is an abbreviation of *minachsinink*, the place of broken stones, referring to the mountains north of the Lehigh river, where his ancestors had their homes. The *Wonalacht'go* of the early historians he identifies with the Nanticokes, and translates it "people following the waves;" that is, living near the ocean.

The chieftaincy of the tribe is still, in theory, hereditary in one family, and in the female line. The ordinary term *sakima*, sachem, is not in use among the Minsi, who call their chief *kikay*, or *kitschikikay* (*kitschi*, great; *kikay*, old, or old man : the *elderman*, or alderman, of the Saxons).

Some peculiarities of the language deserve to be noted.

The German alphabet, employed by the Moravians to reduce it to writing, answered so well that the Moravian missionary, Rev. Mr. Hartmann, at present in charge of the New Fairfield Reservation, Ontario, who does not understand a word of Delaware, told me he had read the books printed in the native tongue to his congregation, and they understood him perfectly. But I soon detected two or three sounds which had escaped Zeisberger and his followers. There is a soft *th* which the German ear could not catch, and a *kth* which was equally difficult, both of frequent occurrence. There is also a slight breathing between the possessives *n'*, my, *k'*, thy, *w'*, his, and the names of the things possessed, which the missionaries sometimes disregarded, and sometimes wrote as a full vowel. But after a little practice I had rarely any difficulty in pronouncing the words in an intelligible manner. This I was obliged to do with the whole dictionary, for although Mr. Anthony speaks his language with perfect ease, he does not read or write it, and has no acquaintance with German or its alphabet.

On one point I cross-examined him carefully.* It is wellknown to linguists that in Algonkin grammar the verb undergoes a vowel change of a peculiar character, which usually throws the sentence into an indefinite or dubitative form. This is a very marked trait, recognized early by the missionary Eliot and others, and the omission of all reference to it by Zeisberger in his Grammar of the Lenâpé has been commented on as a serious oversight. Well, after all my questions, and after explaining the point fully to Mr. Anthony, he insisted that no such change takes place in Delaware verbs. I read to him the forms in Zeisberger's Grammar which are supposed to indicate it, but he explained them all by other reasons, mere irregularities or erroneous expressions.

The intricacies of the Lenâpé verb have never yet been solved, and it is now doubtful if they ever will be, for the language is fast changing and disappearing, at least in both reservations in Canada, and also among the representatives of the tribe at their settlement in Kansas. It is not now, and Mr. Anthony assured me that, so far as he knew, it never was, a custom for parents to correct their children in speaking the language. Probably this is true of most uncivilized tribes. The children of such learn their exceed-

COMPOUND WORDS.

ingly complicated languages with a facility and accuracy which is surprising to the cultivated mind. I can say from experience, that no child learns to speak pure English without incessant correction from parents and teachers.

The general result of my conversations with Mr. Anthony on the grammar of his language led me to estimate at a lower value the knowledge of it displayed in the works of Zeisberger, Ettwein, and Heckewelder. The first and last named no doubt spoke it fluently in some fashion; but they had not the power to analyze it, nor to detect its finer shades of meaning, nor to appreciate many refinements in its word-building, nor to catch many of its semi-notes.

To give an example:—

Heckewelder gave Duponceau a compound which has often been quoted as a striking instance of verbal synthesis. It is *kuligatschis*, and is analyzed by Duponceau thus: *k*, possessive pronoun, second person singular; *uli*, abbreviation of *wulit*, pretty; *gat*, last syllable of *wichgat*, foot or paw; *chis*, diminutive termination; in all, "thy pretty little paw." Now, there is no such word in Lenâpé as *wichgat*. "His foot" is *w'uchsüt*, where the initial *w* is the possessive, and does not belong in the word for foot. But in all likelihood this was not in the compound heard by Heckewelder. What he heard was *k'wulinachkgis*, from, *k*, possessive; *wulit*, pretty; *nachk*, hand, or paw of an animal; *gis*, diminutive termination. He lost the peculiar whistled *w* and the nasalized *n*, sounds unknown to Germans. Duponceau's statement that *gat* is the last syllable of the word for foot is totally erroneous. I am convinced that much of the excessive synthesis, so called, in the Lenâpé arises from a lack of appreciation on the part of the whites of delicate phonetic elements. If I had heard many more of Mr. Anthony's analyses of compounds, I believe I should have reached the conclusion that synthesis in Lenâpé means little beyond juxtaposition with euphonic elision.

PART III.

GRAPHIC SYSTEMS AND LITERATURE.

INTRODUCTORY.

THE intellectual development of a nation attains its fullest expression in language, oral or written. This "divine art" as Plato calls it, claims therefore from the student of man in the aggregate a prolonged attention and the most painstaking analysis. Too frequently one hears among anthropologists the claims of linguistics decried, and the many blunders and over-hasty generalizations of philologists quoted as good reasons for the neglect or distrust of their branch.

The real reason of this attitude I believe to be not so much the mistakes of the linguists, as a strong aversion which I have noticed in many distinguished teachers of physical science to the study of language and the philosophy of expression. The subject is difficult and distasteful to them. Having no aptitude for it, nor real acquaintance with it, they condemn it as of small value and of doubtful results. I have never known a scientific man who was really a well-read philologist who thus under-estimated the position of linguistics in the scheme of anthropology ; but I have known many who, not having such thorough knowledge, depreciated its value in others.

The third and fourth parts of this volume are devoted to language, the third as it appears especially in its written forms, the fourth particularly to the profounder questions of linguistic philosophy. Here again I shall be found in opposition to the majority who have written on these subjects. The claim I make for the largely phonetic character of the Mexican and Maya hieroglyphs is not generally accepted ; and the poetical spirit which I argue exists in many productions of the aboriginal muse will not be favored by those who deny the higher sentiments of humanity to uncivilized man.

I have endeavored by frequent illustration, and reference to the best sources of information, to put the reader in the position to judge for himself; and I shall feel highly gratified if he is prompted to such investigations by what I may say, whether his final conclusions agree with mine or not.

THE PHONETIC ELEMENTS IN THE GRAPHIC SYSTEMS OF THE MAYAS AND MEXICANS.*

ALL who have read the wonderful story of the Spanish conquest of Mexico and Central America will remember that the European invaders came upon various nations who were well acquainted with some method of writing, who were skilled in the manufacture of parchment and paper, and who filled thousands of volumes formed of these materials with the records of their history, the theories of their sciences, and the traditions of their theologies. Aiming at greater permanence than these perishable materials would offer, they also inscribed on plinths of stone, on slabs of hard wood, and on terra cotta tablets, the designs and figures which in the system they adopted served to convey the ideas they wished to transmit to posterity.

In spite of the deliberate and wholesale destruction of these records at the conquest, and their complete neglect for centuries afterwards, there still remain enough, were they collected, to form a respectably large *Corpus Inscriptionum Americanarum.* Within the present century many Mexican and Maya MSS. have for the first time been published, and

---

* Read before the Anthropological Section of the American Association for the Advancement of Science, at Buffalo, August, 1886, and published in the *American Antiquarian* in November of the same year.

the inscriptions on the temples of southern Mexico and Yucatan have been brought to the tables of students by photography and casts, methods which permit no doubt as to their faithfulness.

Nor have there been lacking diligent students who have availed themselves of these facilities to search for the lost key to these mysterious records. It is a pleasure to mention the names of Thomas and Holden in the United States, of De Rosny, Aubin and de Charencey in France, of Förstemann, Seler and Schellhas in Germany, of Ramirez and Orozco in Mexico. But it must frankly be confessed that the results obtained have been inadequate and unsatisfactory. We have not yet passed the threshold of investigation.

The question which forces itself upon our attention as demanding a reply at the very outset, is whether the Aztec and Maya systems of writing were or were not, in whole or in part, *phonetic* systems? Did they appeal, in the first instance, to the *meaning* of the word, or to the *sound* of the word? If to the latter—if, in other words, they were phonetic, or even partially phonetic—then it is vain to attempt any interpretation of these records without a preliminary study of the languages of the nations who were the writers. These languages must moreover be studied in the form in which they were spoken at the period of the conquest, and the course of native thought as expressed in the primitive grammatical structure must be understood and taken into account. I hasten to add that we have abundant materials for such studies.

This essential preliminary question, as to the extent of the phonetic element in the Mexican and Maya systems of writ-

ARRANGEMENT OF PHONETIC SIGNS. 197

ing, is that which I propose to put at present, and to answer it, so far as may be. Hitherto, the greatest diversity of opinion about it has prevailed. Some able writers, such as Valentini and Holden, have questioned the existence of any phonetic elements; but most have been willing to concede that there are such present, though their quantity and quality are by no means clearly defined.

We may assume that both systems under consideration are partly ideographic. Every system of phonetic writing introduces ideograms to some extent, our own among the number. The question is, to what extent?

But before we are prepared to answer this question about the extent of the phonetic element, we must seek to ascertain its character. We are all aware that a phonetic symbol may express the sound either of a whole word of several syllables, or of a single syllable, or of a simple acoustic element. Again, a single phonetic symbol may express several quite diverse sounds, as is familarly exemplified in the first letter of the English alphabet, which represents three very different sounds; and, on the other hand, we may find three, four or more symbols, no wise alike in form or origin, bearing one and the same phonetic value, a fact especially familiar to Egyptologists.

We must further bear in mind that the arrangement to the eye of phonetic symbols is altogether arbitrary. Because a prefix is pronounced first in the order of time and a suffix last, it by no means follows that the order in space of their corresponding symbols shall bear any analogous relation. The idea awakened by the sound of the word is a whole, and one; and so that this sound is represented, the disposition of its component parts is, philosophically speaking, indifferent. When it is remembered that in most American languages, and notably in the Mexican or Nahuatl, there is a tendency to consolidate each phrase into a single word, the importance of this consideration is greatly increased.

As the position of the phonetic parts of the phrase-word may thus be disregarded, yet more indifferent is the order of sequence of the symbols. There is no *a priori* reason why this should be from left to right as in English, or from right to left as in Hebrew; alternately, as in the Boustrophedon of the Greek; or from top to bottom, as in Chinese.

In such an examination as the present one, we must rid our minds of the expectation of finding the phonetic elements in some familiar form, and simply ask whether they are to be found in any form.

We are not without a trustworthy guide in this quest. It is agreed among those who have most carefully studied the subject that there is but one path by which the human mind could have originally proceeded from picture-writing or thought-writing to phonetic or sound-writing. This was through the existence of homophones and homoiophones in a language, of words with the same or similar sounds, but with diverse significations. The deliberate analysis of a language back to its phonetic elements, and the construction upon those of a series of symbols, as was accomplished for the Cherokee by the half-breed Sequoyah, has ever been the product of culture, not a process of primitive evolution.

In this primitive process the sounds which were most frequently repeated, or were otherwise most prominent to the ear, would be those first represented by a figure; and the same figure would come to be employed as an equivalent for this sound and others closely akin to it, even when they had other connections and bore other significations. Hence affixes, suffixes, and monosyllabic words, are those to which we must look as offering the earliest evidences of a connection of figure with sound.

According to the theory here very briefly indicated, I shall examine the Maya and Nahuatl systems of writing, to ascertain if they present any phonetic elements, and of what nature these are.

Turning first to the Maya, I may in passing refer to the disappointment which resulted from the publication of Landa's alphabet by the Abbé Brasseur in 1864. Here was what seemed a complete phonetic alphabet, which should at once unlock the mysteries of the inscriptions on the temples of Yucatan and Chiapas, and enable us to interpret the script of the Dresden and other Codices. Experience proved the utter fallacy of any such hope. His work is no key to the Maya script; but it does indicate that the Maya scribes were able to assign a character to a sound, even a sound so meaningless as that of a single letter.

The failure of the Landa alphabet left many scholars total skeptics as to the phonetic values of any of the Maya characters. To name a conspicuous and recent example, Prof. Leon de Rosny, in his edition of the Codex Cortesianus, published in 1883, appends a Vocabulary of the hieratic signs as far as known; but does not include among them any phonetic signs other than Landa's.

But if we turn to the most recent and closest students of

these records, we find among them a consensus of opinion that a certain degree, though a small degree, of phoneticism must be accepted. Thus our own able representative in this branch, Prof. Cyrus Thomas, announced in 1882, in his *Study of the MS. Troano*,* that several of the day and month characters are, beyond doubt, occasionally phonetic.

Prof. Förstemann, of Dresden, whose work on the Dresden Codex has appeared quite recently, announces his conclusion that the Maya script is essentially ideographic;† but immediately adds that the numerous small figures attached to the main sign are to be considered phonetic, and no matter in what local relation they may stand to this sign, they are to be regarded either as prefixes or suffixes of the word. He does not attempt to work out their possible meaning, but, as he says, leaves that to the future.

Almost identical is the conclusion of Dr. Schellhas, whose essay on the Dresden Codex‡ is a most meritorious study. His final decision is in these words: "The Maya writing is ideographic in principle, and probably avails itself, in order to complete its ideographic hieroglyphs, of a number of fixed phonetic signs."

Some of these signs have been so carefully scrutinized that their phonetic value may be considered to have been determined with reasonable certainty. An interesting example is shown in Fig. 1, for the analysis of which we are indebted to Dr. Schellhas. The quadrilateral figure at the top represents the firmament. One of the squares into which it is

---

* *Study of the MS. Troano*, p. 141.
† *Erläuterungen der Maya Hand-schrift*, etc., p. 2. (Dresden, 1886.)
‡ *Die Maya Hand-schrift der Könige. Bib. zu Dresden.* p. 77; (Berlin, 1886.)

HIEROGLYPH OF THE FIRMAMENT.

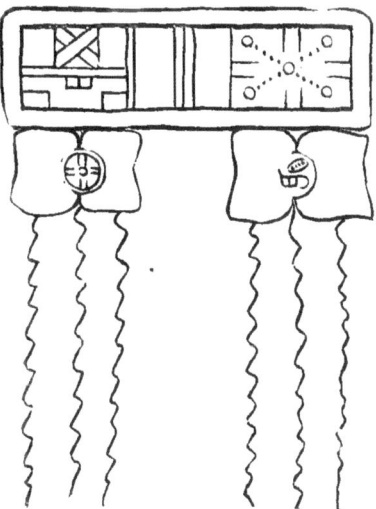

FIG. 1.—The Maya Hieroglyph of the Firmament.

divided portrays the sky in the day time, the other, the starry sky at night. Beneath each are white and black objects, signifying the clouds, from which falling rain is indicated by long zigzag lines. Between the clouds on the left of the figure is the well-known ideogram of the sun, on the right that of the moon. In the Maya language the sun is called *kin*, the moon *u*, and these figures are found elsewhere, not indicating these celestial bodies, but merely the phonetic values, the one of the syllable *kin*, the other of the letter *u*. The two signs given in Landa's alphabet for the letter *u* are really one, separated in transcription, and a variant of the figure for the moon with the wavy line beneath it. The word *u* in Maya is the possessive adjective of the third person, and as such is employed in conjugating verbs, the Maya verbal being really a possessive.

A very common terminal syllable in Maya is *il*. It is called by grammarians "the determinative ending," and is employed to indicate the genitive and ablative relations. Dr. Schellhas considers that this is represented by the signs affixed to the main hieroglyphs shown on Fig. 2.*

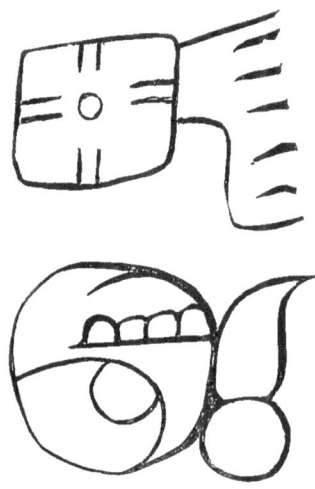

FIG. 2.—Maya Phonetic Terminals.

The upper figure he reads *kinil*, the lower *cim-il*. The two signs are the title to a picture in the Codex Troano representing a storm with destruction of human life. The two words *kin-il cim-il* may be translated "At the time of the killing." The syllable *cim* is expressed in several

---

* *Die Maya Hand-schrift*, etc., p. 47.

MAYA PHONETICS.   203

variants in the Codices, examples of two of which, from the Dresden Codex, are presented in Fig. 3.

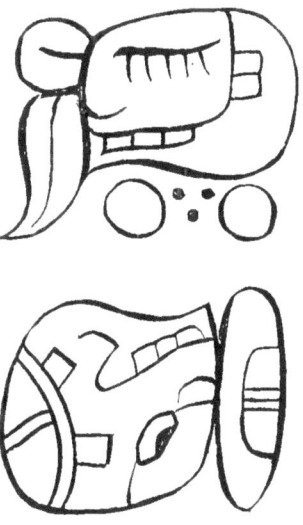

FIG. 3.—Maya Phonetic Terminals.

The signs for the four cardinal points appear to be expressed phonetically. They are represented in Figs. 4 and 5. The words are for North, *xaman*, East, *lakin*, South, *nohil*, West, *chikin*. Of these the syllable *kin* appears in *lakin* and *chikin*, and is represented as above described. The word for North has not been analyzed; that for South has been translated by Prof. Londe Rosny as *ma ya*, the word *ma* meaning hands or arms, the lower as either a fruit or the masculine sign, in either case the phonetic value being alone intended. Both the name and the etymology are, however, doubtful, resting upon late and imperfect authorities.

By pursuing the plan here indicated, that is, by assuming that a figure whose representative value is known, has also a merely phonetic value in other combinations, a certain number of phonetic elements of the Maya tongue have been identified. Prof. Cyrus Thomas, in an article published in

FIGS. 4 and 5.—Signs of the Cardinal Points in Maya.

one of our prominent journals, states that he has "interpreted satisfactorily to himself twelve or fifteen compound characters which appear to be phonetic."*

It is obvious, however, that small progress has been made in this direction compared to the labor expended. By far

---

* *American Antiquarian*, March, 1886.

the greater number of the fixed symbols of the Maya are yet undeciphered. It is acknowledged by all recent students that they cannot be representative, as they recur too frequently. To explain them, there is but one sure course, and that is, by a close analysis of the Maya language to get at the relations of ideas in the native mind as expressed in their own phonetic system.

When we turn to the Mexican system of writing, much more definite and extensive information as to its phonetic elements awaits us. It is possible that at bottom it has really no higher phonetic character, but several facts have combined to give us a better understanding of its structure. In the first place, more examples of it have been preserved, some of these with more or less accurate translations. Again, the earlier writers, those whom we look upon as our historical authorities, have been more explicit and ample in their description of Mexican native literature than of that of Yucatan. Finally, and most important, the Mexican language, the Nahuatl, was studied at an early date, and with surprising thoroughness, by the Catholic priests. Within a generation after the conquest they had completed a quite accurate analysis of its grammatical structure, and had printed a Nahuatl-Spanish dictionary containing more words than are to be found in any English dictionary for a century later.

These intelligent missionaries acquainted themselves with the principles of the Mexican script, and to a limited extent made use of it in their religious instructions, as did also the Spanish scriveners in their legal documents in transactions with the natives. They found the native phonetic writing partly syllabic and partly alphabetic; and it was easy for the priests to devise a wholly alphabetic script on the same plan. An interesting example of this is preserved in the work of Valades, entitled *Rhetorica Christiana*, written about 1570. Familiar objects are represented, chiefly of European introduction. Each has the phonetic value only of the first letter of its Nahuatl name. The plan is extremely simple, and indeed the forms and names of the Hebrew letters seem to indicate that they arose in the same way. Applying it to English, we should spell the word *cat* by a picture of a chair, of an axe, and of a table, each of these being the recognized symbol of its first phonetic element or initial letter. Often any one of several objects whose names begin with the same letter could be used, at choice. This is also illustrated in Valades' alphabet, where, for instance, the letter *E* is represented by four different objects.

As I have observed, the native genius had not arrived at a complete analysis of the phonetic elements of the language; but it was distinctly progressing in that direction. Of the five vowels and fourteen consonants which make up the Nahuatl alphabet, three vowels certainly, and probably three consonants, had reached the stage where they were often expressed as simple letters by the method above described. The vowels were *a*, for which the sign was *atl*, water; *e* represented by a bean, *etl;* and *o* by a footprint, or path, *otli;* the consonants were *p*, represented either by a flag, *pan*, or a mat, *petl; t*, by a stone, *tetl*, or the lips, *tentli;* and *z*, by a lancet, *zo*. These are, however, exceptions. Most of the Nahuatl phonetics were syllabic, sometimes one, sometimes two syllables of the name of the object being employed. When the whole name of an object or most of it was used as a phonetic value, the script remains truly phonetic, but becomes of the nature of a rebus, and this is the character of most of the phonetic Mexican writing.

Every one is familiar with the principle of the rebus. It is where a phrase is represented by pictures of objects whose names bear some resemblance in sound to the words employed. A stock example is that of the gallant who to testify his devotion to the lady of his heart, whose name was Rose Hill, had embroidered on his gown the pictures of a rose, a hill, an eye, a loaf of bread, and a well, which was to be interpreted, "Rose Hill I love well."

In medieval heraldry this system was in extensive use. Armorial bearings were selected, the names of the elements of which expressed that of the family who bore them. Thus Pope Adrian IV, whose name was Nicolas Breakespeare, carried the device of a spear with a broken shaft; the Boltons of England wear arms representing a cask or *tun* pierced by a cross-bow shaft or *bolt;* etc. Such arms were called *canting* arms, the term being derived from the Latin *cantare*, to sing or chant, the arms themselves chanting or announcing the family surname.

We have, so far as I am aware, no scientific term to express this manner of phonetic writing, and I propose for it therefore the adjective *ikonomatic*, from the Greek *eikon*, a figure or image, and *onoma* (genitive, *onomatos*) name,—a writing by means of the names of the figures or images represented. The corresponding noun would be *ikonomatography*. It differs radically from picture-writing (*Bilderschrift*,) for although it is composed of pictures, these were used solely with reference to the sound of their names, not their objective significance.

FIG. 6—Mexican Phonetic Hieroglyphics of the name of Montezuma.

The Mexicans, in their phonetic writing, were never far removed from this ikonomatic stage of development. They combined, however, with it certain clearly defined monosyllabic signs, and the separate alphabetic elements which I have already noted. An examination of the MSS. proves that there was no special disposition of the parts of a word. In other words, they might be arranged from right to left or from left to right, from below upwards or from above downwards; or the one may be placed within the other. It will easily be seen that this greatly increases the difficulty of deciphering these figures.

MEXICAN EXAMPLES

As illustrations of the phoneticism of Mexican writing I show two compounds, quoted by M. Aubin in his well-known essay on the subject. The first is a proper noun, that of the emperor Montezuma (Fig. 6). It should be read from right to left. The picture at the right represents a mouse trap, in Nahuatl, *montli*, with the phonetic value *mo*, or *mon*, the head of the eagle has the value *quauh*, from *quauhtli*; it is transfixed with a lancet, *zo;* and surmounted with a hand, *maitl*, whose phonetic value is *ma;* and these values combined give *mo-quauh-zo-ma*.

FIG. 7.—Mexican Phonetic Hieroglyphics of the name of a Serpent.

The second example is a common noun, the name of a serpent *tecuhtlacozauhqui* (Fig. 7). It is also read from right to left ; the head with the peculiar band and frontal ornament is that of one of the noble class, *tecuhtli* ; at the base of the left figure is a familiar sign for *tla*, and represents two teeth, *tlantli;* they are surmounted by a jar, *comitl* with the value *co;* and this in turn is pierced by a lancet, which here has only its alphabetic value z. The remainder of the word was not expressed in the writing, the above signs being deemed sufficient to convey the idea to the reader.

In presenting these examples I do not bring forward anything new. They are from an essay which has been in print nearly forty years.* Many other examples are to be seen in the great work of Lord Kingsborough, and later in publications in the city of Mexico. The learned Ramirez undertook a dictionary of Nahuatl hieroglyphics which has in part been published; Orozco y Berra in his "History of Ancient Mexico" gathered a great many facts illustrative of the phonetic character of the Mexican script; and within a year Dr. Peñafiel has issued a quarto of considerable size giving ancient local Mexican names with their phonetic representations.†

---

* The first of M. Aubin's Memoirs appeared in 1849, and was the result of studies begun in 1830. A new and enlarged edition has lately been edited by Dr. Hamy: *Mémoires sur la Peinture Didactique et l' Ecriture Figurative des Anci ns Mexicains*. Par. J. M. A. Aubin (Paris 1885.) But Dr. Hamy has traveled very far beyond the limits of a sober appreciation of M. Aubin's results when he writes: "Les recherches de M. Aubin ont réussi à resoudre presque toutes les difficultés que presentait la lecture des hieroglyphes nahuas." (Introduction, p. viii.) He is also in error in supposing (in a note to same page) that Aubin's theory is not well-known to Americanists. Brasseur popularized it in his introductions to his *Histoire du Mexique*. Aubin, in fact, guided by the Spanish writers of the 16th century and the annotators of the Codices, first clearly expressed the general principles of the phonetic picture writing; but his rules and identifications are entirely inadequate to its complete or even partial interpretation.

† Orozco y Berra, *Historia Antigua de Mexico*, (Mexico, 1880). The Atlas to this work contains a large number of of proposed identifications of hieroglyphics. See also by the same writer, *Ensayo de Descifracion Geroglifica* in the *Anales del Museo Nacional*, tom. II. Much of this is founded on Ramirez's studies, who, however, by his own admission, knew little or nothing of the Nahuatl language (as he states in his introduction to the *Codex Chimalpopoca* or *Anales de Quauhtitlan*). Dr. Peñafiel's praiseworthy collection is entitled *Catalogo Alfabetico de los nombres de Lugares pertenecientes al Idioma Nahuatl, Estudio Jeroglifico*. (Mexico, 1885.)

DIFFICULTIES OF INTERPRETATION.

With these aids at command, why has not our progress in the interpretation of the ancient records on stone and paper been more rapid? Why do we stand now almost at the same point as in 1850?

There can be but one answer, and that will immediately suggest itself from the nature of the phoneticism in the Mexican writing. What I have called the *ikonomatic* system of writing can be elucidated only by one who has a wide command of the vocabulary of the language. Consider, for a moment, the difficulty which we experience, with all our knowledge of our native tongue, in solving one of the rebuses which appear in the puzzle columns of periodicals for children; or in interpreting the canting arms in armorial bearings. Not only must we recall the various names of the objects represented, and select from them such as the sense of the context requires, but we must make allowance for extensive omissions, as in one of the examples above quoted (Fig. 7), and for mere similarities of sound, often quite remote, as well as for the abbreviations and conventionalisms of practiced scribes, familiar with their subject and with this method of writing the sounds of their language.

Such difficulties as these can only be overcome by long-continued application to the tongues themselves, and by acquainting one's self intimately with the forms, the methods, and the variations of this truly puzzling graphic system. Every identification is solving an enigma; but once solved, each illustrates the method, confirms its accuracy, and facilitates the learner's progress, and at the same time stimulates him with the joyous sense of difficulties conquered, and with the vision of discovered truth illuminating his onward path.

Although, as I have stated, the general principles of this method were pointed out forty years ago, the prevailing ignorance of the Nahuatl language has prevented any one from successfully deciphering the Mexican script. This ignorance has had even a worse effect. Men who did not know a dozen words of Nahuatl, who were unable to construe a single sentence in the language, have taken upon themselves to condemn Aubin's explanations as visionary and untrue, and to deny wholly the phonetic elements of the Mexican writing. Lacking the essential condition of testing the accuracy of the statement, they have presumed blankly to condemn it!

THE IKONOMATIC METHOD OF PHONETIC WRITING.*

All methods of recording ideas have been divided into two classes, Thought Writing and Sound Writing.

The first, simplest and oldest is Thought Writing. This in turn is subdivided into two forms, Ikonographic and Symbolic Writing. The former is also known as Imitative, Representative or Picture Writing. The object to be held in memory is represented by its picture, drawn with such skill, or lack of skill, as the writer may possess. In Symbolic Writing, a single characteristic part or trait serves to represent the whole object; thus, the track of an animal will stand for the animal itself; a representation of the peculiar round impression of the wolf's foot, or the three-lined track of the wild turkey, being amply sufficient to designate these creatures. Even the rudest savages practice both these forms of writing, and make use of them to scratch on rocks, and paint on bark and hides, the record of their deeds.

It will be observed that Thought Writing has no reference to spoken language; neither the picture of a wolf, nor the representation of his footprint, conveys the slightest

---
* This paper was originally read before the American Philosophical Society in October, 1886, and was published in their *Proceedings*.

notion of the sound of the word *wolf.* How was the enormous leap made from the thought to the sound—in other words, from an ideographic to a phonetic method of writing?

This question has received considerable attention from scholars with reference to the development of the two most important alphabets of the world, the Egyptian and the Chinese. Both these began as simple picture writing, and both progressed to almost complete phoneticism. In both cases, however, the earliest steps are lost, and can be retraced only by indications remaining after a high degree of phonetic power had been reached. On the other hand, in the Mexican and probably in the Maya hieroglyphics, we find a method of writing which is intermediate between the two great classes I have mentioned, and which illustrates in a striking manner the phases through which both the Egyptian and Semitic alphabets passed somewhat before the dawn of history.

To this method, which stands midway between the ikonographic and the alphabetic methods of writing, I have given the name *ikonomatic,* derived from the Greek εικων-ονος, an image, a figure; ονομα-ατος, a name. That which the figure or picture refers to is not the object represented, but the *name* of that object—a *sound,* not a *thing.* But it does not refer to that sound as the name of the object, but precisely the contrary—it is the sound of the name of some other object or idea. Many ideas have no objective representation, and others are much more simply expressed by the use of figures whose names are familiar and of similar sound. Thus, to give a simple example, the infinitive "to hide" could be written by a figure 2, and the picture of a skin or hide. It is this plan on which those familiar puzzles are constructed which are called *rebuses*, and none other than this which served to bridge over the wide gap between Thought and Sound writing. It is, however, not correct to say that it is a writing by *things*, "*rebus;*" but it is by the *names* of things, and hence I have coined the word *ikonomatic*, to express this clearly.

I shall select several illustrations from two widely diverse sources, the one the hieroglyphs of Egypt, the other the heraldry of the Middle Ages, and from these more familiar fields obtain some hints of service in unraveling the intricacies of the Mexican and Maya scrolls.

The general principle which underlies "ikonomatic writing" is the presence in a language of words of different meaning but with the same or similar sounds; that is, of *homophonous* words. The figure which represents one of these is used phonetically to signify the other. There are homophones in all languages; but they abound in some more than in others. For obvious reasons, they are more abundant in languages which tend toward monosyllabism, such as the Chinese and the Maya, and in a less degree the ancient Coptic. In these it is no uncommon occurrence to find four or five quite different meanings to the same word; that is, the same sound has served as the radical for that many different names of diverse objects. The picture of any of these objects would, to the speaker of the language, recall a sound which would have all these significations, and could be employed indifferently for any of them. This circle of meanings would be still more widely extended when mere similarity, not strict identity, was aimed at.

Such was plainly the origin of phoneticism in the Egyptian hieroglyphic inscriptions. Take the word *nefer*. Its most common concrete signification was "a lute," and in the picture writing proper the lute is represented by its figure. But *nefer* had several other significations in Coptic. It meant, a *colt*, a *conscript soldier*, a *door*, and the adjective *good*. The picture of the lute therefore was used to signify every one of these.

It will be observed that this is an example of a pure ikonograph—the picture is that of the object in full, a lute; but precisely in the same way the second class of figures in picture writing, those which are wholly symbolic, may be employed. This, too, finds ample illustration in the Egyptian hieroglyphics. Instead of the picture of a house, the figure of a square was employed, with one side incomplete. Phonetically, this conveyed the sound *per*, which means *house*, and several other things.

It will readily be seen that where a figure represents a number of homophonous words, considerable confusion may result from the difficulty of ascertaining which of these is intended. To meet this, we find both in Egyptian and Chinese writing series of signs which are written but not pronounced, called "determinatives." These indicate the class to which a word has reference. They are ideographic, and of fixed meaning. Thus, after the word *nefer*, when used for conscript, the determinative is the picture of a man, etc.*

---

* The following elements occur in the old Egyptian writing:
    1. Ideographic.—(*a*) Pictures or ikonographs.
        (*b*) Symbols.
        (*c*) Determinatives.

EGYPTIAN PHONETICS.   217

There is little doubt but that all the Egyptian syllabic and alphabetic writing was derived from this early phase, where the governing principle was that of the rebus. At the date of the earliest inscriptions, most of the phonetics were monosyllabic; but in several instances, as *nefer*, above given, *neter*, which represents a banner, and by homophony, a god, and others, the full disyllabic name was preserved to the latest times. The monosyllabic signs were derived from the initial and the accented syllables of the homophones; and the alphabet, so-called, but never recognized as such, by the Egyptians, either from monoliteral words, or from initial sounds. At no period of ancient Egyptian history was one sound constantly represented by one sign. In the so-called Egyptian alphabet, there are four quite different signs for the M, four for the T, three for the N, and so on. This is obviously owing to the independent derivation of these phonetic elements from different figures employed ikonomatically.

There are other peculiarities in the Egyptian script, which are to be explained by the same historic reason. For instance, certain phonetic signs can be used only in definite combinations; others must be assigned fixed positions, as at the beginning or at the end of a group; and, in other cases, two or more different signs, with the same phonetic value, follow one another, the scribe thinking that if the reader was not acquainted with one, he would be with the other. I note these peculiarities, because they may be expected to recur in

2. Phonetic.—(*a*) Words.
(*b*) Syllables.
(*c*) Letters.

other systems of ikonomatic writing, and may serve as hints in interpreting them.

Evidently, one of the earliest stimuli to the development of phonetics was the wish to record proper names, which in themselves had no definite signification, such as those drawn from a foreign language, or those which had lost through time their original sense. In savage conditions every proper name is significant; but in conditions of social life, as developed as that of the Egyptians of the earlier dynasties, and as that of the Mayas and Mexicans in the New World, there are found many names without meaning in the current tongue. These could not be represented by any mode of picture writing. To be recorded at all, they must be written phonetically; and to accomplish this the most obvious plan was to select objects whose names had a similar sound, and by portraying the latter, represent to the ear the former. The Greek names, *Alexander* and *Alexandria*, occurring on the Rosetta Stone, were wholly meaningless to the Egyptian ear; but their scribes succeeded in expressing them very nearly by a series of signs which in origin are rebuses.

This inception of the ikonomatic method, in the effort to express phonetically proper names, is admirably illustrated in mediæval heraldry. Very early in the history of armorial bearings, we find a class of scutal devices called in Latin *arma cantantia*, in English *canting arms*, in French *armes parlantes*. The English term *canting* is from the Latin *cantare*, in its later sense of *chanting* or *announcing*. Armorial bearings of this character present charges, the names of which resemble more or less closely in sound the proper names of the family who carry them.

CANTING ARMS.

Some writers on heraldry have asserted that bearings of this character should be considered as what are known as *assumptive arms*, those which have been *assumed* by families, without just title. Excellent authorities, however, such as Woodham and Lower, have shown that these devices were frequent in the remotest ages of heraldry.* For instance, in the earliest English Roll of Arms extant, recorded in the reign of the third Henry, about the year 1240, nine such charges occur, and still more in the Rolls of the time of Edward the Second. They are also abundant in the heraldry of Spain, of Italy and of Sweden; and analogous examples have been adduced from ancient Rome. In fact, the plan is so obvious that instances could be quoted from every quarter of the globe. In later centuries, such punning allusions to proper names became unpopular in heraldry, and are now considered in bad taste.

To illustrate their character, I will mention a few which are of ancient date. The well-known English family of *Dobells* carry a *hart passant*, and three bells *argent*, thus expressing very accurately their name, *doe-bells*. The equally ancient family of Boltons carry a device representing a cask or *tun*, transfixed by a crossbow or *bolt*. Few canting arms, however, are so perfect as these. The Swinburnes, who are among those mentioned on the Roll of 1240, already referred to, bear three boar-heads, symbolical af *swine;* the Boleynes carry three bulls' heads, which reminds us of Cardinal Wolsey's pronunciation of the name in Shakespeare's Henry VIII, *Bullen:*

---

*See M. A. Lower, *Curiosities of Heraldry*, Chap. vi (London, 1845). An appropriate motto of one of these bearings was: "Non verbis sed *rebus* loquimur."

> "Anne Bullen? No; I'll no Anne Bullens for him;
> There's more in't than fair visage.—Bullen!
> No, we'll no Bullens."—*King Henry VIII, Act III.*

Not rarely the antiquity of such bearings is evidenced by the loss of the allusion in the current language, and recourse must be had to ancient and obsolete words to appreciate it. The English Harrisons display in their shield a hedgehog, which is to be explained by the French *hérisson*, and testifies to their Norman origin. The Sykes of the north of England show a fountain in their shield, whose significance is first ascertained on learning that in the Northumbrian dialect *syke* means a flowing spring or stream. The celebrated *fleurs-de-lys* of the royal house of France are traced back to the first Louis, whose name was pronounced *Loys*, and from the similarity of this to the common name of the flower, the latter was adopted as the charge on his shield.

Hundreds of such examples could be adduced, and the task of examining and analyzing them would not be an altogether vain one, as the principles upon which they were applied are the same which control the development of ikonomatic writing wherever we find it. But I pass from the consideration of these facts of general knowledge to the less known and much misunderstood forms of this writing which are presented in American archæology.

These are best exemplified in the so-called Mexican picture writing. For many years scholars have been divided in opinion whether this was purely ikonographic or partly phonetic. About forty years ago M. Aubin wrote an essay maintaining that it is chiefly phonetic, and laid down rules for its interpretation on this theory. But neither he nor any who undertook to apply his teachings succeeded in offering any acceptable renderings of the Aztec Codices. I am persuaded, however, that the cause of this failure lay, not in the theory of Aubin, but in the two facts, first, that not one of the students who approached this subject was well grounded in the Nahuatl language; and, secondly, that the principles of the interpretation of ikonomatic writing have never been carefully defined, and are extremely difficult, ambiguous and obscure, enough so to discourage any one not specially gifted in the solution of enigmas. At first, every identification is as puzzling as the effort to decipher an artificial rebus.

There are, indeed, some able scholars who still deny that any such phoneticism is to be found in Mexican pictography. To convince such of their error, and to illustrate the methods employed by these native American scribes, I will present and analyze several typical examples from Aztec manuscripts.

Beginning with proper names drawn from other languages, we find that the Nahuas had a number of such, which, of course, had no meaning in their own tongue. One of their documents speaks of the town of the Huastecas, called by that tribe *Tamuch*, which means in their tongue "near the scorpions," and by the Aztecs, in imitation, *Tamuoc*.* As the Huasteca is a Maya dialect, totally distinct from the Nahuatl, this word had no sense to the ears of

---

* *Tam*, near ; *uch*, scorpion. *Diccionario Huasteca-Español*, MS., in my possession. This and most of the other instances quoted are to be found in Lord Kingsborough's great work on Mexico, and also in Dr. Peñafiel's *Catàlogo Alfabetico de os Nombres de Lugares pertenecientes al Idioma Nahuatl* (Mexico, 1885).

the Aztecs. To convey its sound, they portrayed a man holding in his hands a measuring stick, and in the act of measuring. Now, in Nahuatl, the verb "to measure" is *tamachiua;* the measuring stick is *octocatl;* and to make the

FIG. 1.—Tamuoc.

latter plainer, several foot-prints, *xoctli*, are painted upon the measuring stick, giving an example of the repetition of the sound, such as we have already seen was common among the Egyptian scribes.

In another class of proper names, in their own tongue, although they had a meaning in the Nahuatl, the scribe preferred to express them by ikonomatic instead of ikonographic devices. Thus, *Mapachtepec*, means literally,

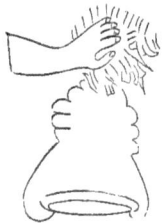

FIG. 2.—Mapachtepec.

"badger hill," or "badger town," but in place of depicting a badger, the native writer made a drawing of a hand grasping a bunch of Spanish moss, the *Tillandsia usneoides*. The hand or arm in Nahuatl is *maitl*, the moss *pachtli;* and taking the first syllables of these two words we obtain *ma pach:* the word *tepec*, locative form of *tepetl*, hill or village, is expressed by the usual conventional ideographic or determinative sign.

In other names, the relative *positions* of the objects are significant, reminding us of the rebus of a well-known town in Massachusetts, celebrated for its educational institutions:

    &
Mass.

which is to be read, "Andover, Massachusetts;" so in the Aztec scrolls, we have *itzmiquilpan* represented by an obsidian knife, *itztli*, and an edible plant, *quilitl*, which are placed above or over (*pan*), the sign for cultivated land, *milli*, thus giving all the elements of the name, the last syllable by position only.

FIG. 3.—Itzmiquilpan.

In one respect I believe the ikonomatic writing of the Mexicans is peculiar; that is, in the phonetic value which it assigns to *colors*. Like the Egyptian, it is polychromatic, but, so far as I know, the Egyptian polychromes never had a phonetic value; they were, in a general way, used by that people as determinatives, from some supposed similarity of hue; thus green indicates a vegetable substance or bronze, yellow, certain woods and some animals, and so on. In heraldry the colors are very important and have well-defined significations, but very seldom, if ever, phonetic ones. Quite the contrary is the case with the Mexican script. It presents abundant instances where the color of the object as portrayed is an integral phonetic element of the sound designed to be conveyed.

To quote examples, the Nahuatl word for yellow is *cuztic* or *coztic*, and when the hieroglyphics express phonetically such proper names as *Acozpa*, *Cozamaloapan*, *Cozhuipilcan*, etc., the monosyllable *coz* is expressed solely by the yellow color which the scribe lays upon his picture. Again, the name *Xiuhuacan*, "the place of grass," is represented by a

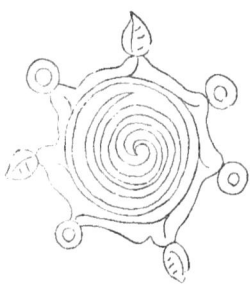

FIG. 4.—Acozpa. (A yellow center surrounded by water drops, *atl*, *a*.)

circle colored pale blue, *xiuhtic*. The name of this tint supplies the phonetic desired. The name of the village *Tlapan* is conveyed by a circle, whose interior is painted red, *tlapalli*, containing the mark of a human foot-print. Such examples are sufficient to prove that in undertaking to decipher the Mexican writing we must regard the color as well as the figure, and be prepared to allow to each a definite phonetic value.

AZTEC PHONETIC SYMBOLS.   225

It must not be understood that all the Aztec writing is made up of phonetic symbols. This is far from being the case. We discover among the hundreds of curious figures which it presents, determinatives, as in the Egyptian in-

FIG. 5.—Tlamapa.

scriptions, and numerous ideograms. Sometimes the ideogram is associated with the phonetic symbol, acting as a sort of determinative to the latter. An interesting example of this is given at the beginning of the "Manuscrito Hieratico," recently published by the Spanish government.* It is the more valuable as an example, as the picture writing is translated into Nahuatl and written in Spanish characters. The date of the document, 1526, leaves no doubt that it is in the same style as the ancient Codices. The page is headed with the picture of a church edifice; underneath is the outline of a human arm, and the legend in Nahuatl is:

In Altepetl y Santa Cruz Tlamapa.

These words mean, "the town of Santa Cruz Tlamapa." The name "*tlamapa*" means "on the hillside," and doubtless originally referred to the position in which the village was situated. But the prefix "*tlama*" usually signifies, "to do something with the arms or hands," derived from *maitl*, hand or arm. Hence, the figure of the extended arm gives this disyllable, *tlama*, which was sufficient to recall the name of the town.

The Aztecs by no means confined the ikonomatic system to proper names. They composed in it words, sentences, and treatises on various subjects. In proportion as it is applied to these connected and lengthy compositions, its processes become more recondite, curious and difficult of interpretation. Without a knowledge of the spoken language considerably more than rudimentary, it would be hopeless for the student to attempt to solve the enigmas which he meets at every step. Yet every well-directed effort will convince him that he is on the right track, and he will con-

---

* It is given in the appendix to the *Ensayo sobre la Interpretacion de la Escritura Hieratica de la America Central*, by De Rosny, translated by D. Juan de Dios de la Rada y Delgada (Madrid, 1884).

stantly be cheered and stimulated to further endeavor by the victories he will win day by day.

The analogy which is presented in so many particulars between Mexican and Maya civilization would lead us to infer that the Maya writing, of which we have a number of examples well preserved, should be unlocked by the same key which has been successfully applied to the Aztec Codices. The latest writers on the Maya manuscripts, while agreeing that they are in part, at least, in phonetic characters, consider them mostly ideographic. But it is to be noted that not one of these writers had any practical acquaintance with the sounds of the Maya language, and scarcely any with its vocabulary. From this it is evident that even were these codices in ikonomatic writing, such investigators could make very little progress in deciphering them, and might readily come to the conclusion that the figures are not phonetic in any sense. Precisely the same position was taken by a number of students of Egyptian antiquity long after the announcement of the discovery of Champollion ; and even within a few years works have been printed denying all phoneticism to the Nilotic inscriptions.

What induces me to believe that much of the Maya script is of the nature of the Mexican is the endeavor, undertaken for a very different purpose, of Professor Valentini to explain the origin of the so-called Maya alphabet, preserved by Bishop Landa, and printed in the editions of his celebrated "Description of Yucatan."* Professor Valentini

---

* Valentini's Essay appeared in the *Proceedings of the American Antiquarian Society*, April, 1880. Landa's work was originally published by the Abbe Brasseur (de Bourbourg) at Paris, 1864, and more accurately at Madrid, 1884, under the supervision of Don Juan de Dios de la Rada y Delgada.

shows by arguments and illustrations, which I think are in the main correct, that when the natives were asked to represent the sounds of the Spanish letters in their method of writing, they selected objects to depict, whose names, or initial sounds, or first syllables, were the same, or akin, to the sounds of the Spanish vowel or consonant heard by them. Sometimes they would give several words, with their corresponding pictures, for the same sound; just as I have shown was the custom of the ancient Egyptians. Thus, for the sound *b* they drew a foot-print, which in their tongue was called *be;* for the sound *a* an obsidian knife, in Maya, *ach*, etc. Valentini thinks also that the letter *e* was delineated by black spots, in Maya *eek*, meaning black, which, if proved by further research, would show that the Mayas, like the Mexicans, attributed phonetic values to the colors they employed in their painted scrolls.

Outside of the two nations mentioned, the natives of the American continent made little advance toward a phonetic system. We have no positive evidence that even the cultivated Tarascas and Zapotecs had anything better than ikonographs; and of the Quiches and Cakchiquels, both near relatives of the Mayas, we only know that they had a written literature of considerable extent, but of the plan by which it was preserved we have only obscure hints. Next to these we should probably place the Chipeway pictography, as preserved on their *meda* sticks, bark records, and *adjidjiatig* or grave-posts. I have examined a number of specimens of these, but have failed to find any evidence that the characters refer to sounds in the language; however, I might not consider it improbable that further researches might disclose some germs of the ikonomatic method of writing even in these primitive examples of the desire of the human intellect to perpetuate its acquisitions, and hand them down to generations yet unborn.

THE WRITING AND RECORDS OF THE ANCIENT MAYAS.*

1.—Introductory.

ONE of the ablest living ethnologists has classified the means of recording knowledge under two general headings—Thought-writing and Sound-writing.† The former is again divided into two forms, the first and earliest of which is by pictures, the second by picture-writing.

The superiority of picture-writing over the mere depicting of an occurrence is that it analyzes the thought and expresses separately its component parts, whereas the picture presents it as a whole. The representations familiar among the North American Indians are usually only pictures, while most of the records of the Aztec communities are in picture-writing.

The genealogical development of Sound-writing begins by the substitution of the sign of one idea for that of another whose sound is nearly or quite the same. Such was the early graphic system of Egypt, and such substantially to-day

---

* Originally published as an introduction to Dr. Cyrus Thomas' *Study of the Manuscript Troano*, issued by the U. S. Geographical and Geological Survey of the Rocky Mountain Region, Washington, 1882, (revised with additions for the present volume).

† Dr. Friedrich Müller, *Grundriss der Sprachwissenchaft*, Band i, pp. 151-156.

EVOLUTION OF THE ALPHABET.

is that of the Chinese. Above stands syllabic writing, this as that of the Japenése, and the semi-syllabic signs of the old Semitic alphabet; while, as the perfected result of these various attempts, we reach at last the invention of a true alphabet, in which a definite figure corresponds to a definite elementary sound.

It is a primary question in American archæology, How far did the most cultivated nations of the western continent ascend this scale of graphic development? This question is as yet unanswered. All agree, however, that the highest evolution took place among the Nahuatl-speaking tribes of Mexico and the Maya race of Yucatan.

I do not go too far in saying that it is proved that the Aztecs used to a certain extent a phonetic system of writing, one in which the figures refer not to the thought, but to the sound of the thought as expressed in spoken language. This has been demonstrated by the researches of M. Aubin, and, of late, by the studies of Señor Orozco y Berra.*

Two evolutionary steps can be distinguished in the Aztec writing. In the earlier the plan is that of the rebus in combination with ideograms, which latter are nothing more than the elements of picture-writing. Examples of this plan are the familiar "tribute rolls" and the names of towns and kings, as shown in several of the codices published by Lord Kingsborough. The second step is where a conventional image is employed to represent the sound of its first

---

* Aubin, *Mémoire sur la Peinture didactique et l'Écriture figurative des anciens Mexicains*, in the introduction to Brasseur (de Bourbourg)'s *Histoire des Nations civilisées du Mexique et de l'Amérique Centrale*, tom. i; Manuel Orozco y Berra *Ensayo de Descifracion geroglifica*, in the *Anales del Museo nacional de México*, tom. i, ii.

syllable. This advances actually to the level of the syllabic alphabet; but it is doubtful if there are any Aztec records entirely, or even largely, in this form of writing. They had only reached the commencement of its development.

The graphic system of the Mayas of Yucatan was very different from that of the Aztecs. No one at all familiar with the two could fail at once to distinguish between the manuscripts of the two nations. They are plainly independent developments.

We know much more about the ancient civilization of Mexico than of Yucatan; we have many more Aztec than Maya manuscripts, and hence we are more at a loss to speak with positiveness about the Maya system of writing than about the Mexican. We must depend on the brief and unsatisfactory statements of the early Spanish writers, and on what little modern research has accomplished, for means to form a correct opinion; and there is at present a justifiable discrepancy of opinion about it among those who have given the subject most attention.

2.—Descriptions by Spanish Writers.

The earliest exploration of the coast of Yucatan was that of Francisco Hernandez de Cordova, in 1517. The year following, a second expedition, under Juan de Grijalva, visited a number of points between the island of Cozumel and the Bahia de Terminos.

Several accounts of Grijalva's voyage have been preserved, but they make no distinct reference to the method of writing they found in use. Some native books were obtained, however, probably from the Mayas, and were sent to Spain, where they were seen by the historian Peter Martyr. He describes them in general terms, and compares the characters in which they were written to the Egyptian hieroglyphics, some of which he had seen in Rome. He supposes that they contain the laws and ceremonies of the people, astronomical calculations, the deeds of their kings, and other events of their history. He also speaks in commendation of the neatness of their general appearance, the skill with which the drawing and painting were carried out. He further mentions that the natives used this method of writing or drawing in the affairs of common life.*

Although Yucatan became thus early known to the Spaniards, it was not until 1541 that a permanent settlement was effected, in which year Francisco de Montejo, the younger, advanced into the central province of Ceh Pech, and established a city on the site of the ancient town called *Ichcanziho*, which means "the five (temples) of many oracles (or serpents)," to which he gave the name *Mérida*, on account of the magnificent ancient edifices he found there.

Previous to this date, however, in 1534, Father Jacobo de Testera, with four other missionaries, proceeded from Tabasco up the west coast to the neighborhood of the Bay of Campeachy. They were received amicably by the natives, and instructed them in the articles of the Christian faith. They also obtained from the chiefs a submission to the King of Spain; and I mention this early missionary expedition for the fact stated that each chief signed this act of submission "with a certain mark, like an autograph." This document

---

* Peter Martyr, Decad. iv, cap. viii.

was subsequently taken to Spain by the celebrated Bishop Las Casas.* It is clear from the account that some definite form of signature was at that time in use among the chiefs.

It might be objected that these signatures were nothing more than rude totem marks, such as were found even among the hunting tribes of the Northern Mississippi Valley. But Las Casas himself, in whose possession the documents were, here comes to our aid to refute this opinion. He was familiar with the picture-writing of Mexico, and recognized in the hieroglyphics of the Mayas something different and superior. He says expressly that these had inscriptions, writings, in certain characters, the like of which were found nowhere else.†

One of the early visitors to Yucatan after the conquest was the Pope's commissary-general, Father Alonzo Ponce, who was there in 1588. Many natives who had grown to adult years in heathenism must have been living then. He makes the following interesting observation:

"The natives of Yucatan are, among all the inhabitants of New Spain, especially deserving of praise for three things: First, that before the Spaniards came they made use of characters and letters, with which they wrote out their histories, their ceremonies, the order of sacrifices to their idols, and their calendars, in books made of bark of a certain tree.

---

* "Se sujetaron de su propria voluntad al Señorio de los Reies de Castilla, recibiendo al Emperador, como Rei de España, por Señor supremo y universal, e hicieron ciertas señales, como Firmas ; las quales, con testimonio de los Religiosos Franciscos, que alli estaban, llevó consigo el buen Obispo de Chiapa, Don Fr. Bartolomé de las Casas, amparo, y defensa de estos Indios, quando se fué á España." Torquemada, *Monarquia Indiana*, lib. xix. cap. xiii.

† "Letreros de ciertos caracteres que en otra ninguna parte." Las Casas, *Historia Apologetica de las Indias Occidentales*. cap. cxxiii.

These were on very long strips, a quarter or a third (of a yard) in width, doubled and folded, so that they resembled a bound book in quarto, a little larger or smaller. These letters and characters were understood only by the priests of the idols (who in that language are called Ahkins) and a few principal natives. Afterwards some of our friars learned to understand and read them, and even wrote them."*

The interesting fact here stated, that some of the early missionaries not only learned to read these characters, but employed them to instruct the Indians, has been authenticated by a recent discovery of a devotional work written in this way.

The earliest historian of Yucatan is Fr. Bernardo de Lizana.† But I do not know of a single complete copy of his work, and only one imperfect copy, which is, or was, in the city of Mexico, from which the Abbé Brasseur (de Bourbourg) copied and republished a few chapters. Lizana was himself not much of an antiquary, but he had in his hands the manuscripts left by Father Alonso de Solana, who came to Yucatan in 1565, and remained there till his death, in 1599. Solana was an able man, acquiring thoroughly the Maya tongue, and left in his writings many notes on the antiquities of the country.‡ Therefore we may put

---

* *Relacion Breve y Verdadera de Algunas Cosas de las muchas que sucedieron al Padre Fray Alonso Ponce, Commissario General, en las Provincias de la Nueva España*, in the *Coleccion de Documentos para la Historia de España*, tom. lviii, p. 392. The other traits he praises in the natives of Yucatan are their freedom from sodomy and cannibalism. (For the text see later, p. 255.)

† Bernardo de Lizana, *Historia de Yucatan. Devocionario de Nuestra Señora de Izamal, y Conquista Espiritual*, 8vo. Pinciæ (Valladolid), 1633.

‡ For these facts see Diego Lopez Cogolludo, *Historia de Yucatan*, lib ix, cap. xv. Cogolludo adds that in his time (1650-'60) Solana's MSS. could not be found; Lizana may have sent them to Spain.

considerable confidence in what Lizana writes on these matters.

The reference which I find in his work to the Maya writings is as follows:

"The most celebrated and revered sanctuary in this land, and that to which they resorted from all parts, was this town and temples of Ytzamal, as they are now called; and that it was founded in most ancient times, and that it is still known who did found it, will be set forth in the next chapter.

"III. The history and the authorities which we can cite are certain ancient characters, scarcely understood by many, and explained by some old Indians, sons of the priests of their gods, who alone knew how to read and expound them, and who were believed in and revered as much as the gods themselves, etc.*"

We have here the positive statement that these hieroglyphic inscriptions were used by the priests for recording their national history, and that by means of them they preserved the recollection of events which took place in a very remote past.

Another valuable early witness, who testifies to the same effect, is the Dr. Don Pedro Sanchez de Aguilar, who was *cura* of Valladolid, in Yucatan, in 1596, and, later, dean of the chapter of the cathedral at Merida. His book, too, is extremely scarce, and I have never seen a copy; but I have

---

* I add the original of the most important passage: "La historia y autores que podemos alegar son unos antiguos caracteres, mal entendidos de muchos, y glossados de unos indios antiguos, que son hijos de los sacerdotes de sus dioses, que son los que solo sabian leer y adivinar, y a quien creian y reverenciavan como á Dioses destos."

copious extracts from it, made by the late Dr. C. Hermann Berendt from a copy in Yucatan. Aguilar writes of the Mayas:

"They had books made from the bark of trees, coated with a white and durable varnish. They were ten or twelve yards long, and were gathered together in folds, like a palm leaf. On these they painted in colors the reckoning of their years, wars, pestilences, hurricanes, inundations, famines, and other events. From one of these books, which I myself took from some of these idolaters, I saw and learned that to one pestilence they gave the name *Mayacimil*, and to another *Ocnakuchil*, which mean 'sudden deaths' and 'times when the crows enter the houses to eat the corpses.' And the inundation they called *Hunyecil*, the submersion of trees."*

The writer leaves it uncertain whether he learned these words directly from the characters of the book or through the explanations of some native.

It has sometimes been said that the early Spanish writers drew a broad line between the picture-writing that they found in America and an alphabetic script. This may be true of other parts, but is not so of Yucatan. These signs, or some of them, are repeatedly referred to as "letters," *letras*.

This is pointedly the case with Father Gabriel de San Buenaventura, a French Franciscan who served in Yucatan about 1670–'80. He published one of the earliest grammars of the language, and also composed a dictionary in three

---
* Pedro Sanchez de Aguilar, *Informe contra Idolorum cultores del Obispado de Yucatan*. 4to. Madrid, 1639, ff. 124.

large volumes, which was not printed. Father Beltran de Santa Rosa quotes from it an interesting tradition preserved by Buenaventura, that among the inventions of the mythical hero-god of the natives, *Itzamna* or *Kinich ahau*, was that of "the letters of the Maya language," with which letters they wrote their books.* Itzamna, of course, dates back to a misty antiquity, but the legend is of value, as showing that the characters used by the natives did, in the opinion of the early missionaries, deserve the name of *letters*.

Father Diego Lopez Cogolludo is the best-known historian of Yucatan. He lived about the middle of the seventeenth century, and says himself that at that time there was little more to be learned about the antiquities of the race. He adds, therefore, substantially nothing to our knowledge of the subject, although he repeats, with positiveness, the statement that the natives "had characters by which they could understand each other in writing, such as those yet seen in great numbers on the ruins of their buildings."†

This is not very full. Yet we know to a certainty that there were quantities of these manuscripts in use in Yucatan for a generation after Cogolludo wrote. To be sure, those in the Christianized districts had been destroyed, wherever the priests could lay their hands on them; but in the southern part of the peninsula, on the islands of Lake Peten and

---

* "El primero quo halló las letras de la lengua Maya é hizó el cómputo de los años, meses y edades, y lo enseño todo a los Indios de esta Provincia, fué un Indios llamado *Kinchahau*, y por otro nombre Tzamna." Fr. Pedro Beltran de Santa Rosa Maria, *Arte del Idioma Maya*, p. 16 (2d ed., Mérida de Yucatan, 1859).

† Diego Lopez Cogolludo, *Historia de Yucatan*, lib. iv, cap. 111. The original is: "No acostumbraban escribir los pleitos, aunque tenian caracteres con que se entendian, de que se ven muchos en las ruinas de los edificios."

adjoining territory, the powerful chief, Canek, ruled a large independent tribe of Itzas. They had removed from the northern provinces of the peninsula somewhere about 1450, probably in consequence of the wars which followed the dissolution of the confederacy whose capital was the ancient city of Mayapan.

Their language was pure Maya, and they had brought with them in their migration, as one of their greatest treasures, the sacred books which contained their ancient history, their calendar and ritual, and the prophecies of their future fate. In the year 1697 they were attacked by the Spaniards, under General Don Martin de Ursua; their capital, on the island of Flores, in Lake Peten, taken by storm; great numbers of them slaughtered or driven into the lake to drown, and the twenty-one temples which were on the island razed to the ground.

A minute and trustworthy account of these events has been given by Don Juan de Villagutierre Soto-Mayor, in the course of which occur several references to the sacred books, which he calls *Analtés.*

The king Canek, he tells us, in reading in his *Analtés*, had found notices of the northern provinces of Yucatan and of the fact that his predecessors had come thence, and had communicated these narratives to his chiefs.*

These books are described as showing "certain characters and figures, painted on certain barks of trees, each leaf or

---

* "Porque lo leia su Rey en sus Analtehes, teniau Noticias de aquellas Provincias de Yucatan (que Analtehes, ò Historias, es una misma cosa) y de que sus Pasados avian salido de ellas." *Historia de la Conquista de la Provincia de el Itza, Reduccion y Progressos de la de el Lacandon,* etc., (folio, Madrid, 1701) lib. vi, cap. iv.

tablet about a quarter (of a yard) wide, and of the thickness of a piece of eight, folded at one edge and the other in the manner of a screen, called by them *Analtehes.*"*

When the island of Flores was captured these books were found stored in the house of the king Canek, containing the account of all that had happened to the tribe.† What disposition was made of them we are not informed.

I have reserved until now a discussion of the description of the Maya writing presented in the well-known work of Diego de Landa, the second bishop of Yucatan. Landa arrived in the province in August, 1549, and died in April, 1579, having passed most of the intervening thirty years there in the discharge of his religious duties. He became well acquainted with the language, which, for that matter, is a comparatively easy one, and though harsh, illiberal, and bitterly fanatic, he paid a certain amount of attention to the arts, religion, and history of the ancient inhabitants.

The notes that he made were copied after his death and reached Spain, where they are now preserved in the library of the Royal Academy of History, Madrid. In 1864 they were published at Paris, with a French translation, by the Abbé Brasseur (de Bourbourg).

Of all writers Landa comes the nearest telling us how the Mayas used their system of writing ; but, unfortunately, he also is so superficial and obscure that his words have given rise to very erroneous theories. His description runs as follows :

---

* *Ibid.*, lib. vii, cap. i.

† Y en su casa tambien tenia de estos Idolos, y Mesa de Sacrificios, y los Analtehes, ò Historias de todo quanto los avia sucedido." *Ibid.*, lib. viii, cap. xiii.

"This people also used certain characters or letters, with which they wrote in their books their ancient matters and their sciences, and with them (*i. e.*, with their characters or letters), and figures (*i. e.*, drawings or pictures), and some signs in the figures, they understood their matters, and could explain them and teach them. We found great numbers in these letters, but as they contained nothing that did not savor of superstition and lies of the devil, we burnt them all, at which the natives grieved most keenly and were greatly pained.

"I will give here an *a*, *b*, *c*, as their clumsiness does not allow more, because they use one character for all the aspirations of the letters, and for marking the parts another, and thus it could go on *in infinitum*, as may be seen in the following example. *Le* means a noose and to hunt with one; to write in their characters, after we had made them understand that there are two letters, they wrote it with three, giving to the aspiration of the *l* the vowel *é*, which it carries before it; and in this they are not wrong so to use it, if they wish to, in their curious manner. After this they add to the end the compound part."*

I need not pursue the quotation. The above words show clearly that the natives did not in their method of writing analyze a word to its primitive phonetic elements. "This," said the bishop, "we had to do for them." Therefore they did not have an alphabet in the sense of the word as we use it.

On the other hand, it is equally clear, from his words and examples, that they had figures which represented sounds,

---

* Diego de Landa, *Relacion de las Cosas de Yucatan*, pp. 316, 318, *seq.*

and that they combined these and added a determinative or an ideogram to represent words or phrases.

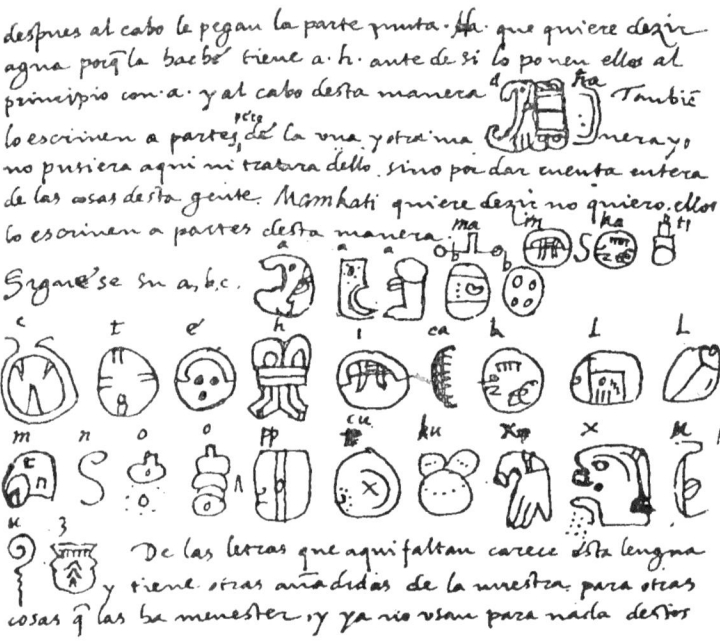

FIG. 1.--Fac Simile of Landa's Manuscript.

The alphabet which he inserts has been engraved and printed several times, but nowhere with the fidelity desirable for so important a monument in American archæology. For that reason I insert a photographic reproduction of it from the original MS. in the library of the Academia de la Historia of Madrid.

A comparison of this with the alphabet as given in Brasseur's edition of Landa discloses several variations of im-

portance. Thus the Abbé places the first form of the letter
C horizontally instead of upright. Again in the MS., the
two figures for the letter *U* stand, the first at the end of one
line, the second at the beginning of the next. From their
strong analogy with the sign of the sky at night, I am of
opinion that they belong together as members of one composite sign, not separately as Brasseur gives them.

Both in it and in the inscriptions, manuscripts, and paintings the forms of the letters are rounded, and a row of them presents the outlines of a number of pebbles cut in two. Hence the system of writing has been called "calculiform," from *calculus*, a pebble. The expression has been criticised, but I agree with Dr. Förstemann in thinking it a very appropriate one. It was suggested, I believe, by the Abbé Brasseur (de Bourbourg).

This alphabet of course, can not be used as the Latin *a, b, c*. It is surprising that any scholar should have ever thought so. It would be an exception, even a contradiction, to the history of the evolution of human intelligence, to find such an alphabet among nations of the stage of cultivation of the Mayas or Aztecs.

The severest criticism which Landa's figures have met has been from Dr. Phillip J. J. Valentini. He discovered that many of the sounds of the Spanish alphabet were represented by signs or pictures of objects whose names in the Maya begin with that sound. Thus he supposes that Landa asked an Indian to write in the native character the Spanish letter *a*, and the Indian drew an obsidian knife, which, says Dr. Valentini, is in the Maya *ach;* in other words, it begins with the vowel *a*. So for the sound *ki*, the Indian gave the sign of the day named *kinich*.

Such is Dr. Valentini's theory of the formation of Landa's alphabet; and not satisfied with lashing with considerable sharpness those who have endeavored by its aid to decipher the manuscripts and mural inscriptions, he goes so far as to term it "a Spanish fabrication."

I shall not enter into a close examination of Dr. Valentini's supposed identification of these figures. It is evident that it has been done by running over the Maya dictionary to find some word beginning with the letter under criticism, the figurative representation of which word might bear some resemblance to Landa's letter. When the Maya fails, such a word is sought for in the Kiche or other dialect of the stock; and the resemblances of the pictures to the supposed originals are sometimes greatly strained.

But I pass by these dubious methods of criticism, as well as several lexicographic objections which might be raised. I believe, indeed, that Dr. Valentini is not wrong in a number of his identifications. But the conclusion I draw is a different one. Instead of proving that this is picture-writing, it indicates that the Mayas used the second or higher grade of phonetic syllabic writing, which, as I have before observed, has been shown by M. Aubin to have been developed to some extent by the Aztecs in some of their histories and connected compositions (see above, page 231). Therefore the importance and authenticity of Landa's alphabet are, I think, vindicated by this attempt to treat it as a "fabrication."*

---

* Dr. Valentini's article was published in the *Proceedings of the American Antiquarian Society*, 1880. More recently Dr. Ed. Seler has condemned the Landa alphabet as "ein Versuch von Ladinos, von in die Spanische Wissenschaft eingeweihten

SUMMARY OF THE QUESTION.

Landa also gives some interesting details about their books. He writes:

"The sciences that they taught were the reckoning of the years, months, and days, the feasts and ceremonies, the administration of their sacraments, the fatal days and seasons, their methods of divination and prophecies, events about to happen, remedies for diseases, their ancient history, together with the art of reading and writing their books with characters which were written, and pictures which represented the things written.

"They wrote their books on a large sheet doubled into folds, which was afterwards inclosed between two boards, which they decorated handsomely. They were written from side to side in columns, as they were folded. They manufactured this paper from the root of a tree and gave it a white surface on which one could write. Some of the principal nobles cultivated these sciences out of a taste for them, and although they did not make public use of them, as did the priests, yet they were the more highly esteemed for this knowledge."*

From the above extracts from Spanish writers we may infer that—

1. The Maya graphic system was recognized from the first to be distinct from the Mexican.
2. It was a hieroglyphic system, known only to the priests and a few nobles.

Eingebornen in der Art, wie sie die Spanier ihre Lettern verwenden sahen, auch mit den Eingebornen geläufigen Bildern und Charaktern zu hantiren." *Verhandlungen der Berliner authropologischen Gesellschaft*, 1887, s. 227· I am far from adopting this sweeping statement, which I believe is contradicted by the whole tenor of Landa's words and the testimony of other writers.

* Diego de Landa, *Relacion de las Cosas de Yucatan*, p. 44.

3. It was employed for a variety of purposes, prominent among which was the preservation of their history and calendar.

4. It was a composite system, containing pictures (*figuras*), ideograms (*caracteres*), and phonetic signs (*letras*).

3.—References from Native Sources.

We might reasonably expect that the Maya language should contain terms relating to their books and writings which would throw light on their methods. So, no doubt, it did. But it was a part of the narrow and crushing policy of the missionaries not only to destroy everything that related to the times of heathendom, but even to drop all words which referred to ancient usages. Hence the dictionaries are more sterile in this respect than we might have supposed.

The verb "to write" is *dzib*, which like the Greek γράφειν, meant also to draw and to paint. From this are derived the terms *dziban*, something written; *dzibal*, a signature, etc.

Another word, meaning to write, or to paint in black, is *zabac*. As a noun, this was in ancient times applied to a black fluid extracted from the *zabacche*, a species of tree, and used for dyeing and painting. In the sense of "to write," *zabac* is no longer found in the language, and instead of its old meaning, it now refers to ordinary ink.

The word for letter or character is *uooh*. This is a primitive root found with the same or a closely allied meaning in other branches of this linguistic stock, as, for instance, in the Kiché and Cakchiquel. As a verb, pret. *uooth*, fut. *uooté*, it also means to form letters, to write; and from the passive form, *uoohal*, we have the participial noun, *uoohan*, something written, a manuscript.

The ordinary word for book, paper, or letter, is *huun*, in which the aspirate is almost mute, and is dropped in the forms denoting possession, as *u uun*, my book, *yuunil Dios*, the book of God, *il* being the so-called "determinative" ending. It occurs to me as not unlikely that *uun*, book, is a syncopated form of *uoohan*, something written, given above. To read a book is *xochun*, literally to *count* a book.

According to Villagutierre Soto-Mayor, the name of the sacred books of the Itzas was *analté*. In the printed *Diccionario de la Lengua Maya*, by Don Juan Pio Perez, this is spelled *anahté*, which seems to be a later form.

The term is not found in several early Maya dictionaries in my possession, of dates previous to 1700. The Abbé Brasseur indeed, in a note to Landa, explains it to mean "a book of wood," but it can have no such signification. Perhaps it should read *hunilté*, this being composed of *hunil*, the "determinative" form of *huun*, a book, and the termination *té*, which added to nouns, gives them a specific sense, *e.g. amayté*, a square figure, from *amay*, an angle; *tzucubté*, a province, from *tzuc*, a portion separated from the rest. It would mean especially the sacred or national books.

The particular class of books which were occupied with the calendar and the ritual were called *tzolanté*, which is a participial noun from the verb *tzol*, passive *tzolal*, to set in order, to arrange, with the suffix *té*. By these books were set in order and arranged the various festivals and fasts.

When the conquest was an accomplished fact and the

priests had got the upper hand, the natives did not dare use their ancient characters. They exposed themselves to the suspicion of heresy and the risk of being burnt alive, as more than once happened. But their strong passion for literature remained, and they gratified it as far as they dared by writing in their own tongue with the Spanish alphabet volumes whose contents are very similar to those described by Landa.

A number of these are still in existence, and offer an interesting field for antiquarian and linguistic study. Although, as I say, they are no longer in the Maya letters, they contain quite a number of ideograms, as the signs of the days and the months, and occasional cartouches and paintings, which show that they were made to resemble the ancient manuscripts as closely as possible.

They also contain not infrequent references to the "writing" of the ancients, and what are alleged to be extracts from the old records, chiefly of a mystic character. The same terms are employed in speaking of the ancient graphic system as of the present one. Thus in one of them, known as "The Book of Chilan Balam of Chumayel," occurs this phrase: *Bay dzibanil tumenel Evangelistas yetel profeta Balam*—"as it was written by the Evangelists, and also by the prophet Balam," this Balam being one of their own celebrated ancient seers.

Among the predictions preserved from a time anterior to the Conquest, there are occasional references to their books and their contents. I quote, as an example, a short prophecy attributed to Ahkul Chel, "priest of the idols." It is found in several of the oldest Maya manuscripts, and is in all probability authentic, as it contains nothing which would lead us to suppose that it was one of the "pious frauds" of the missionaries.

"*Enhi cibte katune yume, maixtan à naaté;
Uatac u talel, mac bin ca ɔabac tu coɔ pop;
Katune yume bin uluc, holom uil tucal ya;
Tali ti xaman, tali ti chikine; ahkinob uil yane yume;
Mac to ahkin, mac to ahbobat, bin alic u than uoohe;
Yheil Bolon Ahau, maixtan à naaté?*"

"The lord of the cycle has been written down, but ye will not understand;

"He has come, who will give the enrolling of the years;

"The lord of the cycle will arrive, he will come on account of his love;

"He came from the north, from the west. There are priests, there are fathers,

"But what priest, what prophet, shall explain the words of the books,

"In the Ninth Ahau, which ye will not understand?"*

---

*I add a few notes on this text:

Enhi is the preterit of the irregular verb, *hal*, to be, pret. *enhi*, fut. *anac*. *Katun yum*, father or lord of the Katun or cycle. Each Katun was under the protection of a special deity or lord, who controlled the events which occurred in it. *Tu coɔ pop*, lit., "for the rolling up of Pop," which was the first month in the Maya year. *Holom* is an archaic future from *hul;* this form in *om* is mentioned by Buenaventura, *Arte de la Lengua Maya*, 1684, and is frequent in the sacred language, but does not occur elsewhere. *Tucal ya*, on account of his love; but *ya* means also "suffering," "wound," and "strength," and there is no clue which of these significations is meant. *Ahkinob;* the original has *lukinob*, which I suspect is an error; it would alter the phrase to mean "In that day there are fathers" or lords, the word *yum*, father, being constantly used for lord or ruler. The *ahkin* was the priest; the *ahbobat* was a diviner or prophet. The 9th Ahau Katun was the period of 20 years which began in 1541, according to most native authors, but according to Landa's reckoning in the year 1561.

From this designedly obscure chant we perceive that the ancient priests inscribed their predictions in books, which were afterward explained to the people. The expression *bin alic u than uoohe*—literally, "he will speak the words of the letters"—seems to point to a phonetic writing, but as it may be used in a figurative sense, I shall not lay stress on it.*

4.—*The Existing Codices.*

The word *Codex* ought to be confined, in American archæology, to manuscripts in the original writing of the natives. Some writers have spoken of the "Codex Chimalpopoca," the "Codex Zumarraga," and the "Codex Perez," which are nothing more than manuscripts either in the native or Spanish tongues written with the Latin alphabet.

Of the Maya Codices known, only four have been published, which I will mention in the order of their appearance.

The Dresden Codex.—This is an important Maya manuscript preserved in the Royal Library at Dresden. How or when it came to Europe is not known. It was obtained from some unknown person in Vienna in 1739.

This Codex corresponds in size, appearance, and manner of folding to the descriptions of the Maya books which I have presented above from Spanish sources. It has thirty-nine leaves, thirty-five of which are colored and inscribed on

---

* In quoting and explaining Maya words and phrases in this article, I have in all instances followed the *Diccionario Maya-Español del Convento de Motul* (Yucatan); a copy of which in manuscript (one of the only two in existence) is in my possession. It was composed about 1580. The still older Maya dictionary of Father Villalpando, printed in Mexico in 1571, is yet in existence in one or two copies, but I have never seen it.

both sides, and four on one side only, so that there are only seventy-four pages of matter. The total length of the sheet is 3.5 meters, and the height of each page is 0.295 meter, the width 0.085 meter.

The first publication of any portion of this Codex was by Alexander von Humboldt, who had five pages of it copied for his work, *Vues des Cordillères et Monumens des Peuples Indigènes de l'Amérique*, issued at Paris in 1813 (not 1810, as the title-page has it). It was next very carefully copied in full by the Italian artist, Agostino Aglio, for the third volume of Lord Kingsborough's great work on *Mexican Antiquities*, the first volume of which appeared in 1831.

From Kingsborough's work a few pages of the Codex have been from time to time republished in other books, which call for no special mention; and two pages were copied from the original in Wuttke's *Geschichte der Schrift*, Leipzig, 1872.

Finally, in 1880, the whole was very admirably chromo-photographed by A. Naumann's establishment at Leipzig, to the number of fifty copies, forty of which were placed on sale. It is the first work which was ever published in chromo-photography, and has, therefore, a high scientific as well as antiquarian interest.

The editor was Dr. E. Förstemann, aulic counselor and librarian-in-chief of the Royal Library. He wrote an introduction (17 pp. 4to.) giving a history of the manuscript, and bibliographical and other notes upon it of much value. One opinion he defends must not be passed by in silence. It is that the Dresden Codex is not one, but parts of two original manuscripts written by different hands.

It appears that it has always been in two unequal fragments, which all previous writers have attributed to an accidental injury to the original. Dr. Förstemann gives a number of reasons for believing that this is not the correct explanation, but that we have here portions of two different books, having general similarity but also many points of diversity.

This separation led to an erroneous (or perhaps erroneous) sequence of the pages in Kingsborough's edition. The artist.Aglio took first one fragment and copied both sides, and then proceeded to the next one; and it is not certain that in either case he begins with the first page in the original order of the book.

The Codex Peresianus, or *Codex Mexicanus, No. II*, of the *Bibliothèque Nationale* of Paris.—This fragment—for it is unfortunately nothing more—was discovered in 1859 by Prof. Leon de Rosny among a mass of old papers in the National Library. It consists of eleven leaves, twenty-two pages, each 9 inches long and $5\frac{1}{4}$ inches wide. The writing is very much defaced, but was evidently of a highly artistic character, probably the most so of any manuscript known. It unquestionably belongs to the Maya manuscripts.

Its origin is unknown. The papers in which it was wrapped bore the name "Perez," in a Spanish hand of the seventeenth century, and hence the name "Peresianus" was given it. By order of the Minister of Public Instruction, ten photographic copies of this Codex, without reduction, were prepared for the use of scholars. None of them were placed on sale, and so far as I know the only one which has found its way to the United States is that in my own library. An ordinary lithographic reproduction was given in the *Archives paléographiques de l'Orient et de l'Amérique*, tome I. (Paris, 1869-'71).

The Codex Tro, or *Troano*.—The publication of this valuable Codex we owe to the enthusiasm of the Abbé Brasseur (de Bourbourg). On his return from Yucatan in 1864 he visited Madrid, and found this Manuscript in the possession of Don Juan de Tro y Ortolano, professor of paleography, and himself a descendent of Hernan Cortes. The abbé named it *Troano*, as a compound of the two names of its owner; but later writers often content themselves by referring to it simply as the *Codex Tro*.

It consists of thirty-five leaves and seventy pages, each of which is larger than a page of the Dresden Codex, but less than one of the *Codex Peresianus*. It was published by chromo-lithography at Paris, in 1869, prefaced by a study on the graphic system of the Mayas by the abbé, and an attempt at a translation. The reproduction, which was carried out under the efficient care of M. Leonce Angrand, is extremely accurate.

The Codex Cortesianus.—This Codex, published at Paris, 1883, under the editorship of Professor Leon de Rosny, presents the closest analogy to the Codex Troano, of which, indeed, it probably formed a part. It has forty-two leaves, closely written in the calculiform character. There is no evidence that it was brought to Spain by Cortes, but from a tradition to that effect, it has received its name.

All four of these codices were written on paper manufactured from the leaves of the maguey plant, such as that in common use in Mexico. In Maya the maguey is called *ci*, the varieties being distinguished by various prefixes. It grows luxuriantly in most parts of Yucatan, and although the favorite tipple of the ancient inhabitants was mead, they were not unacquainted with the intoxicating *pulque*, the liquor from the maguey, if we can judge from their word for a drunkard, *ci-vinic* (*vinic*=man). The old writers were probably in error when they spoke of the books being made of the barks of trees; or, at least, they were not all of that material.

The above-mentioned Manuscripts are the only ones which have been published. I shall not enumerate those which are said to exist in private hands. So long as they are withheld from the examination of scientific men they can add nothing to the general stock of knowledge, and as statements about them are not verifiable, it is useless to make any.

In addition to the Manuscripts, we have the mural paintings and inscriptions found at Palenque, Copan, Chichen Itza, and various ruined cities within the boundaries of the Maya-speaking races. There is no mistaking these inscriptions. They are unquestionably of the same character as the Manuscripts, although it is also easy to perceive variations, which are partly owing to the necessary differences in technique between painting and sculpture: partly, no doubt, to the separation of age and time.

Photographs and "squeezes" have reproduced many of these inscriptions with entire fidelity. We can also depend upon the accurate pencil of Catherwood, whose delineations have never been equalled. But the pictures of Waldeck and some other travelers do not deserve any confidence, and should not be quoted in a discussion of the subject.

THE BOOKS OF CHILAN BALAM.*

CIVILIZATION in ancient America rose to its highest level among the Mayas of Yucatan. Not to speak of the architectural monuments which still remain to attest this, we have the evidence of the earliest missionaries to the fact that they alone, of all the natives of the New World, possess a literature written in "letters and characters," preserved in volumes neatly bound, the paper manufactured from the material derived from fibrous plants, and sized with a durable white varnish.†

---

* Read before the Numismatic and Antiquarian Society of Philadelphia, at its twenty-fourth annual meeting, January 5th, 1882, and published in *The Penn Monthly*.

† Of the numerous authorities which could be quoted on this point, I shall give the words of but one, Father Alonso Ponce, the Pope's Commissary-General, who traveled through Yucatan in 1586, when many natives were still living who had been born before the Conquest (1541). Father Ponce had traveled through Mexico, and, of course, had learned about the Aztec picture-writing, which he distinctly contrasts with the writing of the Mayas. Of the latter, he says: "*Son alabados de tres cosas entre todos los demas de la Nueva España, la una de que en su antiguedad tenian caracteres y letras, con que escribian sus historias y las ceremonias y orden de los sacrificios de sus idolos y su calendario, en libros hechos de corteza de cierto arbol, los cuales eran unas tiras muy largas de quarta o tercia en ancho, qus se doblaban y recogian, y venia á queder á manera de un libo encuardenado en cuartilla, poco mas ó menos. Estas letras y caracteras no las entendian, sino los sacerdotes de los idolos, (que en aquella lengua se llaman 'ahkines,') y algun indio principal. Despues las entendieron y supieron leer algunos frailes nuestros y aun las escribien.*"—("*Relacion*

A few of these books still remain, preserved to us by accident in the great European libraries ; but most of them were destroyed by the monks. Their contents were found to relate chiefly to the pagan ritual, to traditions of the heathen times, to astrological superstitions, and the like. Hence, they were considered deleterious, and were burned wherever discovered.

This annihilation of their sacred books affected the natives most keenly, as we are pointedly informed by Bishop Landa, himself one of the most ruthless of Vandals in this respect.* But already some of the more intelligent had learned the Spanish alphabet, and the missionaries had added a sufficient number of signs to it to express with tolerable accuracy the phonetics of the Maya tongue. Relying on their memories, and no doubt aided by some manuscripts secretly preserved, many natives set to work to write out in this new alphabet the contents of their ancient records. Much was added which had been brought in by the Europeans, and much omitted which had become unintelligible or obsolete since the Conquest ; while, of course, the different writers, varying in skill and knowledge, produced works of very various merit.

Nevertheless, each of these books bore the same name.

Breve y Verdadera de Algunas Cosas de las Muchas que Sucedieron al Padre Fray Alonso Ponce, Comisario-General en las Provincias de la Nueva España," page 392). I know no other author who makes the interesting statement that these characters were actually used by the missionaries to impart instruction to the natives; but I have heard that an example of one such manuscript has been discovered, and is now in the hands of a well-known Americanist.

* "*Se les quemamos todos,*" he writes, "*lo qual á maravilla sentian y les dava pena.*" —"*Relacion de las Cosas de Yucatan,*" page 316.

In whatever village it was written, or by whatever hand, it always was, and to-day still is, called "The Book of Chilan Balam." To distinguish them apart, the name of the village where a copy was found or written, is added. Probably, in the last century, almost every village had one, which was treasured with superstitious veneration. But the opposition of the *padres* to this kind of literature, the decay of ancient sympathies, and especially the long war of races, which since 1847 has desolated so much of the peninsula, have destroyed most of them. There remain, however, either portions or descriptions of not less than sixteen of these curious records. They are known from the names of the villages respectively as the Book of Chilan Balam of Nabula, of Chumayel, of Kàna, of Mani, of Oxkutzcab, of Ixil, of Tihosuco, of Tixcocob, etc., these being the names of various native towns in the peninsula.

When I add that not a single one of these has ever been printed, or even entirely translated into any European tongue, it will be evident to every archæologist and linguist what a rich and unexplored mine of information about this interesting people they may present. It is my intention in this article merely to touch upon a few salient points to illustrate this, leaving a thorough discussion of their origin and contents to the future editor who will bring them to the knowledge of the learned world.

Turning first to the meaning of the name "*Chilan Balam,*" it is not difficult to find its derivation. "*Chilan,*" says Bishop Landa, the second bishop of Yucatan, whose description of the native customs is an invaluable source to us, "was the name of their priests, whose duty it was to teach the sciences, to appoint holy days, to treat the sick, to offer sacrifices, and especially to utter the oracles of the gods. They were so highly honored by the people that usually they were carried on litters on the shoulders of the devotees."* Strictly speaking, in Maya "*chilan*" means "interpreter," "mouth-piece," from "*chij*," "the mouth," and in this ordinary sense frequently occurs in other writings. The word, "*balam*"—literally, "tiger,"—was also applied to a class of priests, and is still in use among the natives of Yucatan as the designation of the protective spirits of fields and towns, as I have shown at length in a previous study of the word as it occurs in the native myths of Guatemala.† "*Chilan Balam*," therefore, is not a proper name, but a title, and in ancient times designated the priest who announced the will of the gods and explained the sacred oracles. This accounts for the universality of the name and the sacredness of its associations.

The dates of the books which have come down to us are various. One of them, "The Book of Chilan Balam of Mani," was undoubtedly composed not later than 1595, as is proved by internal evidence. Various passages in the

---

* *Relacion de las Cosas de Yucatan*, page 160.

† See above, pp. 128 and 172. The terminal letter in both these words—"*chilan*," "*balam*,"—may be either "*n*" or "*m*," the change being one of dialect and local pronunciation. I have followed the older authorities in writing "*Chilan Balam*," the modern preferring "*Chilam Balam*." Señor Eligio Ancona, in his recently published *Historia de Yucatan*, (Vol. i., page 240, note, Merida, 1878), offers the absurd suggestion that the name "*balam*" was given to the native soothsayers by the early missionaries in ridicule, deriving it from the well-known personage in the Old Testament. It is surprising that Señor Ancona, writing in Merida, had never acquainted himself with the Perez manuscripts, nor with those in possession of Bishop Carrillo. Indeed, the most of his treatment of the ancient history of his country is disappointingly superficial.

works of Landa, Lizana, Sanchez Aguilar and Cogolludo—all early historians of Yucatan—prove that many of these native manuscripts existed in the sixteenth century. Several rescripts date from the seventeenth century,—most from the latter half of the eighteenth.

The names of the writers are generally not given, probably because the books, as we have them, are all copies of older manuscripts, with merely the occasional addition of current items of note by the copyist; as, for instance, a malignant epidemic which prevailed in the peninsula in 1673 is mentioned as a present occurrence by the copyist of "The Book of Chilan Balam of Nabula."

I come now to the contents of these curious works. What they contain may conveniently be classified under four headings:

Astrological and prophetic matters;
Ancient chronology and history;
Medical recipes and directions;
Later history and Christian teachings.

The last-mentioned consist of translations of the "*Doctrina*," Bible stories, narratives of events after the Conquest, etc., which I shall dismiss as of least interest.

The astrology appears partly to be reminiscences of that of their ancient heathendom, partly that borrowed from the European almanacs of the century 1550–1650. These, as is well known, were crammed with predictions and divinations. A careful analysis, based on a comparison with the Spanish almanacs of that time, would doubtless reveal how much was taken from them, and it would be fair to presume that the remainder was a survival of ancient native theories.

But there are not wanting actual prophecies of a much more striking character. These were attributed to the ancient priests and to a date long preceding the advent of Christianity. Some of them have been printed in translations in the "*Historias*" of Lizana and Cogolludo, and of some the originals were published by the late Abbé Brasseur de Bourbourg, in the second volume of the reports of the "*Mission Scientificque au Mexique et dans l' Amérique Centrale.*" Their authenticity has been met with considerable skepticism by Waitz and others, particularly as they seem to predict the arrival of the Christians from the East and the introduction of the worship of the cross.

It appears to me that this incredulity is uncalled for. It is known that at the close of each of their larger divisions of time (the so-called "*katuns*,") a "*chilan*," or inspired diviner, uttered a prediction of the character of the year or epoch which was about to begin. Like other would-be prophets, he had doubtless learned that it is wiser to predict evil than good, inasmuch as the probabilities of evil in this worried world of ours outweigh those of good; and when the evil comes his words are remembered to his credit, while if, perchance, his gloomy forecasts are not realized, no one will bear him a grudge that he has been at fault. The temper of this people was, moreover, gloomy, and it suited them to hear of threatened danger and destruction by foreign foes. But, alas! for them. The worst that the boding words of the oracle foretold was as nothing to the dire event which overtook them—the destruction of their nation, their temples and their freedom, 'neath the iron heel of the Spanish conqueror. As the wise Goethe says:

A NATIVE PROPHECY.

*"Seltsam ist Prophetenlied,
Doch mehr seltsam was geschieht."*

As to the supposed reference to the cross and its worship, it may be remarked that the native word translated "cross" by the missionaries, simply means "a piece of wood set upright," and may well have had a different and special signification in the old days.

By way of a specimen of these prophecies, I quote one from "The Book of Chilan Balam of Chumayel," saying at once that for the translation I have depended upon a comparison of the Spanish version of Lizana, who was blindly prejudiced, and that in French of the Abbé Brasseur de Bourbourg, who knew next to nothing about Maya, with the original. It will be easily understood, therefore, that it is rather a paraphrase than a literal rendering. The original is in short, aphoristic sentences, and was, no doubt, chanted with a rude rhythm:

> "What time the sun shall brightest shine,
> Tearful will be the eyes of the king.
> Four ages yet shall be inscribed,
> Then shall come the holy priest, the holy god
> With grief I speak what now I see.
> Watch well the road, ye dwellers of Itza.
> The master of the earth shall come to us.
> Thus prophesies Nahau Pech, the seer,
> In the days of the fourth age,
> At the time of its beginning."

Such are the obscure and ominous words of the ancient oracle. If the date is authentic, it would be about 1480—the "fourth age" in the Maya system of computing time being a period of either twenty or twenty-four years at the close of the fifteenth century.

It is, however, of little importance whether these are accurate copies of the ancient prophecies; they remain, at least, faithful imitations of them, composed in the same spirit and form which the native priests were wont to employ. A number are given much longer than the above, and containing various curious references to ancient usages.

Another value they have in common with all the rest of the text of these books, and it is one which will be properly appreciated by any student of languages. They are, by common consent of all competent authorities, the genuine productions of native minds, cast in the idiomatic forms of the native tongue by those born to its use. No matter how fluent a foreigner becomes in a language not his own, he can never use it as does one who has been familiar with it from childhood. This general maxim is ten-fold true when we apply it to a European learning an American language. The flow of thought, as exhibited in these two linguistic families, is in such different directions that no amount of practice can render one equally accurate in both. Hence the importance of studying a tongue as it is employed by natives; and hence the very high estimate I place on these "Books of Chilan Balam" as linguistic material—an estimate much increased by the great rarity of independent compositions in their own tongues by members of the native races of this continent.

I now approach what I consider the peculiar value of these records, apart from the linguistic mould in which they are cast; and that is the light they throw upon the chronological system and ancient history of the Mayas. To a limited extent, this has already been brought before the public. The late Don Pio Perez gave to Mr. Stephens, when in Yucatan, an essay on the method of computing time among the ancient Mayas, and also a brief synopsis of Maya history, apparently going back to the third or fourth century of the Christian era. Both were published by Mr. Stephens in the appendix to his "Travels in Yucatan," and have appeared repeatedly since in English, Spanish and French.* They have, up to the present, constituted almost our sole sources of information on these interesting points. Don Pio Perez was rather vague as to whence he derived his knowledge. He refers to "ancient manuscripts," "old authorities," and the like; but, as the Abbè Brasseur de Bourbourg justly complains, he rarely quotes their words, and gives no descriptions as to what they were or how he gained access to them.† In fact, the whole of Señor Perez's information was derived from these "Books of Chilan Balam;" and without wishing at all to detract from his reputation as an antiquary and a Maya scholar, I am obliged to say that he has dealt with them as scholars so often do with their authorities; that is, having framed his theories, he quoted what he found in their favor and neglected to refer to what he observed was against them.

---

* For example, in the *Registro Yucateco, Tome III; Diccionario Universal de Historia y Geografia, Tome VIII.* (Mexico, 1855); *Diccionario Historico de Yucatan,* Tome I. (Merida, 1866); in the appendix to Landa's *Cosas de Yucatan* (Paris, 1864), etc. The epochs, or *katuns*, of Maya history have been recently again analyzed by Dr. Felipe Valentini, in an essay in the German and English languages, the latter in the *Proceedings* of the American Antiquarian Society, 1880.

† The Abbé's criticism occurs in the note to page 406 of his edition of Landa's *Cosas de Yucatan.*

Thus, it is a cardinal question in Yucatecan archæology as to whether the epoch or age by which the great cycle (the *ahau katun*,) was reckoned, embraced twenty or twenty-four years. Contrary to all the Spanish authorities, Perez declared for twenty-four years, supporting himself by "the manuscripts." It is true there are three of the "Books of Chilan Balam"—those of Mani, Kána and Oxkutzcab,—which are distinctly in favor of twenty-four years; but, on the other hand, there are four or five others which are clearly for the period of twenty years, and of these Don Perez said nothing, although copies of more than one of them were in his library. So of the epochs, or *katuns*, of Maya history ; there are three or more copies in these books which he does not seem to have compared with the one he furnished Stephens. His labor will have to be repeated according to the methods of modern criticism, and with the additional material obtained since he wrote.

Another valuable feature in these records is the hints they furnish of the hieroglyphic system of the Mayas. Almost our only authority heretofore has been the essay of Landa. It has suffered somewhat in credit because we had no means of verifying his statements and comparing the characters he gives. Dr. Valentini has even gone so far as to attack some of his assertions as "fabrications." This is an amount of skepticism which exceeds both justice and probability.

The chronological portions of the "Books of Chilan Balam" are partly written with the ancient signs of the days, months and epochs, and they furnish us, also, delineations of the "wheels" which the natives used for computing time. The former are so important to the student of Maya hieroglyphics, that I have added photographic reproductions of them to this paper, giving also representations of those of Landa for comparison. It will be observed that the signs of the days are distinctly similar in the majority of cases, but that those of the months are hardly alike.

The hieroglyphs of the days taken from the "*Codex Troano*," an ancient Maya book written before the Conquest, probably about 1400, are also added to illustrate the variations which occurred in the hands of different scribes. Those from the "Books of Chilan Balam" are copied from a manuscript known to Maya scholars as the "*Codice Perez*," of undoubted authenticity and antiquity."*

The result of the comparison I thus institute is a triumphant refutation of the doubts and slurs which have been cast on Bishop Landa's work, and vindicate for it a very high degree of accuracy.

The hieroglyphics for the months are quite complicated, and in the "Books of Chilan Balam" are rudely drawn; but, for all that, two or three of them are evidently identical with those in the calendar preserved by Landa. Some years ago, Professor de Rosny expressed himself in great doubt as to the fidelity in the tracing of these hieroglyphs of the months, principally because he could not find them in the two codices at his command.† As he observes, they are

---

*It is described at length by Don Crescencio Carrillo y Ancona, in his, '*Disertacion sobre la Historia de la Lengua Maya*' (Merida, 1870).

†"*Je dois déclarer que l'examen dans tous leurs détails du 'Codex Troano' et du 'Codex Peresianus' m'invite de la façon la plus sérieuse à n'accepter ces signes, tout au moins au point de vue de l'exactitude de leur tracé, qu' avec une certaine réserve.*"— Leon de Rosny's *Essai sur le Déchiffrement de l'Ecriture Hiératique de l'Amérique Centrale*, page 21 (Paris, 1876). By the "*Codex Peresianus*," he does not mean the "*Codice Perez*," but the Maya manuscript in the Bibliothêque Nationale. The identity of the names is confusing and unfortunate.

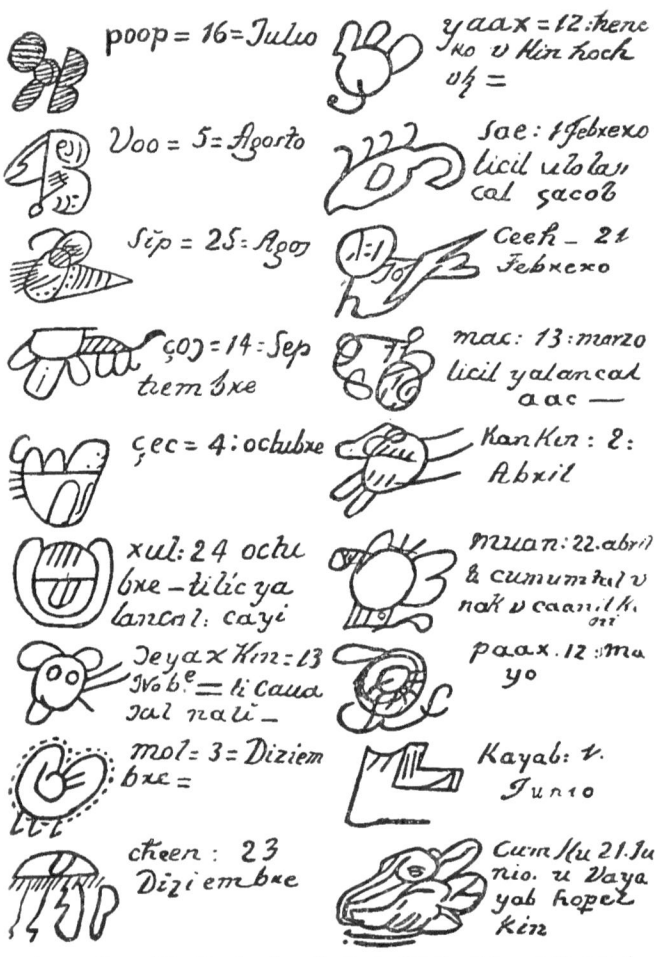

FIG. 1.—Signs of the Months, from the Book of Chilan Balam of Chumayel.

SIGNS OF THE MONTHS.

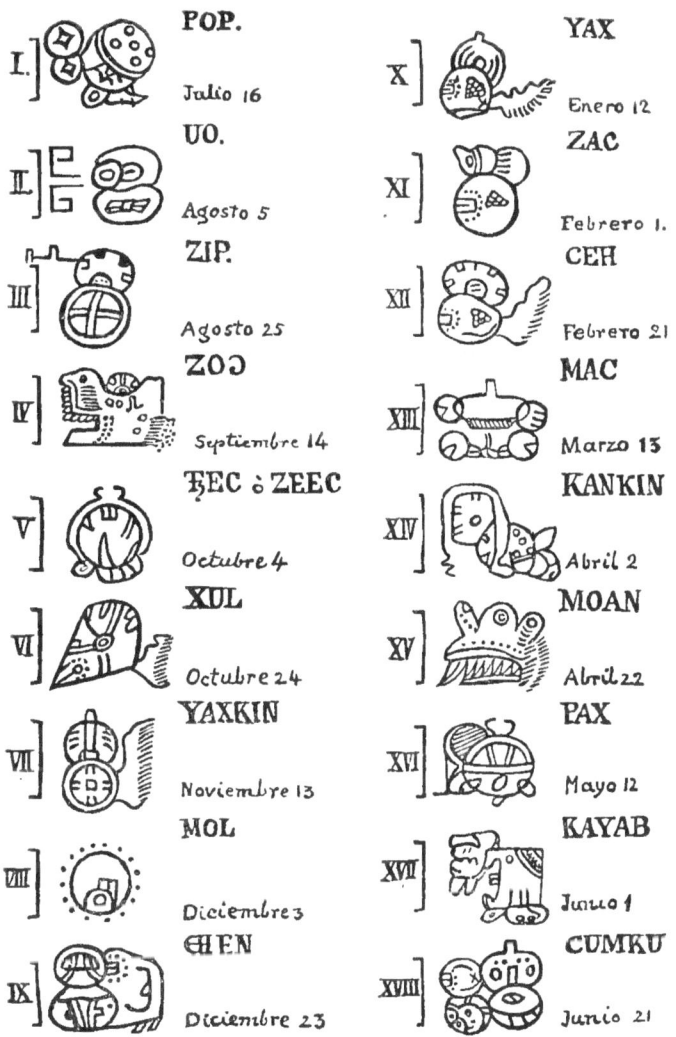

FIG. 2.—Signs of the Months, as given by Bishop Landa.

composite signs, and this goes to explain the discrepancy; for it may be regarded as established that the Maya script permitted the use of several signs for the same sound, and the sculptor or scribe was not obliged to represent the same word always by the same figure.

In close relation to chronology is the system of numeration and arithmetical signs. These are discussed with considerable fulness, especially in the "Book of Chilan Balam of Káua." The numerals are represented by exactly the same figures as we find in the Maya manuscripts of the libraries of Dresden, Pesth, Paris and Madrid; that is, by points or dots up to five, and the fives by single straight lines, which may be indiscriminately drawn vertically or horizontally. The same book contains a table of multiplication in Spanish and Maya, which settles some disputed points in the use of the vigesimal system by the Mayas.

A curious chapter in several of the books, especially those of Káua and Mani, is that on the thirteen *ahau katuns*, or epochs, of the greater cycle of the Mayas. This cycle embraced thirteen periods, which, as I have before remarked, are computed by some at twenty years each, by others at twenty-four years each. Each of these *katuns* was presided over by a chief or king, that being the meaning of the word *ahau*. The books above mentioned give both the name and the portrait, drawn and colored by the rude hand of the native artist, of each of these kings, and they suggest several interesting analogies.

They are, in the first place, identical, with one exception, with those on an ancient native painting, an engraving of which is given by Father Cogolludo in his "History of

Yucatan," and explained by him as the representation of an occurrence which took place after the Spaniards arrived in the peninsula. Evidently, the native in whose hands the worthy father found it, fearing that he partook of the fanaticism which had led the missionaries to the destruction of so many records of their nation, deceived him as to its purport, and gave him an explanation which imparted to the scroll the character of a harmless history.

The one exception is the last or thirteenth chief. Cogolludo appends to this the name of an Indian who probably did fall a victim to his friendship to the Spaniards. This name, as a sort of guarantee for the rest of his story, the native scribe inserted in place of the genuine one. The peculiarity of the figure is that it has an arrow or dagger driven into its eye. Not only is this mentioned by Cogolludo's informant, but it is represented in the paintings in both the "Books of Chilan Balam" above noted, and also, by a fortunate coincidence, in one of the calendar pages of the "*Codex Troano*," plate xxiii., in a remarkable cartouche, which, from a wholly independent course of reasoning, was some time since identified by the well-known antiquary, Professor Cyrus Thomas, of Illinois, as a cartouche of one of the *ahau katuns*, and probably of the last of them. It gives me much pleasure to add such conclusive proof of the sagacity of his supposition.*

There is other evidence to show that the engraving in Cogolludo is a relic of the purest ancient Maya symbolism—

---

* "The Manuscript Troano," published in *The American Naturalist*, August, 1881, page 640. This manuscript or codex was published in chromo-lithograph, Paris, 1879, by the French Government.

SIGNS OF THE DAYS.

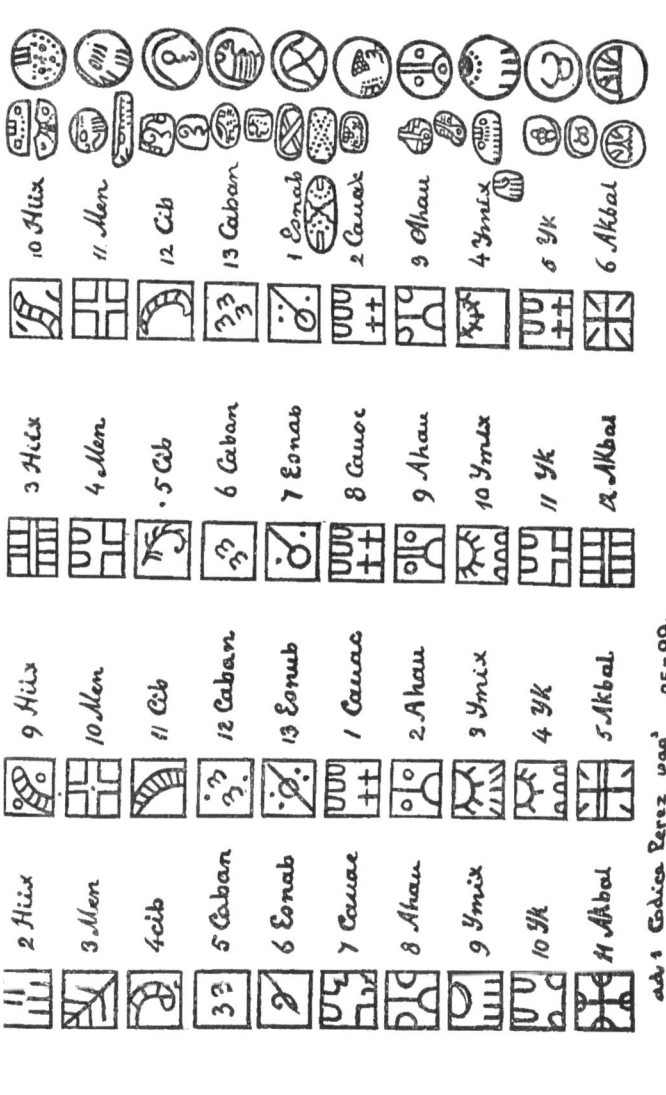

FIG. 3.—SIGNS OF THE DAYS. The second is from the "*Codex Troano.*" The remaining four are from the Book of Chilan Balam of Káua.

one of the most interesting which have been preserved to us; but to enter upon its explanation in this connection would be too far from my present topic.

A favorite theme with the writers of the "Books of Chilan Balam" was the cure of diseases. Bishop Landa explains the "*chilanes*" as "sorcerers and doctors," and adds that one of their prominent duties was to diagnose diseases and point out their appropriate remedies.* As we might expect, therefore, considerable prominence is given to the description of symptoms and suggestions for their alleviation. Bleeding and the administration of preparations of native plants are the usual prescriptions; but there are others which have probably been borrowed from some domestic medicine-book of European origin.

The late Don Pio Perez gave a great deal of attention to collecting these native recipes, and his manuscripts were carefully examined by Dr. Berendt, who combined all the necessary knowledge, botanical, linguistic and medical, and who has left a large manuscript, entitled "*Recetarios de Indios*," which presents the subject fully. He considers the scientific value of these remedies to be next to nothing, and the language in which they are recorded to be distinctly inferior to that of the remainder of the "Books of Chilan Balam." Hence, he believes that this portion of the ancient records was supplanted some time in the last century by medical notions introduced from European sources. Such, in fact, is the statement of the copyists of the books them-

---

* "*Declarar las necesidades y sus remedios.*"—*Relacion de las Cosas de Yucatan*, page 160. Like much of Landa's Spanish, this use of the word "*necesidad*" is colloquial, and not classical.

selves, as these recipes, etc., are sometimes found in a separate volume, entitled "The Book of the Jew,"—*El Libro del Judio.*" Who this alleged Jewish physician was, who left so wide-spread and durable a renown among the Yucatecan natives, none of the archæologists has been able to find out.*

The language and style of most of these books are aphoristic, elliptical and obscure. The Maya language has naturally undergone considerable alteration since they were written; therefore, even to competent readers of ordinary Maya, they are not readily intelligible. Fortunately, however, there are in existence excellent dictionaries, which, were they published, would be sufficient for this purpose.

---

*A *Medicina Domestica,* under the name of "Don Ricardo Ossado, (alias, *el Judio,*)" was published at Merida in 1834; but this appears to have been merely a bookseller's device to aid the sale of the book by attributing it to the "great unknown."

ON THE "STONE OF THE GIANTS."*

AT the last meeting of this Society, a photograph was received of the *Piedra de los Gigantes*, or "Stone of the Giants." now situated at Escamela, near the city of Orizaba, Mexico. It was obligingly forwarded by the Mexican antiquary, Father Damaso Sotomayor, and was referred by the Society to me for a possible interpretation of the figures represented.

The sender accompained the envoy with a copy of a newspaper published in Orizaba, entitled *El Siglo que Acaba*, which contained a lengthy interpretation of the figure by Father Sotomayor in accordance with the principles laid down in his recently published work on the decipherment of Aztec hieroglyphics.† The Father sees in the inscribed figures a mystical allusion to the coming of Christ to the Gentiles, and to the occurrences supposed in Hebrew myth to have taken place in the Garden of Eden. As I cannot agree in the remotest with his hypothesis, I shall say nothing further about it, but proceed to give what I consider the true significance of the inscribed figures.

I should preface my remarks by mentioning that this stone

---
* Read before the Numismatic and Antiquarian Society of Philadelphia in 1889.
† *Los Aztecas*, Mexico, 1888.

is not a recent discovery in Mexican archæology. It was examined by Captain Dupaix in the year 1808, and is figured in the illustrations to his voluminous narrative.* The figure he gives is however so erroneous that it yields but a faint idea of the real character and meaning of the drawing. It omits the ornament on the breast, and also the lines along the right of the giant's face, which as I shall show are distinctive traits. It gives him a girdle where none is delineated, and the relative size and proportions of all the three figures are quite distorted. Dupaix informs us, however, of several particulars which the Rev. Sotomayor omitted to state. From the former's description we learn that the stone, or rather rock, on which the inscription is found is roughly triangular in shape, presenting a nearly staight border of thirty feet on each side. It is hard and uniform in texture, and of a dark color. The length or height of the principal figure is twenty-seven feet, and the incised lines which designate the various objects are deeply and clearly cut. In the present position of the stone, which is the same as that stated by Captain Dupaix, the head of the principal figure, called "the giant," lies toward the east, while the right hand is extended toward the north and the left toward the west. It is open to doubt whether this disposition was accidental or intentional, as there is reason to believe that the stone is not

---

* Dupaix, *Antiquités Mexicaines*. 1st Exped., p. 7, Pl. vi, vii, fig. 6, 7. At that time the flat surface of the rock was the floor of a cabin built upon it. At present the cabin has disappeared. Mr. Bandelier does not seem to have visited this stone when he was at Orizaba, although he refers to Dupaix's explorations. *Report of an Archæological Tour in Mexico in 1881*, p. 26 (Boston, 1884). Nor does M. H. Strebel, though he also refers to it, give any fresh information about it. See his *Alt-Mexiko*, Band I, s. 30.

now in its original position, or not in that for which it was intended.

Along the base of the stone, which is in thickness some five feet, at the feet of the giant, there are a series of figures inscribed which are now almost obliterated ; at least the photographs sent the Society give no clear idea of them, and the cuts of Dupaix are plainly for the most part fanciful. Their presence there, however, proves that the block was not intended to have been set up on edge, or inserted vertically into a wall, as either of these arrangements would have obscured these hieroglyphs.*

I now approach the decipherment of the inscriptions. Any one versed in the signs of the Mexican calendar will at once perceive that it contains the date of a certain year and day. On the left of the giant is seen a rabbit surrounded with ten circular depressions. These depressions are the well-known Aztec marks for numerals, and the rabbit represents one of the four astronomic signs by which they adjusted their chronologic cycle of fifty-two years. The three others were a house, a reed, and a flint. Each one of these recurred thirteen times in their cycle, making, as I have said, a term of fifty-two years in all. A year was designated by one of the four names with its appropriate number; as "3 house," "12 flint," "4 reed," etc., the sequence being regularly preserved.

The days were arranged in zones or weeks of twenty, the different series being numbered, and also named from a

---

* One appears to be a gigantic full face ; another an animal like a frog, with extended legs ; two others are geometrical designs, the outlines of which have evidently been recently freshened with a steel implement. Future observers should be on their guard that this procedure shall not have mutilated the early workmanship.

sequence of eighteen astronomical signs called "wind," "lizard," "snake," "deer," etc. The five days lacking to complete the 365 were intercalated. A second or ritual system had thirteen weeks of twenty days each; but as thirteen times twenty makes only two hundred and sixty, in this computation there remained 105 days to be named and numbered. Their device to accomplish this was simple: they merely recommenced the numbering and naming of the weeks for this remainder, adding a third series of appellations drawn from a list of nine signs, called "rulers of the night." At the close of the solar year they recommenced as at the beginning of the previous year.*

With these facts in our mind, we can approach our task with confidence. The stone bears a carefully dated record, with the year and day clearly set forth. The year is represented to the left of the figure, and is that numbered "ten" under the sign of the rabbit, in Nahuatl, *xihuitl matlactli tochtli;* the day of the year is numbered "one" under the sign of the fish, *ce cipactli.*

These precise dates recurred once, and only once, every fifty-two years; and had recurred only once between the year of our era 1450 and the Spanish conquest of Mexico in 1519–20. We may begin our investigations with that one epoch, as from other circumstances, such as local tradition†

---

* It is needless to expand this explanation of the Aztec Calendar; but it is worth while to warn the student of the subject that the problem is an intricate one and has never yet been satisfactorily solved, because the information presented is both incomplete and contradictory. I consider the most instructive discussion of the Calendar is that in Orozco y Berra, *Historia Antigua de Mexico*, Lib. iv., Cap. 1–6.

† Father Sotomayor, in the newspaper account above referred to, states that tradition assigned the inscription to the time of Cortes' march to the City of Mexico; a

and the character of the work, it is not likely that the inscription was previous to the middle of the fifteenth century. Within the period named, the year "10 rabbit" of the Aztec calendar corresponded with the year 1502 of the Gregorian calendar. It is more difficult to fix the day, as the mathematical problems relating to the Aztec diurnal reckonings are extremely complicated, and have not yet been satisfactorily worked out; but it is, I think, safe to say, that according to both the most probable computations the day "one fish"—*ce cipactli*—occurred in the first month of the year 1502, which month coincided in whole or in part with our February.

Such is the date on the inscription. Now, what is intimated to have occurred on that date? The clue to this is furnished by the figure of the giant.

On looking at it closely we perceive that it represents an ogre of horrid mien with a death-head grin and formidable teeth, his hair wild and long, the locks falling down upon the neck; and suspended on the breast as an ornament is the bone of a human lower jaw with its incisor teeth. The left leg is thrown forward as in the act of walking, and the arms are uplifted, the hands open, and the fingers extended, as at the moment of seizing the prey or the victim. The lines about the umbilicus represent the knot of the girdle which supported the *maxtli* or breech-cloth.

There is no doubt as to which personage of the Aztec pantheon this fear-inspiring figure represents; it is *Tzon*-

---

date which he quite properly ridicules as impossible. The vicinity of Orizaba was, moreover, not a part of the Mexican State until some time after the middle of the 15th century. See Bandelier, *Archæological Tour in Mexico*, pp. 22, sqq.

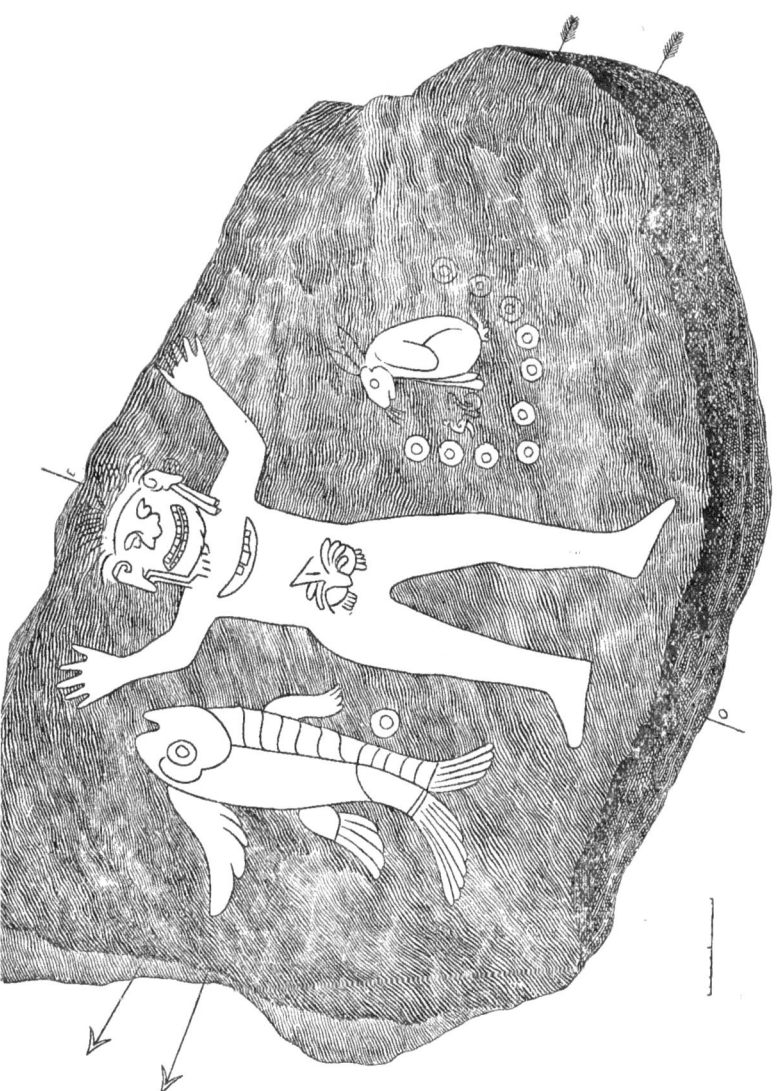

FIG. 1. The Stone of the Giants.

temoc Mictlantecutli, "the Lord of the Realm of the Dead, He of the Falling Hair," the dread god of death and the dead.* His distinctive marks are there, the death-head, the falling hair, the jaw bone, the terrible aspect, the giant size.

There can be no question but that the *Piedra de los Gigantes* establishes a date of death; that it is a necrological tablet, a mortuary monument, and from its size and workmanship, that it was intended as a memorial of the decease of some very important personage in ancient Mexico.

Provided with these deductions from the stone itself, let us turn to the records of old Mexico and see if they corroborate the opinion stated. Fortunately we possess several of these venerable documents, chronicles of the empire before Cortes destroyed it, written in the hieroglyphs which the inventive genius of the natives had devised. Taking two of these chronicles, the one known as the *Codex Telleriano-Remensis*, the other as the *Codex Vaticanus*,† and turning to the year numbered "ten" under the sign of the rabbit, I find that both present the same record, which I copy in the following figure.

---

* *Tzontemoc*, a compound of *tzontli*, hair, and *temoa*, to fall; *mictlan*, locative from *mictli*, to die; *tecutli*, lord, noble. For a description of this deity see Sahagun, *Historia de la Nueva España*, Lib. iii, Appendix, chap. I. I have elsewhere suggested that the falling hair had reference to the long slanting rays of the setting sun. See above, p. 146.

† Both are reproduced in Kingsborough's *Mexican Antiquities*. But I would warn against the explanations in Spanish of the *Codex Telleriano-Remensis*. They are the work of some ignorant and careless clerk, who often applies the explanation of one plate and date to another, through sheer negligence.

EXPLANATION OF HIEROGLYPHS.

FIG. 2. Extract from the Vatican Codex.

You will observe the sign of the year, the rabbit, shown merely by his head for brevity. The ten dots which give its number are beside it. Immediately beneath is a curious quadruped with what are intended as water-drops dripping from him. The animal is the hedge-hog and the figure is to be construed *iconomatically*, that is, it must be read as a rebus through the medium of the Nahuatl language. In that language water is *atl*, in composition *a*, and hedge-hog is *uitzotl*. Combine these and you get *ahuitzotl*, or, with the reverential termination, *ahuitzotzin*. This was the name of the ruler or emperor, if you allow the word, of ancient Mexico before the accession to the throne of that Montezuma whom the Spanish *conquistador* Cortes put to death. His hieroglyph, as I have described it, is well known in Mexican codices.*

Returning to the page from the chronicle, we observe that the hieroglyph of Ahuitzotzin is placed immediately over a corpse swathed in its mummy cloths, as was the custom of interment with the highest classes in Mexico. This signifies that the death of Ahuitzotzin took place in that year. Adjacent to it is the figure of his successor, his name iconomatically represented by the head-dress of the nobles; the *tecuhtli*, giving the middle syllables of "Mo-*tecuh*-zoma." † Beneath is also the figure of the new ruler, with the outlines of a flower and a house, which would be translated by the iconomatic system *xochicalli* or *xochicalco;* but the significance of these does not concern us here.

This page of the Codices gives us therefore a record of a death in the year "10 *tochtli*"—1502—of the utmost importance. No previous ruler had brought ancient Mexico to such a height of glory and power. "In his reign," says Orozco y Berra, "Mexico reached its utmost extension. Tributes were levied in all directions, and fabulous riches poured into the capital city."‡ The death of the ruler was therefore an event of the profoundest national significance. We may well believe that it would be commemorated by some artistic work commensurate with its importance; and

---

* I would refer to an explanation of this system published by me in the *Proceedings of the American Philosophical Society*, for 1886.

† The phonetic significance of this symbol is well established. See Aubin in the Introduction to Brasseur, *Histoire des Nations Civilisées de la Mexique*, Tome I, p. lxix.

‡ *Historia Antigua de Mexico*, Tomo III. p. 426.

this I claim was the purpose of the *Piedra de los Gigantes* of Escamela.

But we may add further and convincing testimony to this interpretation. The day of the month *ce cipactli*, 1 Fish, is engraved to the right of the figure as connected with the event commemorated. Now, although I have not found in the records the exact day of Ahuitzotzin's death, I do find that the native historian Ixtlilxochitl assigns this very day, *ce cipactli*, 1 Fish, as that of the accession of Montezuma;[*] and another native historian, Chimalpahin, states distinctly that this took place "immediately" after the death of his predecessor on the throne.[†] It may possibly have been on the very day of Ahuitzotzin's decease, as still another native writer, Tezozomoc, informs us that this was not sudden, but the slow result of a wound on the head.[‡]

It is indeed remarkable that we should find the precise dates, the year and the day of the year, depicted on this stone, and also recorded by various native writers, as connected with the demise of the emperor Ahuitzotzin. These coincidences are of such a nature that they leave no doubt that *La Piedra de los Gigantes* of Escamela is a necrologic tablet commemorating the death of the emperor Ahuitzotzin some time in February, 1502.

---

[*] Ixtlilxochitl, *Historia Chichimeca*, cap. 70. He errs in assigning it to the year 1503, as all the other narratives of importance are against him.

[†] *Annales de Chimalpahin*, p. 173 (Ed. Siméon, Paris, 1889). His words are "auh ça niman ihcuac oucan in hual motlatocalli in Moteuhcçomatzin," which Siméon renders "Immédiatement apres," etc.

[‡] Tezozomoc, *Cronica Mexicana*, cap. 81. This writer adds that the emperor expected his approaching end, and made a number of preparations with regard to it. The *Anales de Cuauhtitlan*, p. 80, places the events of 10 *tochtli* under the following year 11 *acatl*, and the reverse. It reads "murio el señor de Tenochtitlan, Ahuitzotzin, le sucedio immediatamente Moteuczomatzin."

NATIVE AMERICAN POETRY.*

IN our modern civilization we are apt to consider that a taste for poetry is a mark of high culture, something which belongs exclusively to trained mental fibre and educated perceptions. It causes us, therefore, some surprise when we study the psychology of savage tribes, to find them almost everywhere passionate lovers of verse and measure, of music and song. This fact, well established by the researches of ethnology, was recognized by more than one keen thinker before ethnology was born. In the last century that erratic genius, Hamann, known in German literature as "the magician of the north," penned the memorable words, "Poetry is the common mother-tongue of the human race," and insisted that to attain its noblest flights, "we must return to the infancy of the race, and to the simplicity of a childlike faith," a dictum warmly espoused by the philosophic Herder and by the enthusiasm of the young Goethe. Later on, that profoundest of psychologists, Wilhelm von Humboldt, reflecting on the problems presented by the origin of languages, expressed his conviction that man as a zoological species is a singing animal, like many birds; that

---

*Selections from an Address read before the Numismatic and Antiquarian Society of Philadelphia, in 1886.

his vocal organs turn to song as their appropriate function with a like spontaneity as his mind turns to thought or his eyes to the light.

If we inquire into the psychological principle which makes rhythm agreeable to the ear, we shall find that this principle is that of *repetition*. I could carry the analysis still further, and demonstrate to you that the physiological principle of all pleasure is expressed in the formula—"maximum action with minimum effort;" and that the nerves of audition are most successfully acted upon in accordance with this law by limited repetitions with harmonious intervals. All metres, all rhythm, all forms of alliteration and assonance, are but varied applications of the principle of harmonious repetition ; and the poet, as a poet, as an artist, must be rated, and practically always is rated, by the skill with which he employs the resources of repetition. Lofty thoughts, beautiful metaphors, delicate allusions, these are his extraneous aids, and by no means his exclusive property ; but the form is his own, be it quantity, rhyme, alliteration or accent.

I have felt it necessary to state very briefly these general principles, in order to place in its proper light that form of poetry which is most prevalent among the native tribes of America. You will not find among them any developed examples of either rhyme or alliteration; their dialects do not admit of fixed vocalic quantity, like the Latin; even accent and assonance, which are the more imperfect resources of the poetic art, are generally absent. What, then, in a literary analysis, constitutes their poetic form ?

I answer, *repetition* in its simplest expressions. These are two. The same verse may be repeated over and over again;

or the wording of the verses may be changed, but each may be accompanied by a burden or refrain, which is repeated by the singer or the chorus. These are the two fundamental characteristics of aboriginal poetry, and are found everywhere on the American continent. The refrain is usually interjectional and meaningless; and the verses are often repeated without alteration, four or five times over.

We may, if we choose, begin our survey of the continent with its extreme northernmost inhabitants, the Eskimo, whose abode is along the inhospitable shores of the Arctic sea. One might think that the eternal snows which surround them, the vast glaciers which chill the air for miles beyond their limits, would also freeze out and kill all fire of poesy. Quite the contrary. I doubt if throughout the American continent I could quote you a more thoroughly poetic people, one taking a greater delight in song, than these same boreal, blubber-eating, ice-bound Eskimo. Their great delight is in long tales of magic and adventure, and in improvisation. An Eskimo hunter, with a ready power to string together verse after verse of their peculiar poetry, soon extends his fame beyond the confines of his native village, and becomes known for many a league up and down the shore. Often in the long winter nights, genuine tourneys of song are organized between the champions of villages, not unlike those which took place in fair Provence in the palmy days of *la gaye science*. More than this, I have been assured by Dr. Franz Boas, who recently passed two years among the Eskimo of Baffin's Land, living with them as one of them, that it is nothing uncommon for downright hostile feelings, personal grudges, to be settled by the opponents meeting on a fixed occasion and singing satirical and abusive songs at each other. He who comes out best, raising the most laughter at his antagonist's expense, is considered to have conquered, and his enemy accepts the defeat. These controversial songs have been called by the Danish writers "nith songs," from the word *nith*, which is also old English, and means cursing and contention.

The distinguished traveler, Dr. Heinrich Rink, who has passed nineteen winters in Greenland, has furnished me the originals, with translations, of several of these nith songs.

As an example, I will read you one which took place between two rivals, *Savdlat* and *Pulangit-Sissok*. Savdlat lived to the north, Pulangit-Sissok to the south. To appreciate the satire, you must know that an Eskimo gentleman prides himself chiefly on two points: first, that he speaks his own tongue with precisely the right accent, which, I need not say, he considers to be the accent of his own village, wherever that may be; and secondly, that he is a skillful boatman.

Savdlat begins the poetic duel in these words:

SAVDLAT AND PULANGIT-SISSOK.

SAVDLAT—

The South shore, O yes, the South shore, I know it;
Once I lived there and met Pulangit-Sissok,
A fat fellow who lived on halibut; O yes, I know him.
Those South-shore folk can't talk;
They don't know how to pronounce our language;
Truly they are dull fellows;
They don't even talk alike;
Some have one accent, some another;

Nobody can understand them ;
They can scarcely understand each other.

PULANGIT-SISSOK—

O yes, Savdlat and I are old acquaintances ;
He wished me extremely well at times ;
Once I know he wished I was the best boatman on the shore ;
It was a rough day, and I in mercy took his boat in tow ;
Ha ! ha ! Savdlat, thou didst cry most pitiful ;
Thou wast awfully afeared ;
In truth, thou wast nearly upset ;
And hadst to keep hold of my boat strings,
And give me part of thy load.
O yes, Savdlat and I are old acquaintances.

A similar humorous strain is very marked in most of the Eskimo songs. Indeed, I know no other tribe in America where the genuine fun-loving spirit bubbles forth so freely. In Mexico and Central America, in the midst of beautiful scenery and where the flowery earth basks in the lap of an eternal spring, the tone of most of the songs is sad and lugubrious; or, if humorous, with a satirical, bitter, unhealthy humor, a *Schadenfreude*, which is far from wholesome merriment. Dr. Berendt, who spent seventeen years in studying the languages of Central America, has pointedly called attention to the great predominance of words in them expressing painful, over those expressing pleasurable emotions. It teaches us how little the happiness of man depends upon his environment, that the merriest of the American nations is found precisely where according to our usual notions almost every cheering and enlivening element is withdrawn from life, where darkness, cold, and destitution have undisputed rule.

But I will not continue with such generalizations, attractive though they are. Let me relieve their dryness by a little Eskimo song, the full Eskimo text of which you will find printed in Dr. Rink's work entitled "Tales of the Eskimo." As usual, each line is followed by an interjectional burden, which I shall repeat only in part. The song is called

THE SONG OF KUK-OOK, THE BAD BOY.

This is the song of Kuk-ook, the bad boy.
  Imakayah—hayah,
  Imakayah—hah—hayah.
I am going to run away from home, hayah,
In a great big boat, hayah,
To hunt for a sweet little girl, hayah;
I shall get her some beads, hayah;
The kind that look like boiled ones, hayah;
Then after a while, hayah,
I shall come back home, hayah,
I shall call all my relations together, hayah,
And shall give them all a good thrashing, hayah;
Then I shall go and get married, hayah,
I shall marry two girls at once, hayah;
One of the sweet little darlings, hayah,
I shall dress in spotted seal-skins, hayah,
And the other dear little pet, hayah,
Shall wear skins of the hooded seal only, hayah.

But you must not derive the idea from these specimens that the Eskimos are triflers and jesters only. Some of their poetical productions reveal a true and deep appreciation of the marvellous, the impressive, and the beautiful scenes which their land and climate present. Prominent features in their tales and chants are the flashing, variegated aurora, whose shooting streamers they fable to be the souls of departed heroes; the milky way, gleaming in the still Arctic night, which they regard as the bridge by which the souls of the good and brave mount to the place of joy; the vast, glittering, soundless snowfields; and the mighty, crashing glacier, splintering from his shoreward cliffs the ice mountains which float down to the great ocean.

As an instance of this appreciation of natural scenery I shall read you a song obtained by Dr. Rink, at the small trading station of Arsut on the southern coast of Greenland, near Frederickshaab. Close to Arsut stands Mt. Koonak, whose precipitous sides rise fully four thousand feet above the billows of the Atlantic which dash against its foot. It is the play of the clouds about the mountain which inspires the poet:

MOUNT KOONAK: A SONG OF ARSUT.

>I look toward the south, to great Mount Koonak,
>To great Mount Koonak, there to the south;
>I watch the clouds that gather round him;
>I contemplate their shining brightness;
>They spread abroad upon great Koonak;
>They climb up his seaward flanks;
>See how they shift and change;
>Watch them there to the south;
>How the one makes beautiful the other;
>How they mount his southern slopes,
>Hiding him from the stormy sea,
>Each lending beauty to the other.

No doubt there were and are many historical or traditional

songs among the natives; but I should have little hope of deriving from them much information of a really historical character. Their references to occurrences are very vague, and rather in the form of suggestion than narration. The auditors are supposed to be familiar with the story, and a single name or prominent word is enough to recall it to their minds.

I may illustrate this by a short Pawnee song sent me by Mr. Dunbar, whose intimate acquaintance with the language and customs of that tribe lends entire authority to all he writes about them.

About 1820 the Pawnees captured a young girl from their enemies the Paducas, and according to custom, prepared to burn her alive. On the appointed day she was fastened to the stake, and the village gathered around in order to commence the tortures which were to precede her death. At that moment a young Pawnee brave, by name *Pitale-Sharu*, whose heart had been touched with pity and perhaps with love, dashed madly into the ring with two fleet horses. In a moment with his ready knife he had slit the thongs which fastened the girl to the stake, had thrown her on one horse, himself on the other, and was speeding away on the prairie toward her father's village. The Pawnees were literally stricken dumb. They retired silently to their cabins, and when, three days later, Pitale-Sharu returned to the village, no man challenged his action. All regarded it as an act of divine inspiration, even to inquire about which would be sacrilege. This act is remembered to this day in the tribe, and commemorated in the following song:

A PAWNEE COMMEMORATIVE SONG.

> Well, he foretold this,
> Well, he foretold this,
> Yes, he foretold this;
>   I, Pitale-Sharu,
>   Am arrived here.
> Well, he foretold this,
> Yes, he foretold this,
>   I, Pitale Sharu,
>   Am arrived here.

One of the Pawnee war-songs has a curious metaphysical turn. It is one which is sung when a warrior undertakes to perform some particularly daring individual exploit, which may well cost him his life. The words seem to call upon the gods to decide whether this mortal life is only an illusion, or a divine truth under the guidance of divine intelligence.

PAWNEE WAR-SONG.

> Let us see, is this real,
> Let us see, is this real,
> Let us see, is this real,
> Let us see, is this real,
> This life I am living?
> Ye gods, who dwell everywhere,
> Let us see, is this real,
> This life I am living?

The so-called Indian medicine-songs cannot be understood without a thorough insight into the habits and superstitions of these peoples, and it would only fatigue you were I to repeat them to you.

I prefer to turn to some of the less esoteric productions of the native muse, to some of its expressions of those emotions which are common to mankind everywhere, and which everywhere seek their expression in meter and rhythm.

A recent German traveler, Mr. Theodore Baker, furnishes me with a couple of simple, unpretending but genuinely aboriginal songs which he heard among the Kioway Indians. One is a

SONG OF A KIOWAY MOTHER WHOSE SON HAS GONE TO WAR.

> Young men there are in plenty,
>   But I love only one;
> Him I've not seen for long,
>   Though he is my only son.
>
> When he comes, I'll haste to meet him,
>   I think of him all night;
> He too will be glad to see me,
>   His eyes will gleam with delight.

The second example from the Kioways is a song of true love in the ordinary sense. Such are rare among the North American Indians anywhere. Most of their chants in relation to the other sex are erotic, not emotional; and this holds equally true of those which in some tribes on certain occasions are addressed by the women to the men. The one I give you from the Kioway is not open to this censure:

A KIOWAY LOVE-SONG.

> I sat and wept on the hill-side,
>   I wept till the darkness fell
> I wept for a maiden afar off
>   A maiden who loves me well

> The moons are passing, and some moon
> I shall see my home long-lost,
> And of all the greetings that meet me,
> My maiden's will gladden me most.

A specimen of a characteristic Chipeway love-song is given in one of the works of the late Henry R. Schoolcraft. It was chanted by the lover, at night, in front of the dwelling of the girl he would captivate. The song is in four verses, and it will be noticed that each verse approaches nearer and nearer the final request. It should be understood that each verse was to be repeated several times, so as to give the fair one an opportunity to express her approval or disapproval by some of those signs which belong to the freemasonry of love the world over. If the sign was negative and repelling, the singer abruptly ceased his chant and retired, concealed by the darkness of the night; but if he was encouraged, or heard without rebuke, he continued, in hope that at the close of the song timid fingers would partially draw aside the curtain which closes the lodge door, and that his prayer would be granted.

The serenade runs as follows:

SERENADE SONG OF A CHIPEWAY LOVER TO HIS MISTRESS.

> I would walk into somebody's dwelling,
> Into somebody's dwelling would I walk.
>
> Into *thy* darkened dwelling, my beloved,
> Some night would I walk, would I walk.
>
> Some night at this season, my beloved,
> Into thy darkened dwelling would I walk.

> On this very night, my beloved,
> Into thy darkened dwelling would I walk.

While dealing with these amatory effusions, I will add one or two from another part of the map, from the tribes who make their home in our sister republic, Mexico. You are aware that there are many tribes there barely tinged with European culture or religion. They retain the ancestral tongues and modes of thought. The sword and whip of the Spaniard compelled an external obedience to church and state, but the deference to either was reluctant, and in the minimum degree. Consequently, there also the field for research is rich and practically uncultivated. To employ a native metaphor, frequent in the Aztec poets, I will cause you to smell the fragrance of a few of the flowers I have gathered from those meads.

My late friend, Dr. Berendt, personally known, I doubt not, to some present, obtained a curious Aztec love-song from the lips of an Indian girl in the Sierra of Tamaulipas. It is particularly noticeable from the strange, mystical conceit it contains that to the person who truly loves, the mere bodily presence or absence of the beloved object is unimportant, nay, not even noticed. The literal translation of this song is as follows:

> I know not whether thou hast been absent:
> I lie down with thee, I rise up with thee,
> In my dreams thou art with me.
> If my ear drops tremble in my ears,
> I know it is thou moving within my heart.

This rough rendering has been put into metrical form as follows:

A MODERN AZTEC LOVE-SONG.

I knew it not that thou hadst absent been,
So full thy presence all my soul had left;
By night, by day, in quiet or changing scene,
'Tis thee alone I see, sense of all else bereft.
And when the tinkling pendants sway and ring,
'Tis thou who in my heart dost move and sing.

In another love-song in the same language I have met a conceit which I distinctly remember to have read in some old English poet, that of a lover who complains that his heart has been gathered in along with her flowers by a maiden picking roses.

The literal translation of this song reads thus:

On a certain mountain side,
Where they pluck flowers,
I saw a pretty maiden,
Who plucked from me my heart.
Whither thou goest,
There go I.

As a metrical expansion of this couplet the following has been suggested:

AZTEC LOVE-SONG.

Do you know that mountain side
Where they gather roses?
There I strolled one eventide
In the garden closes.
Soon I met a lovely maid
Fairer than all fancies,
Quick she gathered in my heart
With her buds and pansies,

> But take heed, my pretty may,
> In reaping and in sowing,
> Once with thee, I'll ever stay,
> And go where thou art going.

Perhaps the refinement of some of these sentiments may excite skepticism. It is a favorite doctrine among a certain class of writers that delicacy of sexual feeling is quite unknown among savage tribes, that, indeed, the universal law is that mere bestiality prevails, more or less kept in bounds by superstition and tribal law. I am well acquainted with this theory of several popular philosophers, and do not in the least accept it. Any such dogmatic assertion is unscientific. Delicacy of sentiment bears no sort of constant relation to culture. Every man present knows this. He can name among his acquaintances men of unusual culture who are coarse voluptuaries, and others of the humblest education who have the delicacy of a refined woman. So it is with families, and so it is with tribes. I have illustrated this lately by an analysis of the words meaning "to love" in all its senses in five leading American linguistic stocks, and have shown by the irrefragable proof of language how much they differ in this respect, and how much also the same tribe may differ from itself at various periods of its growth. As the result of this and similar studies I may assure you that there is no occasion for questioning the existence of highly delicate sentiments among some of the American tribes.

As I found the Mexican love poems the most delicate, so I have found their war songs the most stirring. We have a number of specimens written down in the native tongue shortly after the conquest. They have never been translated or published, but I will give you a rendering of one in my possession which, from intrinsic evidence, was written about 1510. I say *written* advisedly, for the nation who sang these songs possessed a phonetic alphabet, and wrote many volumes of poems by its aid. Their historian, Bernardino de Sahagun, especially mentions that the works used for the instruction of youth in their schools contained " poems written in antique characters."

The first of my selections is supposed to be addressed by the poet to certain friends of his who were unwilling to go to war.

A WAR-SONG OF THE OTOMIS.

1. It grieves me, dear friends, that you walk not with me in spirit, that I have not your company in the scenes of joy and pleasure, that never more in union do we seek the same paths.

2. Do you really see me, dear friends? Will no God take the blindness from your eyes? What is life on earth? Can the dead return? No, they live far within the heavens, in a place of joy.

3. The joy of the Lord. the Giver of Life, is where the warriors sing, and the smoke of the war-fire rises up; where the flowers of the shields spread abroad their leaves; where deeds of valor shake the earth; where the fatal flowers of death cover the fields.

4. The battle is there, the beginning of the battle is there, in the open fields, where the smoke of the war-fire winds around and curls upward from the fatal war-flowers which adorn you, ye friends and warriors of the Chichimecs.

5. Let not my soul dread that open field; I earnestly desire the beginning of the slaughter, my soul longs for the murderous fray.

6. O you who stand there in the battle, I earnestly desire the beginning of the slaughter, my soul longs for the murderous fray.

7. The war-cloud rises upward, it rises into the blue sky where dwells the Giver of Life; in it blossom forth the flowers of prowess and valor, beneath it, in the battle field, the children ripen to maturity.

8. Rejoice with me, dear friends, and do ye rejoice, ye children, going forth to the open field of battle; let us rejoice and revel amid these shields, flowers of the murderous fray.

The song which I have just read, like most which I bring before you, has no name of author. The poet has passed to an eternal oblivion, though his work remains. More fortunate is the composer of the next one I shall read you. It is a poem by an Aztec prince and bard who bore the sonorous appellation, *Tetlapan Quetzanitzin*. I can tell you little about him. At the time Cortes entered the City of Mexico, Tetlapan Quetzanitzin was ruler of one of its suburbs, Tlacopan or Tacuba. At the interview when the daring Spaniard seized upon the person of Montezuma and made him a captive, this Tetlapan was one of the attendants of the Aztec monarch, and it is recorded of him that he made his escape and disappeared. I have found no mention of his subsequent adventures.

This war-song is one of two of his poems which have survived the wreck of the ancient literature. It is highly metaphorical. You might at first think it a drinking song; but the drunkenness it refers to is the intoxication of battle, the *Berserkerwuth* of the Norse Vikings; the flowers which he sings are the war-shields with their gay ornaments; and the fertile plains which he lauds are those which are watered with the blood of heroes. Finally, I should tell you that the white wine he speaks of was a sacred beverage among the Mexicans, set forth at certain solemn festivals. Like the rest of their wine, it was manufactured from the maguey.

A WAR-SONG OF TETLAPAN QUETZANITZIN (1519).

1. Why did it grieve you, O friends, why did it pain you, that you were drunk with the wine? Arise from your stupor, O friends, come hither and sing; let us seek for homes in some flowery land; forget your drunkenness.

2. The precept is old that one should quaff the strong white wine in the moment of difficulty, as when one enters the battle-plain, when he goes forth to the place of shattered stones, where the precious stones are splintered, the emeralds, the turquoises, the youths, the children. Therefore, friends and brothers, quaff now the flowing white wine.

3. Let us drink together amid the flowers, let us build our houses among the flowers, where the fragrant blossoms cast abroad their odors as a fountain its waters, where the breath of the dew-laden flowers makes sweet the air; there it is that nobility and strength will make glorious our houses, there the flowers of war bloom over a fertile land.

4. O friends, do you not hear me? Let us go, let us go, let us pour forth the white wine, the strong wine of battle; let us drink the wine which is as sweet as the dew of roses, let it intoxicate our souls, let our souls be steeped in its delights, let them be enriched as in some opulent place, some fertile land. Why does it trouble you? Come with me, and listen to my song.

Alongside of these specimens from Mexico, I put a war-song of the Peruvians. It is from the drama of *Ollanta*, a production dating from shortly before the conquest, and one of the most interesting monuments of American native literature. The hero, Ollanta, a warrior of renown but of humble parentage, had, on the strength of his successes against the enemy, applied for the hand of the Inca's daughter, and had been rejected with scorn. All his loyalty and allegiance turn to hatred, and he sings his war-song against his native country and its ruler in these words:

A WAR-SONG OF OLLANTA.

> O Cuzco, beautiful city,
> Henceforward I shall be thy enemy.
> I shall break the walls of thy bosom,
> I shall tear out thy heart
> And fling it to the vultures.
> Thy cruel king shall witness
> My thousands of warriors,
> Armed and led by me,
> Gather, like a cloud of curses,
> Against thy citadel.
> The sky shall be red with thy burning,
> Bloody shall thy couch be,
> And thy king shall perish with thee.
> Gasping in death, with my hand on his throat,
> We shall see if again he will say:
> "Thou art unworthy of my daughter,
> Never shall she be thine."

A variety of poetic production of frequent occurrence among the aborigines is the prophetic. You are aware that it is by no means peculiar to them; the oracle at Delphi, the sibylline leaves in the Capitol, the words of the Hebrew seers, even the forecasts of Nostradamus, were usually cast in poetic form. The effort to lift the veil of futurity is one ineradicable from the human breast, and faith in its possibility is universal. Those prophets who are wise, those augurs who pass the wink to each other, favor great obscurity and ambiguity in their communications, or else express themselves in such commonplaces as that man is mortal; that all beauty fadeth; that power is transitory, and the like. We find both kinds flourished in ancient America. You may remember that Montezuma in his first interview with Cortes told the Spanish invader that the arrival of a white and bearded conqueror from the East had long been predicted by Mexican soothsayers. Similar prophecies were current in Yucatan, in Peru, and in other portions of the continent. They are all easily explained, and there is no occasion either to question the fact, or to seek for them any supernatural inspiration. It would lead me away from my theme to enter into a discussion of their meaning, but I should like to read you two brief examples of them. Both are from the Maya language of Yucatan, and I have no doubt both antedate the conquest. The first, according to an expression in the poem itself, was composed in the year 1469. It was the prediction of a Maya priest at the close of the indiction or cycle which terminated in that year of our chronology.

THE PROPHECY OF PECH, PRIEST OF CHICHEN-ITZA (1469).

Ye men of Itzá, hearken to the tidings,
Listen to the forecaste of this cycle's end;
Four have been the ages of the world's progressing,
Now the fourth is ending, and its end is near.
A mighty lord is coming, see you give him honor;
A potent lord approaches, to whom all must bow;
I, the prophet, warn you, keep in mind my boding,
Men of Itzá, mark it, and await your lord.

The second example of these mystic chants which I shall give you is from a curious native production called, "The Book of Chilan Balam," a repertory of wild imaginings and scraps of ancient and modern magical lore, which is the very Bible of the Maya Indians. Although I have a copy of it, I have been unable to translate any large portion of it, and my correspondents in Yucatan, though some of them speak Maya as readily as Spanish, find the expressions too archaic and obscure to be intelligible. This particular song is that of the priest and soothsayer Chilan, from whom the sacred book takes its name. There is every reason to believe that it dates from the fifteenth century.

RECITAL OF THE PRIEST CHILAN.

Eat, eat, while there is bread,
Drink, drink, while there is water;
A day comes when dust shall darken the air,
When a blight shall wither the land,
When a cloud shall arise,
When a mountain shall be lifted up,
When a strong man shall seize the city,
When ruin shall fall upon all things,
When the tender leaf shall be destroyed,
When eyes shall be closed in death;
When there shall be three signs on a tree,
Father, son and grandson hanging dead on the same tree;
When the battle flag shall be raised,
And the people scattered abroad in the forests.

Such poems properly belong to the mythologic class. This class was fully represented in the productions of the primitive bards, but chiefly owing to the prejudices of the early missionaries, the examples remaining are few.

I could continue to bring before you specimens of this quaint and ancient lore. My garner is by no means emptied. But probably I have said enough for my purpose. You see that the study of the aboriginal poetry of our continent opens up an unexpectedly rich field for investigation. It throws a new light not only on the folk songs of other nations, but on the general history of the growth of the poetic faculty. More than this, it elevates our opinion of the nations whom we are accustomed to call by the terms savage and barbarous. We are taught that in much which we are inclined to claim as our special prerogatives, they too have an interest. In the most precious possessions of the race, in its aspirations for the infinite and the forever true, they also have a share. They likewise partake, and in no mean degree, of that sweetest heritage of man, the glorious gift of song, "the vision and the faculty divine."

PART IV.

LINGUISTIC.

INTRODUCTORY.

THE processes, psychical and logical, which lie at the basis and modify the forms of articulate speech, have yet to be defined and classified in a manner to secure the general acceptance of scholars. While these processes are operative and recognizable in all languages, it has ever seemed to me that they are more apparent and transparent in the unwritten tongues of savage tribes. As the stream is more diaphanous near its source, as the problem of organic life is more readily studied in the lowest groups of animals and vegetables, by such analogies we are prompted to select the uncultured speech of the rudest of our race to discover the laws of growth in human expression.

Though such laws are not precisely the same throughout space and time, they unquestionably partake of the same uniformity as we note in other natural phenomena, and no language has yet been reported which stands alone in its formation.

Perhaps the general laws under which languages should

be grouped have already been defined as closely as the subject permits. The labors of Wilhelm von Humboldt, as expanded by Professor Steinthal, would appear to present the most comprehensive and satisfactory classification yet attempted. Such is the conclusion to which my own studies of the subject have led me, and in the first three essays of this Part, I have set forth in considerable detail the application of this opinion to the languages of America. Especially in the second essay, I have attempted to popularize a profounder philosophic analysis of these tongues than has heretofore appeared in works on the subject.

The essay on "The Earliest Form of Human Speech" offers a series of inferences drawn from the study of American tongues as to the general characteristics of the articulate utterances of the species when it first became possessed—by some slow evolutionary process—of the power of conveying ideas by intelligible sounds. It is an application of facts drawn from a limited number of languages to the linguistic status of the whole species at an indeterminately remote period, but is, I think, a fair use of the materials offered.

The analysis of words for the affections is the theme of the essay on "The Conception of Love in some American Languages." It is an example of the use to which linguistics may be put in the science of racial psychology; while the essay on the words for linear measures in certain tongues illustrates what knowledge as to the condition of a nation's arts may be obtained by a scrutiny of its lexicon.

The next essay, on the curious hoax perpetrated on some European and American linguists by the manufacture of a novel American tongue by some French students, is an instance, not wholly unprecedented, of misplaced ingenuity on the one side, and easy credulity on the other. It belongs among the "curiosities of literature."

Professional linguists will probably consider the most important generalization debated in this Part that of the identity or diversity of the agglutinative and incorporative processes of tongues. These two processes are considered as forms of but one by most of the present French school; but I have maintained their radical distinction, following the German writers above mentioned; and I have further insisted that the incorporative plan is that especially prominent in American languages.

AMERICAN LANGUAGES, AND WHY WE SHOULD STUDY THEM.*

Contents.—Indian geographic names—Language a guide to ethnology—Reveals the growth of arts and the psychologic processes of a people—Illustration from the Lenâpe tongue—Structure of language best studied in savage tongues—Rank of American tongues—Characteristic traits; pronominal forms; idea of personality; polysynthesis; incorporation; holophrasis; origin of these—Lucidity of American tongues; their vocabularies; power of expressing abstract ideas—Conclusion.

I APPEAR before you this evening to enter a plea for one of the most neglected branches of learning, for a study usually considered hopelessly dry and unproductive—that of American aboriginal languages.

It might be thought that such a topic, in America and among Americans, would attract a reasonably large number of students. The interest which attaches to our native soil and to the homes of our ancestors might be supposed to extend to the languages of those nations who for uncounted generations possessed the land which we have occupied relatively so short a time.

---

* An Address delivered by request before the Historical Societies of Pennsylvania and New York, in 1885. It was printed in the *Pennsylvania Magazine of History and Biography* for that year.

This supposition would seem the more reasonable in view of the fact that in one sense these languages have not died out among us. True, they are no longer media of intercourse, but they survive in thousands of geographical names all over our land. In the state of Connecticut alone there are over six hundred, and even more in Pennsylvania.

Certainly it would be a most legitimate anxiety which should direct itself to the preservation of the correct forms and precise meanings of these numerous and peculiarly national designations. One would think that this alone would not fail to excite something more than a languid curiosity in American linguistics, at least in our institutions of learning and societies for historical research.

That this subject has received so slight attention I attribute to the comparatively recent understanding of the value of the study of languages in general, and more particularly to the fact that no one, so far as I know, has set forth the purposes for which we should investigate these tongues, and the results which we expect to reach by means of them. This it is my present purpose to attempt, so far as it can be accomplished in the scope of an evening address.

The time has not long passed when the only good reasons for studying a language were held to be either that we might thereby acquaint ourselves with its literature; or that certain business, trading, or political interests might be subserved; or that the nation speaking it might be made acquainted with the blessings of civilization and Christianity. These were all good and sufficient reasons, but I cannot adduce any one of them in support of my plea to-night: for the languages I shall speak of have no literature; all transactions with their people can be carried on as well or better in European tongues; and, in fact, many of these peoples are no longer in existence — they have died out or amalgamated with others. What I have to argue for is the study of the dead languages of extinct and barbarous tribes.

You will readily see that my arguments must be drawn from other considerations than those of immediate utility. I must seek them in the broader fields of ethnology and philosophy; I must appeal to your interest in man as a race, as a member of a common species, as possessing in all his families and tribes the same mind, the same soul. Language is almost our only clue to discover the kinship of those countless scattered hordes who roamed the forests of this broad continent. Their traditions are vague or lost, written records they had none, their customs and arts are misleading, their religions misunderstood; their languages alone remain to testify to a oneness of blood often seemingly repudiated by an internecine hostility.

I am well aware of the limits which a wise caution assigns to the employment of linguistics in ethnology, and I am only too familiar with the many foolish, unscientific attempts to employ it with reference to the American race. But in spite of all this, I repeat that it is the surest and almost our only means to trace the ancient connection and migrations of nations in America.

Through its aid alone we have reached a positive knowledge that most of the area of South America, including the whole of the West Indies, was occupied by three great families of nations, not one of which had formed any important settlement on the northern continent. By similar evidence we know that the tribe which greeted Penn, when he landed on the site of this city where I now speak, was a member of the one vast family—the great Algonkin stock—whose various clans extended from the palmetto swamps of Carolina to the snow-clad hills of Labrador, and from the easternmost cape of Newfoundland to the peaks of the Rocky Mountains, over 20° of latitude and 50° of longitude. We also know that the general trend of migration in the northern continent has been from north to south, and that this is true not only of the more savage tribes, as the Algonkins, Iroquois, and Athapascas, but also of those who, in the favored southern lands, approached a form of civilization, the Aztecs, the Mayas, and the Quiches. These and many minor ethnologic facts have already been obtained by the study of American languages.

But such external information is only a small part of what they are capable of disclosing. We can turn them, like the reflector of a microscope, on the secret and hidden mysteries of the aboriginal man, and discover his inmost motives, his impulses, his concealed hopes and fears, those that gave rise to his customs and laws, his schemes of social life, his superstitions and his religions.

Personal names, family names, titles, forms of salutation, methods of address, terms of endearment, respect, and reproach, words expressing the emotions, these are what infallibly reveal the daily social family life of a community, and the way in which its members regard one another. They are precisely as correct when applied to the investigation of the American race as elsewhere, and they are the more valuable just there, because his deep-seated distrust of the white invaders—for which, let us acknowledge, he had abundant cause—led the Indian to practice concealment and equivocation on these personal topics.

In no other way can the history of the development of his arts be reached. You are doubtless aware that diligent students of the Aryan languages have succeeded in faithfully depicting the arts and habits of that ancient community in which the common ancestors of Greek and Roman, Persian and Dane, Brahmin and Irishman, dwelt together as of one blood and one speech. This has been done by ascertaining what household words are common to all these tongues, and therefore must have been in use among the primeval horde from which they are all descended. The method is conclusive, and yields positive results. There is no reason why it should not be addressed to American languages, and we may be sure that it would be most fruitful. How valuable it would be to take even a few words, as maize, tobacco, pipe, bow, arrow, and the like, each representing a widespread art or custom, and trace their derivations and affinities through the languages of the whole continent! We may be sure that striking and unexpected results would be obtained.

These languages also offer an entertaining field to the psychologist.

On account of their transparency, as I may call it, the clearness with which they retain the primitive forms of their radicals, they allow us to trace out the growth of words, and thus reveal the operations of the native mind by a series of witnesses whose testimony cannot be questioned. Often curious associations of ideas are thus disclosed, very instructive to the student of mankind. Many illustrations of this could be given, but I do not wish to assail your ears by a host of unknown sounds, so I shall content myself with one, and that taken from the language of the Lenâpé, or Delaware Indians.

I shall endeavor to trace out one single radical in that language, and show you how many, and how strangely diverse ideas were built up upon it.

The radical which I select is the personal pronoun of the first person, *I*, Latin *Ego*. In Delaware this is a single syllable, a slight nasal, *Nĕ*, or *Ni*.

Let me premise by informing you that this is both a personal and a possessive pronoun; it means both *I* and *mine*. It is both singular and plural, both *I* and *we*, *mine* and *our*.

The changes of the application of this root are made by adding suffixes to it.

I begin with *ni'hillan*, literally, "mine, it is so," or "she, it, is truly mine," the accent being on the first syllable, *ni'*, mine. But the common meaning of this verb in Delaware is more significant of ownership than this tame expression. It is an active, animate verb, and means, "I beat, or strike, somebody." To the rude minds of the framers of that tongue, ownership meant the right to beat what one owned.

We might hope this sense was confined to the lower animals; but not so. Change the accent from the first to the second syllable, *ni'hillan*, to *nihil'lan*, and you have the animate active verb with an intensive force, which signifies "to beat to death," "to kill some person;" and from this, by another suffix, you have *nihil'lowen*, to murder, and *nihil'-*

lowet, murderer. The bad sense of the root is here pushed to its uttermost.

But the root also developed in a nobler direction. Add to *ni'hillan* the termination *ape*, which means a male, and you have *nihillape*, literally, "I, it is true, a man," which, as an adjective, means free, independent, one's own master, "I am my own man." From this are derived the noun, *nihillapewit*, a freeman; the verb *nihillapewin*, to be free; and the abstract, *nihillasowagan*, freedom, liberty, independence. These are glorious words; but I can go even farther. From this same theme is derived the verb *nihillape-wheu*, to set free, to liberate, to redeem; and from this the missionaries framed the word *nihillape-whoalid*, the Redeemer, the Saviour.

Here is an unexpected antithesis, the words for a murderer and the Saviour both from one root! It illustrates how strange is the concatenation of human thoughts.

These are by no means all the derivatives from the root *ni*, I.

When reduplicated as *nĕnĕ*, it has a plural and strengthened form, like "our own." With a pardonable and well-nigh universal weakness, which we share with them, the nation who spoke the language believed themselves the first created of mortals and the most favored by the Creator. Hence whatever they designated as "ours" was both older and better than others of its kind. Hence *nenni* came to mean ancient, primordial, indigenous, and as such it is a frequent prefix in the Delaware language. Again, as they considered themselves the first and only true men, others being barbarians, enemies, or strangers, *nenno* was understood to be one of us, a man like ourselves, of our nation.

In their different dialects the sounds of *n*, *l*, and *r* were alternated, so that while Thomas Campanius, who translated the Catechism into Delaware about 1645, wrote that word *rhennus*, later writers have given it *lenno*, and translate it "man." This is the word which we find in the name Lenni Lenape, which, by its derivation, means "we, we men." The antecedent *lenni* is superfluous. The proper name of the Delaware nation was and still is *Len âpé*, "we men," or "our men," and those critics who have maintained that this was a misnomer, introduced by Mr. Heckewelder, have been mistaken in their facts.*

I have not done with the root *në*. I might go on and show you how it is at the base of the demonstrative pronouns, this, that, those, in Delaware; how it is the radical of the words for thinking, reflecting, and meditating; how it also gives rise to words expressing similarity and identity; how it means to be foremost, to stand ahead of others; and finally, how it signifies to come to me, to unify or congregate together. But doubtless I have trespassed on your ears long enough with unfamilar words.

Such suggestions as these will give you some idea of the value of American languages to American ethnology. But I should be doing injustice to my subject were I to confine my arguments in favor of their study to this horizon. If they are essential to a comprehension of the red race, not less so are they to the science of linguistics in general. This science deals not with languages, but with *language*. It looks at the idiom of a nation, not as a dry catalogue of words and grammatical rules, but as the living expression

---

* For another derivation, see *ante*, p. 182.

of the thinking power of man, as the highest manifestation of that spiritual energy which has lifted him from the level of the brute, the complete definition of which, in its origin and evolution, is the loftiest aim of universal history. As the intention of all speech is the expression of thought, and as the final purpose of all thinking is the discovery of truth, so the ideal of language, the point toward which it strives, is the absolute form for the realization of intellectual function.

In this high quest no tongue can be overlooked, none can be left out of account. One is just as important as another. Gœthe once said that he who knows but one language knows none; we may extend the apothegm, and say that so long as there is a single language on the globe not understood and analyzed, the science of language will be incomplete and illusory. It has often proved the case that the investigation of a single, narrow, obscure dialect has changed the most important theories of history. What has done more than anything else to overthrow, or, at least, seriously to shake, the time-honored notion that the White Race first came from Central Asia? It was the study of the Lithuanian dialect on the Baltic Sea, a language of peasants, without literature or culture, but which displays forms more archaic than the Sanscrit. What has led to a complete change of views as to the prehistoric population of Southern Europe? The study of the Basque, a language unknown out of a few secluded valleys in the Pyrenees.

There are many reasons why unwritten languages, like those of America, are more interesting, more promising in results, to the student of linguistics, than those which for generations have been cast in the conventional moulds of written speech.

Their structure is more direct, simple, transparent; they reveal more clearly the laws of the linguistic powers in their daily exercise; they are less tied down to hereditary formulæ and meaningless repetitions.

Would we explain the complicated structure of highly-organized tongues like our own, would we learn the laws which have assigned to it its material and formal elements, we must turn to the naïve speech of savages, there to see in their nakedness those processes which are too obscure in our own.

If the much-debated question of the origin of language engages us, we must seek its solution in the simple radicals of savage idioms; and if we wish to institute a comparison between the relative powers of languages, we can by no means omit them from our list. They offer to us the raw material, the essential and indispensable requisites of articulate communication.

As the structure of a language reflects in a measure, and as, on the other hand, it in a measure controls and directs the mental workings of those who speak it, the student of psychology must occupy himself with the speech of the most illiterate races in order to understand their theory of things, their notions of what is about them. They teach him the undisturbed evolution of the untrained mind.

As the biologist in pursuit of that marvellous something which we call "the vital principle" turns from the complex organisms of the higher animals and plants to life in its simplest expression in microbes and single cells, so in the future will the linguist find that he is nearest the solution of the most weighty problems of his science when he directs his attention to the least cultivated languages.

Convinced as I am of the correctness of this analogy, I venture to predict that in the future the analysis of the American languages will be regarded as one of the most important fields in linguistic study, and will modify most materially the findings of that science. And I make this prediction the more confidently, as I am supported in it by the great authority of Wilhelm von Humboldt, who for twenty years devoted himself to their investigation.

As I am advocating so warmly that more attention should be devoted to these languages, it is but fair that you should require me to say something descriptive about them, to explain some of their peculiarities of structure. To do this properly I should require not the fag end of one lecture, but a whole course of lectures. Yet perhaps I can say enough now to show you how much there is in them worth studying.

Before I turn to this, however, I should like to combat a prejudice which I fear you may entertain. It is that same ancient prejudice which led the old Greeks to call all those who did not speak their sonorous idioms *barbarians;* for that word meant nothing more nor less than babblers ($\beta\alpha\lambda$-$\beta\alpha\lambda o\iota$), people who spoke an unintelligible tongue. Modern civilized nations hold that prejudice yet, in the sense that each insists that his own language is the best one extant, the highest in the scale, and that wherein others differ from it in structure they are inferior.

So unfortunately placed is this prejudice with reference to

my subject, that in the very volume issued by our government at Washington to encourage the study of the Indian languages, there is a long essay to prove that English is the noblest, most perfect language in the world, while all the native languages are, in comparison, of a very low grade indeed!*

The essayist draws his arguments chiefly from the absence of inflections in English. Yet many of the profoundest linguists of this century have maintained that a fully inflected language, like the Greek or Latin, is for that very reason ahead of all others. We may suspect that when a writer lauds his native tongue at the expense of others, he is influenced by a prejudice in its favor and an absence of facility in the others.

Those best acquainted with American tongues praise them most highly for flexibility, accuracy, and resources of expression. They place some of them above any Aryan language. But what is this to those who do not know them? To him who cannot bend the bow of Ulysses it naturally seems a useless and awkward weapon.

I do not ask you to accept this opinion either; but I do ask that you rid your minds of bias, and that you do not condemn a tongue because it differs widely from that which you speak.

American tongues do, indeed, differ very widely from those familiar to Aryan ears. Not that they are all alike in structure. That was a hasty generalization, dating from a time when they were less known. Yet the great majority

---

* *Introduction to the Study of Indian Languages.* By J. W. Powell (second edition, Washington, 1880).

of them have certain characteristics in common, sufficient to place them in a linguistic class by themselves. I shall name and explain some of these.

As of the first importance I would mention the prominence they assign to pronouns and pronominal forms. Indeed, an eminent linguist has been so impressed with this feature that he has proposed to classify them distinctively as "pronominal languages." They have many classes of pronouns, sometimes as many as eighteen, which is more than twice as many as the Greek. There is often no distinction between a noun and a verb other than the pronoun which governs it. That is, if a word is employed with one form of the pronoun it becomes a noun, if with another pronoun, it becomes a verb.

We have something of the same kind in English. In the phrase, "I love," love is a verb; but in "my love," it is a noun. It is noteworthy that this treatment of words as either nouns or verbs, as we please to employ them, was carried further by Shakespeare than by any other English writer. He seemed to divine in such a trait of language vast resources for varied and pointed expression. If I may venture a suggestion as to how it does confer peculiar strength to expressions, it is that it brings into especial prominence the idea of Personality; it directs all subjects of discourse by the notion of an individual, a living, personal unit. This imparts vividness to narratives, and directness and life to propositions.

Of these pronouns, that of the first person is usually the most developed. From it, in many dialects, are derived the demonstratives and relatives, which in Aryan languages were taken from the third person. This prominence of the *Ego*, this confidence in self, is a trait of the race as well as of their speech. It forms part of that savage independence of character which prevented them coalescing into great nations, and led them to prefer death to servitude.

Another characteristic, which at one time was supposed to be universal on this continent, is what Mr. Peter Du Ponceau named *polysynthesis*. He meant by this a power of running several words into one, dropping parts of them and retaining only the significant syllables. Long descriptive names of all objects of civilized life new to the Indians were thus coined with the greatest ease. Some of these are curious enough. The Pavant Indians call a school house by one word, which means "a stopping-place where sorcery is practiced;" their notion of book-learning being that it belongs to the uncanny arts. The Delaware word for horse means "the four-footed animal which carries on his back."

This method of coining words is, however, by no means universal in American languages. It prevails in most of those in British America and the United States, in Aztec and various South American idioms; but in others, as the dialects found in Yucatan and Guatemala, and in the Tupi of Brazil, the Otomi of Mexico, and the Klamath of the Pacific coast, it is scarcely or not at all present.

Another trait, however, which was confounded with this by Mr. Du Ponceau, but really belongs in a different category of grammatical structure, is truly distinctive of the languages of the continent, and I am not sure that any one of them has been shown to be wholly devoid of it. This is what is called *incorporation*. It includes in the verb, or in the verbal expression, the object and manner of the action.

This is effected by making the subject of the verb an inseparable prefix, and by inserting between it and the verb itself, or sometimes directly in the latter, between its syllables, the object, direct or remote, and the particles indicating mode. The time or tense particles, on the other hand, will be placed at one end of this compound, either as prefixes or suffixes, thus placing the whole expression strictly within the limits of a verbal form of speech.

Both the above characteristics, I mean Polysynthesis and Incorporation, are unconscious efforts to carry out a certain theory of speech which has aptly enough been termed *holophrasis*, or the putting the whole of a phrase into a single word. This is the aim of each of them, though each endeavors to accomplish it by different means. Incorporation confines itself exclusively to verbal forms, while polysynthesis embraces both nouns and verbs.

Suppose we carry the analysis further, and see if we can obtain an answer to the query,—Why did this effort at blending forms of speech obtain so widely? Such an inquiry will indicate how valuable to linguistic search would prove the study of this group of langauges.

I think there is no doubt but that it points unmistakably to that very ancient, to that primordial period of human utterance when men had not yet learned to connect words into sentences, when their utmost efforts at articulate speech did not go beyond single words, which, aided by gestures and signs, served to convey their limited intellectual converse. Such single vocables did not belong to any particular part of speech. There was no grammar to that antique tongue. Its disconnected exclamations mean whole sentences in themselves.

A large part of the human race, notably, but not exclusively, the aborigines of this continent, continued the tradition of this mode of expression in the structure of their tongues, long after the union of thought and sound in audible speech had been brought to a high degree of perfection.

Although I thus regard one of the most prominent peculiarities of American languages as a survival from an exceedingly low stage of human development, it by no means follows that this is an evidence of their inferiority.

The Chinese, who made no effort to combine the primitive vocables into one, but range them nakedly side by side, succeeded no better than the American Indians; and there is not much beyond assertion to prove that the Aryans, who, through their inflections, marked the relation of each word in the sentence by numerous tags of case, gender, number, etc., got any nearer the ideal perfection of language.

If we apply what is certainly a very fair test, to wit: the uses to which a language is and can be put, I cannot see that a well-developed American tongue, such as the Aztec or the Algonkin, in any way falls short of, say French or English.

It is true that in many of these tongues there is no distinction made between expressions, which with us are carefully separated, and are so in thought. Thus, in the Tupi of Brazil and elsewhere, there is but one word for the three expressions, "his father," "he is a father," and "he has a father;" in many, the simple form of the verb may convey three different ideas, as in Ute, where the word for "he seizes" means also "the seizer," and as a descriptive noun, "a bear," the animal which seizes.

This has been charged against these languages as a lack of "differentiation." Grammatically, this is so; but the same charge applies with almost equal force to the English language, where the same word may belong to any of four, five, even six parts of speech, dependent entirely on the connection in which it is used.

As a set-off, the American languages avoid confusions of expression which prevail in European tongues.

Thus in none of these latter, when I say "the love of God," "l'amour de Dieu," "amor Dei," can you understand what I mean. You do not know whether I intend the love which we have or should have toward God, or God's love toward us. Yet in the Mexican language (and many other American tongues) these two quite opposite ideas are so clearly distinguished that, as Father Carochi warns the readers of his *Mexican Grammar*, to confound them would not merely be a grievous solecism in speech, but a formidable heresy as well.

Another example. What can you make out of this sentence, which is strictly correct by English grammar: "John told Robert's son that he must help him?" You can make nothing out of it. It may have any one of six different meanings, depending on the persons referred to by the pronouns "he" and "him." No such lamentable confusion could occur in any American tongue known to me. The Chippeway, for instance, has three pronouns of the third person, which designate the near and the remote antecedents with the most lucid accuracy.

There is another point that I must mention in this connection, because I find that it has almost always been overlooked or misunderstood by critics of these languages. These have been free in condemning the synthetic forms of construction. But they seem to be ignorant that their use is largely optional. Thus, in Mexican, one can arrange the same sentence in an analytic or a synthetic form, and this is also the case, in a less degree, in the Algonkin. By this means a remarkable richness is added to the language. The higher the grade of synthesis employed, the more striking, elevated, and pointed becomes the expression. In common life long compounds are rare, while in the native Mexican poetry each line is often but one word.

Turning now from the structure of these languages to their vocabularies, I must correct a widespread notion that they are scanty in extent and deficient in the means to express lofty or abstract ideas.

Of course, there are many tracts of thought and learning familiar to us now which were utterly unknown to the American aborigines, and not less so to our own forefathers a few centuries ago. It would be very unfair to compare the dictionary of an Indian language with the last edition of Webster's Unabridged. But take the English dictionaries of the latter half of the sixteenth century, before Spenser and Shakespeare wrote, and compare them with the Mexican vocabulary of Molina, which contains about 13,000 words, or with the Maya vocabulary of the convent of Motul, which presents over 20,000, both prepared at that date, and your procedure will be just, and you will find it not disadvantageous to the American side of the question.

The deficiency in abstract terms is generally true of these languages. They did not have them, because they had no use for them—and the more blessed was their condition. European languages have been loaded with several thousand such by metaphysics and mysticism, and it has required many generations to discover that they are empty windbags, full of sound and signifying nothing.

Yet it is well known to students that the power of forming abstracts is possessed in a remarkable degree by many native languages. The most recondite formulæ of dogmatic religion, such as the definition of the Trinity and the difference between consubstantiation and transubstantiation, have been translated into many of them without introducing foreign words, and in entire conformity with their grammatical structure. Indeed, Dr. Augustin de la Rosa, of the University of Guadalajara, says the Mexican is peculiarly adapted to render these metaphysical subtleties.

I have been astonished that some writers should bring up the primary meaning of a word in an American language in order to infer the coarseness of its secondary meaning. This is a strangely unfair proceeding, and could be directed with equal effect against our own tongues. Thus, I read lately a traveler who spoke hardly of and Indian tribe because their word for "to love" was a derivative from that meaning "to buy," and thence "to prize." But what did the Latin *amare*, and the English *to love*, first mean? Carnally living together is what they first meant, and this is not a nobler derivation than that of the Indian. Even yet, when the most polished of European nations, that one which most exalts *la grande passion*, does not distinguish in language between loving their wives and liking their dinners, but uses the same word for both emotions, it is scarcely wise for us to indulge in much latitude of inference from such etymologies.

Such is the general character of American languages, and such are the reasons why they should be preserved and studied. The field is vast and demands many laborers to reap all the fruit that it promises. It is believed at present that there are about two hundred wholly independent stocks of languages among the aborigines of this continent. They vary most widely in vocabulary, and seemingly scarcely less so in grammar.

Besides this, each of these stocks is subdivided into dialects, each distinguished by its own series of phonetic changes, and its own new words. What an opportunity is thus offered for the study of the natural evolution of language, unfettered by the petrifying art of writing!

This is the case which I present to you, and for which I earnestly solicit your consideration. And that I may add weight to my appeal, I close by quoting the words of one of America's most distinguished scientists, Professor William Dwight Whitney, of Yale College, who writes to this effect:

"The study of American languages is the most fruitful and the most important branch of American Archæology."

WILHELM VON HUMBOLDT'S RESEARCHES IN AMERICAN LANGUAGES.*

Contents.—What led Humboldt toward the American tongues—Progress of his studies—Fundamental doctrine of his philosophy of language—His theory of the evolution of languages—Opinion on American languages—His criterion of the relative perfection of languages—Not abundance of forms—Nor verbal richness—American tongues not degenerations—Humboldt's classification of languages—Psychological origin of Incorporation in language—Its shortcomings—In simple sentences—In compound sentences—Absence of true formal elements—The nature of the American verb.

THE foundations of the Philosophy of Language were laid by Wilhelm von Humboldt (born June 22, 1767, died April 8, 1835). The principles he advocated have frequently been misunderstood, and some of them have been

---

* This essay is extracted from a more general discussion of Humboldt's linguistic philosophy which I read before the American Philosophical Society in 1885, and which was printed in their *Proceedings* for that year. Humboldt's great work was his Introduction to his essay on the Kawi language under the title: *Ueber die Verschiedenheit des menschlichen Sprachbaues und ihren Einfluss auf die geistige Entwickelung des Menschengeschlechts.* Prof. Adler translates this, "The Structural Differences of Human Speech and their Influence on the Intellectual Development of the Human Race." The word *geistige*, however, includes emotional as well as intellectual things. Of the many commentators on this masterly production, I have used particularly the following:

Die Elemente der Philosophischen Sprachwissenschaft Wilhelm von Humboldt's.

modified, or even controverted, by more extended research; but a careful survey of the tendencies of modern thought in this field will show that the philosophic scheme of the nature and growth of languages which he set forth, is gradually reasserting its sway after having been neglected and denied through the preponderance of the so-called "naturalistic" school during the last quarter of a century.

The time seems ripe, therefore, to bring the general principles of his philosophy to the knowledge of American scholars, as applied by himself to the analysis of American languages.

These languages occupied Humboldt's attention earnestly and for many years. He was first led to their study by his brother Alexander, who presented him with the large linguistic collection amassed during his travels in South and North America.

While Prussian Minister in Rome (1802–8) Wilhelm ransacked the library of the *Collegio Romano* for rare or unpublished works on American tongues; he obtained from the ex-Jesuit Forneri all the information the latter could give about the Yurari, a tongue spoken on the Meta river,

---

In systematischer Entwicklung dargestellt und kritisch erläutert, von Dr. Max Schasler, Berlin, 1847.

Die Sprachwissenschaft Wilhelm von Humboldt's und die Hegel'sche Philosophie, von Dr. H. Steinthal, Berlin, 1848. The same eminent linguist treats especially of Humboldt's teachings in *Grammatik, Logik und Psychologie, ihre Principien und ihr Verhältniss zu einander*, pp. 123-135 (Berlin, 1855); in his well-known volume *Characteristik der Hauptsächlichsten Typen des Sprachbaues*, pp. 20-70 (Berlin, 1860); in his oration *Ueber Wilhelm von Humboldt* (Berlin, 1883); and elsewhere.

Wilhelm von Humboldt's Linguistical Studies. By C. J. Adler, A. M. (New York, 1866). This is the only attempt beside my own, so far as I know, to present Humboldt's philosophy of language to English readers. It is meritorious, but certainly in some passages Prof. Adler failed to catch Humboldt's meaning.

New Granada;* and he secured accurate copies of all the manuscript material on these idioms left by the diligent collector and linguist, the Abbé Hervas.

A few years later, in 1812, we find him writing to his friend Baron Alexander von Rennenkampff, then in St. Petersburg: "I have selected the American languages as the special subject of my investigations. They have the closest relationship of any with the tongues of north-eastern Asia; and I beg you therefore to obtain for me all the dictionaries and grammars of the latter which you can." †

It is probable from this extract that Humboldt was then studying these languages from that limited, ethnographic point of view, from which he wrote his essay on the Basque tongue, the announcement of which appeared, indeed, in that year, 1812, although the work itself was not issued until 1821.

Ten years more of study and reflection taught him a far loftier flight. He came to look upon each language as an organism, all its parts bearing harmonious relations to each other, standing in a definite connection with the intellectual and emotional development of the nation speaking it. Each language again bears the relation to language in general that the species does to the genus, or the genus to the order, and by a comprehensive process of analysis he hoped to arrive at those fundamental laws of articulate speech which

---

* *Ueber die Verschiedenheit*, etc., Bd. vi, s. 271, note. I may say, once for all, that my references, unless otherwise stated, are to the edition of Humboldt's *Gesammelte Werke*, edited by his brother, Berlin, 1841–1852.

† *Aus Wilhelm von Humboldt's letzten Lebensjahren. Eine Mittheilung bisher unbekannter Briefe*, von Theodor Distel, p. 19 (Leipzig, 1883).

form the Philosophy of Language, and which, as they are also the laws of human thought, at a certain point coincide, he believed, with those of the Philosophy of History.

In the completion of this vast scheme, he contined to attach the utmost importance to the American languages.

His illustrations were constantly drawn from them, and they were ever the subject of his earnest studies. He prized them as in certain respects the most valuable of all to the philosophic student of human speech.

Thus, in 1826, he announced before the Berlin Academy that he was preparing an exhaustive work on the "Organism of Language," for which he had selected the American languages exclusively, as best suited for this purpose. "The languages of a great continent," he writes, "peopled by numerous nationalities, probably never subject to foreign influence, offer for this branch of linguistic study specially favorable material. There are in America as many as thirty little known languages for which we have means of study, each of which is like a new natural species, besides many others whose data are less ample."*

In his memoir, read two years later, "On the Origin of Grammatic Forms, and their Influence on the Development of Ideas," he chose most of his examples from the idioms of the New World;† and the year following, he read the monograph on the Verb in American languages, which I refer to on a later page.

---

* From his memoir *Ueber das vergleichende Sprachstudium in Beziehung auf die verschiedenen Epochen der Sprachentwicklung*, Bd. iii, s. 249.

† He draws examples from the Carib, Lule, Tupi, Mbaya, Huasteca, Nahuatl, Tamanaca, Abipone, and Mixteca; *Ueber das Entstehen der grammatischen Formen, und ihren Einfluss auf die Ideenentwicklung*, Bd. iii, ss. 269-306.

In a subsequent communication, he announced his special study of this group as still in preparation. It was, however, never completed. His earnest desire to reach the fundamental laws of language led him into a long series of investigations into the systems of recorded speech, phonetic hieroglyphics and alphabetic writing, on which he read memoirs of great acuteness.

In one of these he again mentions his studies of the American tongues, and takes occasion to vindicate them from the current charge of being of a low grade in the linguistic scale. "It is certainly unjust," he writes, "to call the American languages rude or savage, although their structure is widely different from those perfectly formed."*

In 1828, there is a published letter from him making an appointment with the Abbé Thavenet, missionary to the Canadian Algonkins, then in Paris, "to enjoy the pleasure of conversing with him on his interesting studies of the Algonkin language." † And a private letter tells us that in 1831 he applied himself with new zeal to mastering the intricacies of Mexican grammar. ‡

All these years he was working to complete the researches which led him to the far-reaching generalization which is at the basis of his linguistic philosophy.

Let me state in a few words what this philosophy teaches. It aims to establish as a fundamental truth that *the*

---

* *Ueber die Buchstabenschrift und ihren Zusammenhang mit dem Sprachbau*, Bd. vi, s. 526.

† This letter is printed in the memoir of Prof. E. Teza, *Intorno agli Studi del Thavenet sulla Lingua Algonchina*, in the *Annali delle Università toscane*, Tomo xviii (Pisa, 1880).

‡ Compare Prof. Adler's Essay, above mentioned, p. 11.

diversity of structure in languages is both the necessary antecedent and the necessary consequent of the evolution of the human mind.*

In the establishment of this thesis he begins with a subtle analysis of the nature of speech in general, and then proceeds to define the reciprocal influences which thought exerts upon it, and it upon thought.

It will readily be seen that a corollary of this theorem is that the Science of Language is and must be the most instructive, the indispensable guide in the study of the mental evolution of the human race. Humboldt recognized this fully. He taught that in its highest sense the philosophy of language is one with the philosophy of history. The science of language misses its purpose unless it seeks its chief end in explaining the intellectual growth of the race.†

Each separate tongue is "a thought-world in tones" established between the minds of those who speak it and the objective world without.‡ Each mirrors in itself the spirit of the nation to which it belongs. But it has also an earlier

---

* This is found expressed nowhere else so clearly as at the beginning of § 13, where the author writes: "Der Zweck dieser Einleitung, die Sprachen, in der Verschiedenartigkeit ihres Baues, als die nothwendige Grundlage der Fortbildung des menschlichen Geistes darzustellen, und den wechselseitigen Einfluss des Einen auf das Andre zu erörtern, hat mich genöthigt, in die Natur der Sprache überhaupt einzugehen." Bd. vi, s. 106.

† "Das Studium der verschiedenen Sprachen des Erdbodens verfehlt seine Bestimmung, wenn es nicht immer den Gang der geistigen Bildung im Auge behält, und darin seinen eigentlichen Zweck sucht." *Ueber den Zusammenhang der Schrift mit der Sprache*, Bd. vi, s. 428.

‡ "Eine Gedankenwelt an Töne geheftet." *Ueber die Buchstabenschrift und ihre Zusammenhang mit dem Sprachbau*, Bd. vi, s. 530.

and independent origin; it is the product of the conceptions of antecedent generations, and thus exerts a formative and directive influence on the national mind, an influence not slight, but more potent than that which the national mind exerts upon it.*

He fully recognized a progress, an organic growth, in human speech. This growth may be from two sources, one the cultivation of a tongue within the nation by enriching its vocabulary, separating and classifying its elements, fixing its expressions, and thus adapting it to wider uses; the second, by forcible amalgamation with another tongue.

The latter exerts always a more profound and often a more beneficial influence. The organism of both tongues may be destroyed, but the dissolvent force is also an organic and vital one, and from the ruins of both constructs a speech of grander plans and with wider views. "The seemingly aimless and confused interminglings of primitive tribes sowed the seed for the flowers of speech and song which flourished in centuries long posterior."

The immediate causes of the improvement of a language through forcible admixture with another, are: that it is obliged to drop all unneccessary accessory elements in a proposition; that the relations of ideas must be expressed by conventional and not significant syllables; and that the limitations of thought imposed by the genius of the language are violently broken down, and the mind is thus given wider play for its faculties.

Such influences, however, do not act in accordance with

---

* This cardinal point in Humboldt's philosophy is very clearly set forth in his essay, *Ueber die Aufgabe des Geschichtschreibers*. Bd, i, s. 23, and elsewhere.

fixed laws of growth. There are no such laws which are of universal application. The development of the Mongolian or Aryan tongues is not at all that of the American. The goal is one and the same, but the paths to it are infinite. For this reason each group or class of languages must be studied by itself, and its own peculiar developmental laws be ascertained by searching its history.*

With reference to the growth of American languages, it was Humboldt's view that they manifest the utmost refractoriness both to external influences and to internal modifications. They reveal a marvellous tenacity of traditional words and forms, not only in dialects, but even in particular classes of the community, men having different expressions from women, the old from the young, the higher from the lower classes. These are maintained with scrupulous exactitude through generations, and three centuries of daily commingling with the white race have scarcely altered their grammar or phonetics.

Nor is this referable to the contrast between an Aryan and an American language. The same immiscibility is shown between themselves. "Even where many radically different languages are located closely together, as in Mexico, I have not found a single example where one exercised a constructive or formative influence on the other. But it is by the encounter of great and contrasted differences that languages gain strength, riches, and completeness. Only thus are the perceptive powers, the imagination and the feelings impelled to enrich and extend the means of expres-

---

* This reasoning is developed in the essay, *Ueber das Vergleichende Sprachstudium*, etc., *Gesammelte Werke*, Bd. iii, ss. 241–268; and see Ibid, s. 270.

sion, which, if left to the labors of the understanding alone, are liable to be but meagre and arid."*

Humboldt's one criterion of a language was its tendency to *quicken and stimulate mental action*. He maintained that this is secured just in proportion as the grammatical structure favors clear definition of the individual idea apart from its relations; in other words, as it separates the material from the inflectional elements of speech. Clear thinking, he argued, means progressive thinking. Therefore he assigned a lower position both to those tongues which inseparably connect the idea with its relations, as most American languages, and to those which, like the Chinese and in a less degree the modern English, have scarcely any formal elements at all, but depend upon the position of words (placement) to signify their relations. But he warns us that it is of importance to recognize fully "that grammatical principles dwell rather in the mind of the speaker than in the material and mechanism of his language," and that the power of expressing ideas in any tongue depends much more on the intellectual capacity of the speaker than the structure of the tongue itself.

He censures the common error (common now as it was in his day) that the abundance and regularity of forms in a language is a mark of excellence. This very multiplicity, this excessive superfluity, is a burden and a drawback, and obscures the integration of the thought by attaching to it a quantity of needless qualifications. Thus, in the language of the Abipones, the pronoun is different as the person

---

* See the essay *Ueber die Buchstabenschrift und ihren Zusammenhang mit dem Sprachbau, Ges. Werke*, Bd. vi, ss. 551-2.

spoken of is conceived as present, absent, sitting, walking, lying or running—all quite unnecessary specifications.*

In some languages much appears as form which, on close scrutiny, is nothing of the kind.

This misunderstanding has reigned almost universally in the treatment of American tongues. The grammars which have been written upon them proceed generally on the principles of Latin, and apply a series of grammatical names to the forms explained, entirely inappropriate to them, and misleading. Our first duty in taking up such a grammar as, for instance, that of an American language, is to dismiss the whole of the arrangement of the "parts of speech," and by an analysis of words and phrases, to ascertain by what collocation of elements they express logical, significant relations.†

For example, in the Carib tongue, the grammars give *aveiridaco* as the second person singular, subjunctive imperfect, "if thou wert." Analyze this, and we discover that *a* is the possessive pronoun "thy;" *veiri* is "to be" or "being" (in a place); and *daco* is a particle of definite time. Hence, the literal rendering is "on the day of thy being." The so-called imperfect subjunctive turns out to be a verbal noun with a preposition. In many American languages the

---

* *Ueber das Entstehen der grammatischen Formen*, etc., *Werke*, Bd. iii, s. 292.

† Speaking of such "imperfect" languages, he gives the following wise suggestion for their study: "Ihr einfaches Geheimniss, welches den Weg anzeigt, auf welchem man sie, mit gänzlicher Vergessenheit unserer Grammatik, immer zuerst zu enträthseln versuchen muss, ist, das in sich Bedeutende unmittelbar an einander zu reihen." *Ueber das Vergleichende Sprachstudium*, etc., *Werke*, Bd. iii, s. 255; and for a practical illustration of his method, see the essay, *Ueber das Entstehen der grammatischen Formen*, etc., Bd. iii, s. 274.

hypothetical supposition expressed in the Latin subjunctive is indicated by the same circumlocution.

Again, the infinitive, in its classical sense, is unknown in most, probably in all, American languages. In the Tupi of Brazil and frequently elsewhere it is simply a noun; *caru* is both "to eat" and "food;" *che caru ai-pota*, "I wish to eat," literally "my food I wish."

Many writers continue to maintain that a criterion of a language is its lexicographic richness—the number of words it possesses. Even recently, Prof. Max Müller has applied such a test to American languages, and, finding that one of the Fuegian dialects is reported to have nearly thirty thousand words, he maintains that this is a proof that these savages are a degenerate remnant of some much more highly developed ancestry. Founding his opinion largely on similar facts, Alexander von Humboldt applied the expression to the American nations that they are "des débris échappés à un naufrage commun."

Such, however, was not the opinion of his brother Wilhelm. He sounded the depths of linguistic philosophy far more deeply than to accept mere abundance of words as proof of richness in a language. Many savage languages have twenty words signifying to eat particular things, but no word meaning "to eat" in general; the Eskimo language has different words for fishing for each kind of fish, but no word "to fish," in a general sense. Such apparent richness is, in fact, actual poverty.

Humboldt taught that the quality, not merely the quanity, of words was the decisive measure of verbal wealth. Such quality depends on the relations of concrete words, on the one hand, to primitive objective perceptions at their root, and, on the other, to the abstract general ideas of which they are particular representatives; and besides this, on the relations which the spoken word, the articulate sound, bears to the philosophic laws of the formation of language in general.*

In his letter to Abel-Remusat he discusses the theory that the American languages point to a once higher condition of civilization, and are the corrupted idioms of deteriorated races. He denies that there is linguistic evidence of any such theory. These languages, he says, possess a remarkable regularity of structure, and very few anomalies. Their grammar does not present any visible traces of corrupting intermixtures.†

Humboldt's classification of languages was based on the relation of the word to the sentence, which, expressed in logic, would mean the relation of the simple idea to the proposition. He taught that the plans on which languages combine words into sentences are a basic character of their structure, and divide them into classes as distinct and as decisive of their future, as those of vertebrate and invertebrate animals in natural history.

These plans are four in number:

1. By Isolation.

The words are placed in juxtaposition, without change.

---

* His teachings on this point, of which I give the barest outline, are developed in sections 12 and 13 of his Introduction, *Ueber die Verschiedenheit*, etc. Steinthal's critical remarks on these sections (in his *Charakteristik der haupt. Typen des Sprachbaues*) seem to me unsatisfactory, and he even does not appear to grasp the chain of Humboldt's reasoning.

† *Lettre à M. Abel-Remusat*, Werke, Bd. vii, s. 353.

Their relations are expressed by their location only (placement). The typical example of this is the Chinese.

2. By Agglutination.

The sentence is formed by suffixing to the word expressive of the main idea a number of others, more or less altered, expressing the relations. Examples of this are the Eskimo of North America, and the Northern Asiatic dialects.

3. By Incorporation.

The leading word of the sentence is divided, and the accessory words either included in it or attached to it with abbreviated forms, so that the whole sentence assumes the form and sound of one word.

4. By Inflection.

Each word of the sentence indicates by its own form the character and relation to the main proposition of the idea it represents. Sanscrit, Greek and Latin are familiar examples of inflected tongues.

It is possible to suppose that all four of these forms were developed from some primitive condition of utterance unknown to us, just as naturalists believe that all organic species were developed out of a homogeneous protoplasmic mass; but it is as hard to see how any one of them *in its present form* could pass over into another, as to understand how a radiate could change into a mollusk.

Of the four plans mentioned, Incorporation is that characteristic of, *though not confined to*, American tongues.

The psychological origin of this plan is explained rather curiously by Humboldt, as the result of an *exaltation of the imaginative over the intellectual elements of mind*. By this method, the linguistic faculty strives to present to the understanding the whole thought in the most compact form possible, thus to facilitate its comprehension; and this it does, because a thought presented in one word is more vivid and stimulating to the imagination, more individual and picturesque, than when narrated in a number of words.*

Incorporation may appear in a higher or a lower grade, but its intention is everywhere the effort to convey in one word the whole proposition. The verb, as that part of speech which especially conveys the synthetic action of the mental operation, is that which is selected as the stem of this word-sentence; all the other parts are subordinate accessories, devoid of syntactic value.

The higher grade of incorporation includes both subject, object and verb in one word, and if for any reason the object is not included, the scheme of the sentence is still maintained in the verb, and the object is placed outside, as in apposition, without case ending, and under a form different from its original and simple one.

This will readily be understood from the following examples from the Mexican language.

The sentence *ni-naca-qua* is one word, and means "I, flesh, eat." If it is desired to express the object independently, the expression becomes *ni-c-qua-in-nacatl*, "I it eat, the flesh." The termination *tl* does not belong to the root of the noun, but is added to show that it is in an external and, as it were, unnatural position. Both the direct and remote object can thus be incorporated, and if they are not,

---

* "Daher ist das Einschliessen in Ein Wort mehr Sache der Einbildungskraft, die Trennung mehr die des Verstandes." *Ueber die Verschiedenheit*, etc,, s. 327. Compare also, s. 326 and 166.

but separately appended, the scheme of the sentence is still preserved; as *ni-te-tla-maca*, literally, "I, to somebody, something, give." How closely these accessories are incorporated is illustrated by the fact that the tense-augments are not added to the stem, but to the whole word; *o-ni-c-te-maca-e*, where the *o* is the prefix of the perfect.

In these languages, every element in the sentence which is not incorporated in the verb has, in fact, no syntax at all. The verbal exhausts all the formal portion of the language. The relations of the other words are intimated by their position. Thus *ni-tlaçotlaz-nequia*, I wished to love, is literally, "I, I shall love, I wished." *Tlaçotlaz* is the first person singular of the future; *ni-nequia*, I wished; which is divided, and the future form inserted. The same expression may stand thus: *ni-c-nequia-tlaço-tlaz*, where the *c* is an intercalated relative pronoun, and the literal rendering is, "I it wished, I shall love."

In the Lule language the construction with an infinitive is simply that the two verbs follow each other in the same person, as *caic tucuec*, "I am accustomed to eat," literally, "I am accustomed, I eat."

None of these devices fulfils all the uses of the infinitive, and hence they are all inferior to it.

In languages which lack formal elements, the deficiency must be supplied by the mind. Words are merely placed in juxtaposition, and their relationship guessed at. Thus, when a language constructs its cases merely by prefixing prepositions to the unaltered noun, there is no grammatical form; in the Mbaya language *e-tiboa* is translated "through me," but it is really "I, through;" *l'emani*, is rendered "he wishes," but it is strictly, "he, wish."

In such languages the same collocation of words often corresponds to quite different meanings, as the precise relation of the thoughts is not defined by any formal elements. This is well illustrated in the Tupi tongue. The word *uba* is "father;" with the pronoun of the third person prefixed it is *tuba*, literally "he, father." This may mean either "his father," or "he is a father," or "he has a father," just as the sense of the rest of the sentence requires.

Certainly a language which thus leaves confounded together ideas so distinct as these, is inferior to one which discriminates them; and this is why the formal elements of a tongue are so important to intellectual growth. The Tupis may be an energetic and skillful people, but with their language they can never take a position as masters in the realm of ideas.

The absence of the passive in most American tongues is supplied by similar inadequate collocations of words. In Huasteca, for example, *nana tanin tahjal*, is translated "I am treated by him;" actually it is, "I, me, treats he." This is not a passive, but simply the idea of the Ego connected with the idea of another acting upon it.

This is vastly below the level of inflected speech; for it cannot be too strenuously maintained that the grammatical relations of spoken language are the more perfect and favorable to intellectual growth, the more closely they correspond to the logical relations of thought.

Sometimes what appears as inflection turns out on examination to be merely adjunction. Thus in the Mbaya tongue there are such verbal forms as *daladi*, thou wilt throw, *nilabuite*, he has spun, where the *d* is the sign of the future, and the *n* of the perfect. These look like inflections; but in fact, *d* is simply a relic of *quide*, hereafter, later, and *n* stands in the same relation to *quine*, which means "and also."

To become true formal elements, all such adjuncts must have completely lost their independent signification; because if they retain it, their material content requires qualification and relation just as any other stem-word.

A few American languages may have reached this stage. In the Mexican there are the terminals *ya* or *a* in the imperfect, the augment *o* in the preterit and others in the future. In the Tamanaca the present ends in *a*, the preterit in *e*, the future in *c*. "There is nothing in either of these tongues to show that these tense-signs have independent meaning, and therefore there is no reason why they should not be classed with those of the Greek and Sanscrit as true inflectional elements."*

The theory of Incorporation, it will be noted, is to express the whole proposition, as nearly as possible, in one word; and what part of it cannot be thus expressed, is left without any syntax whatever. Not only does this apply to individual words in a sentence, but it extends to the various clauses of a compound sentence, such as in Aryan languages show their relation to the leading clauses by means of prepositions, conjunctions and relative pronouns.

When the methods are analyzed by which the major and minor clauses are assigned their respective values in these tongues, it is very plain what difficulties of expression the

---

* "Der Mexikanischen kann man am Verbum, in welchem die Zeiten durch einzelne Endbuchstaben und zum Theil offenbar symbolisch bezeichnet werden, Flexionen und ein gewisses Streben nach Sanskritischer Worteinheit nicht absprechen." *Ueber die Verschiedenheit*, etc., *Werke*, Bd. vi, s. 176.

system of Incorporation involves. Few of them have any true connecting word of either of the three classes above mentioned. They depend on scarcely veiled material words, simply placed in juxtaposition.

It is probable that the prepositions and conjunctions of all languages were at first significant words, and the degree to which they have lost their primary significations and have become purely formal elements expressing relation, is one of the measures of the grammatical evolution of a tongue. In most American idioms their origin from substantives is readily recognizable. Frequently these substantives refer to parts of the body, and this, in passing, suggests the antiquity of this class of words and their value in comparison.

In Maya *tan* means in, toward, among; but it is also the breast or front of the body. The Mexican has three classes of prepositions—the first, whose origin from a substantive cannot be detected; the second, where an unknown and a known element are combined; the third, where the substantive is perfectly clear. An example of the last mentioned is *itic*, in, compounded of *ite*, belly, and the locative particle *c;* the phrase *ilhuicatl itic*, in heaven, is literally "in the belly of heaven." Precisely the same is the Cakchiquel *pamcah*, literally, "belly, heaven"=in heaven. In Mexican, *notepotzco* is "behind me," literally, "my back, at;" this corresponds again to the Cakchiquel *chuih*, behind me, from *chi*, at, *u*, my, *vih*, shoulder-blades. The Mixteca prepositions present the crude nature of their origin without disguise, *chisi huahi*, belly, house—that is, in front of the house; *sata huahi*, back, house—behind the house.

The conjunctions are equally transparent. "And" in

Maya is *yetel*, in Mexican *ihuan*. One would suppose that such an indispensable connective would long since have been worn down to an insoluble entity. On the contrary, both these words retain their perfect material meaning. *Yetel* is a compound of *y*, his, *et*, companion, and *el*, the definite termination of nouns. *Ihuan* is the possessive, *i*, and *huan*, associate companion, used also as a termination to form a certain class of plurals.

The deficiency in true conjunctions and relative pronouns is met in many American languages by a reversal of the plan of expression with us. The relative clause becomes the principal one. There is a certain logical justice in this; for if we reflect, it will appear evident that the major proposition is in our construction presented as one of the conditions of the minor. "I shall drown, if I fall in the water," means that, of the various results of my falling in the water, one of them will be that I shall drown. "I follow the road which you described," means that you described a road, and one of the results of this act of yours was that I follow it.

This explains the plan of constructing compound sentences in Qquichua. Instead of saying "I shall follow the road which you describe," the construction is, "You describe, this road I shall follow;" and instead of "I shall drown if I fall in the water," it would be, "I fall in the water, I shall drown."

The Mexican language introduces the relative clause by the word *in*, which is an article and demonstrative pronoun, or, if the proposition is a conditional one, by *intla*, which really signifies "within this," and conveys the sense that the major is included within the conditions of the minor clause.

The Cakchiquel conditional particle is *vue*, if, which appears to be simply the particle of affirmation "yes," employed to give extension to the minor clause, which, as a rule, is placed first.

Or a conventional arrangement of words may be adopted which will convey the idea of certain dependent clauses, as those expressing similitude, as is often the case in Mexican.

About 1822 Humboldt read a memoir before the Berlin Academy on "The American Verb," which remained unpublished either in German or English until I translated and printed it in the Proceedings of the American Philosophical Society in 1885. At its close he sums up his results, and this summary will form an appropriate conclusion to the present review of his labors in the field of American linguistics:

"If we reflect on the structure of the various verbal forms here analyzed, certain general conclusions are reached, which are calculated to throw light upon the whole organism of these languages.

"The leading and governing part of speech in them is the Pronoun; every subject of discourse is connected with the idea of Personality.

"Noun and Verb are not separated; they first become so through the pronoun attached to them.

"The employment of the Pronoun is two-fold, one applying to the Noun, the other to the Verb. Both, however, convey the idea of belonging to a person—in the noun appearing as Possession, in the verb as Energy. But it is on this point, on whether these ideas are confused and obscure, or whether they are defined and clear, that the grammatical perfection of a language depends. The just discrimination of the kinds of pronouns is therefore conclusive, and in this respect we must yield the decided pre-eminence to the Mexican.

"It follows that the speaker must constantly make up his verbs, instead of using those already on hand ; and also that the structure of the verb must be identical throughout the language, that there must be only one conjugation, and that the verbs, except a few irregular ones, can possess no peculiarities.

"This is different in the Greek, Latin and ancient Indian. In these tongues many verbs must be studied separately, as they have numerous exceptions, phonetic changes, deficiencies, etc., and in other respects carry with them a marked individuality.

"The difference between these cultivated and those rude languages is chiefly merely one of time, and of the more or less fortunate mixture of dialects; though it certainly also depends in a measure on the original mental powers of the nations.

"Those whose languages we have here analyzed are, in speaking, constantly putting together elementary parts ; they connect nothing firmly, because they follow the changing requirements of the moment, joining together only what these requirements demand, and often leave connected through habit that which clear thinking would necessarily divide.

"Hence no just division of words can arise, such as is demanded by accurate and appropriate thought, which requires that each word must have a fixed and certain content and a defined grammatical form, and as is also demanded by the highest phonetic laws.

"Nations richly endowed in mind and sense will have an instinct for such correct divisions ; the incessant moving to and fro of elementary parts of speech will be distasteful to them ; they will seek true individuality in the words they use ; therefore they will connect them firmly, they will not accumulate too much in one, and they will only leave that connected which is so in thought, and not merely in usage or habit."

SOME CHARACTERISTICS OF AMERICAN LANGUAGES.*

Contents.—Study of the human species on the geographic system—Have American languages any common trait?—Duponceau's theory of polysynthesis—Humboldt on Polysynthesis and Incorporation—Francis Lieber on Holophrasis—Prof. Steinthal on the incorporative plan—Lucien Adam's criticism of it—Prof. Müller's inadequate statement—Major Powell's omission to consider it—Definitions of polysynthesis, incorporation and holophrasis—Illustrations—Critical application of the theory to the Othomi language—To the Bri-bri language—To the Tupi-Guarani dialects—To the Mutsun—Conclusions—Addendum: critique by M. Adam on this essay.

AS the careful study of the position of man toward his surroundings advances, it becomes more and more evident that like other members of the higher fauna, he bears many and close correlations to the geographical area he inhabits. Hence the present tendency of anthropology is to return to the classification proposed by Linnæus, which, in a broad way, subdivides the human species with reference to the continental areas mainly inhabited by it in the earliest historic times. This is found to accord with color, and to give five sub-species or races, the White or European, the Black

---

* Read before the American Philosophical Society in 1885, and revised from the *Proceedings* of that year.

or African, the Yellow or Mongolian (Asiatic), the Brown or Malayan (Oceanic), and the Red or American Races.

No ethnologist nowadays will seek to establish fixed and absolute lines between these. They shade into one another in all their peculiarities, and no one has traits entirely unknown in the others. Yet, in the mass, the characteristics of each are prominent, permanent and unmistakable; and to deny them on account of occasional exceptions is to betray an inability to estimate the relative value of scientific facts.

Does this racial similarity extend to language? On the surface, apparently not. Only one of the races named—the Malayan—is monoglottic. All the others seem to speak tongues with no genetic relationship, at least none indicated by etymology. The profounder study of language, however, leads to a different conclusion—to one which, as cautiously expressed by a recent writer, teaches that "every large, connected, terrestrial area developed only one, or scarcely more than one, fundamental linguistic type, and this with such marked individuality that rarely did any of its languages depart from the general scheme."*

This similarity is not to be looked for in likeness between words, but in the inner structural development of tongues. To ascertain and estimate such identities is a far more delicate undertaking than to compare columns of words in vocabularies; but it is proportionately more valuable.

---

* "Diese thatsachen scheinen darauf hinzudeuten, dass jeder grössere in sich zusammenhängende ländercomplex nur einen oder doch nur ganz wenige sprachgrundtypen herausbildet, so eigenartig, dass selten eine sprache ganz aus dem allgemeinen rahmen heraustritt." Dr. Heinrich Winkler, *Uralaltaische Völker und Sprachen*, s. 147 (Berlin, 1884).

Nor should we expect it to be absolute. The example of the Basque in a pure white nation in Western Europe warns us that there are exceptions which, though they may find a historic explanation, forbid us all dogmatic assertion. They are so few, however, that I quote Dr. Winkler's words as the correct expression of the latest linguistic science, and I wish that some investigator would make it the motto of his study of American tongues.

The task—no light one—which such an investigator would have, would be, first to ascertain what structural traits form the ground plan or plans (if there are more than one) of the languages of the New World. Upon this ground-plan he would find very different edifices have been erected, which, nevertheless, can be classified into groups, each group marked by traits common to every member of it. These traits and groups he must carefully define. Then would come the separate question as to whether this community of traits has a genetic explanation or not. If the decision were affirmative, we might expect conclusions that would carry us much further than etymological comparisons, and might form a scientific basis for the classification of American nations.

Possibly some one or two features might be discovered which though not peculiar to American tongues, nor fully present in every one of them, yet would extend an influence over them all, and impart to them in the aggregate a certain aspect which could fairly be called distinctive. Such features are claimed to have been found in the grammatic processes of *polysynthesis* and *incorporation*.

Peter Stephen Duponceau, at one time President of the

American Philosophical Society, was the first to assert that there was a prevailing unity of grammatic schemes in American tongues. His first published utterance was in 1819, when he distinguished, though not with desirable lucidity, between the two varieties of synthetic construction, the one (incorporation) applicable to verbal forms of expression, the other (polysynthesis) to nominal expressions. His words are—

"A *polysynthetic* or *syntactic* construction of language is that in which the greatest number of ideas are comprised in the least number of words. This is done principally in two ways. 1. By a mode of compounding locutions which is not confined to joining two words together, as in Greek, or varying the inflection or termination of a radical word as in most European languages, but by interweaving together the most significant sounds or syllables of each simple word, so as to form a compound that will awaken in the mind at once all the ideas singly expressed by the words from which they are taken. 2. By an analogous combination [of] the various parts of speech, particularly by means of the verb, so that its various forms and inflections will express not only the principal action, but the greatest possible number of the moral ideas and physical objects connected with it, and will combine itself to the greatest extent with those conceptions which are the subject of other parts of speech, and in other languages require to be expressed by separate and distinct words. Such I take to be the general character of the Indian languages."*

---

* *Report of the Corresponding Secretary to the Committee, of his progress in the Investigation committed to him of the General Character and Forms of the Languages*

HUMBOLDT'S OPINION. 353

Duponceau's opinion found an able supporter in Wilhelm von Humboldt, who, as already shown, placed the American languages among those acting on the incorporative plan—*das Einverleibungssystem.* The spirit of this system he defines to be, "to impress the unity of the sentence on the understanding by treating it, not as a whole composed of various words, but as one word." A perfect type of incorporation will group all the elements of the sentence in and around the verbal, as this alone is the bond of union between the several ideas. The designation of time and manner, that is, the tense and mode signs, will include both the object and subject of the verb, thus subordinating them to the notion of action. It is "an indispensable basis" of this system that there should be a difference in the form of words when incorporated and when not. This applies in a measure to nouns and verbals, but especially to pronouns, and Humboldt names it as "the characteristic tendency" of American languages, and one directly drawn from their incorporative plan, that the personal pronouns, both subjective and objective, used in connection with the verbs, are of a different form from the independent personal pronouns, either greatly abbreviated or from wholly different roots. Outside of the verbal thus formed as the central point of the sentence, there is no syntax, no inflections, no declension of nouns or adjectives.*

Humboldt was far from saying that the incorporative

---

of the American Indians Read (12th Jan., 1819) in the *Transactions of the Historical and Literary Committee of the American Philosophical Society.* Vol. i, 1819, pp. xxx, xxxi.

* See *Ueber die Verschiedenheit*, etc., pp. 170-173, 325-6, etc.

system was exclusively seen in American languages, any more than that of isolation in Chinese, or flexion in Aryan speech. On the contrary, he distinctly states that every language he had examined shows traces of all three plans; but the preponderance of one plan over the other is so marked and so distinctive that they afford us the best means known for the morphological classification of languages, especially as these traits arise from psychological operations widely diverse, and of no small influence on the development of the intellect.

Dr. Francis Lieber, in an essay on "The Plan of Thought in American Languages,"* objected to the terms *polysynthesis* and *incorporation* that "they begin at the wrong end; for these names indicate that that which has been separated is put together, as if man began with analysis, whereas he ends with it." He therefore proposed the noun *holophrasis* with its adjective *holophrastic*, not as a substitute for the terms he criticised, but to express the meaning or purpose of these processes, which is, to convey the whole of a sentence or proposition in one word. Polysynthesis, he explains, indicates a purely etymological process, holophrasis " refers to the meaning of the word considered in a philosophical point of view."

If we regard incorporation and polysynthesis as structural processes of language aiming to accomplish a certain theoretical form of speech, then it will be convenient to have this word *holophrasis* to designate this theoretical

---

* Published in H. R. Schoolcraft's *History and Statistics of the Indian Tribes of the United States*. Vol. ii, pp. 346-349 (Washington, 1853).

form, which is, in short, the expression of the whole proposition in a single word.

The eminent linguist Professor H. Steinthal, has developed the theory of incorporation more fully than any other writer. He expresses himself without reserve of the opinion that all American languages are constructed on this same plan, more or less developed.

I need not make long quotations from a work so well-known as his *Charakteristik der hauptsächlichsten Typen des Sprachbaues*, one section of which, about thirty pages in length, is devoted to a searching and admirable presentation of the characteristics of the incorporative plan as shown in American languages. But I may give with brevity what he regards as the most striking features of this plan. These are especially three :—

1. The construction of words by a mixed system of derivation and new formation.

2. The objective relation is treated as a species of possession; and

3. The possessive relation is regarded as the leading and substantial one, and controls the form of expression.

The first of these corresponds to what I should call *polysynthesis;* the others to *incorporation* in the limited sense of the term.

Some special studies on this subject have been published by M. Lucien Adam, and he claims for them that they have refuted and overturned the thesis of Duponceau, Humboldt, and Steinthal, to the effect that there is a process called *incorporative* or *polysynthetic*, which can be traced in all American languages, and though not in all points confined to them, may fairly and profitably be taken as characteristic of them, and indicative of the psychological processes which underlie them. This opinion M. Adam speaks of as a "stereotyped phrase which is alsolutely false."*

So rude an iconoclasm as this must attract our careful consideration. Let us ask what M. Adam understands by the terms *polysynthesis* and *incorporation*. To our surprise, we shall find that in two works published in the same year, he advances definitions by no means identical. Thus, in his "Examination of Sixteen American Languages," he says, "*Polysynthesis* consists essentially in the affixing of subordinate personal pronouns to the noun, the preposition and the verb." In his "Study of Six Languages," he writes: "By *polysynthesis* I understand the expression in one word of the relations of cause and effect, or of subject and object."†

Certainly these two definitions are not convertible, and we are almost constrained to suspect that the writer who gives them was not clear in his own mind as to the nature of the process. At any rate, they differ widely from the plan or method set forth by Humboldt and Steinthal as characteristic of American languages. M. Adam in showing that

---

* " Je suis donc autorisé à conclure qu'il faut tenir pour absolument fausse cette proposition devenue faute d'y avoir regardé de près, une sorte de clichè: que si les langues Américaines diffèrent entre elles par la lexique, elles possedent néanmoins en commun une seule et même grammaire " *Examen grammatical comparé de seize langues Américaines*, in the Compte-rendu of the Congrès international des Américanistes, 1877, Tome ii, p. 242. As no one ever maintained the unity of American grammar outside of the *Einverleibungssystem*, it must be to this theory only that M. Adam alludes.

† *Etudes sur Six Langues Américaines*, p. 3 (Paris, 1878); and compare his *Examen Grammatical* above quoted, p. 74, 243.

polysynthesis in his understanding of the term is not confined to or characteristic of American tongues, missed the point, and fell into an *ignoratio elenchi*.

Equally narrow is his definition of incorporation. He writes, "When the object is intercalated between the subject and the verbal theme, there is *incorporation*." If this is to be understood as an explanation of the German expression, *Einverleibung*, then it has been pared down until nothing but the stem is left.

As to Dr. Lieber's suggestion of *holophrastic* as an adjective expressing the plan of thought at the basis of polysynthesis and incorporation, M. Adam summarily dismisses it as "a pedantic succedaneum" to our linguistic vocabulary.

I cannot acknowledge that the propositions so carefully worked up by Humboldt and Steinthal have been refuted by M. Adam; I must say, indeed, that the jejune significance he attaches to the incorporative process seems to show that he did not grasp it as a structural motive in language, and a wide-reaching psychologic process.

Professor Friedrich Müller, whose studies of American languages are among the most extended and profitable of the present time, has not given to this peculiar feature the attention we might reasonably expect. Indeed, there appears in the standard treatise on the science of language which he has published, almost the same vagueness as to the nature of incorporation which I have pointed out in the writings of M. Adam. Thus, on one page he defines incorporating languages as those which "do away with the distinction between the word and the sentence;" while on another he explains incorporation as "the including of the object within the body of the verb."* He calls it "a peculiarity of most American languages, but not of all." That the structural process of incorporation is by no means exhausted by the reception of the object within the body of the verb, even that this is not requisite to incorporation, I shall endeavor to show.

Finally, I may close this brief review of the history of these doctrines with a reference to the fact that neither of them appears anywhere mentioned in the official "Introduction to the Study of Indian Languages," issued by the United States Bureau of Ethnology! How the author of that work, Major J. W. Powell, Director of the Bureau, could have written a treatise on the study of American languages, and have not a word to say about these doctrines, the most salient and characteristic features of the group, is to me as inexplicable as it is extraordinary. He certainly could not have supposed that Duponceau's theory was completely dead and laid to rest, for Steinthal, the most eminent philosophic linguist of the age, still teaches in Berlin, and teaches what I have already quoted from him about these traits. What is more, Major Powell does not even refer to this structural plan, nor include it in what he terms the "grammatic processes" which he explains.† This is indeed the play of "Hamlet" with the part of Hamlet omitted!

I believe that for the scientific study of language, and especially of American languages, it will be profitable to restore and clearly to differentiate the distinction between

---

* *Grundriss der Sprachwissenschaft*, Von Dr. Friedrich Müller. Compare Bd. i., s. 68, und Bd. ii, s. 182.

† *Introduction to the Study of Indian Languages*. By J. W. Powell, p. 55, Second edition. Washington, 1880.

polysynthesis and incorporation, dimly perceived by Duponceau and expressed by him in the words already quoted. With these may be retained the neologism of Lieber, *holophrasis*, and the three defined as follows:

Polysynthesis is a method of word-building, applicable either to nominals or verbals, which not only employs juxtaposition with aphæresis, syncope, apocope, etc., but also words, forms of words and significant phonetic elements which have no separate existence apart from such compounds. This latter peculiarity marks it off altogether from the processes of agglutination and collocation.

Incorporation, *Einverleibung*, is a structural process confined to verbals, by which the nominal or pronominal elements of the proposition are subordinated to the verbal elements, either in form or position; in the former case having no independent existence in the language in the form required by the verb, and in the latter case being included within the specific verbal signs of tense and mood. In a fully incorporative language the verbal exhausts the syntax of the grammar, all other parts of speech remaining in isolation and without structural connection.

Holophrasis does not refer to structural peculiarities of language, but to the psychologic impulse which lies at the root of polysynthesis and incorporation. It is the same in both instances—the effort to express the whole proposition in one word. This in turn is instigated by the stronger stimulus which the imagination receives from an idea conveyed in one word rather than in many.

A few illustrations will aid in impressing these definitions on the mind.

As *polysynthetic* elements, we have the inseparable possessive pronouns which in many languages are attached to the names of the parts of the human body and to the words for near relatives; also the so-called "generic formatives," particles which are prefixed, suffixed, or inserted to indicate to what class or material objects belong; also the "numeral terminations" affixed to the ordinal numbers to indicate the nature of the objects counted; the negative, diminutive and amplificative particles which convey certain conceptions of a general character, and so on. These are constantly used in word-building, but are generally not words themselves, having no independent status in the language. They may be single letters, or even merely vowel-changes and consonantal substitutions; but they have well-defined significance.

In *incorporation* the object may be united to the verbal theme either as a prefix, suffix or infix; or, as in Nahuatl, etc., a pronominal representative of it may be thus attached to the verb, while the object itself is placed in isolated apposition.

The subject is usually a pronoun inseparably connected, or at least included within the tense-sign; to this the nominal subject stands in apposition. Both subjective and objective pronouns are apt to have a different form from either the independent personals or possessives, and this difference of form may be accepted as *a priori* evidence of the incorporative plan of structure—though there are other possible origins for it. The tense and mode signs are generally separable, and, especially in the compound tense, are seen to apply not only to the verb itself, but to the whole scope of its action, the tense sign for instance preceding the subject.

Some further observations will set these peculiarities in a yet clearer light.

Although in polysynthesis we speak of prefixes, suffixes, and juxtaposition, we are not to understand these terms as the same as in connection with the Aryan or with the agglutinative languages. In polysynthetic tongues they are not intended to form words, but sentences; not to express an idea, but a proposition. This is a fundamental logical distinction between the two classes of languages.

With certain prefixes, as those indicating possession, the form of the word itself alters, as in Mexican, *amatl*, book, *no*, mine, but *namauh*, my book. In a similar manner suffixes or post-positions affect the form of the words to which they are added.

As the holophrastic method makes no provision for the syntax of the sentence outside of the expression of action (*i. e.*, the verbal and what it embraces), nouns and adjectives are not declined. The "cases" which appear in many grammars of American languages are usually indications of space or direction, or of possession, and not case-endings in the sense of Aryan grammar.

. A further consequence of the same method is the absence of true relative pronouns, of copulative conjunctions, and generally of the machinery of dependent clauses. The devices to introduce subordinate propositions I have referred to in a previous essay (above, p. 346).

As the effort to speak in sentences rather than in words entails constant variation in these word-sentences, there arise both an enormous increase in verbal forms and a multiplication of expressions for ideas closely allied. This is the cause of the apparently endless conjugations of many such tongues, and also of the exuberance of their vocabularies in words of closely similar signification. It is an ancient error—which, however, I find repeated in the official "Introduction to the Study of Indian Languages," issued by our Bureau of Ethnology—that the primitive condition of languages is one "where few ideas are expressed by few words." On the contrary, languages structurally at the bottom of the scale have an enormous and useless excess of words. The savage tribes of the plains will call a color by three or four different words as it appears on different objects. The Eskimo has about twenty words for fishing, depending on the nature of the fish pursued. All this arises from the "holophrastic" plan of thought.

It will be seen from these explanations that the definition of Incorporation as given by M. Lucien Adam (quoted above) is erroneous, and that of Professor Müller is inadequate. The former reduces it to a mere matter of position or placement; the latter either does not distinguish it from polysynthesis, or limits it to only one of its several expressions.

In fact, Incorporation may take place with any one of the six possible modifications of the grammatical formula, "subject + verb + object." It is quite indifferent to its theory which of these comes first, which last; although the most usual formula is either,

$$\text{subject} + \text{object} + \text{verb, or,}$$
$$\text{object} + \text{subject} + \text{verb};$$

EXAMPLE OF NOUNS.

the verb being understood to be the verbal theme only—not its tense and mode signs. Where either of the above arrangements occurs, we may consider it to be an indication of the incorporative tendency; but as mere position is insufficient evidence, Incorporation may be present in other arrangements of the elements of the proposition.

As a fair example of polysynthesis in nouns, we may select the word for "cross" in the Cree. The Indians render it by "praying-stick" or "holy wood," and their word for "our praying-sticks" (crosses) is:

N"t'ayamihewâttikuminânak.

This is analyzed as follows:

n't', possessive pronoun, $\frac{1}{2}$ person plural.

ayami, something relating to religion.

he, indicative termination of the foregoing.

w, a connective.

âttik, suffix indicating wooden or of wood.

u, a connective.

m, sign of possession.

i, a connective.

nân, termination of $\frac{1}{3}$ person plural.

ak, termination of animate plural (the cross is spoken of as animate by a figure of speech).

Not a single one of the above elements can be employed as an independent word. They are all only the raw material to weave into and make up words.

As a characteristic specimen of incorporation we may select this Nahuatl word-sentence:

onictemacac,

I have given something to somebody:

which is analyzed as follows:

o, augment of the preterit, a tense sign.

ni, pronoun, subject, 1st person.

c, "semi-pronoun," object, 3d person.

te, "inanimate semi-pronoun," object, 3d person.

maca, theme of the verb, "to give."

c, suffix of the preterit, a tense sign.

Here it will be observed that between the tense-signs, which are logically the essential limitations of the action, are included both the agent and the near and remote objects of the action.

In the modifications of meaning they undergo, American verbal themes may be divided into two great classes, either as they express these modifications (1) by suffixes to an unchanging radical, or (2) by internal changes of their radical.

The last mentioned are most characteristic of synthetic tongues. In all pure dialects of the Algonkin the vowel of the verbal root undergoes a peculiar change called "flattening" when the proposition passes from the "positive" to the "suppositive" mood.* The same principle is strikingly illustrated in the Choctaw language, as the following example will show:*

takchi, to tie (active, definite).

takchi, to be tying (active, distinctive).

---

* This obscure feature in Algonkin Grammar has not yet been satisfactorily explained. Compare Baraga, *Grammar of the Otchipwe Language*, p. 116 (Montreal, 1878), and A. Lacombe, *Grammaire de la Langue des Cris*, p. 155 (Montreal, 1874).

† See *Grammar of the Chòctaw Languages*. By the Rev. Cyrus Byington. Edited by D. G. Brinton, pp. 35, 36 (Philadelphia, 1870).

tak'chi, to *tie* (active, emphatic).
taiakchi, to tie tightly (active, intesive).
tahakchi, to keep tying (active, frequentative).
tahkchi, to tie at once (active immediate).
tullakchi, to be tied (passive definite).
tallakchi, to be the one tied (passive distinctive), etc., etc.

This example is, however, left far behind by the Qquichua of Peru, which by a series of so-called "verbal particles" affixed to the verbal theme confers an almost endless variety of modification on its verbs. Thus Anchorena in his Grammar gives the form and shades of meaning of 675 modifications of the verb *munay*, to love.*

These verbal particles are not other words, as adverbs, etc., qualifying the meaning of the verb and merely added to it, but have no independent existence in the language. Von Tschudi, whose admirable analysis of this interesting tongue cannot be too highly praised, explains them as "verbal roots which never reached independent development, or fragments handed down from some earlier epoch of the evolution of the language."† They are therefore true synthetic elements in the sense of Duponceau's definition, and not at all examples of collocation or juxtaposition.

While the genius of American languages is such that they permit and many of them favor the formation of long compounds which express the whole of a sentence in one word, this is by no means necessary. Most of the examples of words of ten, twenty or more syllables are not genuine

---

* *Gramática Quechua, ó del Idioma del Imperio de los Incas.* Por el Dr. José Dionisio Anchorena, pp. 163-177 (Lima, 1874).

† *Organismus der Khetsua-Sprache.* Von J. J. von Tschudi, p. 368 (Leipzig, 1884).

native words, but novelties manufactured by the missionaries. In ordinary intercourse such compounds are not in use, and the speech is comparatively simple.

Of two of the most synthetic languages, the Algonkin and the Nahuatl, we have express testimony from experts that they can be employed in simple or compound forms, as the speaker prefers. The Abbé Lacombe observes that in Cree "sometimes one can employ very long words to express a whole phrase, although the same ideas can be easily rendered by periphrasis."* In the syllabus of the lectures on the Nahuatl by Prof. Agustin de la Rosa, of the University of Guadalaxara, I note that he explains when the Nahuatl is to be employed in a synthetic, and when in an analytic form.†

I shall now proceed to examine those American tongues which have been authoritatively declared to be exceptions to the general rules of American grammar, as being devoid of the incorporative and polysynthetic character.

THE OTHOMI.‡

As I have said, the Othomi was the stumbling block of

---

* "Ces exemples font comprendre combien quelquefois on peut rendre des mots tres longs, pour exprimer tonte une phrase, quoiqn' aussi on puisse facilement rendre les mêmes idées par des périphrases." Lacombe, *Grammaire de la Langue des Cris*, p. 11 (Montreal, 1874).

† "Se explicara la razon filosófica de los dos modos de usar las palabras en Mexicano, uno componiendo de varias palabras uno solo, y otro dejandolas separadas y enlazandolas solo por regimen." From the programme of Prof. A. de la Rosa's course in 1870.

‡ The original authorities I have consulted on the Othomi are:
Reglas de Orthographia, Diccionario, y Arte del Idioma Othomi. By Luis de Neve y Molina (Mexico, 1767).
De Lingua Othomitorum Dissertatio. By Emmanuel Naxera (Philadelphia, 1835).
Catecismo en Lengua Otomi. By Francisco Perez (Mexico, 1834).

Mr. Duponceau, and led him to abandon his theory of polysythesis as a characteristic of American tongues. Although in his earlier writings he expressly names it as one of the illustrations suporting his theory, later in life the information he derived from Señor Emmanuel Naxera led him to regard it as an isolating and monosyllabic language, quite on a par with the Chinese. He expressed this change of view in the frankest manner, and since that time writers have spoken of the Othomi as a marked exception in structure to the general rules of synthesis in American tongues. This continues to be the case even in the latest writings, as, for instance, in the recently published *Anthropologie du Mexique*, of Dr. Hamy.*

Let us examine the grounds of this opinion.

The Othomis are an ancient and extended family, who from the remotest traditional epochs occupied the central valleys and mountains of Mexico north of the Aztecs and Tezcucans. Their language, called by themselves *nhiân*

---

* He speaks of the Othomi in these terms:—"Une langue aux allures toutes spéciales, fondamentalement distincte de toutes les langues qni se parlent aujourd' hui sur le continent américain." *Mission Scientifique au Mexique*, Pt. i. Anthropologie, p. 32 (Paris, 1884). This is the precise opinion, strongly expressed, that it is my object to controvert. Many other writers have maintained it. Thus Count Piccolomini in the *Prolegomena* to his version of Neve's Othomi Grammar says: "La loro lingua che con nessuna altra del mondo conosciuto ha la menoma analogia, è semplice. * * * La formazione dei loro verbi, nomi ed altri derivati ha molta semplecità," etc. *Grammatica della Lingua Otomi*, p. 3 (Roma, 1841). This writer also offers an illustration of how imperfectly Duponceau's theory of polysynthesis has been understood. Not only does Piccolomini deny it for the Otomi, but he denies that it is anything more than merely running several words together with some phonetic syncopation. See the *Annotations* at the close of his Othomi Grammar, *hiû*, the fixed or current speech* (*nhiân*, speech, *hiû*, stable, fixed), presents extraordinary phonetic difficulties on account of its nasals, gutturals and explosives.

It is one of a group of related dialects which may be arranged as follows:

- The Othomi.
- The Mazahua.
- The Pame and its dialects.
- The Meco or Jonaz.

It was the opinion of M. Charencey, that another member of this group was the Pirinda or Matlazinca; a position combatted by Señor Pimentel, who acknowledges some common property in words, but considers them merely borrowed.†

Naxera made the statement that the Mazahua is monosyllabic, an error in which his copyists have obediently followed him; but Pimentel pointedly contradicts this assertion and shows that it is a mistake, both for the Mazahua and for the Pame and its dialects.‡

We may begin our study of the language with an examination of the

TENSE-SIGNS IN OTHOMI.

PRESENT TENSE.

1. I wish,   *di nee.*
2. Thou wishest, *gui nee.*
3. He wishes,   *y nee.*

---

* This is the orthography of Neve. The terminal vowels are both nasals; *nhian* is from the radical *hiâ*, to breathe, breath.

† See the "Comparacion del Othomi con el Mazahna y el Pirinda," in the *Cuadro Descriptivo y Comparativo de las Lenguas Indigenas de México*, por Francisco Pimentel. Tomo iii, pp. 431-445 (Mexico, 1875).

‡ See Pimentel, *Cuadro Descriptivo*, etc. Tomo iii, pp. 426 and 455.

PAST AORIST.

1. I wished, *da nee.*
2. Thou wished, *ga nee.*
3. He wished, *bi nee.*

PERFECT.

1. I have wished, *xta nee.*
2. Thou hast wished, *xca nee.*
3. He has wished, *xpi nee.*

PLUPERFECT.

1. I had wished, *xta nee hma.*
2. Thou hadst wished, *xca nee hma.*
3. He had wished, *xpi nee hma.*

FIRST FUTURE.

1. I shall wish, *ga nee.*
2. Thou wilt wish, *gui nee.*
3. He will wish, *da nee.*

SECOND FUTURE.

1. I shall have wished, *gua xta nee.*
2. Thou wilt have wished, *gua xca nee.*
3. He will have wished, *gua xpi nee.*

The pronouns here employed are neither the ordinary personals nor possessives (though the Othomi admits of a possessive conjugation), but are verbal pronouns, strictly analogous to those found in various other American languages. The radicals are:

I, *d—.*
Thou, *g—.*
He, it, *b—.*

In the present, the first and second are prefixed to what is really the simple concrete form of the verb, *y-nee*. In the past tenses the personal signs are variously united with particles denoting past time or the past, as *a*, the end, to finish, *ma* and *hma*, yesterday, and the prefix *x*, which is very noteworthy as being precisely the same in sound and use which we find in the Cakchiquel past and future tenses. It is pronounced *sh* (as in *sh*ove) and precedes the whole verbal, including subject, object, and theme; while in the pluperfect, the second sign of past time *hma* is a suffix to the collective expression.

The future third person is given by Neve as *da*, but by Perez as *di*, which latter is apparently from the future particle *ni* given by Neve. In the second future, the distinctive particle *gua* precedes the whole verbal, thus inclosing the subject with the theme in the tense-sign, strictly according to the principles of the incorporative conjugation.

This incorporative character is still more marked in the objective conjugations, or "transitions." The object, indeed, follows the verb, but is not only incorporated with it, but in the compound tense is included within the double tense signs.

Thus, I find in Perez's Catechism,

di   *ûn-ba*   *magetzi*,
He will   give-them   heaven.

In this sentence, *di* is the personal pronoun combined with the future sign; and the verb is *ûn-ni*, to give to another, which is compounded with the personal *ba*, them, drops its final syllable, forming a true synthesis.

In the phrase,

xpi   *ûn-ba*   *hma*   *magetzi*,
he had   give them   (had)   heaven,

both subject and object, the latter inclosed in a synthesis with the radical of the theme, the former phonetically altered and coalesced with a tense particle, are included in the double tense-sign, *x-hma*. This is as real an example of incorporation as can be found in any American language.

Ordinary synthesis of words, other than verbs, is by no means rare in Othomi. Simple juxtaposition, which Naxera states to be the rule, is not all universal. Such a statement by him leads us to suspect that he had only that elementary knowledge of the tongue which Neve refers to in a forcible passage in his *Reglas*. He writes: "A good share of the difficulty of this tongue lies in its custom of syncope; and because the tyros who make use of it do not syncopate it, their compositions are so rough and lacking in harmony to the ears of the natives that the latter count their talk as no better than that of horse-jockeys, as we would say."*

The extent of this sycopation is occasionally to such a degree that only a fragment of the original word is retained. As:

> The charcoal-vendor, *na māthiâ*.

Here *na* is a demonstrative particle like the Aztec *in*, and *māthiâ* is a compound of *pà*, to sell, and *théhñâ*, charcoal.

The expression,

> *y mahny oqha*, he loves God,

is to be analyzed,

---

* "Parte de la dificultad de este idioma consiste en la syncopa, pues el no syncopar los principiantes artistas, es causa de que sus periodos y oraciones sean tan rispidos, y faltos de harmonia, por cuyo motivo los nativos los murmuran, y tienen (como vulgarmente decimos), por quartreros." *Reglas de Orthographia*, etc., p. 146.

y *mâhdi* *nuny* *oqha;*
he   loves   him   God;

where we perceive not only synthesis, but the object standing in apposition to the pronoun representing it which is incorporated with the verb.

So: *yot-gua*, light here; from *yotti*, to light, *nugua*, here.

These examples from many given in Neve's work seem to me to prove beyond cavil that the Othomi exhibits, when properly spoken, precisely the same theories of incorporation and polysynthesis as the other American languages, although undoubtedly its more monosyllabic character and the extreme complexity of its phonetics do not permit of a development of these peculiarities to the same degree as many.

Nor am I alone in this opinion. It has already been announced by the Count de Charencey, as the result of his comparison of this tongue with the Mazahua and Pirinda. "The Othomi," he writes, "has all the appearance of a language which was at first incorporative, and which, worn down by attrition and linguistic decay, has at length come to simulate a language of juxtaposition."*

Some other peculiarities of the language, though not directly bearing on the question, point in the same direction. A certain class of compound verbs are said by Neve to have a possessive declension. Thus, of the two words *puengui*, he draws, and *hiâ*, breath, is formed the verb *buehiâ*, which is conjugated by using the verb in the indefinite third per-

---

* "L'Othomi nous a tout l'air d'une langue primitivement incorporante, et qui, parvenu au dernier degré d'usure et délabrement, a fini par prendre les allures d'un dialecte à juxtaposition." *Mélanges de Philologie et de Paléographie Américaine.* Par le Comte de Charencey, p. 80 (Paris, 1883).

son and inserting the possessives *ma, ni, na,* my, thy, his; thus,

>*ybuemahia*, I breathe.
>*ybuenihia*, thou breathest.
>*ybuenahia*, he breathes.*

Literally this would be "it-is-drawing, my breath," etc.

In the Mazahua dialects there is a remarkable change in the objective conjugations (transitions) where the whole form of the verb appears to alter. In this language $ti =$ I; *ki* or *khe* = thou.

>I give, *ti une*.
>I give thee, *ti dakke*.
>He will give us, *ti yakme*.†

The last example is not fully explained by my authorities; but it shows the verbal change.

Something like this occurs in the Pame dialects. They reveal a manifest indifference to the integrity of the theme, characteristic of polysynthetic languages. Thus, our only authority on the Pame, Father Juan Guadalupe Soriano, gives the preterit forms of the verb "to aid:"

>*Ku pait*, I aided.
>*Ki gait*, thou aidedest.
>*Ku mait*, he aided.

So, of "to burn:"

>*Knu aum*, I burned.
>*Kuddu du taum*, they burned.‡

A large number of such changes run through the conjuga-

---

* Neve, *Reglas* etc., pp. 159, 160.

† Pimentel, *Cuadro Descriptivo*, Tom. iii, p. 424.

‡ Pimentel, *Cuadro Descriptivo*, Tomo iii, p. 462.

tion. Pimentel calls them phonetic changes, but they are certainly, in some instances, true syntheses.

All these traits of the Othomi and its related dialects serve to place them unquestionably within the general plan of structure of American languages.

THE BRI-BRI LANGUAGE.

The late Mr. Wm. M. Gabb, who was the first to furnish any satisfactory information about it and its allied dialects in Costa Rica, introduces the Bri-Bri language, spoken in the highlands of that State, by quoting the words of Alexander von Humboldt to the effect that "a multiplicity of tenses characterizes the rudest American languages." On this, Mr. Gabb comments: "This certainly does not apply to the Costa Rican family, which is equally remarkable for the simplicity of its inflections."*

This statement, offered with such confidence, has been accepted and passed on without close examination by several unusually careful linguists. Thus Professor Friedrich Müller, in his brief description of the Bri-Bri (taken exclusively from Gabb's work), inserts the observation—"The simple structure of this idiom is sufficient to contradict the theories generally received about American languages."† And M. Lucien Adam has lately instanced its verbs as notable examples of inflectional simplicity.‡ The

---

* Wm. M. Gabb, *On the Indian Tribes and Languages of Costa Rica*, in the Proceedings of the American Philosophical Society for 1875, p. 532.

† "Dessen einfacher Bau die über die Amerikanischen Sprachen im Allgemeinen verbreiteten Theorien zu widerlegen im Stande ist." *Grundriss der Sprachwissenschaft*, ii Band, s. 318 (Wien, 1882).

‡ *Le Taensa a-t-il été forgé de toutes Pièces?* Réponse à M. Daniel G. Brinton, Par Lucien Adam, p. 19 (Paris, Maisonneuve et Cie, 1885).

study of this group of tongues becomes, therefore, of peculiar importance to my present topic.

Since Mr. Gabb published his memoir, some independent material, grammatical as well as lexicographical, has been furnished by the Rt. Rev. B. A. Thiel, Bishop of Costa Rica,* and I have obtained, in addition, several MS. vocabularies and notes on the language prepared by Prof. P. J. J. Valentini and others.

The stock is divided into three groups of related dialects, as follows:—

I. The Brunka, Bronka or Boruca, now in southwestern Costa Rica, but believed by Gabb to have been the earliest of the stock to occupy the soil, and to have been crowded out by later arrivals.

II. The Tiribi and Terraba, principally on the head-waters of the Rio Telorio and south of the mountains.

III. The Bri-Bri and Cabecar on the head-waters of the Rio Tiliri. The Biceitas (Vizeitas) or Cachis, near the mouth of the same stream, are off-shoots of the Bri-Bris; so also are the small tribes at Orosi and Tucurrique, who were removed to those localities by the Spaniards.

The Bri-Bri and Cabecar, although dialects of the same original speech, are not sufficiently alike to be mutually intelligible. The Cabecars occupied the land before the Bri-Bris, but were conquered and are now subject to them. It is probable that their dialect is more archaic.

The Bri-Bri is a language of extreme poverty, and as

---

* *Apuntes Lexicograficos de las Lenguas y Dialectos de los Indios de Costa-Rica*. Por Bernardo Augusto Thiel, Obispo de Costa-Rica, (San José de Costa-Rica, 1882. Imprenta Nacional).

spoken at present is plainly corrupt. Gabb estimates the whole number of words it contains as probably not exceeding fifteen hundred. Some of these, though Gabb thinks not very many, are borrowed from the Spanish; but it is significant, that among them is the pronoun "that," the Spanish *ese*.

Let us now examine the Bri-Bri verb, said to be so singularly simple. We are at once struck by Mr. Gabb's remark (just after he has been speaking of their unparalleled simplicity) that the inflections he gives "have been verified with as much care as the difficulties of the case would admit." Evidently, then, there were difficulties. What they are, becomes apparent when we attempt to analyze the forms of the eighteen brief paradigms which he gives.

The personal pronouns are

je, I.   *sa*, we.
be, thou.   *ha*, you.
ye, he, etc.   *ye-pa*, they.

These are both nominative and objective, personal and, with the suffix *cha*, possessives.

The tenses are usually, not always, indicated by suffixes to the theme; but these vary, and no rule is given for them, nor is it stated whether the same theme can be used with them all. Thus,

To burn, *i-norka*,   Present, *i-nyor-ket-ke*.
To cook, *i-lu'*.   "   *i-luk*.
To start, *i-be-te*.   "   *i-be-te*.

Here are three forms for the present, not explained. Are they three conjugations, or do they express three shades of meaning, like the three English presents? I suspect the latter, for under *ikiana*, to want, Gabb remarks that the form in *-etke*, means "he *wants* you," *i. e.*, is emphatic.

The past aorist has two terminations, one in *-na*, and one in *-e*, about the uses and meanings of which we are left equally in the dark.

The future is utterly inexplicable. Even Prof. Müller, just after his note calling attention to the "great simplicity" of the tongue, is obliged to give up this tense with the observation, "the structural laws regulating the formation of the future are still in obscurity!" Was it not somewhat premature to dwell on the simplicity of a tongue whose simplest tenses he acknowledges himself unable to analyze?

The futures of some verbs will reveal the difficulties of this tense:—

To burn, *i-nyor-ka;*   future, *i-nyor-wanc-ka.*
To cook, *i-lu';*   "   *i-lu'.*
To start, *i-bete;*   "   *i-bete.*
To want, *i-ki-ana;*   "   *i-kie.*
To count, *ishtaung;*   "   *mia shta'we.*

In the last example *mia* is the future of the verb *imia*, to go, and is used as an auxiliary.

The explanation I have to suggest for these varying forms is, either that they represent in fact that very "multiplicity of tense-formations" which Humboldt alluded to, and which were too subtle to be apprehended by Mr. Gabb within the time he devoted to the study of the language; or that they are in modern Bri-Bri, which I have shown is noticeably corrupted, survivals of these formations, but are now largely disregarded by the natives themselves.

Signs of the incorporative plan are not wanting in the

tongue. Thus in the objective conjugation not only is the object placed between subject and verb, but the latter may undergo visible synthetic changes. Thus:

>Je be sueng.
>I thee see.
>Ke je be wai su-na.
>Not I thee (?) see-did.

In the latter sentence *na* is the sign of the past aorist, and the verb in synthesis with it drops its last syllable. The *wai* Gabb could not explain. It will be noticed that the negative precedes the whole verbal form, thus indicating that it is treated as a collective idea (holophrastically).

Prepositions always appear as suffixes to nouns, which, in composition, may suffer elision. This is strictly similar to the Nahuatl and other synthetic tongues.

Other examples of developed synthesis are not uncommon, as—

>away, *imibak*, from *imia* to go, *jebak*, already.
>very hot, *palina*, from *ba* + *ilinia*.

The opinion that the Bri-Bri is at present a considerably corrupted and worn-down dialect of a group of originally highly synthetic tongues is borne out by an examination of the scanty materials we have of its nearest relations.

Thus in the Terraba we find the same superfluous richness of pronominal forms which occurs in many South American tongues, one indicating that the person is sitting, another that he is standing, a third that he is walking.*

The Brunka has several distinct forms in the present tense:

>I eat, *cha adeh*, and *atqui chan* (*atqui* = I).

---

*Gabb, ubi suprá, p. 539.

Although Bishop Thiel supplies a number of verbal forms from this dialect, the plan of their construction is not obvious. This is seen from a comparison of the present and perfect tenses in various words. The pronouns are—

For instance:
1 { *atqui*, I.
3 { *ique*, he.

BRUNKA VERBAL FORMS.

To kill (radical, *ai*).
Present, I kill, *cha atqui i aira*.
Perfect, he has killed, *iang i aic*.
To die (radical, *cojt*).
Present, I die, *còjo drah*.
Perfect, he has died, *cojt crah*.
To hear (radical, *dòj*).
Present, I hear, *aari dòj ograh*.
Perfect, I have heard, *aqui dòj crah*.
To forget.
Present, I forget, *asqui chita uringera*.
Perfect, I have forgotten, *ochita uringea*.

These examples are sufficient to show that the Brunka conjugations are neither regular nor simple, and such is the emphatic statement of Bishop Thiel, both of it and all these allied dialects. In his introduction he states that he is not yet ready to offer a grammar of these tongues, though well supplied with lexicographical materials, and that "*their verbs are especially difficult.*"*

---

* " Especial dificultad ofrecen los verbos." *Apuntes Lexicograficos*, etc. Introd. p. iv. This expression is conclusive as to the incorrectness of the opinion of M. Adam, and Prof. Müller above quoted, and shows how easily even justly eminent

The Cabecar dialect, in which he gives several native funeral poems, without translations, is apparently more complicated than the Bri-Bri. The words of the songs are long and seem much syncopated.

THE TUPI-GUARANI DIALECTS.

Several writers of the highest position have asserted that these dialects, spoken over so large a portion of the territory of Brazil, are neither polysynthetic nor incorporative. Thus the late Prof. Charles F. Hartt in his "Notes on the Lingoa Geral or Modern Tupi," expressed himself: "Unlike the North American Indian tongues, the languages of the Tupi-Guarani family are not polysynthetic in structure."* With scarcely less positiveness Professor Fredrich Müller writes: "The objective conjugation of the Tupi-Guarani does not show the incorporation usually seen in American languages, but rather a mere collocation."†

It is, I acknowledge, somewhat hazardous to venture an opinion contrary to such excellent authorities. But I must say, that while, no doubt, the Tupi in its structure differs widely from the Algonkin or Nahuatl, it yet seems to present unmistakable signs of an incorporative and polysynthetic character, such as would be difficult to parallel outside of America.

I am encouraged to maintain this by the recent example of the erudite Dr. Amaro Cavalcanti, himself well and prac-

---

linguists may fall into error about tongues of which they have limited means of knowledge. The proper course in such a case is evidently to be cautious about venturing positive assertions.

* *Transactions of the American Philological Association*, 1872, p. 58.

† *Grundriss der Sprachwissenschaft*, Bd. ii, p. 387.

tically versed in the spoken Tupi of to-day, who has issued a learned treatise to prove that "the Brazilian dialects present undoubtedly all the supposed characteristics of an agglutinative language, and belong to the same group as the numerous other dialects or tongues of America."* Dr. Cavalcanti does not, indeed, distinguish so clearly between agglutinative and incorporative languages as I should wish, but the trend of his work is altogether parallel to the arguments I am about to advance.

Fortunately, we do not suffer from a lack of materials to study the Tupi, ancient and modern. There are plenty of dictionaries, grammars and texts in it, and even an "Ollendorff's Method." for those who prefer that intellectual (!) system.†

All recent writers agree that the modern Tupi has been materially changed by long contact with the whites. The traders and missionaries have exerted a disintegrating effect on its ancient forms, to some of which I shall have occasion to refer.

---

* *The Brazilian Language and its Agglutination.* By Amaro Cavalcanti, LL. B., etc., p. 5 (Rio Janeiro, 1883).

† The most valuable for linguistic researches are the following :

Arte de Grammatica da Lingua mais usada na Costa do Brazil. By Joseph de Anchieta. This is the oldest authority, Anchieta having commenced as missionary to the Tupis in 1556.

Arte, Vocabulario y Tesoro de la Lengua Guarani, ó mas bien Tupi. By Antonio Ruiz de Montoya. An admirable work representing the southern Tupi as it was in the first half of the seventeenth century.

Both the above have been republished in recent years. Of modern writings I would particularly name :

Apontamentos sobre o Abañeénga tambem chamado Guarani ou Tupi. By Dr. B. C. D'A. Nogueira (Rio Janeiro, 1876).

O Selvagem i Curso da Lingua Geral. By Dr. Couto de Magalhaes (Rio de Janeiro, 1876).

Turning our attention first to its synthetic character, one cannot but be surprised after reading Prof. Hartt's opinion above quoted to find him a few pages later introducing us to the following example of "word-building of a more than usually polysynthetic character."*

akáyu, head; *ayú*, bad.

akayayú, crazy.

muakayayu, to seduce (make crazy).

xayumuakayayú, I make myself crazy, etc.

Such examples, however, are not rare, as may be seen by turning over the leaves of Montoya's *Tesoro de la Lengua Guarani*. The most noticeable and most *American* peculiarity of such compounds is that they are not collocations of words, as are the agglutinative compounds of the Ural-Altaic tongues, but of particles and phonetic elements which have no separate life in the language.

Father Montoya calls special attention to this in the first words of his *Advertencia* to his *Tesoro*. He says:—"The foundation of this language consists of particles which frequently have no meaning if taken alone; but when compounded with the whole or parts of others (for they cut them up a great deal in composition) they form significant expressions; for this reason there are no independent verbs in the language, as they are built up of these particles with nouns or pronouns. Thus, *ñemboé* is composed of the three particles *ñe, mo, e*. The *ñe* is reciprocal; *mo* an active particle; *e* indicates skill; and the whole means 'to exercise oneself,' which we translate, 'to learn,' or 'to teach,' indeterminately; but with the personal sign added, *anemboe*, 'I learn.'"

---

* *Notes on the Lingoa Geral*, as above, p. 71.

This analysis, which Montoya carries much further, reminds us forcibly of the extraordinarily acute analysis of the Cree (Algonkin) by Mr. James Howse.* Undoubtedly the two tongues have been built up from significant particles (not words) in the same manner.

Some of these particles convey a peculiar turn to the whole sentence, difficult to express in our tongues. Thus the element *é* attached to the last syllable of a compound gives an oppositive sense to the whole expression; for example, *ajur*, "I come" simply; but if the question follows: "Who ordered you to come?" the answer might be, *ajuré*, "I come of my own accord; nobody ordered me."†

Cavalcanti observes that many of these formative elements which existed in the old Tupi have now fallen out of use.‡ This is one of several evidences of a change in structure in the language, a loss of its more pliable and creative powers.

This synthesis is also displayed in the Tupi, as in the Cree, by the inseparable union of certain nouns with pronouns. The latter are constantly united with terms of consanguinity and generally with those of members of the body, the form of the noun undergoing material modifications. Thus:

tete, body; *cete*, his body; *xerete*, my body.
tuba, father; *oguba*, his father; *xerub*, my father.
mymbaba, domestic animal; *gueymba*, his domestic animal,
tera, name; *guera*, his name.

---

*James Howse, *A Grammar of the Cree Language* (London, 1844). A remarkable production which has never received the attention from linguists which it merits.

†Anchieta, *Arte de Grammatica*, etc., p. 75.

‡ *The Brazilian Language*, etc., pp. 48-9.

Postpositions are in a similar manner sometimes merged into the nouns or pronouns which they limit. Thus: *tenonde*, before ; *guenonde*, before him.

It appears to me that the substratum, the structural theory, of such a tongue is decidedly polysynthetic and not agglutinative, still less analytic.

Let us now inquire whether there are any signs of the incorporative process in Tupi.

We are at once struck with the peculiarity that there are two special sets of pronouns used with verbals, one set subjective, and the other objective, several of which *cannot be employed in any other construction.** This is almost diagnostic of the holophrastic method of speech. The pronouns in such cases are evidently regarded by the language-faculty as subordinate accessories to the verbal, and whether they are phonetically merged in it or not is a secondary question.

The Tupi pronouns (confining myself to the singular number for the sake of brevity) are as follows:

		Verbal affixes.	
Independent personals.	Possessives.	Subject.	Object.
ixe or *xe*.	*se* or *xe*.	*a*.	*xe*.
inde or *ne*.	*ne* or *re*.	*re, yepe*.	*oro*.
ae or *o*.	*ae* or *i*.	*o*.	*ae* or *i*.

The verbal affixes are united to the theme with various phonetic changes, and so intimately as to form one word. The grammars give such example as:—

areco, I hold ;   *guereco*, they hold him.
ahcnoi, I call ;   *xerenoi*, they call me.
ayaca, I dispute him ;   *oroaca*, I dispute thee.

---

* See Anchieta, *Arte de Grammatica*, etc., p. 52.

In the first person singular, the two pronominal forms *xe* and *a* are usually merged in the synthesis *xa;* as *xamehen*, I love.

Another feature pointing to the incorporative plan is the location of the object. The rule in the old language was to place the object in all instances *before* the verb, that is, between the verb and its subject when the latter was other than a personal suffix. Dr. Cavalcanti says that this is now in a measure changed, so that when the object is of the third person it is placed after the verb, although in the first and second persons the old rule still holds good.* Thus the ancient Tupis would say:

> *boia aè o-sou,*
> snake him he-bites.

But in the modern tongue it is:

> *boia o-sou aé*
> snake he-bites him.

With the other persons the rule is still for the object to precede and to be attached to the theme:

> *xeoroinca*, I thee kill.
> *xepeinca*, I you kill.
> *xeincayepe*, me killest thou.

Many highly complex verbal forms seem to me to illustrate a close incorporative tendency. Let us analyze for instance the word,

> *xeremimboe*,

which means "him whom I teach" or "that which I teach." Its theme is the verbal *mboe*, which in the extract

---

* *The Brazilian Language*, etc., p. 111.

I have above made from Montoya is shown to be a synthesis of the three elementary particles *ñe*, *mo*, and *e*; *xe* is the possessive form of the personal pronoun, "my"; it is followed by the participial expression *temi* or *tembi*, which, according to Montoya, is equivalent to "illud quod facio;" its terminal vowel is syncopated with the relative *y* or *i*, "him, it"; so the separate parts of the expression are:—

$$xe+tembi+y+ñe+mo+e.$$

I shall not pursue the examination of the Tupi further. It were, of course, easy to multiply examples. But I am willing to leave the case as it stands, and to ask linguists whether, in view of the above, it was not a premature judgment that pronounced it a tongue neither polysynthetic nor incorporative.

THE MUTSUN.

This is also one of the languages which has been announced as "neither polysynthetic nor incorporative," and the construction of its verb as "simple to the last degree."*

We know the tongue only through the Grammar and Phrase-Book of Father de la Cuesta, who acknowledges himself to be very imperfectly acquainted with it.† With its associated dialects, it was spoken near the site of the present city of San Francisco, California.

---

* "Kein polysynthesis und keine incorporation," says Dr. Heinrich Winkler (*Uralaltaische Völker und Sprachen*, p. 149), who apparently has obtained all his knowledge of it from the two pages devoted to it by Professor Friedrich Müller, who introduces it as "äusserst einfach." *Grundriss der Sprachwissenschaft*, Bd. ii, p. 257.

† *Grammatica Mutsun* ; Por el R. P. F. F. Arroyo de la Cuesta ; and *Vocabulario Mutsun*, by the same, both in Shea's "Library of American Linguistics."

Looking first at the verb, its "extreme simplicity" is not so apparent as the statements about it would lead us to expect.

In the first place, the naked verbal theme undergoes a variety of changes by insertion and suffixes, like those of the Quiche and Qquechua, which modify its meaning. Thus:

Ara, to give.
Arsa, to give to many, or to give much.
Arapu, to give to oneself.
Arasi, to order to give, etc., etc.

Again:

Oio, to catch.
Oiñi, to come to catch.
Oimu, to catch another, etc.

The author enumerates thirty-one forms thus derived from each verb, some conjugated like it, some irregularly. With regard to tenses, he gives eight preterits and four futures; and it cannot be said that they are formed simply by adding adverbs of time, as the theme itself takes a different form in several of them, *aran*, *aras*, *aragts*, etc. In the reflexive conjugation the pronoun follows the verb and is united with it: As,

aragneca, I give myself,

where *ca* is a suffixed form of *can*, I ; *ne* represents *nenissia*, oneself; the *g* is apparently a connective; and the theme is *ara*. This is quite in the order of the polysynthetic theory and is also incorporative.

Such syntheses are prominent in imperative forms. Thus from the above-mentioned verb, *oio*, to catch, we have,

> *oiomityuts*, Gather thou for me, .

in which *mit* is apparently the second person *men*, with a postposition *tsa*, *mintsa;* while *yuts* is a verbal fragment from *yuyuts*, which the author explains to mean "to set about," or "to get done." This imperative, therefore, is a verbal noun in synthesis with an interjection, "get done with thy gathering." It is a marked case of polysynthesis. A number of such are found in the Mutsun phrases given, as :

> *Rugemitithsyuts cannis*, Give me arrows.

In this compound *cannis*, is for *can* + *huas*, me + for; *yuts* is the imperative interjection for *yuyuts;* the remainder of the word is not clear. The phrase is given elsewhere

> *Rugemitit*, Give (thou) me arrows.

Without going further into this language, of which we know so little, it will be evident that it is very far from simple, and that it is certainly highly synthetic in various features.

CONCLUSIONS.

The conclusions to which the above study leads may be briefly summarized as follows:

1. The structural processes of incorporation and polysynthesis are much more influential elements in the morphology of language than has been conceded by some recent writers.

2. They are clearly apparent in a number of American languages where their presence has been heretofore denied.

3. Athough so long as we are without the means of examing all American tongues, it will be premature to assert that these processes prevail in all, nevertheless it is safe to say

CONCLUSIONS.

that their absence has not been demonstrated in any of which we have sufficient and authentic material on which to base a decision.

4. The opinion of Duponceau and Humboldt, therefore, that these processes belong to the ground-plan of American languages, and are their leading characteristics, must still be regarded as a correct generalization.

[ADDENDUM.

Critique by M. Lucien Adam on the above.

Shortly after the above essay appeared in the *Proceedings* of the American Philosophical Society, its arguments and conclusions were vigorously attacked by M. Lucien Adam in the *Revue de Linguistique et de Philologie Comparée*, Tome XIX (Paris, 1886). He begins by pointing out that examples of incorporation may be found in tongues of the Old World—which has never been denied (see above, pp. 353-4). Having acknowledged the incompleteness of his own definitions, he intimates that those I give are calculated rather to sustain my theory than to prove a linguistic trait. He then proceeds to lengthy and minute criticisms of the analyses I have made of the examples given under the several languages discussed. I am quite willing to concede that with the imperfect grammars and lexicons of these tongues so far published, I may have tripped at times in such analyses; but I am far from acknowledging that all those of M. Adam are correct, and I am quite certain that in some he is mistaken. The question, however, is one not possible to discuss in this place, and I must leave it; but I would refer the earnest student to the acute and learned article of M. Adam, which is much the most thorough yet written on the negative side of the debate.]

THE EARLIEST FORM OF HUMAN SPEECH, AS REVEALED BY AMERICAN TONGUES.*

ARCHÆOLOGISTS tell us that the manufacturers of those rude stone implements called palæoliths wandered up and down the world while a period of something like two hundred thousand years was unrolling its eventless centuries. Many believe that these early artisans had not the power of articulate expression to convey their emotions or ideas; if such they had, they were confined to inarticulate grunts and cries.

Haeckel proposed for the species at this period of its existence the designation *Homo alalus,* speechless man. Anatomists have come forward to show that the inferior maxillary bones disinterred in the caves of La Naulette and Schipka are so formed that their original possessors could not have had the power of articulation.† But the latest investigators of this point have reached an opposite conclusion.‡ We must, however, concede that the oral com-

---

* Read before the American Philosophical Society in 1888, and published in their *Proceedings* under the title "The Language of Palæolithic Man."

†"L'homme chelleen n' avait pas la parole," Mortillet, *La Prehistorique Antiquité de l' Homme,* p. 250 (Paris, 1883).

‡ See Dr. H. Steinthal, *Der Ursprung der Sprache,* s. 264, et seq. (Berlin, 1888), who rehearses the discussion of the point with sufficient fullness.

munication of men during that long epoch was of a very rudimentary character; it is contrary to every theory of intellectual evolution to suppose that they possessed a speech approaching anything near even the lowest organized of the linguistic stocks now in existence. By an attentive consideration of some of these lowest stocks, can we not form a somewhat correct conception of what was the character of the rudimentary utterances of the race? I think we can, but, as I believe I am the first to attempt such a picture, I offer it with becoming diffidence.

The physiological possibility that palæolithic man possessed a language has, as I have said, been already vindicated; and that he was intellecually capable of speech could, I think, scarcely be denied by any one who will contemplate the conceptions of symmetry, the technical skill, and the wise adaptation to use, manifested in some of the oldest specimens of his art; as for example the axes disinterred from the ancient strata of San Isidro, near Madrid, those found forty feet deep in the post-glacial gravels near Trenton, New Jersey, or some of those figured by De Mortillet as derived from the beds of the Somme in France.* We have evidence that at that period man made use of fire; that he raised shelters to protect himself from the weather; that he possessed some means of navigating the streams; that he could occasionally overcome powerful and ferocious beasts; that he already paid some attention to ornamenting his person; that he lived in communities; and that his migrations were ex-

---

*See, for instance, Plate X of Mortillet, *Musée Préhistorique:* Cartailhac, *Ages Préhistoriques de l' Espagne*, plate on p. 27.

tensive.* In view of all this, is it not highly improbable that he was destitute of any vocal powers of expressing his plans and desires? I maintain that we should dismiss the *Homo alalus*, as a scientific romance which has served its time.

More than this, I believe that by a judicious study of existing languages, especially those which have suffered little by admixture or by distant removals, we can picture with reasonable fidelity the character of the earliest tongues spoken by man, the speech of the Palæolithic Age.

This primitive utterance was, of course, not the same everywhere. It varied indefinitely. But for all that it is almost certain that in all localities it proceeded on analogous lines of development, just as languages have everywhere and at all times since. By studying simple and isolated languages, those which have suffered least by contact with others, or by alterations in conditions of culture, we can catch some glimpses of the character of man's earliest significant expression, the "baby-talk of the race," if I may use the expression. I have gleaned a certain number of such traits in the field of American linguistics, and present them to you as curiosities, which, like other curiosities, have considerable significance to those who will master their full purport.

The question I am about to consider, is, you will observe, quite different from that which concerns itself with the origin of *linguistic stocks*. Many of these unquestionaly arose long after man had acquired well-developed lan-

---

* I have collected the evidence for this in an Essay on Prehistoric Archæology, in the *Iconographic Encyclopedia*, Vol. ii.

guages, and when the cerebral convolutions whose activity is manifested in articulate expression had acquired a high grade of development through hereditary training. How such stocks may have arisen has been lucidly set forth by my learned friend Mr. Horatio Hale. He demonstrates by many examples that in the present cerebral evolution of man, infants develop an articulate language with the same natural facility that any other species of animal does the vocal utterances peculiar to its kind.*

But in this essay I am contemplating man as he was before hundreds of generations of speaking ancestors had evolved such cerebral powers.

I begin with some observations on the phonetic elements. These are no other than what we call the alphabet, the simple sounds which combined together make up the words of a language. In all European tongues, the mere letters of the alphabet, by themselves, have no meaning and convey no idea; furthermore, their value in a word is fixed; and, thirdly, arranged in a word, they are sufficient to convey its sound and sense to one acquainted with their values.

Judged by certain American examples, all three of these seemingly fundamental characteristics of the phonetic elements were absent in primitive speech, and have become stable only by a long process of growth. We find tongues in which the primary sounds are themselves significant, and yet at the same time are highly variable; and we find many examples in which they are inadequate to convey the sense of the articulate sound.

---

* See his address on "The Origin of Languages and the Antiquity of Speaking Man," in the *Proceedings of the American Association for the Advancement of Science*, Vol. xxxv, p. 279.

As exemplifying these peculiarities I take the Tinné or Athapascan, spoken widely in British America, and of which the Apache and Navaho in the United States are branches. You know that in English the vowels A, E, I, O, U, and the consonants, as such, F, S, K, and the others, convey to your mind no meaning, are not attached to any idea or train of ideas. This is altogether different in the Tinné. We are informed by Bishop Faraud,* a thorough master of that tongue, that its significant radicals are the five primitive vowel sounds, A, E, I, O, U. Of these A expresses matter, E existence, I force or energy, O existence doubtful, and U existence absent, non-existence, negation or succession. These vowels are "put in action," as he phrases it, by single or double consonants, "which have more or less value in proportion as the vowel is more or less strong." These consonantal sounds, as we learn at length from the works on this language by Father Petitot, are also materially significant. They are numerous, being sixty-three in all, and are divided into nine different classes, each of which conveys a series of related or associated ideas in the native mind.

Thus, the labials express the ideas of time and space, as age, length, distance, and also whiteness, the last mentioned, perhaps, through association with the white hair of age, or the endless snowfields of their winter. The dentals express all that relates to force terminating, hence uselessness, inanity, privation, smallness, feebleness; and also greatness, elevation, the motor power. The nasals convey the general notion of motion in repetition; hence, rotation, reduplication, gravitation, and, by a singularly

---

* *Dix-huit Ans chez les Sauvages*, p. 85.

logical association, organic life. The gutturals indicate motion in curves; hence, sinuousness, flexibility, ebullition, roundness, and by a linear figure different from that which underlies the Latin *rectitudo*, justness, correctness. The H, either as an aspirate or an hiatus, introduces the ideas of command and subjection, elevation and prostration, and the like.*

You will observe that in some of these cases the signification of a sound includes both a notion and its opposite, as greatness and smallness. This is an interesting feature, to which I shall refer later.

Turn now to another language, the Cree. Geographically it is contiguous to the Tinné; but, says Bishop Faraud, who spoke them both fluently, they resemble each other no more than the French does the Chinese. Nevertheless, we discover this same peculiarity of materially significant phonetic elements. Howse, in his *Cree Grammar*, observes that the guttural K and the labial W constitute the essential part of all intensive terms in that language, "whether the same be attributive, formative, or personal accident." Indeed, he maintains that the articulate sounds of the Cree all express relative powers, feebleness or force, independent of their position with reference to other sounds.

You may inquire whether in the different groups of American tongues the same or a similar signification is attached to any one sound, or to the sounds of any one organ. If it were so, it would give countenance to those theories which maintain that there is some fixed relation between sound and sense in the radicals of languages. I must reply that I have

---

* Petitot, *Dictionnaire de la Langue Déné Dindjié*, Introduction.

found very little evidence for this theory; and yet some. For example, the N sound expresses the notion of the *ego*, of myself-ness, in a great many tongues, far apart geographically and linguistically. It is found at the basis of the personal pronoun of the first person and of the words for *man* in numerous dialects in North and South America. Again, the K sound is almost as widely associated with the ideas of *otherness*, and is at the base of the personal pronoun of the second person singular and of the expressions for superhuman personalities, the divine existence.* It is essentially demonstrative in its power.

Again, in a long array of tongues in various parts of the world, the subjective relation is expressed by the M sound, as has been pointed out by Dr. Winkler; and other examples could be added. Many of these it is impossible to attribute to derivation from a common source. Some writers maintain that sounds have a subjective and fixed relation to ideas; others call such coincidences "blind chance," but these should remember that chance itself means merely the action of laws not yet discovered.

You might suppose that this distinction, I mean that between *self* and *other*, between *I*, *thou* and *he*, is fundamental, that speech could not proceed without it. You would be mistaken. American languages furnish conclusive evidence that for unnumbered generations mankind got along well enough without any such discrimination. One

---

*On the astonishingly wide distribution of the *n* and *k* sounds as primitive demonstratives, compare H. Winkler, *Uralaltaische Völker und Sprachen*, s. 86, 87, (Berlin, 1884). For other comparisons, see Tolmie and Dawson, *Vocabularies of Inds. of British Columbia*, p. 128.

and the same monosyllable served for all three persons and both numbers. The meaning of this monosyllable was undoubtedly "any living human being." Only after a long time did it become differentiated by the addition of locative particles into the notions, "I—living human being," "Thou—living human being," "He—living human being," and so on. Even a language spoken by so cultured a people as the ancient Peruvians bears unmistakable traces of this process, as has been shown by Von Tschudi in his admirable analysis of that tongue; and the language of the Baures of Bolivia still presents examples of verbs conjugated without pronouns or pronominal affixes.*

The extraordinary development of the pronouns in many American languages—some have as many as eighteen different forms, as the person is contemplated as standing, lying, in motion, at rest, alone, in company, etc., etc.—this multiplicity of forms, I say, is proof to the scientific linguist that these tongues have but recently developed this grammatical category. Wherever we find overgrowth, the soil is new and the crop rank.

In spite of the significance attached to the phonetic elements, they are, in many American languages, singularly vague and fluctuating. If in English we were to pronounce

---

* "Es hat offenbar eine Zeit gegeben, in der *ka* alleiniges Pron. pers. für alle drei Personen war, erst allmählig entwickelten sich *ño ka*, ego, *ka m*, tu, *ka y*, ille." J. J. von Tschudi, *Organismus der Khetsua Sprache*, s. 184 (Leipzig, 1884). In the language of the Baures of Bolivia when the verb takes the negative termination *apico*, the pronominal signs are discarded; thus, *era*, to drink, a drink ; *erapico*=I, thou, he, we, you, they, do not drink. Magio, *Arte de la Lengua de los Indios Baures*, p. 82 (Paris, 1880). This reveals a time when both affirmative and negative verbals dispensed with pronouns altogether.

three words, *loll, nor, roll,* indifferently as one or the other, you see what violence we should do to the theory of our alphabet. Yet analogous examples are constant in many American languages. Their consonants are "alternating," in large groups, their vowels "permutable." M. Petitot calls this phenomenon "literal affinity," and shows that in the Tinné it takes place not only between consonants of the same group, the labials for instance, but of different groups, as labials with dentals, and dentals with nasals. These differences are not merely dialectic; they are found in the same village, the same family, the same person. They are not peculiar to the Tinné; they recur in the Klamath. Dr. Behrendt was puzzled with them in the Chapanec. "No other language," he writes, "has left me in such doubt as this one. The same person pronounces the same word differently; and when his attention is called to it, will insist that it is the same. Thus, for devil he will give *Titambi* and *Sisaimbui;* for hell, *Nakupaju* and *Nakapoti.*"* Speaking of the Guarani, Father Montoya says: "There is in this language a constant changing of the letters, for which no sufficient rules can be given."† And Dr. Darapsky in his recently published study of the Araucanian of Chile gives the following equation of permutable letters in that tongue:

$$B=W=F=U=\acute{U}=I=E=G=GH=HU.\ddagger$$

The laws of the conversion of sounds of the one organ into those of another have not yet been discovered; but the

---

* *Apuntes sobre la Lengua Chapaneca, MS.*
† *Arte de la Lengua Guarani,* p. 93.
‡ *La Lengua Araucana,* p. 15 (*Santiago de Chile,* 1888).

above examples, which are by no means isolated ones, serve to admonish us that the phonetic elements of primitive speech probably had no fixedness.

There is another oddity about some of these consonantal sounds which I may notice in passing. Some of them are not true elementary sounds; they cannot stand alone, but must always have another consonant associated with them. Thus, the labial *B* is common in Guarani; but it must always be preceded by an *M*. In Nahuatl the liquid *L* is frequent; but it is the initial of no word in that language. The Nahuas apparently could not pronounce it, unless some other articulate sound preceded it.

Albornoz, in his *Grammar of the Chapanec Tongue*,* states that the natives cannot pronounce an initial *B*, *G*, *Y*, or *D*, without uttering an *N* sound before it.

The third point in the phonology of these tongues to which I alluded is the frequency with which the phonetic elements, as graphically expressed, are inadequate to convey the idea. I may quote a remark by Howse in his *Cree Grammar*, which is true probably of all primitive speech, "Emphasis, accent and modifications of vocal expression; which are inadequately expressed in writing, seem to constitute an essential, perhaps the vital part of Indian language." In such modifications I include tone, accent, stress, vocal inflection, quantity and pause. These are with much difficulty or not at all includable in a graphic method, and yet are frequently significant. Take the pause or hiatus. I have already mentioned that in Tinné it correlates a whole series of ideas. M. Belcourt, in his Grammar of the

---

* Albornoz, *Arte de la Langua Chapaneca*, p. 10.

Sauteux, an Algonkin dialect, states that the pause may completely change the meaning of a word and place it in another class; it is also essential in that language in the formation of the tenses.* This is the case in the Guarani of South America. Montoya illustrates it by the example: *Peru o'u*, Peter ate it; but *Peru ou*, Peter came; quite another thing, you will observe.†

The stress laid on a vowel-sound often alters its meaning. In the Sauteux, Belcourt points out that this constitutes the only distinction between the first and second persons in participles. In the Nahuatl this alone distinguishes many plural forms from their singulars; and many similar examples could be cited.

With difficulties of this nature to encounter, a person accustomed to the definite phonology of European tongues is naturally at a loss. The Spanish scholar Uricoechea expresses this in relating his efforts to learn the Chibcha of New Granada, a tongue also characterized by these fluctuating phonetics. He visited the region where it is still spoken with a grammar and phrase-book in his hand, and found to his disappointment that they could not understand one word he said. He then employed a native who spoke Spanish, and with him practiced some phrases until he believed he had them perfect. Another disappointment—not one of them was understood. He returned to his teacher and again repeated them; but what was his dismay when

---

* *Principes de la Langue des Sauvages appellés Sauteux.* Introd.

† *Arte de la Lengua Guarani, ó mas bien Tupi.* Por el P. Antonio Ruiz de Montoya, p. 100.

not even his teacher recognized a single word! After that Uricoechea gave up the attempt.*

Leaving now the domain of phonology and turning to that of lexicography, I will point out to you a very curious phenomenon in primitive speech. I have already alluded to it in quoting M. Petitot's remark that in Tinné a sound often means both a notion and its opposite; that, for instance, the same word may express good and bad, and another both high and low. To use M. Petitot's own words, "a certain number of consonants have the power of expressing a given order of ideas or things, and also the contradictory of this order." In Tinné, a great many words for opposite ideas are the same or nearly the same, derived from the same significant elements. Thus, *son* good, *sona* bad; *tezo*, sweet, *tezon* bitter; *ya* immense, *ya* very small; *inla* one time, *inlasin* every time; and so on.

This union of opposite significations reappears in the ultimate radicals of the Cree language. These, says Mr. Howse,† whose *Grammar* I again quote, express *Being* in its positive and negative modes: "These opposite modes are expressed by modifications of the same element, furnishing two classes of terms widely different from each other in signification." In Cree the leading substantive radical is *eth*, which originally meant both Being and Not-Being. In the present language *eth* remains as the current positive, *ith* as the current privative. *It* means within, *ut* without; and like parallelisms run through many expressions, indicating

---

* *Grammatica de la Lengua Chibcha.* Introd.

† See Howse. *Grammar of the Cree Language*, pp. 16, 134, 135, 169, etc.

that numerous series of opposite ideas are developments from the same original sounds.

I have found a number of such examples in the Nahuatl of Mexico, and I am persuaded that they are very usual in American tongues. Dr. Carl Abel has pointed out many in the ancient Coptic, and I doubt not they were characteristic of all primitive speech.

To explain their presence we must reflect on the nature of the human mind, and the ascertained laws of thought. One of these fundamental and necessary laws of thought, that usually called the second, was expressed by the older logicians in the phrase *Omnis determinatio est negatio*, and by their modern followers in the formula, "A is not *not-A;*" in other words, a quality, an idea, an element of knowledge, can rise into cognition only by being limited by that which it is not. That by which it is limited is known in logic as its privative. In a work published some years ago I pointed out that this privative is not an independent thought, as some have maintained, but that the positive and its privative are really two aspects of the same thought.* This highly important distinction explains how in primitive speech, before the idea had risen into clear cognition, both it and its privative were expressed by the same sound; and when it did rise into such cognition, and then into expression, the original unity

---

* *The Religious Sentiment; Its Source and Aim. A Contribution to the Science of Religion.* By D. G. Brinton, p. 31 (New York, 1876). The statement in the text can be algebraically demonstrated in the mathematical form of logic as set forth by Prof. Boole, thus: $A = $ not (not $-A$); which, in its mathematical expression becomes, $x = x^2$. Whence by transposition and substitution we derive, $x^2 = 1$; in which equation $1 = A$. See Boole. *An Investigation into the Laws of Thought* (London, 1854).

is exhibited by the identity of the radical. Thus it happens that from such an unexpected quarter as an analysis of Cree grammar do we obtain a confirmation of the starting point of the logic of Hegel in his proposition that the identity of the *Being* and the *Not-being* is the ultimate equation of thought.

The gradual development of grammar is strikingly illustrated in these languages. Their most prominent trait is what is called *incorporation*. Subject, verb, direct object and remote object, are all expressed in one word. Some have claimed that there are American languages of which this is not true; but I think I have shown in an essay published some time ago,* that this opinion arises from our insufficient knowledge of the alleged exceptions. At any rate, this incorporation was undoubtedly a trait of primitive speech in America and elsewhere. Primitive man, said Herder, was like a baby; he wanted to say all at once. He condensed his whole sentence into a single word. Archdeacon Hunter, in his *Lecture on the Cree Language*, gives as an example the scriptural phrase, "I shall have you for my disciples," which, in that tongue, is expressed by one word.†

So far as I have been able to analyze these primitive sentence-words, they always express *being in relation;* and hence they partake of the nature of verbs rather than nouns. In this conclusion I am obliged to differ with the eminent linguist Professor Steinthal, who, in his profound exposition of the relations of psychology to grammar, maintains that

---

* *On Polysynthesis and Incorporation*, in *Proceedings* of the American Philosophical Society, 1885. (See the preceding essay.)

† *On the Grammatical Construction of the Cree Language*, p. 12 (London, 1875).

while the primitive sentence was a single word, that word was a noun, a name.*

It is evident that the primitive man did not connect his sentences. One followed the other disjointedly, unconnectedly. This is so plainly marked in American tongues that the machinery for connecting sentences is absent. This machinery consists properly of the relative pronoun and the conjunction. You will be surprised to hear that there is no American language, none that I know, which possesses either of these parts of speech. That which does duty for the conjunction in the Maya and Nahuatl, for instance, is a noun meaning associate or companion, with a prefixed possessive.†

Equally foreign to primitive speech was any expression of *time* in connection with verbal forms; in other words, there was no such thing as tenses. We are so accustomed to link actions to time, past, present, or future, that it is a little difficult to understand how this accessory can be omitted in intelligible discourse. It is perfectly evident, however, from the study of many American tongues, that at one period of their growth they possessed for a long interval only one tense, which served indifferently for past, present, and future; ‡ and even yet most of them form the past and future

---

* Steinthal, *Gramatik, Logik und Psychologie*, s. 325.

† In Maya the conjunction "and" is rendered by *yetl*, a compound of the possessive pronoun, third person singular *y*, and *etl*, companion. The Nahuatl, *ihuan*, is precisely the same in composition.

‡ "Die meisten amerikanischen Sprachen haben die Eigenthümlichkeit, dass in der Regel die Haupttempora in Anwenduug kommen und unter diesen besonders das Präsens, selbst wenn von einer bestimmten, besonders aber von einer unbestimmten Vergangenheit gesprochen wird." J. J. von Tschudi, *Organismus der Khetsua Sprache*, s. 189. The same tense is also employed for future occurrences.

by purely material means, as the addition of an adverb of time, by accent, quantity or repetition, and in others the tense relation is still unknown.*

In some tongues, the Omagua of the upper Orinoco for example, there is no sort of connection between the verbal stem and its signs of tense, mode or person. They have not even any fixed order. In such languages there is no difference in sound between the words for "I marry," and "my wife;" "I eat," and "my food;" between "Paul dies," "Paul died," "Paul will die," and "Paul is dead." † Through such tongues we can distinctly perceive a time when the verb had neither tense, mode, nor person; when it was not even a verb nor yet a verbal, but an epicene sound which could be adapted to any service of speech.

It is also evident that things were not thought of, or talked of, out of their natural relations. There are still in most American tongues large classes of words, such as the parts of the body and terms of kinship, which cannot stand alone. They must always be accompanied by a pronoun expressing relation.

Few American tongues have any adjectives, the Cree, for instance, not a dozen in all. Prepositions are equally rare, and articles are not found. These facts testify that what are called "the grammatical categories" were wholly absent in the primitive speech of man.

What classical grammarians call "the historical present," will illustrate this employment of a single tense for past and future time.

*The Chiquita of Bolivia is an extreme example. "La distinction du passé, du présent et du futur n'existe pas dans cette langue étrange." *Arte y Vocabulario de la Lengua Chiquita.* Por. L. Adam, y V. Henry, p. x.

† *On the Verb in American Languages.* By Wilhelm von Humboldt. Translated by D. G. Brinton, in *Proceedings of the American Philosophical Society*, 1885.

So also were those adjectives which are called *numerals*. There are American tongues which have no words for any numerals whatever. The numerical concepts one, two, three, four, cannot be expressed in these languages for lack of terms with any such meaning.* This was a great puzzle to the missionaries when they undertook to expound to their flocks the doctrine of the Trinity. They were in worse case even than the missionary to an Oregon tribe, who, to convey the notion of *soul* to his hearers, could find no word in their language nearer to it than one which meant "the lower gut."

A very interesting chapter in the study of these tongues is that which reveals the evolution of specific distinctions, those inductive generalizations under which primitive man classified the objects of the universe about him. These distinctions were either grammatical or logical, that is, either formal or material. That most widely seen in America is a division of all existence into those which are considered living and those considered not living. This constitutes the second great generalization of the primitive mind, the first, as I have said, having been that into Being and Not-being. The distinctions of Living and Not-living gave rise to the *animate* and *inanimate* conjugations. A grammatical sex distinction, which is the prevailing one in the grammars of the Aryan tongues, does not exist in any American dialect known to me.†

---

* A striking example is the Chiquita of Bolivia. "No se puede en chiquito, ni contar dos, tres, cuatro, etc., ni decir segundo, tercero, etc." *Arte y Vocabulario de la Lengua Chiquita*, p. 19 (Paris, 1880).

† Those distinctions, apparently of sex, called by M. Lucien Adam *anthropic* and *metanthropic*, *arrhenic* and *metarrhenic*, found in certain American tongues, belong

It is true that abstract general terms are absent or rare in the most primitive tongues. On the other hand, we find in them a great many classificatory particles. These correspond only remotely to anything known in Aryan speech, and seem far more abstract than generic nouns. I will illustrate what they are by an example taken from the Hidatsa, a dialect of the Dakota.

The word for sled in that dialect is *midu-maidutsada*. The first part of this compound, *midu*, means anything of wood or into which wood enters. Fire is *midé* because it is kept up with wood. With the phonetic laxity which I have before noted, the first syllable *mi* may as correctly be pronounced *bi* or *wi*. It is a common nominal prefix, of vague significance, but seems to classify objects as distinctives. *Ma* designates objects whose immediate use is not expressed; *i* denotes instrument or material; *du*, conveys that the cause of the action is not specified; *tsa* intimates the action is that of separating; *da*, that this is done quickly (*tsa-da*, to slide).*

Thus by the juxtaposition of one classificatory particle after another, seven in number, all of them logical universals, the savage makes up the name of the specific object.

This system was probably the first adopted by man when he began to set in order his perceptions within the categories of his understanding, with the aim of giving them vocal ex-

---

to the material, not the formal part of the language, and, strictly speaking, are distinctions not really based on sexual considerations. See Adam, *Du Genre dans les Diverses Langues* (Paris, 1883).

*Washington Matthews, *Grammar and Dictionary of the Language of the Hidatsa* (New York, 1873). In a letter received since the first publication of this essay, Dr. Matthews writes that the analysis in the text is quite correct.

pression. It is a plan which we find most highly developed in the rudest languages, and therefore we may reasonably believe that it characterized prehistoric speech.

The question has been put by psychological grammarians, which one of the senses most helped man in the creation of language—or to express it in modern scientific parlance, was primitive man a *visuaire* or an *auditaire?* Did he model his sounds after what he heard, or what he saw? The former opinion has been the more popular, and has given rise to the imitative or "onomatopoetic" theory of language. No doubt there is a certain degree of truth in this, but the analysis of American tongues leans decidedly toward classing primitive man among the *visuaires*. His earliest significant sounds seem to have been expressive of motion and rest, energy and its absence, space and direction, color and form, and the like. A different opinion has been maintained by Darwin and by many who have studied the problems presented by the origin of words from a merely physical or physiological standpoint, but a careful investigation shows that it was the sense of sight rather than of hearing which was the prompter to vocal utterance. But the consideration of the source of primitive significant sounds lies without the bounds of my present study.

It will be seen from these remarks that the primitive speech of man was far more rudimentary than any language known to us. It had no grammatical form; so fluctuating were its phonetics, and so much depended on gesture, tone, and stress, that its words could not have been reduced to writing, nor arranged in alphabetic sequence; these words often signified logical contradictories, and which of the antithetic meanings was intended could be guessed only from the accent or sign; it possessed no prepositions nor conjunctions, no numerals, no pronouns of any kind, no forms to express singular or plural, male or female, past or present; the different vowel-sounds and the different consonantal groups conveyed specific significance, and were of more import than the syllables which they formed. The concept of time came much later than that of space, and for a long while was absent.

THE CONCEPTION OF LOVE IN SOME AMERICAN LANGUAGES.*

"THE words which denote love, describing a sentiment at once powerful and delicate, reveal the inmost heart of those who created them. The vital importance attached to this sentiment renders these beautiful words especially adapted to point out the exceeding value of language as a true autobiography of nations."

This quotation is from an essay by a thoughtful writer, Dr. Carl Abel, in which he has gathered from four languages, the Latin, English, Hebrew and Russian, their expressions for this sweet emotion, and subjected them to a careful analysis.† The perusal of his article has led me to make some similar examinations of American languages; but with this difference in method, that while Dr. Abel takes the languages named in the fullness of their development and does not occupy himself with the genesis of the terms of affection, I shall give more particular attention to their history and derivation as furnishing illustrations of the origin and growth of those altruistic sentiments which are revealed in their strongest expression in the emotions of friendship and love.

---
* Extract from a paper read before the American Philosophical Society in 1886.
† *Linguistic Essays*, by Carl Abel, Ph. D. (London, 1882).

Upon these sentiments are based those acts which unite man to man in amicable fellowship and mutual interchange of kindly offices, thus creating a nobler social compact than that which rests merely on increased power of defence or aggression. These sentiments are those which bind parent to child and child to parent, and thus supply the foundation upon which the family in the true significance of the term should rest. These are they which, directed toward the ruler or the state, find expression in personal loyalty and patriotic devotion. Surpassing all in fervor and potency, these sentiments, when exhibited in love between the sexes, direct the greater part of the activity of each individual life, mould the forms of the social relations, and control the perpetuation of the species. Finally, in their last and highest manifestations, these sentiments are those which have suggested to the purest and clearest intellects both the most exalted intellectual condition of man, and the most sublime definition of divinity.* These are good reasons, therefore, why we should scan with more than usual closeness the terms for the conception of love in the languages of nations.

Another purpose which I shall have in view will be to illustrate by these words the wonderful parallelism which everywhere presents itself in the operations of the human mind, and to show how it is governed by the same associations of ideas both in the new and the old worlds.

---

*I scarcely need say that I refer to the marvelous words of St. John: ὁ μη αγαπων, ουκ εγνω τον Θεον, οτι ὁ Θεος αγαπη εστιν (1 John iv, 8); and to the *amor intellectualis*, the golden crown of the philosophy of Spinoza as developed in the last book of his *Ethica*.

As a preparation for the latter object, let us take a glance at the derivation of the principal words expressing love in the Aryan languages. The most prominent of them may be traced back to one of two ruling ideas, the one intimating a similarity or likeness between the persons loving, the other a wish or desire. The former conveys the notion that the feeling is mutual, the latter that it is stronger on one side than on the other.

These diverse origins are well illustrated by the French *aimer* and the English *love*. *Aimer*, from the Latin *amare*, brings us to the Greek αμα, ομος, both of which spring from the Sanscrit *som;* from which in turn the Germans get their words *sammt*, along with, and *zusammen*, together; while we obtain from this root almost without change our words *similar* and *same*. Etymologically, therefore, those who love are alike; they are the *same* in such respects that they are attracted to one another, on the proverbial principle that "birds of a feather flock together."

Now turning to the word *love*, German *liebe*, Russian *lubov*, *lubity*, we find that it leads us quite a different road. It is traced back without any material change to the Sanscrit *lobha*, covetousness, the ancient Coptic λιβε, to want, to desire. In this origin we see the passion portrayed as a yearning to possess the loved object; and in the higher sense to enjoy the presence and sympathy of the beloved, to hold sweet communion with him or her.

A class of ideas closely akin to this are conveyed in such words as "attached to," "attraction," "affection," and the like, which make use of the figure of speech that the lover is fastened to, drawn toward, or bound up with the beloved object. We often express this metaphor in full in such phrases as "the bonds of friendship," etc.

This third class of words, although in the history of language they are frequently of later growth than the two former, probably express the sentiment which underlies both these, and that is a dim, unconscious sense of the unity which is revealed to man most perfectly in the purest and highest love, which at its sublimest height does away with the antagonism of independent personality, and blends the *I* and the *thou* in a oneness of existence.

Although in this, its completest expression, we must seek examples solely between persons of opposite sex, it will be well to consider in an examination like the present the love between men, which is called friendship, that between parents and children, and that toward the gods, the givers of all good things. The words conveying such sentiments will illustrate many features of the religious and social life of the nations using them.

I. THE ALGONKIN.

I begin with this group of dialects, once widely spread thoughout the St. Lawrence valley and the regions adjoining; and among them I select especially the Cree and the Chipeway, partly because we know more about them, and partly because they probably represent the common tongue in its oldest and purest type. They are closely allied, the same roots appearing in both with slight phonetic variations.

In both of them the ordinary words for love and friendship are derived from the same monosyllabic root, *sak*. On this, according to the inflectional laws of the dialects, are built up the terms for the love of man to woman, a lover, love in the abstract, friend, friendship, and the like. It is also occasionally used by the missionaries for the love of man to God and of God to man.*

In the Chipeway this root has but one form, *sagi;* but in Cree it has two, a weak and a strong form, *saki* and *sakk*. The meaning of the latter is more particularly to fasten to, to attach to. From it are derived the words for string or cord, the verbs "to tie," "to fasten," etc.; and also some of the coarsest words to express the sexual relation.† Both these roots are traced back to the primary element of the Algonkin language expressed by the letters *sak* or *s—k*. This conveys the generic notion of force or power exerted by one over another,‡ and is apparently precisely identical with the fundamental meaning of the Latin *afficio*, "to affect one in some manner by active agency,"§ from which word, I need hardly add, were derived *affectus* and *affectio* and our "affection;" thus we at once meet with an absolute parallelism in the working of the Aryan Italic and the American Algonkin mind.

The Cree has several words which are confined to parental and filial love and that which the gods have for men. These

---

* Chipeway: *nin sagiiwin*, I love; *sagiiwewin*, love; *saiagiiwed*, a lover.
Cree: *sâkihituwin*, friendship; *manitowi sâkihewewin*, the love of God. The words from the Chipeway are from Baraga's *Otchipwe Dictionary;* those from the Cree from Lacombe's *Dictionnaire de la langue des Cris*, except when otherwise noted.

† Chipeway: *sagibidjigan*, a string or cord.
Cree: *sakkappitew*, he fastens, he ties; *sakkahigun*, a nail; *sakkistiwok*, coeunt, copulati suut.

‡ See Joseph Howse, *Grammar of the Cree Language*, p. 165.

§ See the remarks in Andrew's *Latin Lexicon, s. v.*

are built up on the disyllabic radical *espi* or *aspi*, which is an instrumental particle signifying "by means of, with the aid of."* Toward the gods, such words refer to those who aid us; toward children those whom their parents aid; and from children toward parents, again, those from whom aid is received.

For love between men, friendship, the Cree employs some words from the radical *sâki;* but more frequently those compounded with the root *wit* or *witch*, which means "in company with,"† and is the precise analogue of the syllable *com* (Latin, *con*) in the English words companion, comrade, compeer, confederate, etc.; it conveys the idea of association in life and action, and that association a voluntary and pleasure-giving one.

In the Chipeway there is a series of expressions for family love and friendship which in their origin carry us back to the same psychological process which developed the Latin *amare* from the Sanscrit *sam* (see above). They may be illustrated by the melodious term, which in that dialect means both friendship and relationship, *inawendawin*. This is an abstract verbal noun from the theme *ni inawa*, I resemble him, which is built up from the radicle *in*. This particle denotes a certain prevailing way or manner, and appears both in Cree and Chipeway in a variety of words.‡ The

---

* Cree: *espiteyimit kije-manito*, for the love of God; *espiteyimatijk*, for the love of the children.

† Cree: *ni wittjiwâgan*, my friend; *wi'chettuwin*, a confraternity, or society.

‡ Chipeway: *inawema*, I am his relative, or, his friend.

Cree: *ijinâkusiw*, he has such an appearance. This particle of similarity is considered by Howse to be "one of the four primary generic nouns" of the Algonkin language. *Grammar of the Cree Language*, p. 135.

principle of similarity is thus fully expressed as the basis of friendship. To see how apparent this is we have but to remember the English, "I like him," *i. e.*, there is something in him *like* me.

The feebler sentiment of merely liking a person or thing is expressed in the Chipeway by a derivative from the adjective *mino*, good, well, and signifies that he or it seems good to me.*

The highest form of love, however, that which embraces all men and all beings, that whose conception is conveyed in the Greek ἀγάπη, we find expressed in both the dialects by derivation from a root different from any I have mentioned. It is in its dialectic forms *kis*, *keche*, or *kiji*, and in its origin it is an intensive interjectional expression of pleasure, indicative of what gives joy.† Concretely it signifies what is completed, permanent, powerful, perfected, perfect. As friendship and love yield the most exalted pleasure, from this root the natives drew a fund of words to express fondness, attachment, hospitality, charity; and from the same worthy source they selected that adjective which they applied to the greatest and most benevolent divinity.‡

---

* Chipeway: *nin minenima*, I like (him, her, it).

† See Howse, *Grammar of the Cree Lang.*, p. 157. *Keche* (*kees*) as an interjection of pleasure, he considers in antithesis to *ak* (compare German *ach!*) as an interjection of pain, and cites abundant examples.

‡ Chipeway: *nin kijewadis*, I am amicable, benevolent; *kijewadisiwin*, charity, benevolence, benignity, compassion; *kije manitowin*, God-head, divine nature.

Cree: *kisatew*, he is devoted to (him, her); *kisew*, she loves (her children); *kisewatisiwin*, charity, the highest virtue; *kise manito*, "l'esprit charitable, Dieu," and numerous others.

II. THE NAHUATL.

The Nahuatl, Mexican or Aztec language was spoken extensively throughout Mexico and Central America, and every tribe who used it could boast of a degree of culture considerably above that of any of the Algonkin communities. Such being the case, it is rather surprising to note how extremely poor in comparison is the Nahuatl in independent radicals denoting love or affection. In fact, there is only one word in the language which positively has this signification, and it, with its derivatives, is called upon to express every variety of love, human and divine, carnal and chaste, between men and between the sexes, and by human beings toward inanimate things.

This word is *tlazótla*, he loves. It is no easy matter to trace its history. By well known laws of Nahuatl etymology we know that the root is *zo*. We have from this same root several other words of curiously diverse meanings. Thus, *izo*, to bleed, to draw blood, either for health, or, as was the custom of those nations, as a sacrifice before idols; *izolini*, to grow old, to wear out, applied to garments; *tlazoti*, to offer for sale at a high price; and *zozo*, to string together, as the natives did flowers, peppers, beads, etc. Now, what idea served as the common starting-point of all these expressions? The answer is that we find it in the word *zo* as applied to a sharp-pointed instrument, a thorn, or a bone or stone awl, used in the earliest times for puncturing or transfixing objects. From this came *zozo*, to transfix with such an instrument, and string on a cord; *izoliui*, to be full of holes, as if repeatedly punctured, and thus worn out; and *izo*, to bleed, because that was done by puncturing the flesh with the thorns of the maguey or sharp obsidian points.*

But how do we bring these into connection with the sentiment of love and its verbal expression? We might indeed seek an illustration of the transfer from classical mythology, and adduce the keen-pointed arrows of Cupid, the darts of love, as pointing out the connection. But I fear this would be crediting the ancient Nahuas with finer feelings than they deserve. I gravely doubt that they felt the shafts of the tender passion with any such susceptibility as to employ this metaphor. Much more likely is it that *tlazótla*, to love, is derived directly from the noun *tlazôtl*, which means something strung with or fastened to another. This brings us directly back to the sense of "attached to" in English, and to that of the root *saki* in Algonkin, the idea of being bound to another by ties of emotion and affection.

But there is one feature in this derivation which tells seriously against the national psychology of the Nahuas; this, their only word for love, is not derived, as is the Algonkin, from the primary meaning of the root, but from a secondary and later signification. This hints ominously at the probability that the ancient tongue had for a long time no word at all to express this, the highest and noblest emotion of the

---

* The following words and meanings are from Carochi's Grammar and Molina's Dictionary of this tongue :

ço, punzar, sangrar.

çoço, ensartar, como flores, cuentas, etc.

çotica, estar ensartada la cuenta, etc.

tlaçotl, cosa ensartada.

The original meaning of *zo*, a pointed tool or awl, is not given by Molina, but is repeatedly expressed in the phonetic picture-writing of the Aztecs.

human heart, and that consequently this emotion itself had not risen to consciousness in the national mind.

But the omissions of the fathers were more than atoned for by the efforts of their children. I know no more instructive instance in the history of language to illlustrate how original defects are amended in periods of higher culture by the linguistic faculty, than this precise point in the genesis of the Nahuatl tongue. The Nahuas, when they approached the upper levels of emotional development, found their tongue singularly poor in radicals conveying such conceptions. As the literal and material portions of their speech offered them such inadequate means of expression, they turned toward its tropical and formal portions, and in those realms reached a degree of development in this direction which far surpasses that in any other language known to me.

In the formal portion of the language they were not satisfied with one, but adopted a variety of devices to this end. Thus: all verbs expressing emotion may have an intensive termination suffixed, imparting to them additional force; again, certain prefixes indicating civility, respect and affection may be employed in the imperative and optative moods; again, a higher synthetic construction may be employed in the sentence, by which the idea expressed is emphasized, a device in constant use in their poetry; and especially the strength of emotion is indicated by suffixing a series of terminations expressing contempt, reverence or love. The latter are wonderfully characteristic of Nahuatl speech. They are not confined to verbs and nouns, but may be added to adjectives, pronouns, participles, and even to adverbs and postpositions. Thus every word in the sentence is made to carry its burden of affection to the ear of the beloved object!

Add to these facilities the remarkable power of the Nahuatl to impart tropical and figurative senses to words by the employment of rhetorical resources, and to present them as one idea by means of the peculiarities of its construction, and we shall not consider as overdrawn the expression of Professor De la Rosa when he writes: "There can be no question but that in the manifestation in words of the various emotions, the Nahuatl finds no rival, not only among the languages of modern Europe, but in the Greek itself."*

The Nahuatl word for friendship is *icniuhtli*. This is a compound of the preposition *ic*, with ; the noun-ending *tli;* and the adverbial *yuh*, or *noyuh*, which means "of the same kind." The word, therefore, has the same fundamental conception as the Latin *amicus* and the Cree *inawema*, but it was not developed into a verbal to express the suffering of the passion itself.†

III. THE MAYA.

The whole peninsula of Yucatan was inhabited by the Mayas, and tribes speaking related dialects of their tongue lived in Guatemala, Chipapas, and on the Gulf Shore

---

* *Estudio de la Filosofia y Riqueza de la Lengua Mexicana.* Par Agostiu de la Rosa, p. 78 (Guadalajara, 1877).

† There is another word in Nahuatl of similar derivation. It is *pohui*, to make much of a person, to like one. The root is *po*, which carries with it the idea of sameness, similarity or equality; as *itelpocapo*, a boy like himself. (Paredes, *Promptuario Manual Mexicano*, p. 140.)

north of Vera Cruz. All these depended chiefly on agriculture for subsistence, were builders of stone houses, and made use of a system of written records. Their tongue, therefore, deserves special consideration as that of a nation with strong natural tendencies to development.

In turning to the word for love in the Maya vocabulary, we are at once struck with the presence of a connected series of words expressing this emotion, while at the same time they, or others closely akin to them and from the same root, mean pain, injury, difficulty, suffering, wounds and misery. Both are formed by the usual rules from the monosyllable *ya*.*

Were the ancient Mayas so sensitive to love's wounds and the pangs of passion as to derive their very words for suffering from the name of this sentiment?

No; that solution is too unlikely for our acceptance. More probable is it that we have here an illustration of the development of language from interjectional cries. In fact, we may be said to have the proof of it, for we discover that this monosyllable *ya* is still retained in the language as a verb, with the signification "to feel anything deeply, whether as a pain or as a pleasure."† Its derivatives were developed

---

* Thus:

ya or *yail*, love; pain, sickness, a wound; difficult, laborious.
yate, to love.
yacunah, to love.
yaili, painfully, laboriously.
yalal, to taste; to have relations with a woman.
yatzil, love, charity; something difficult or painful.

† "*Ya:* sentir mucho una cosa.
yamab: sin sentir [the *ma* is the negative].
Diccionario Maya-Español del Convento de Motul. (MS. in my possession).

with both meanings, and as love and friendship are the highest forms of pleasure, the word *ya* in its happier senses became confined to them.

It seems to have sufficed to express the conception in all its forms, for the writers in the language apply it to the love of the sexes, to that between parents and children, that among friends, also to that which men feel toward God, and that which He is asserted to feel toward men.*

The Mayas, therefore, were superior to the Nahuas in possessing a radical word which expressed the joy of love; and they must be placed above even the early Aryans in that this radical was in significance purely psychical, referring strictly to a mental state, and neither to similarity nor desire.

It is noteworthy that this interjectional root, although belonging to the substructure of the language, does not appear with the meaning of love in the dialects of the Maya stock. In them the words for this sentiment are derived from other roots.

Thus among the Huastecas, residing on the Gulf of Mexico, north of Vera Cruz, the word for love is *canezal*. It is employed for both human and divine love, and also means anything precious and to be carefully guarded as of advant-

---

* Thus:
    yahtetabal cah tumen Dios, we are loved by God.
    u yacunah Dios toon, the love of God to us.
    yacunahil Dios, the love with which God is loved.
    mehenbit yacunah, filial love.
    bakil yacunah, carnal love.
    All from the *Diccionario de Motul* (MS.).

age to the possessor.* There is no difficulty in following its development when we turn to the Maya, which preserves the most numerous ancient forms and meanings of any dialect of this stock. In it we discover that the verb *can* means "to affect another in some way, to give another either by physical contact or example a virtue, vice, disease or attribute,"† Here again we come upon the precise correlative of the Latin *afficio*, from which proceeds our "affection," etc.

The Guatemalan tribes, the principal of which were and are the Quiches and Cakchiquels, did not accept either *ya* or *can* as the root from which to build their expressions for the sentiment of love. In both these dialects the word for to love is *logoh*. It also means "to buy," and this has led a recent writer to hold up to ridicule the Spanish missionaries who chose this word to express both human and divine love. Dr. Stoll, the writer referred to, intimates that it had no other meaning than "to buy" in the pure original tongue, and that the only word for the passion is *ah*, to want, to desire.‡ In this he does not display his usual accuracy, for we find *logoh* used in the sense "to like," "to love," in the *Annals of the Cakchiquels*, written by a native who had grown to manhood before the Spaniards first entered his country.§

---

* Thus:

tatu canel ixallé, my beloved wife.

ma a canezal a Dios, dost thou love God?

Diccionario Huasteca Español, por Carlos de Tapia Zenteno (Mex., 1767).

† A number of examples are given in the *Diccionario de Motul* (MS).

‡ "Der blosse Begriff derjenigen Liebe, welche das lateinische Zeitwort *amare* ausdrückt, dem Cakchiquel Indianer fremd ist. *Zur Ethnographie der Republik Guatemala*. Von Otto Stoll, M. D., p. 146 (Zurich, 1884).

§ *Xelogox ka chiri ruma Akahal vinak*, "they were loved by the Akahal men."

That the verb *logoh* means, both in origin and later use, "to buy," as well as "to love," is undoubtedly true. Its root *logh* is identical with the Maya *loh*, which has the meanings "to exchange, to buy, to redeem, to emancipate." It was the word selected by the Franciscan missionaries to express the redemption of the world by Christ, and was applied to the redemption of captives and slaves. It might be suggested that it bears a reference to "marriage by purchase;" but I think that "to buy," and "to love," may be construed as developments of the same idea of *prizing highly*. When we say that a person is *appreciated*, we really say that he has had a proper price put upon him. The Latin *carus*, which Cicero calls *ipsum verbum amoris*,* means costly in price as well as beloved; and the tender English "dear" means quite as often that the object is expensive to buy, as that we dote very much upon it. Nor need we go outside of American languages for illustrations; in Nahuatl *tlazóti* means to offer for sale at a high price; and in Huasteca *canel*, from the same root as *canezal*, to love, means something precious in a pecuniary sense, as well as an object of the affections. Other instances will present themselves when we come to examine some of the South American

---

Annals of the Cakchiquels, p. 126 (Vol. VI of Brinton's Library of Aboriginal American Literature). In the Quiche *Popol Vuh* the word has the same meaning, as (page 102):

chi log u vach, their beloved face.

In fact, the word Dr. Stoll gives as that now usual among the Cakchiquels for "to love"=to desire, in the *Popol Vuh* is applied to the price paid for wives (p. 304):

rahil pu mial, the price of their daughters.

This word may be a derivative from the Maya *ya*, above mentioned.

* *De Naturâ Deorum*, I, 44.

tongues. But from what I have already given, it is evident that there is nothing contradictory in the double meaning of the verb *logoh*.

IV. THE QQUICHUA.

The ancient Peruvians who spoke the Qquichua language had organized a system of government and a complex social fabric unsurpassed by any on the continent. The numerous specimens of their arts which have been preserved testify strongly to the licentiousness of their manners, standing in this respect in marked contrast to the Aztecs, whose art was pure. It must be regarded as distinctly in connection with this that we find a similar contrast in their languages. We have seen that in the Nahuatl there appears to have been no word with a primary signification "to love" or any such conception. The Qquichua, on the contrary, is probably the richest language on the continent, not only in separate words denoting affection, but in modifications of these by imparting to them delicate shades of meaning through the addition of particles. As an evidence of the latter, it is enough to cite the fact that Dr. Anchorena, in his grammar of the tongue, sets forth nearly six hundred combinations of the word *munay*, to love!*

The Qquichua is fortunate in other respects; it has some literature of its own, and its structure has been carefully studied by competent scholars; it is possible, therefore, to examine its locutions in a more satisfactory manner than is the case with most American languages. Its most celebrated literary monument is the drama of *Ollanta*, supposed

---

* *Gramática Quechua*, por Dr. J. D. Anchorena, pp. 163-177 (Lima, 1874).

to have been composed about the time of the conquest. It has been repeatedly edited and translated, most accurately by Pacheco Zegarra.* His text may be considered as the standard of the pure ancient tongue.

Of Qquichua words for the affections, that in widest use is the one above quoted, *munay*. It is as universal in its application as its English equivalent, being applied to filial and parental love as well as to that of the sexes, to affection between persons of the same sex, and to the love of God. No other word of the class has such a wide significance. It ranges from an expression of the warmest emotion down to that faint announcement of a preference which is conveyed in the English, " I should prefer."†

On looking for its earlier and concrete sense, we find that *munay* expressed merely a sense of want, an appetite and the accompanying desire of satisfying it, hence the will, or the the wish, not subjectively, but in the objective manifestation.‡ Therefore it is in origin nearly equivalent to the earliest meaning of " love," as seen in the Sanscrit and the Coptic.

---

* *Ollanta : Drame en vers Quechuas du Temps des Incas.* Traduit et commenté par Gavino Pacheco Zegarra (Paris, 1878).

† Thus, from the *Ollanta :*
Ollantaytan munar ccanqui, thou lovest Ollanta ! (line 277).
munacusccallay, my well beloved! (the Inca to his daughter, line 344).
munayman, I should prefer (line 1606).
Holguin, in his *Vocabulario de la Lengua Qquichua*, gives:
Dios munay, the love of God.
munaricuy, unchaste love.

‡ Holguin (u. s.) gives the definitions :
munana, la voluntad que es potentia.
munay, voluntad, el querer, el gusto, appetito ó amor que es acto.

While *munay* is thus to love on reasonable grounds and with definite purpose, blind, unreasoning, absorbing passion is expressed by *huaylluni*. This is nearly always confined to sexual love, and conveys the idea of the sentiment showing itself in action by those sweet signs and marks of devotion which are so highly prized by the loving heart. The origin of this word indicates its sentient and spontaneous character. Its radical is the interjection *huay*, which among that people is an inarticulate cry of tenderness and affection.*

The verb *lluylluy* means literally to be tender or soft, as fruit, or the young of animals; and applied to the sentiments, to love with tenderness, to have as a darling, to caress lovingly. It has less of sexuality in it than the word last mentioned, and is applied by girls to each other, and as a term of family fondness. It is on a parallel with the English "dear," "to hold dear," etc.†

In the later compositions in Qquichua the favorite word for love is *ccuyay*. Originally this expression meant to pity, and in this sense it occurs in the drama of Ollanta ; but also even there as a term signifying the passion of love apart from any idea of compassion.‡ In the later songs, those

---

* From the *Ollanta:*
 Huay ccoyailay, Huay mamallay,
 Ay, huayliucusccay ccosallay.
 Oh, my queen! Oh my mother!
 Oh, my husband so beloved! (305, 306).
 These lines show both the word and its derivation.
† From the *Ollanta:*
 ña llulluspa, caress thee, are fond of thee (934).
‡ From the *Ollanta:*
 ccuyaccuscallay, my beloved one (1758).
 ccuyaska, compassionate (1765).

whose composition may be placed in this century, it is preferred to *munay* as the most appropriate term for the love between the sexes.* From it also is derived the word for charity and benevolence.

As *munay* is considered to refer to natural affection felt within the mind, *mayhuay* is that ostentatious sentiment which displays itself in words of tenderness and acts of endearment, but leaves it an open question whether these are anything more than simulated signs of emotion.†

This list is not exhaustive of the tender words in the Qquichua; but it will serve to show that the tongue was rich in them, and that the ancient Peruvians recognized many degrees and forms of this moving sentiment.

What is also noteworthy is the presence in this language of the most philosophical term for friendship in its widest sense that can be quoted from any American language. It is *runaccuyay*, compounded of *ccuyani*, mentioned above, and *runa*, man—the love of mankind. This compound, however, does not occur in the Ollanta drama, and it may have been manufactured by the missionaries. The usual term is *maciy*, which means merely "associate," or *kochomaciy*, a table-companion or *convive*.

V. THE TUPI-GUARANI.

The linguistic stock which has the widest extension in South America is that which is represented in Southern Brazil by the Guarani, and in Central and Northern by the Tupi or Lingoa Geral. The latter is spoken along the Ama-

---

* See the Qquichua love songs, *harahui* and *huaynu*, as they are called, given by Anchorena in his *Gramática Quechua*, pp. 131-135.

† See Holguin, *Vocabulario Qquichua*, s. v. *mayhuay* and *mayhuayccuni*.

zon and its tributaries for a distance of twenty-five hundred miles. It is by no means identical with the Guarani, but the near relationship of the two is unmistakable. The Guarani presents the simpler and more primitive forms, and may be held to present the more archaic type.

The word for love in the Guarani is *aihu*, in another form *haihu*, the initial *h* being dropped in composition. This expression is employed for all the varieties of the sentiment, between men, between the sexes, and for that which is regarded as divine.* For "a friend," they have no other term than one which means a visitor or guest; and from this their expression for "friendship" is derived, which really means "hospitality."†

Verbal combinations in Guarani are usually simple, and I do not think we can be far wrong in looking upon *aihu* as a union of the two primary words *ai* and *hu*. The former, *ai*, means self or the same; and the latter, *hu*, is the verb to find, or, to be present.‡ "To love," in Guarani, therefore, would mean, "to find oneself in another," or, less metaphysically, "to discover in another a likeness to one's self." This again is precisely the primary signification of the Latin *amare;* and if the sentiment impressed in that way the bar-

---

* Thus :

Tupa nande raihu, God loves us.

Tupa nande haihu, the love which we have for God.

ahaihu, I love her (him, it).

† *yecotiaha*, friend ; compounded of *coti*, a dwelling, and *aha*, to go,—a goer to a dwelling, a visitor. This, and the other Guarani words given, are taken from Ruiz de Montoya's *Tesoro de la Lengua Guarani* (ed. Vienna, 1876).

‡ Another possible derivation would be from *ahii*, desire, appetite (Spanish, *gana*); and *hu*, in the sense of being present. This would express a longing, a lust, like love (see above).

barous ancient Aryans, there is no reason why it would not have struck the Guaranis in the same manner.

In the Tupi or Lingua Geral the word for love is evidently but a dialectic variation of that in Guarani. It is given by some authors as *çaiçu*, plainly a form of *haihu;* and by others as *çauçu*.* These forms cannot be analyzed in the Tupi itself, which illustrates its more modern type.

There are other dialects of this widespread stem, but it would not be worth while to follow this expression further in its diverse forms. It is interesting, however, to note that which appears in the Arawack, spoken in Guiana. In that tongue to love is *kanisin*, in which the radical is *ani* or *ansi*. Now we find that *ani* means "of a kind," peculiar to, belonging to, etc. Once more it is the notion of similarity, of "birds of a feather," which underlies the expression for the conception of love.†

CONCLUSIONS.

If, now, we review the ground we have gone over, and classify the conception of love as revealed in the languages under discussion, we find that their original modes of expression were as follows:

---

* I find *çaiçu* given by Dr. Couto de Magelhaes in his *Cours da Lingoa Geral segundo Ollendorf* (Rio de Janeiro, 1876); *saisu* by Dr. Amaro Cavalcanti in *The Brazilian Language and its Agglutination* (Rio Janeiro, 1883); *çauçub* by Dias, *Diccionario da Lingua Tupy* (Leipzig, 1858), and by Dr. E. F. França in his *Chrestomathia da Lingua Brasilica* (Leipzig, 1859).

† "*Ani*, es gehört, ist eigen; *ta ani*, nach seiner Art." *Arawackisch-Deutsches Wörterbuch*. This dictionary, published anonymously at Paris, in 1882, in Tome viii of the *Bibliotheque Linguistique Américaine*, is the production of the Moravian Missionary, Rev. T. S. Schuhmann. See *The Literary Works of the Foreign Missionaries of the Moravian Church*. By the Rev. G. H. Reichelt. Translated and annotated by Bishop Edmund de Schweinitz, p. 13 (Bethlehēm, 1886).

1. Inarticulate cries of emotion (Cree, Maya, Qquichua).
2. Assertions of sameness or similarity (Cree, Nahuatl, Tupi, Arawack).
3. Assertions of conjunction or union (Cree, Nahuatl, Maya).
4. Assertions of a wish, desire or longing (Cree, Cakchiquel, Qquichua, Tupi).

These categories are not exhaustive of the words which I have brought forward, but they include most of them, and probably were this investigation extended to embrace numerous other tongues, we should find that in them all the principal expressions for the sentiment of love are drawn from one or other of these fundamental notions. A most instructive fact is that these notions are those which underlie the majority of the words for love in the great Aryan family of languages. They thus reveal the parallel paths which the human mind everywhere pursued in giving articulate expression to the passions and emotions of the soul. In this sense there is a oneness in all languages, which speaks conclusively for the oneness in the sentient and intellectual attributes of the species.

We may also investigate these categories, thus shown to be practically universal, from another point of view. We may inquire which of them comes the nearest to the correct expression of love in its highest philosophic meaning. Was this meaning apprehended, however dimly, by man in the very infancy of his speech-inventing faculty?

In another work, published some years ago, I have attempted a philosophic analysis of the sentiment of love. Quoting from some of the subtlest dissectors of human motive, I have shown that they pronounce love to be "the volition of the end," or "the resting in an object as an end." These rather obscure scholastic formulas I have attempted to explain by the definition: "Love is the mental impression of rational action whose end is in itself."* As every end or purpose of action implies the will or wish to that end, those expressions for love are most truly philosophic which expressthe will, the desire, the yearning after the object. The fourth, therefore, of the above categories is that which presents the highest forms of expression of this conception. That it also expresses lower forms is true, but this merely illustrates the evolution of the human mind as expressed in language. Love is ever the wish; but while in lower races and coarser natures this wish is for an object which in turn is but a means to an end, for example, sensual gratification, in the higher this object is the end itself, beyond which the soul does not seek to go, in which it rests, and with which both reason and emotion find the satisfaction of boundless activity without incurring the danger of satiety.

---

* *The Religious Sentiment, its Source and Aim; a Contribution to the Science and Philosophy of Religion*, p. 60 (New York, 1876).

THE LINEAL MEASURES OF THE SEMI-CIVILIZED NATIONS OF MEXICO AND CENTRAL AMERICA.

POSITIVE progress in constructive art can be accurately estimated by the kind and perfection of the instruments of precision employed by the artists. A correct theory of architecture or of sculpture must have as its foundation a correct system of weights and measures, and recognized units and standards of gravity and extension. Where these are not found, all is guess-work, and a more or less haphazard rule-of-thumb.

In a study of the art-products of Mexico and Central America, it has occurred to me that we may with advantage call linguistics to our aid, and attempt to ascertain, by an analysis of the words for weights and measures, what units, if any, were employed by those who constructed the massive works in that region, which still remain for our astonishment. The tongues I shall examine are the Maya of Yucatan, its related dialect the Cakchiquel of Guatemala, and the Nahuatl or Aztec of Mexico. The most striking monuments of art in North America are found in the territories where these where spoken at the time of the Conquest. The Cakchiquel may be considered to include the Quiche and the

* From the *Proceedings* of the American Philosophical Society for 1885.

Tzutuhil, both of which are closely associated to it as dialects of the same mother tongue.

THE MAYAS.

The generic word in Maya for both measuring and weighing, and for measures and weights, is at present *ppiz*, the radical sense of which is "to put in order," "to arrange definite limits." Its apparent similarity to the Spanish *pesar*, French *peser*, etc., seems accidental, as it is in Maya the root of various words meaning battle, to fight, etc., from the "order of battle," observed on such occasions. Any weight or measure is spoken of as *ppizib*, to measure land is *ppiz-luum*, a foot measure *ppiz-oc* etc. But I am quite certain that the original scope of the word did not include weight, as there is no evidence that the ancient Mayas knew anything about a system of estimating quantity by gravity. If the word is not from the Spanish *pesar*, it has extended its meaning since the conquest.

The Maya measures are derived directly, and almost exclusively, from the human body, and largely from the hand and foot.

Oc, the foot; *chekoc*, the footstep, the print or length of the foot, is a measure of length. Other forms of the same are *chekel*, *chekeb*, *chekeb-oc*, etc.; and this abundance of synonyms would seem to show that the measure of a foot was very familiar and frequent. The verb is *chekoc* (*tah*, *té*), as in the phrase:

Chekocté y otoch Ku.
He measured by feet His house God.

i. e. He measured by feet the church. From this was distinguished—

Xukab, paces or strides, a word confined to the paces of man. The verb is *Xukab* (*tah, té*), to step off, to measure by paces.

Quite a series of measures were recognized from the ground (or, as some say, from the point of the foot) to the upper portions of the body.

Hun cal coy u-xul (one to the neck of the ankle its-end), extending from the ground to the narrowest portion of the ankle.

Hun ppuloc u-xul (one calf-of-the-leg its-end), from the ground to the highest portion of the calf of the leg. The word *xul* means end or limit, and is used often adverbially, as in the phrase *uay u-xul*, literally "here its end," or "thus far" (Span. *hasta aquí*).

Hun pixib, the distance from the ground (or point of the toes) to the knee-cap. From *piix*, the knee. Also called *hun hol piix*, from *hol*, head, the knee-cap being called "the knee-head."

Hun hachabex, one girdle, from the ground to the belt or girdle, to which the skirt was fashioned (from *hach*, to tie, to fasten). The same measure was called *hun theth*, the word *theth* being applied to the knot of the girdle.

Hun tanam, from the ground to the border of the true ribs; from *tanam*, the liver. The *Diccionario de Motul* gives the example, *hun tanam in ual*, one *tanam* (is) my corn, *i. e.*, my corn reaches to my chest. It adds that the measure is from the point of the foot to the chest.

Hun tzem, a measure from the ground to a line drawn from one mamma to the other.

Hun cal u-xul, one neck its-end, from the ground to the border (upper or lower) of the neck.

Hun chi, from the mouth, *chi*, to the ground.

Hun holom, one head, from the top of the head to the ground. This is also called *hun uallah*, one time the stature or height of a man, from a root meaning "to draw to a point," "to finish off." The Spanish writers say that one *uallah* was equal to about three *varas*, and was used as a square measure in meting corn fields.* The Spanish *vara* differed as much as the English ell, and to the writer in question could not have represented quite two feet. Elsewhere he defines the *vara* as half a *braza* or fathom. (See below, *betan*.)

The hand in Maya is expressed by the word *kab*, which also means the arm, and is more correctly therefore translated by the anatomical term "upper extremity." This is not an uncommon example in American tongues. When it is necessary to define the hand specifically the Mayas say *u cheel kab*, "the branch of the arm," and for the fingers *u nii kab*, "the points (literally, noses) of the arm" or upper extremity.

The shortest measurements known to them appear to have been finger-breadths, which are expressed by the phrase *u nii kab*. The thumb was called *u nā kab*, literally "the mother of the hand" or arm, and as a measure of length the distance from the first joint to the end of the nail was in use and designated by the same term.

With the hand open and the fingers extended, there were three different measures or spans recognized by the Mayas.

---

* *Diccionario del Convento de Motul*, MS., s. v.

1. The *nāb*, from the tip of the thumb to the tip of the middle finger.

2. The *ɔecnab*, or little *nāb*, from the tip of the thumb to the tip of the index finger. This is the span yet most in use by the native inhabitants of Yucatan (Dr. Berendt).

3. The *chi nāb*, or the *nāb* which extends to the edge, from the tip of the thumb to the tip of the little finger (Pio Perez).

The *kok* was a hand measure formed by closing the fingers and extending the thumb. Measuring from the outer border of the hand to the end of the thumb, it would be about seven inches.

The *cuc* or *noch cuc* (*noch* is a term applied to a bony prominence, in this instance to the olecranon) was the cubit, and was measured from the summit of the olecranon to the end of the fingers, about eighteen inches.

The most important of the longer measures was the *zap* or *zapal*. It was the distance between the extremities of the extended arms, and is usually put down at a fathom or six feet.

The half of it was called *betan* or *pātan*, meaning "to the middle of the chest." Canes and cords were cut of the fixed length of the *zap* and bore the name *xapalche*, *zap*-sticks, as our *yard-stick* (*che* = stick), and *hilppiz*, measuring rods (*hil*, a species of cane, and *ppiz*, to measure, *Dicc. Motul*).

On this as a unit, the customary land measure was based. It was the *kaan*, one shorter, *hun kaan tah ox zapalche*, a *kaan* of three *zap*, and one longer, *hun kaan tah can zapalche*, a *kaan* of four *zap*. The former is stated to be thirty-six fathoms square, the latter forty-eight fathoms square. Twenty *kaan* made a *vinic*, man, that amount of land being considered the area requisite to support one family in maize.

The uncertainty about this measure is increased by the evident error of Bishop Landa, or more probably his copyist, in making the *vinic* equal to 400 square feet, which even in the most favored soils would never support a family. He probably said "400 feet square," which in that climate would be sufficient. The *kaan* is said by Spanish writers to be equal to the Mexican *mecate*, which contains 5184 square feet. I acknowledge, however, that I have not reconciled all the statements reported by authors about these land measures.

Greater measures of length are rarely mentioned. Journeys were measured by *lub*, which the Spaniards translated "leagues," but by derivation it means "resting places," and I have not ascertained that it had a fixed length.

The Mayas were given to the drawing of maps, and the towns had the boundaries of their common lands laid out in definite lines. I have manuscripts, some dated as early in 1542, which describe these town lands. In most of them only the courses are given, but not the distances. In one, a title to a domain in Acanceh, there are distances given, but in a measure quite unknown to me, *sicina*, preceded by the numeral and its termination indicating measures, *hulucppiz sicina*, eleven sicinas.*

The maps indicate relative position only, and were evidently not designed by a scale, or laid off in proportion to distance. The distinguished Yucatecan antiquary, the Rev.

---

* *Acanceh Cheltun. Titulo de un solar y Monte in Acanceh*, 1767, MS.

Don Crescencio Carrillo, in his essay on the cartography of the ancient Mayas,* apparently came to the same conclusion, as he does not not mention any method of measurement.

I do not know of any measurements undertaken in Yucatan to ascertain the metrical standard employed by the ancient architects. It is true that Dr. Augustus LePlongeon asserts positively that they knew and used *the metric system*, and that the metre and its divisions are the only dimensions that can be applied to the remains of the edifices.† But apart from the eccentricity of this statement, I do not see from Dr. LePlongeon's own measurements that the metre is in any sense a common divisor for them.

From the linguistic evidence, I incline to believe that the *oc*, the foot, was their chief lineal unit. This name was also applied to the seventh day of the series of twenty which made up the Maya month; and there may be some connection between these facts and the frequent recurrence of the number seven in the details of their edifices.‡

THE CAKCHIQUELS.

The root-word for measuring length is, in Cakchiquel, *et*. Its primitive meaning is, a sign, a mark, a characteristic. From this root are derived the verbal *etah*, to measure length, to lay out a plan, to define limits; *etal*, a sign, mark,

---

* *Geografia Maya. Anales del Museo Nacional de Mexico*, Tomo ii, p. 435.

† "The metre is the *only measure of dimension* which agrees with that adopted by these most ancient artists and architects."—Dr. Le Plongeon, *Mayapan and Maya Inscriptions*, in *Proceedings* of the American Antiquarian Society, April, 1881.

‡ Nearly all the monuments of Yucatan bear evidence that the Mayas had a predilection for the number *seven*," etc. Le Plongeon, *Vestiges of the Mayas*, p. 63 (New York, 1881). Of course, this may have other symbolic meanings also.

limit; *etabal*, measuring field; *etamah*, to know, *i. e.*, to recognize the signs and characters of things; *etamanizah*, to cause to know, to teach, to instruct, etc.

My authorities do not furnish evidence that the Cakchiquels used the foot as the unit of measurement, differing in this from the Mayas. They had, however, like the latter, a series of measurements from the ground to certain points of the body, and they used a special terminal particle, *bem* (probably from *be*, to go), "up to" to indicate such measurements, as *vexibem*, up to the girdle (*vex*, girdle, *i*, connective, *bem*, up to, or "it goes to").

These body measures, as far as I have found them named, are as follows:

quequebem, from the ground to the knee.

ru-vach a, from the ground to the middle of the thigh; literally "its front, the thigh," *ru*, its, *vach*, face, front, *a*, the muscles of the thigh).)

vexibem, from the ground to the girdle, *vex*.

qaalqaxibem, from the ground to the first true ribs.

kulim, from the ground to the neck (*kul*).

The more exact Cakchiquel measures were derived from the upper extremity. The smallest was the finger breadth, and was spoken of as one, two, three, four fingers, *han ca, cay ca, ox ca, cah ca* (*ca* = finger). This was used in connection with the measure called *tuvic*, the same that I have described as the Maya *kok*, obtained by closing the hand and extending the thumb. They combined these in such expressions as *ca tuvic raqin han ca*, two *tuvics* with (plus) one finger breadth.*

---

* Coto, *Diccionario de la Lengua Cakchiquel*, MS.

CAKCHIQUEL MEASURES.

The span of the Cakchiquels was solely that obtained by extending the thumb and fingers and including the space between the extremities of the thumb and *middle* finger. It was called *qutu*, from the radical *qut*, which means to show, to make manifest, and is hence akin in meaning to the root *et*, mentioned above.

The cubit, *chumay*, was measured from the point of the elbow to the extremities of the fingers. We are expressly informed by Father Coto that this was a customary building measure. "When they build their houses they use this cubit to measure the length of the logs. They also measure ropes in the same manner, and say, *Tin chumaih retaxic riqam*, I lay out in cubits the rope with which I am to measure."

The different measures drawn from the arms were:

chumay, from the elbow to the end of the fingers of the same hand.

hahmehl, from the elbow to the ends of the fingers of the opposite hand, the arms being outstretched.

telen, from the point of the shoulder of one side to the ends of the fingers of the outstretched arm on the other side.

tzam telen, from the point of the shoulder to the ends of the fingers on the same side. *Tzam* means nose, point, beak, etc.

ru vach qux, from the middle of the breast to the end of the outstretched hand.

hah, from the tips of the fingers of one hand to those of the other, the arms outstretched.

Another measure was from the point of the shoulder to the wrist.

The *hah*, or fathom, was one of the units of land measure, and the corn fields and cacao plantations were surveyed and laid out with ropes, *qam*, marked off in fathoms. The fields are described as of five ropes, ten ropes, etc., but I have not found how many fathoms each rope contained.

Another unit of land measure in frequent use was the *maaoh*. This was the circumference of the human figure. A man stood erect, his feet together, and both arms extended. The end of a rope was placed under his feet and its slack passed over one hand, then on top of his head, then over the other hand, and finally brought to touch the beginning. This gives somewhat less than three times the height. This singular unit is described by both Varea and Coto as in common use by the natives.

There were no accurate measures of long distances. As among the Mayas, journeys were counted by resting places, called in Cakchiquel *uxlanibal*, literally "breathing places," from *uxla*, the breath, itself, a derivative of the radical *ux*, to exist, to be, to live, the breath being taken as the most evident sign of life.

There was originally no word in Cakchiquel meaning "to weigh," as in a balance, and therefore they adopted the Spanish *peso*, as *tin pesoih*, I weigh. Nor, although they constructed stone walls of considerable height, did they have any knowledge of the plumb line or plummet. The name they gave it even shows that they had no idea what its use was, as they called it "the piece of metal for fastening together," supposing it to be an aid in cementing the stone work, rather than in adjusting its lines.*

---

* Coto, *Diccionario*, MS., s. v. "Ploma de albañil."

The Aztecs.

In turning to the Mexicans or Aztecs, some interesting problems present themselves. As far as I can judge by the Nahuatl language, measures drawn from the upper extremity were of secondary importance, and were not the bases of their metrical standards, and, as I shall show, this is borne out by a series of proofs from other directions.

The fingers, *mapilli*, appear to have been customary measures. They are mentioned in the early writers as one equal to an inch. The name *mapilli*, is a synthesis of *maitl*, hand, and *pilli*, child, offspring, addition, etc,

The span was called *miztetl* or *miztitl*, a word of obvious derivation, meaning "between the finger nails," from *iztetl*, finger nail. This span, however, was not like ours, from the extremity of the thumb to the extremity of the little finger, nor yet like that of the Cakchiquels, from the extremity of the thumb to that of the middle finger, but like that now in use among the Mayas (see above), from the extremity of the thumb to that of the index finger.*

There were four measures from the point of the elbow; one to the wrist of the same arm, a second to the wrist of the opposite arm, a third to the ends of the fingers of the same arm, and the fourth to the ends of the fingers of the opposite arm, the arms always considered as extended at right angles to the body. The terms for these are given somewhat confusedly in my authorities, but I believe the following are correct.

1. From the elbow to the wrist of the same arm; *cemmat-*

---

*"Cuanto se mide con el pulgar y el indice." Molina, *Vocabulario de la Lengua Mexicana*.

zotzopatzli, "a little arm measure," from *ce*, a, one, *ma* from *maitl*, arm or hand, *tzotzoca*, small, inferior, *patzoa*, to make small, to diminish.

2. From the elbow to the wrist of the opposite arm, *cemmitl*, an arrow, a shaft, from *ce*, and *mitl*, arrow, this distance being the approved length of an arrow. We may compare the old English expression, a "cloth-yard shaft."

3. From the elbow to the ends of the fingers of the same arm, *cemmolicpitl*, one elbow, *ce*, one, *molicpitl*, elbow. This is the cubit.

4. From the elbow to the ends of the fingers of the opposite arm.

The following were the arm measures:

Cemaçolli, from the tip of the shoulder to the end of the hand (*ce*, one, *maçoa*, to extend the arm).

Cemmatl, from the tip of the fingers of one hand to those of the other. Although this word is apparently a synthesis of *ce*, one, *maitl*, arm, and means "one arm," it is uniformly rendered by the early writers *una braza*, a fathom.

Cenyollotli, from the middle of the breast to the end of the fingers (*ce*, one, *yollotl*, breast).

It is known that the Aztecs had a standard measure of length which they employed in laying out grounds and constructing buildings. It was called the *octacatl*, but neither the derivation of this word, nor the exact length of the measure it represented, has been positively ascertained. The first syllable, *oc*, it will be noticed, is the same as the Maya word for foot, and in Nahuatl *xocopalli* is "the sole of the foot." This was used as a measure by the decimal system, and there were in Nahuatl two separate and apparently original words to express a measure of ten foot-lengths. One was:

Matla xocpallatamachiualoni, which formidable synthesis is analyzed as follows: *matla*, from *matlactli*, ten, *xocpal*, from *xocpalli*, foot-soles, *tamachiuia*, to measure (from *machiotl*, a sign or mark, like the Cakchiquel *etal*), *l*, for *lo*, sign of the passive, *oni*, a verbal termination "equivalent to the Latin *bilis* or *dus*."* Thus the word means that which is measurable by ten foot-lengths.

The second word was *matlacyxitlatamachiualoni*.

The composition of this is similar to the former, except that in the place of the perhaps foreign root *xoc*, foot, *yxitl*, foot, is used, which seems to have been the proper Nahuatl term.

As these words prove that the foot-length was one of the standards of the Aztecs, it remains to be seen whether they enlighten us as to the *octacatl*. I quote in connection an interesting passage by the native historian, Fernando de Alva Ixtlilxochitl in his *Historia Chichimeca*, published in Lord Kingsborough's great work on Mexico (Vol. ix., p. 242). Ixtlilxochitl is describing the vast communal dwelling built by the Tezcucan chieftain Nezahualcoyotl, capable of accommodating over two thousand persons. He writes: "These houses were in length from east to west four hundred and eleven and a half [native] measures, which reduced to our [Spanish] measures make twelve hundred and thirty-four and a half yards (*varas*), and in breadth, from north to south three hundred and twenty-six measures, which are nine hundred and seventy-eight yards."

---

*Carochi, *Arte de la Lengua Mexicana*, p. 123.

This passage has been analyzed by the learned antiquary, Señor Orozco y Berra.* The native measure referred to by Ixtlilxochitl was that of Tezcuco, which was identical with that of Mexico. The yard was the *vara de Burgos*, which had been ordered to be adopted throughout the colony by an ordinance of the viceroy Antonio de Mendoza. This vara was in length 0.838 metre, and, as according to the chronicler, the native measurement was just three times this ($411\frac{1}{2} \times 3 = 1234\frac{1}{2}$, and $326 \times 3 = 978$), it must have been 2.514 metre. This is equal in our measure to 9.842 feet, or, say, nine feet ten inches.

This would make the *octacatl* identical with those long-named ten-foot measures, which, as I have shown, were multiples of the length of the foot, as is proved by an analysis of their component words.

This result is as interesting as it is new, since it demonstrates that the metrical unit of ancient Mexico was the same as that of ancient Rome—the length of the foot-print.

Some testimony of another kind may be brought to illustrate this point.

In 1864, the Mexican government appointed a commission to survey the celebrated ruins of Teotihuacan, ander the care of Don Ramon Almaraz. At the suggestion of Señor Orozco, this able engineer ran a number of lines of construction to determine what had been the metrical standard of the builders. His decision was that it was "about" met. 0.8, or, say, $31\frac{1}{2}$ inches.† This is very close to an even

---

* Orozco y Berra, *Historia Antigua de la Conquista de Mexico*, Tomo i, pp. 557-8, (Mexico, 1880).

† *Memoria de los Trabajos ejecutados por la comision scientifica de Pachuca en el año*

third of the *octacatl*, and would thus be a common divisor of lengths laid off by it.

I may here turn aside from my immediate topic to compare these metrical standards with that of the Mound-Builders of the Ohio valley.

In the *American Antiquarian*, April, 1881, Prof. W. J. McGee applied Mr. Petrie's arithmetical system of "inductive metrology" to a large number of measurements of mounds and earthworks in Iowa, with the result of ascertaining a common standard of 25.716 inches.

In 1883, Col. Charles Whittlesey, of Cleveland, analyzed eighty-seven measurements of Ohio earthworks by the method of even divisors and concluded that thirty inches was about the length, or was one of the multiples, of their metrical standard.*

Moreover, fifty-seven per cent. of all the lines were divisible without remainder by ten feet. How much of this may have been owing to the tendency of hurried measurers to average on fives and tens, I cannot say; but leaving this out of the question, there is a probability that a ten foot-length rule was used by the "mound-builders" to lay out their works.

It may not be out of place to add a suggestion here as to the applicability of the methods of inductive metrology to American monuments. The proportions given above by Ixtlilxochitl, it will be noted, are strikingly irregular

---

de 1861, p. 357, quoted by Orozco. Almaraz's words are not at all precise: "la unidad lineal, con pequeñas modificaciones, debió ser cosa de o. m 8, ó cuatro palmos próximamente."

* *The Metrical Standard of the Mound-Builders*. Reduced by the Method of Even Divisors. By Col. Chas. Whittlesey (Cleveland, 1883).

(411½, 326). Was this accident or design? Very likely the latter, based upon some superstitious or astrological motive. It is far from a solitary example. It recurs everywhere in the remarkable ruins of Mitla. "Careful attention," says Mr. Louis H. Aymé, "has been paid to make the whole asymmetrical. * * * This asymmetry of Mitla is not accidental, I am certain, but made designedly. M. Désiré Charnay tells me he has observed the same thing at Palenque." These examples should be a warning against placing implicit reliance on the mathematical procedures for obtaining the lineal standards of these forgotten nations.*

Whatever the lineal standard of the Aztecs may have been, we have ample evidence that it was widely recognized, very exact, and officially defined and protected. In the great market of Mexico, to which thousands flocked from the neighboring country (seventy thousand in a day, says Cortes, but we can cut this down one-half in allowance for the exaggeration of an enthusiast), there were regularly appointed government officers to examine the measures used by the merchants and compare them with the correct standard. Did they fall short, the measures were broken and the merchant severely punished as an enemy to the public weal.†

The road-measures of the Aztecs was by the stops of the carriers, as we have seen was also the case in Guatemala. In Nahuatl these were called *neceuilli*, resting places, or

---

* *Notes on Mitla*, in *Proceedings of the American Antiquarian Society*, April, 1882, p. 97.

† See Herrera, *Decadas de Indias*, Dec. ii, Lib. vii, cap. xvi, and Dec. iii, Lib. iv. cap. xvii. "Castigaban mucho alque falseaba medidas, diciendo que era enemigo de todos i ladron publico," etc.

netlatolli, sitting places; and distances were reckoned numerically by these, as one, two, three, etc., resting places. Although this seems a vague and inaccurate method, usage had attached comparatively definite ideas of distance to these terms. Father Duran tells us that along the highways there were posts or stones erected with marks upon them showing how many of these stops there were to the next market-towns—a sort of mile-stones, in fact. As the competition between the various markets was very active, each set up its own posts, giving its distance, and adding a curse on all who did not attend, or were led away by the superior attractions of its rivals.*

So far as I have learned, the lineal measures above mentioned were those applied to estimate superficies. In some of the plans of fields, etc., handed down, the size is marked by the native numerals on one side of the plan, which are understood to indicate the square measure of the included tract. The word in Nahuatl meaning to survey or measure lands is *tlalpoa*, literally "to count land," from *tlalli* land, *poa* to count.

The Aztecs were entirely ignorant of balances, scales or weights. Cortes says distinctly that when he visited the great market of Mexico-Tenochtitlan, he saw all articles sold by number and measure, and nothing by weight.†

---

* " Habian terminos señalados de cuantas leguas habian de acudir á los mercados," etc. Diego Duran, *Historia de la Nueva España*, Vol. ii, pp, 215, 217. Both the terms in the text are translated *legua* in Molina's Vocabulary, so that it is probable that the resting places were something near two and a half to three miles apart,

† " Todo lo venden por cuenta y medida, excepto que fasta agora no se ha visto vender cosa alguna por peso." *Cartas y Relaciones de Hernan Cortes*, p. 105. (Ed. Gayangos.)

The historian Herrera confirms this from other authorities, and adds that when grass or hay was sold, it was estimated by the length of a cord which could be passed around the bundle.*

The plumb-line must have been unknown to the Mexicans also. They called it *temetztepilolli*, "the piece of lead which is hung from on high," from *temetzli*, lead, and *piloa*, to fasten something high up. Lead was not unknown to the Aztecs before the conquest. They collected it in the Provinces of Tlachco and Itzmiquilpan, but did not esteem it of much value, and their first knowledge of it as a plummet must have been when they saw it in the hands of the Spaniards. Hence their knowledge of the instrument itself could not have been earlier.

The conclusions to which the above facts tend are as follows:

1. In the Maya system of lineal measures, foot, hand, and body measures were nearly equally prominent, but the foot unit was the customary standard.

2. In the Cakchiquel system, hand and body measures were almost exclusively used, and of these, those of the hand prevailed.

3. In the Aztec system, body measurements were unimportant, hand and arm measures held a secondary position, while the foot measure was adopted as the official and obligatory standard both in commerce and architecture.

---

* "Tenian medida para todas las cosas; hasta la ierva, que era tanta, quanta se podia atar con una cuerda de una braza por un tomin." Herrera, *Decadas de Indias*, Dec. ii, Lib. vii, cap. xvi. In another passage where this historian speaks of weights (Dec. iii, Lib. iv, cap. xvii), it is one of his not infrequent slips of the pen.

4. The Aztec terms for their lineal standard being apparently of Maya origin, suggest that their standard was derived from that nation.

5. Neither of the three nations was acquainted with a system of estimation by weight, nor with the use of the plumb-line, nor with an accurate measure of long distances.

THE CURIOUS HOAX OF THE TAENSA LANGUAGE.*

ONE might think it a difficult task to manufacture a new language "from the whole cloth;" but, in fact, it is no great labor. We have but to remember that within the last dozen years more than a dozen "world-languages" have been framed and offered for acceptance, and we at once perceive that a moderate knowledge of tongues and some linguistic ingenuity are all that is required.

It is an innocent amusement so long as no fraudulent use is made of the manufactured product; but the temptation to play a practical joke, and to palm off a deception on overeager linguists, is as great in languages as it is in archæology—and every antiquary knows how suspiciously he has to scrutinize each new specimen.

A curious hoax, which deceived some of the best linguists of Europe and America, was perpetrated about a decade ago by two young French seminarists, Jean Parisot and A. Dejouy. Interested by reading Châteaubriand, and by various publications on American languages which appeared in France about that time, they made up a short grammar and a list of words of what they called the *Tansa* language, from a name they found in Châteaubriand's *Voyage en Amerique*, and into this invented tongue they translated the Lord's

Prayer, the Creed, an Algonkin hymn published in Paris, and other material.

At first, the two students pursued this occupation merely as an amusement, but it soon occurred to them that more could be made of it; so M. Parisot sent a batch of the alleged "fragments" of the "Tansa" to the publishers, Maisonneuve et Cie, Paris, for publication. The manuscripts were passed over to M. Julien Vinson, editor of the *Révue de Linguistique*, who addressed the young author for further particulars. M. Parisot replied that these pieces were copies of originals obtained many years before by his grandfather, from what source he knew not, and on the strength of this vague statement, they duly appeared in the *Révue*.

Their publication attracted the attention of the eminent French linguist, M. Lucien Adam, who had long occupied himself with American tongues, and he entered into correspondence with M. Parisot. The latter's stock meanwhile had considerably increased. He and his friend had published at Epinal, apparently privately, a small pamphlet, with an introductory note in bad Spanish, containing a number of "songs" in the "Taensa," as they now called their language. They claimed in the note that the songs had been obtained by a traveler in America, in the year 1827 or 1828, "in the Taensa town, on the banks of the Mississippi or the Alabama" (!)*

---

* A copy of this curious production called *Cancionero Americano* is in the Library of the Bureau of Ethnology at Washington. The introductory note is as follows:

"Esos cantos, escogidos en el año mil y ocho cientos veinte y siete, ó veinte y ocho, por un viagero en America, y despues hallados en sus papeles, no vinieron jamás, siquiera por lo que podemos saber, conocidos del publico sabio. Estos son

With this abundant material at hand, young Parisot replied cheerfully to M. Adam, and supplied that scientist with "copy" from the alleged ancestral MSS. quite enough to fill a goodly volume of grammar, songs, lexicon, and the various paraphernalia of a linguistic apparatus, all of which eager M. Adam and his collaborator, Mr. A. S. Gatschet, the expert linguist attached to our Bureau of Ethnology, received in good faith and without a suspicion of the joker who victimized them; and what is more singular, without having a doubt excited by the many and gross blunders of the young seminarist.

Their joint work reached the United States in 1883, and for two years was received both here and in Europe as a genuine production. My attention was first attracted to it in 1883, and then I referred to it as a "strange" production; but I did not give it a close examination until the close of 1884. This examination led me to prepare the following article, which was published in the *American Antiquarian* for March, 1885:

THE TAENSA GRAMMAR AND DICTIONARY.

A Deception Exposed.

The student of American languages is under many obligations to the editors and publishers of the *Bibliothéque Linguistique Américaine*, nine volumes of which have been is-

---

los mismos cantos del Pueblo Taensa, para las orillas del Misisipi ó del Alabama, todos escritos en el dulce y pulido dialecto de aquel pueblo. Todos los amigos de la ciencia han de sentir el precio de esta pequeña colleccion."

It will be noticed that the Spanish is full of errors, as *esos* for *estos*, *hallados* for *encontrados*, *para las orillas* for *por las orillas*; and *sentir el precio* does not mean *appreciate*, as the author would say, but "regret the price."

sued by the firm of Maisonneuve et Cie., Paris. Most of these contain valuable authentic original material, from approved sources, and edited with judgment. The exception to this rule is the volume last issued, which from its character deserves more than a passing criticism.

This volume bears the following title: *Grammaire et Vocabulaire de la Langue Taensa, avec Textes Traduits et Commentés par J. D. Haumonté, Parisot, L. Adam.* Pp. 19, 111. It contains what professes to be a grammar of the Taensas Indians, who lived near the banks of the lower Mississippi, in the parish of that name in Louisiana, when it was first discovered, but who have long since become extinct. Following the grammar are the "Texts," a remarkable series of native songs in the alleged Taensa tongue, with a French translation, accompanied by a commentary and a vocabulary.

All this array has been received by scholars without question. It looks so extremely scientific and satisfactory that no one has dared assail its authenticity. Moreover, the book appears with an historical introduction by Mr. Albert S. Gatschet, of our Bureau of Ethnology, and one of the editors is M. Lucien Adam, a gentleman who stands at the head of European Americanists. Mr. Gatschet, moreover, fully recognizes the authenticity of the whole in his latest work, and up to the present I know of no one who has doubted it, either in this country or in Europe.

It is, therefore, only after a great deal of consideration and hesitation that I now give publicity to the opinion I have long entertained, that a gross deception has been somewhere practiced is the preparation of this book, and that it is not at all what it purports to be. Let it be understood that I distinctly exculpate the gentlemen I have named from any share in this; they can only be charged with the venial error of allowing their enthusiasm for knowledge to get the better of their critical acumen.

I shall proceed to give with as much brevity as possible the reasons which have led me to reject the pretended character of this work.

And first I may note that both the history of the alleged original manuscript and the method in which it has been presented are to the last degree unsatisfactory. About the former, M. Haumonté tells us that among the papers of his grandfather, who died as mayor of Plombères, in 1872, he found a manuscript in Spanish, without date or name of author, and that it is this manuscript "translated and arranged," which is the work before us. M. Adam adds that for his part he had revised this translation and advised the omission of certain passages not "profitable to science." I have been informed by a private source that M. Adam was not shown the original Spanish manuscript, although he asked to see it. We are deprived therefore of any expert opinion as to the age of the manuscript, or its authorship.

We naturally ask, how did this manuscript come to be in Spanish? No one has been able to point out in the voluminous histories of the Spanish Missions a single reference to any among the Taensas. Moreover, this tribe was constantly under French observation from its first discovery by La Salle in 1682, until its entire destruction and disappearance about 1730-40, as is minutely recorded by Charlevoix, who even adds the name of the planter who obtained the concession of their lands. With the knowledge we have of the early Louisiana colony, it would have been next to impossible for a Spanish monk to have lived with them long enough to have acquired their language, and no mention to have been made of him in the French accounts. That a Spaniard, not a monk, should have attempted it, would have excited still more attention from national distrust.

This preliminary ground of skepticism is not removed by turning to the grammar itself. As M. Adam remarks, the language is one "of extreme simplicity," such simplicity that it excites more than the feeling of astonishment. How much liberty M. Haumonté allowed himself in his translation he unfortunately does not inform us; but I suppose that he scarcely went so far as to offer original opinions on the pronunciation of a language which no man has heard spoken for more than a century. If he did not, then the writer of the original manuscript must have been a pretty good linguist for his day, since he explains the pronunciation of the Taensa by the French, the English, the German, and the Spanish ! ! (p. 4). I suppose the references on p. 11, to the Nahuatl, Kechua and Algonkin tongues are by the translator, though we are not so told; at any rate, they are by some one who has given a certain amount of study to American languages, and could get up one not wholly unlike them. There is, however, just enough unlikeness to all others in the so-called Taensa to make us accept it "with all reserves," as the French say. That an American language should have a distinctively grammatical gender, that it should have a true relative pronoun, that its numeral system should be based on the nine units in the extraordinarily simple manner here proposed, that it should have three forms of the plural, that its verbs should present the singular simplicity of these,—these traits are indeed not impossible, but they are too unusual not to demand the best of evidence.

But the evidence which leaves no doubt as to the humbuggery in this whole business is found in the so-called "Cancionero Taensa," or Taensa Poems. There are eleven of these, and according to M. Adam, "they give us unexpected information about the manners, customs and social condition of the Taensas." If he had also added, still more unexpected information about the physical geography of Louisiana, he would have spoken yet more to the point. For instance, our botanists will be charmed to learn that the sugar maple flourishes in the Louisiana swamps, and that it furnished a favorite food of the natives. It is repeatedly referred to (pp. 31, 34, 45, 67). They will also learn that the sugar cane was raised by the Taensas, although the books say it was introduced into Louisiana by the Jesuits in 1761 (p. 45). The potato and rice, apples and bananas, were also familiar to them, and the white birch and wild rice are described as flourishing around the bayous of the lower Mississippi ! It may be urged that these are all mistranslations of misunderstood native words. To this I reply, what sort of editing is that which not only could commit such unpardonable blunders, but send them forth to the scientific world without a hint that they do not pretend to be anything more than guesses?

But no such apology can be made. The author of this fabrication had not taken the simplest precaution to make his statements coincide with facts. How dense was his ignorance of the climate of Louisiana is manifested in the pretended "Calendar of the Taensas," which is printed on p. 41 of his book. He tells us that their year began at the vernal equinox and consisted of twelve or thirteen months named as follows:

1. Moon of the sugar maples (April).
2. Moon of flowers (May).
3. Moon of strawberries (June).
4. Moon of heat (July).
5. Moon of fruits (August).
6. Moon of the summer hunts (September).
7. Moon of leaves, (falling leaves) (October).
8. Moon of cold (November).
6. Moon of whiteness (i. e. of snow) (December).
10. Moon of fogs (January).
11. Moon of winter hunts (February).
12. Moon of birds (returning).   } (March).
13. Moon of green (returning green). }

How absurd on the face of it, such a calendar would be for the climate of Tensas Parish, La., need not be urged. The wonder is that any intelligent editor would pass it over without hesitation. The not infrequent references to snow and ice might and ought to have put him on his guard.

The text and vocabulary teem with such impossibilities; while the style of the alleged original songs is utterly unlike that reported from any other native tribe. It much more closely resembles the stilted and tumid imitations of supposed savage simplicity, common enough among French writers of the eighteenth century.

As a fair example of the nonsense of the whole, I will translate the last song given in the book, that called

THE MARRIAGE SONG.

1. The chief of the Chactas has come to the land of the warriors "I come." "Thou comest."

2. Around his body is a beautiful garment, he wears large leggings, sandals, tablets of white wood, feathers behind his head and behind his shoulders, on his head the antlers of a deer, a heavy war club in his right hand.

3. What is the wish of the great warrior who has come?

4. He wishes to speak to the chief of the numerous and powerful Taensas.

5. Let the warrior enter the house of the old men. The chief is seated in the midst of the old men. He will certainly hear thee. Enter the house of the old men.

6. Great chief, old man, I enter. Thou comest. Enter; bring him in. What wishes the foreign warrior? Speak, thou who hast come.

7. Old men, ancient men, I am the chief of many men; at ten days' journey up the river there lies the land of poplars, the land of the wild rice, which belongs to the brave warriors, the brothers of the Taensas.

8. They said to me—since thou hast not chosen a bride, go to the Taensas our brothers, ask of them a bride; for the Chactas are strong; we will ask a bride of the Taensas.

9. That is well; but speak, warrior, are the Chactas numerous?

10. Count; they are six hundred, and I am stronger than ten.

11. That is well; but speak, do they know how to hunt the buffalo and the deer? does the squirrel run in your great forests?

12. The land of the wild rice has no great forests, but cows, stags and elks dwell in our land in great numbers.

13. What plants grow in your country?

14. Poplars, the slupe tree, the myrtle grow there, we have the

sugar maple, ebony to make collars, the oak from which to make war clubs; our hills have magnolias whose shining leaves cover our houses.

15. That is well; the Taensas have neither the slupe tree nor the ebony, but they have the wax tree and the vine: has the land of the wild rice these also?

16. The Taensas are strong and rich, the Chactas are strong also, they are the brothers of the Taensas.

17. The Taensas love the brave Chactas, they will give you a bride; but say, dost thou come alone? dost thou bring bridal presents.

18. Twenty warriors are with me, and *bulls drag a wain*.

19. Let six, seven, twenty Taensa warriors go forth to meet those who come. For thee, we will let thee see the bride, she is my daughter, of me, the great chief; she is young; she is beautiful as the lily of the waters; she is straight as the white birch; her eyes are like unto the tears of gum that distil from the trees; she knows how to prepare the meats for the warriors and the sap of the sugar maple; she knows how to knit the fishing nets and keep in order the weapons of war—we will show thee the bride.

20. The strangers have arrived, the bulls have dragged up the wain. The warrior offers his presents to the bride, paint for her eyes, fine woven stuff, scalps of enemies, collars, beautiful bracelets, rings for her feet, and swathing-bands for her first born.

21. The father of the bride and the old man receive skins, horns of deer, solid bows and sharpened arrows.

22. Now let the people repose during the night; at sunrise there shall be a feast; then you shall take the bride in marriage.

And this is the song of the marriage.

The assurance which has offered this as a genuine composition of a Louisiana Indian is only equalled by the docility with which it has been accepted by Americanists. The marks of fraud upon it are like Falstaff's lies—"gross as a mountain, open, palpable." The Choctaws are located ten days' journey up the Mississippi in the wild rice region about the headwaters of the stream, whereas they were the immediate neighbors of the real Taensas, and dwelt when first discovered in the middle and southern parts of the present State of Mississippi. The sugar maple is made to grow in the Louisiana swamps, the broad-leaved magnolia and the ebony in Minnesota. The latter is described as the land of the myrtle, and the former of the vine. The northern warrior brings feet-rings and infant clothing as presents, while the southern bride knows all about boiling maple sap, and is like a white birch. But the author's knowledge of aboriginal customs stands out most prominently when he has the up-river chief come with an ox-cart and boast of his cows! After that passage I need say nothing more. He is indeed ignorant who does not know that not a single draft animal, and not one kept for its milk, was ever found among the natives of the Mississippi valley.

I have made other notes tending in the same direction, but it is scarcely necessary for me to proceed further. If the whole of this pretended Taensa language has been fabricated, it would not be the first time in literary history that such a fraud has been perpetrated. In the last century, George Psalmanazar framed a grammar of a fictitious language in Formosa, which had no existence whatever. So it seems to be with the Taensa; not a scrap of it can be found elsewhere, not a trace of any such tongue remains in Louisiana. What is more, all the old writers distinctly deny that this tribe had any independent language. M. De Montigny, who was among them in 1699, Father Gravier, who was also at their towns, and Du Pratz, the historian,

THE MANUSCRIPT LOST. 463

all say positively that the Taensas spoke the Natchez language and were part of the same people. We have ample specimens of the Natchez, and it is nothing like this alleged Taensa. Moreover, we have in old writers the names of the Taensa villages furnished by the Taensas themselves, and they are nowise akin to the matter of this grammar, but are of Chahta-Muskoki derivation.

What I have now said is I think sufficient to brand this grammar and its associated texts as deceptions practiced on the scientific world. If it concerns the editors and introducers of that work to discover who practiced and is responsible for that deception, let the original manuscript be produced and submitted to experts; if this is not done, let the book be hereafter pilloried as an imposture.

As soon as I could obtain reprints of the above article I forwarded them to M. Adam and others interested in American languages, and M. Adam at once took measures to obtain from the now "Abbé" Parisot the original MSS. That young ecclesiastic, however, professed entire ignorance of their whereabouts; he had wholly forgotten what disposition he had made of this portion of his grandfather's papers! He also charged M. Adam with having worked over (*remanié*) his material; and finally disclaimed all responsibility concerning it.

In spite, however, of his very unsatisfactory statements, M. Adam declined to recognize the fabrication of the tongue, and expressed himself so at length in a brochure entitled, *Le Taensa a-t-il été forgé de toutes Pièces? Reponse* à M. Daniel G. Brinton (pp. 22, Maissonneuve Frères et Ch. Leclerc, Paris, 1885). The argument which he made use of will be seen from the following reply which I published in *The American Antiquarian*, September, 1885:

THE TAENSA GRAMMAR AND DICTIONARY.

The criticism on the Taensa Grammar published in the *American Antiquarian* last March has led to a reply from M. Lucien Adam, the principal editor, under the following title: "*Le Taensa a-t-il-été forgé de toutes Pièces?*" As the question at issue is one of material importance to American archæology, I shall state M. Adam's arguments in defense of the Grammar.

It will be remembered that the criticism published last March closed with an urgent call for the production of the original MS., which M. Adam himself had never seen. To meet this, M. Adam as soon as practicable applied to M. Parisot, who alleged that he had translated the Grammar from the Spanish original, to produce that original. This M. Parisot professed himself unable to do; although only two or three years have elapsed, he cannot remember what he did with it, and he thinks it possible that it is lost or destroyed! The investigations, however, reveal two facts quite clearly: first, that the original MS., if there was one, was not in Spanish as asserted, and was not in the handwriting of M. Parisot's grandfather, as was also asserted, as the latter was certainly not the kind of man to occupy himself with any such document. He kept a sort of boardinghouse, and the suggestion now is that one of his temporary guests left this supposed MS. at his house. As its existence is still in doubt, this uncertainty about its origin need not further concern us.

The more important question is whether the language as presented in the Grammar and texts bears internal evidence of authenticity or not.

M. Adam begins with the texts, the so-called poems. To my surprise, M. Adam, so far as they pretend to be native productions, tosses them overboard without the slightest compunction. "In my own mind," he writes, "I have always considered them the work of some disciple of the Jesuit Fathers, who had taken a fancy to the Taensa poetry." This emphatic rejection of their aboriginal origin has led me to look over the volume again, as it seemed to me that if such was the opinion of the learned editor he should certainly have hinted it to his readers. Not the slightest intimation of the kind can be found in its pages.

The original MS. having disappeared, and the texts having been ruled out as at best the botch-work of some European, M. Adam takes his stand on the Grammar and maintains its authenticity with earnestness.

I named in my criticism six points in the grammatical structure of the alleged Taensa, specifying them as so extremely rare in American languages, that it demanded the best evidence to suppose that they all were present in this extraordinary tongue.

These points are discussed with much acuteness and fairness by M. Adam, and his arguments within these limits are considered convincing by so eminent an authority as Professor Friederich Müller, of Vienna, to whom they were submitted, and whose letter concerning them he publishes. What M. Adam does is to show that each of the peculiarities named finds a parallel in other American tongues, or he claims that the point is not properly taken. As I never denied the former, but merely called attention to the rarity of such features, the question is, whether the evidence is sufficient to suppose that several of them existed 'in this tongue; while as to the correctness of my characterization of Taensa Grammar, scholars will decide that for themselves.

It will be seen from the above that, even if some substructure will be shown to have existed for this Taensa Grammar and texts (which, individually, I still deny), it has been presented to the scientific world under conditions which were far from adequate to the legitimate demands of students.

M. Adam in the tone of his reply is very fair and uniformly courteous, except in his last sentence, where he cannot resist the temptation to have a fling at us for the supposed trait which Barnum and his compeers have conferred upon us among those who do not know us. "Permettez-moi de vous dire," he writes, "que la France n'est point la terre classique du *humbug*." Has M. Adam forgotten that George Psalmanazar, he who in the last century manufactured a langurge out of the whole cloth, grammar and dictionary and all, was a Frenchman born and bred? And that if the author of the Taensa volume has done the same, his only predecessor in this peculiar industry is one of his own nation?

THE HOAX ACKNOWLEDGED.

M. Adam continued his praiseworthy efforts to unearth the imaginary originals of the Abbé Parisot's hoax, but with the results one can easily anticipate—they were not forthcoming.*

The discussion continued in a desultory manner for some time, and Mr. Gatschet made the most strenuous efforts during his official journeys as government linguist in the southwest and in the Indian territory to find evidence showing that he had not been taken in by the ingenious French seminarists; but his continued silence was evidence enough that none such came to his ken.

In 1886 Professor Julien Vinson reviewed the question for the *Révue de Linguistique*, and delivered what may be considered the final verdict in the case. It is to the effect that the whole alleged language of the Taensas,—grammar, vocabulary, prose and poetry—is a fabrication by a couple of artful students to impose on the learned. I may close with the Professor's own closing words:

"Que restera-t-il du *taensa?* A mon avis, une mystification sans grande portée et *much ado about nothing.*"

---

*The discussion elicited the following additional brochures from M. Adam:

Le Taensa n'a pas été forgé de toutes pièces. Lettre de M. *Friedrich Müller à Lucien Adam,* pp. 4.

Dom Parisot ne produira pas le Manuscrit Taensa. Lettre à M. Victor Henry, pp. 13.

INDEX OF AUTHORS AND AUTHORITIES.

Abbot, C. C., 27, 32, 53, 185.
Abel-Remusat, 339.
Abel, Carl, 402, 410.
Adair, James, 71, 78.
Adam, Lucien, 36, 355-7, 374, 379, 389, 405, 406, 453, *sq.*
Adler, C. J., 328, 329.
Aglio, Agostino, 250.
Aguilar, Pedro Sanchez de, 236.
Albornoz, R. F., 399.
Alcazar, Padre, 76.
Almaraz, Ramon, 446.
Ameghino, Fiorentino, 31.
Anales de Chimalpahin, 283.
Anales de Cuauhtitlan, 86, 90, 210, 283.
Anales del Museo Nacional, 210, 439.
Anchieta, Joseph de, 381, *sq.*
Anchorena, Jose D., 365, 425, 428.
"Ancient Nahuatl Poems," 97, 154.
Ancona, Eligio, 258.
Andrews, 414.
Angrand, Leonce, 84, 253.
Annals of the Kakchiquels, 100, 423
Anthony, A. S., 181-192.
Archives paléographiques de l'Orient et de l'Amérique, 253.

Aubin, J. M. A., 196, 209, 210, 212, 220, 231, 282.
Avé Lallemant, Dr. R., 64.
Aymé, Louis H., 448.

Babbitt, Frances, 54.
Baeza, Bart. G. de, 164, 166.
Baker, Theodore, 293.
Bandelier, A. F., 275, 278.
Baraga, Frederic, 131, 364, 414.
Bartram, John, 75.
Bartram, William, 71, 76, 78.
Beach, W. W., 45.
Beauvois, E., 148.
Belcourt, Père, 399, 400.
Berendt, C. H., 119, 164, 171, 175, 179, 237, 272, 288, 295, 398.
Beverly, Robert, 70.
Bibliothéque Linguistique Americaine, 454.
Bichat, 57.
Biedma, his narrative, 72, 74.
Bienvenida, Lorenzo de, 26.
Blomes, Richard, 76.
Blumenbach, F. J., 38, 56, 57.
Boas, Franz, 22, 64, 286.
Books of the Jew, MS., 273.
Boole, Professor, 402.
Borde, M. de la, 123.
Boturini, B., 116.

INDEX OF AUTHORS AND AUTHORITIES.

Bourbourg, Brasseur de, *see* Brasseur.
Brasseur (de Bourbourg), C., 84, 105, 107, 120, 126, 128, 167, 170, 199, 210, 227, 231, 243, 263, 282.
Bristock, his fabulous narrative, 76.
Buenaventura, Gabriel de San, 237, 249.
Buschmann, J. C. E., 23, 92, 93.
Byington, Cyrus, 364.

Campanius, Thomas, 315.
Cancionero, Americano, 453.
Carochi, Horacio, 325, 418.
Carrillo, Crescencio, 258, 265, 439.
Carrillo, Estanislao, 164.
Cartailhac, Emile de, 391.
Casas, Bartolome de las, 124, 234.
Catherwood, Frederick, 254.
Cavalcanti, Amaro, 380-385, 430.
Cerou, Francisco, 107.
Champollion, 227.
Charencey, H. de, 59, 84, 167, 196, 372.
Charlevoix, P. F. X., 69, 456.
Charnay, D., 83, 86, 89, 97, 448.
Chateaubriand, 452.
Chilan Balam, Book of, 248, 254 *sqq.*, 303.
Chimalpahiu, D. F. de, 283.
Chronicles of the Mayas, 99, 100.
Cicero, M. T., 127, 424.
Clavigero, F., 84.
Codex Bolognensis, 158.
Codex Chimalpopoca, 210, 221.
Codex Cortesianus, 198, 253.
Codex Dresdensis, 199, 200, 250, *sq.*
Codex Mexicanus, No. II., 252.
Codex Peresianus, 252, 265.
Codex Poinsett, 154.

Codex Ramirez, the, 84, 89, 90, 91, 92.
Codex Telleriano-Remensis, 280.
Codex Troano, 114, 200, 202, 230, 253, 265.
Codex Vaticanus, 155, 280.
Codex Zumarraga, 250.
Codice Perez, 265.
Cogolludo, D. L., 127, 168, 235, 238, 268.
Colden, C., 68.
Coleccion de Documentos para la Historia de España, 235.
Comte, Auguste, 57.
Copway, George, 154.
Cortes, H. de, 448, 449.
Coto, Thomas, 106, 107, 110, 111 *sq.*, 440 *sq.*
Cresson, H. T., 41, 53.
Cuesta, Arroyo de la, 386-388.
Culin, Stewart, 151.
Cuoq, J. A., 132.
Cushing, Frank, 108.
Cuvier, G., 38, 57, 61.

Darapsky, Dr., 398.
Darwin, Charles, 39, 43, 408.
Dawson, J. William, 44.
Dawson, George M., 395.
Dead, Book of the, 136-140.
Dejouy, A., 452 *sq.*
Dias, 430.
Diccionario Historico de Yucatan, 263.
Diccionario Huasteca - Español, MS., 221.
Diccionario Maya - Español de Motul, MS., *see* Motul.
Dictionaire Galibi, 123.
Distel, Theodore, 330.
D'Orbigny, Alcide, 39.

INDEX OF AUTHORS AND AUTHORITIES. 471

Dorsey, J. O., 108.
Dumont, M., 77, 78.
Dumoutier, M., 150.
Dunbar, John B., 291.
Dupaix, Captain, 275, 276.
Duponceau, P. S., 36, 94, 191, 321, 351, 389.
Du Pratz, Lepage, 462.
Duran, Diego, 88, 89, 99, 159, 449.

Ehrenreich, Paul, 38, 65.
Eliot, John, 190.
El Siglo que Acaba, 274.
Ettwein, J., 183, 191.

Faraud, Henry, 21, 394, 395.
Fernandez, Alonzo, 124.
Finch, Prof., 70.
Flint, Earl, 28, 42.
Foley, Dr., 57.
Forneri, R. P., 329.
Förstermann, Dr. E., 200, 243, 251.
Foster, J. W., 67.
França, E. F., 430.
Gabb, William M., 374–378.
Gage, Thomas, 170.
Gallatin, Albert, 88, 100.
Garcia y Garcia, Ap. 165.
Gatschet, A. S., 75, 454 *sq.*
Gayangos, P. de, 449.
Goethe, J. W. von, 260, 284, 316.
Granados y Galvez, I. J., 117.
Gravier, P., 462.
Guzman, Pantaleon de, 107, 128.

Haeckel, E., 390.
Hale, Horatio, 35, 393.
Hamann, 284.
Hamy, E. T., 148, 140, 210, 367.
Harpe, M. de la, 77.
Hartmann, W., 189.

Hartt, Charles F., 380, 382.
Haumonte, J. D., 455 *sq.*
Haynes. H. W., 18, 31.
Heckewelder, John, 191, 315.
Hegel, 403.
Henry, V., 405, 467.
Herder, 284, 403.
Herrera, Antonio de, 89, 91, 92, 448, 450.
Hervas, Abbé, 330.
Hervé, Georges, 62.
Holden, 196, 197.
Holguin, R. P., 426, 428.
Holmes, W. H., 148.
Hovelacque, Abel, 62.
Howse, James, 36, 383, 395, 399, 401, 414, 415.
Humboldt, Alexander von, 20, 33, 60, 251, 338, 374, 377.
Humboldt, Wilhelm von, 36, 284, 318, 328–348, 353, 405.
Hunter, Archdeacon, 403.

Iconographic Encyclopædia, The, 52.
Ixtlilxochitl, F., 84, 87, 90, 92, 97, 283, 445.

Jesuits, Relations des, 78.
Jones, C. C., 79, 80.
Kalm, Peter, 185.
Kane, Paul, 69.
Kingsborough, Lord, 84, 87, 90, 99, 155, 210, 221, 231, 251, 280, 445.
Kollmann, J., 40.

Lacombe, Al., 131, 364, 366, 414.
Lafitau, J. F., 69.
Landa, Diegode, 119, 127, 159, 166, 199, 227, 240 *sq.*, 256, 257, 265, 438.

Lang, Andrew, 102.
Leland, Charles G., 130, 133.
Le Plongeon, A., 439.
Lieber, Francis, 355, 357.
Lindstrom, 183.
Linnæus, C., 38, 349.
Lizaua, Bernardo de, 235, 260, 261.
Lower, M. A., 219.
Lopez, J. M., 164.
Luchan, von, 149.
Lund, Dr., 29.

Macedo, F. de, 148, 157, 159.
MacLean, J. P., 67.
Magalhaes, Dr. Couto de, 381, 430.
Magio, R. P., 397.
Mallery, Garrick, 156, 159.
Manuscrito Hieratico, 225.
Martyr, Peter, 233.
Matthews, Washington, 62, 407.
McGee, W. J., 447.
Meigs, James A., 63.
Mendoza, Gumesindo, 59.
Michel, F., 21.
Mitre, Bartolome, 26, 27.
Molina, Alonso de, 93, 325, 418, 443.
Montesinos, H., 23.
Montigny, M. de, 462.
Montoya, Ruiz de, 381–5, 398, 400, 429.
Morgan, Lewis A., 44, 45, 60.
Morgues, Le Moyne de, 75.
Morse, E. G., 60.
Mortillet, G. de, 390, 391.
Motolinia, P., 85, 99.
Motul, Diccionario de, MS., 119, 127, 177, 250, 325, 421 *sq.*, 435 *sq.*
Müller, Frederick, 230, 357, 374, 379, 380, 386, 465.
Müller, Max, 338.

Narvaez, Pamfilo de, 72.
Naxera, Emanuel, 366, 371.
Neve y Molina, Luis de, 366, 370, 371.
Nikkanoche, Oceola, his narrative, 77.
Nogueira, D. C. Da., 381.
Nostradamus, Michael, 301.

Ollanta, Drama of, 300, 425 *sq.*
Olshausen, 149.
Orozco y Berra, 23, 84, 87, 90, 95, 196, 210, 231, 277, 282, 446.
Ossado, Ricardo, 273.

Paredes, R. P., 420.
Parisot, J., 452 *sq.*
Peñafiel, Antonio, 210.
Perez, Francisco, 366, 370.
Perez, Pio, 120, 263, 264, 272.
Peschel, Oscar, 64.
Petit, Pere C., 77.
Petitot, Emile, 21, 58, 394, 398, 401.
Petrie, Prof., 447.
Piccolomini, Count, 367.
Pickering, Charles, 33.
Pickett, Thomas E., 82.
Pierret, Paul, 138.
Pimentel, Francisco, 368, 373.
Platzmann, Julius, 58.
Ponce, Alonzo, 234, 255.
"Popol Vuh," the, 105 *sq.*, 171, 424.
Powell, J. W., 68, 319, 358.
Pratz, Le Page du, 78.
Prescott, W. H., 84.
Psalmanazar, George, 462, 466.
Putnam, F. A., 53.

Rada y Delgada, J. de D., 226, 227.

INDEX OF AUTHORS AND AUTHORITIES. 473

Rajendalala, 146.
Ramirez, J. F., 23, 88, 196, 210.
Ramusio, 72, note.
Rand, S. T., 130.
Ranke, Dr., 64.
Rau, Charles, 31.
Recetarios de Indios, MS., 272.
Reichelt, G. H., 430.
Registro Yucateco, 164, 263.
Rennenkampff, A. von, 330.
Rink, Heinrich, 287, 289.
Romans, Bernard, 78.
Rosa, Agostin de la, 326, 366, 420.
Rosny, Leon de, 196, 199, 226, 252, 253, 265.
Ruiz de Montoya, Antonio, 381 sq.

Saint Hilaire, J. G. de, 164.
Santa Rosa, Beltran de, 238.
Sahagun, Bernardino de, 84, 86, 88, 93, 94, 97, 142, 280, 298.
Saz, P., 122.
Schasler, Max, 329.
Schellhas, Dr., 196, 200, 202.
Scherzer, Karl, 114.
Schoolcraft, H. R., 69, 133, 294, 354.
Schuhmann, T. S., 430.
Schweinitz, E. de, 430.
Seler, Ed., 196, 244.
Sequoyah, 198.
Shakespeare, W., 127, 219, 220, 320.
Shea, John G., 386.
Short, John T., 67.
Siméon, Rémi, 94, 283.
Smith, Spencer, 81.
Solana, Alonso de, 235.
Soriano, Juan G., 373.
Sosa, F. de P., 164.
Sotomayor, Damaso, 272, 277.

Sotomayor, J. de Villagutierre de, 239, 247.
Spinoza, B., 411.
Squier, E. G., 69, 81, 133.
Steinen, Karl von den, 34.
Steinthal, H., 329, 355, 390, 403.
Stephens, J. L., 164, 168, 263.
Stoll, Dr. Otto, 35, 100, 109, 112, 122, 423.
Storm, Gustav, 22.
Strebel, M. H., 275.
Sungimoto, K., 151.

Tanner, John, 157.
Tapia Zenteno, Carlos de, 423.
Taylor, S., 70.
Ten Kate, Dr. H. F. C., 66.
Testera, Jacobo de, 233.
Tetlapan Quetzanitzin, 299.
Teza, E., 332.
Tezozomoc, A., 23, 89, 93, 143, 283.
Thavenet, Abbé, 332.
Thiel, B. A., 375, 379.
Thomas, Cyrus, 82, 106, 200, 204, 230, 269.
Timberlake, Lieutenant, 71.
Tolmie, W. F., 396.
Topinard, Paul, 64.
Torquemada, J. de, 94, 234.
Tro y Ortolano, Juan de, 252.
Tschudi, J. J. von, 365, 397, 404.

Uricoechea, E., 400, 401.

Vaca, Cabeza de, 72.
Valades, D., 206.
Valentini, P. J. J., 197, 227, 228, 243, 263, 375.
Varea, Francisco, 106, 110, 129, 442.
Vedas, the, 142.
Vega, Garcilasso de la, 73, 77.
Veitia, E., 84, 90, 97.

Vico, R. P., 110.
Villacañas, Benito de, 107.
Villalpando, R. P., 250.
Villagutierre Soto-Mayor, Juan de, 239, 247.
Vinson, Julien, 453, 467.
Virchow, Rudolph, 63, 64, 153, 158.

Waitz, Theo., 260.
Waldeck, Baron de, 254.
Whitney, William D., 327.
Whittlesey, Charles, 447.
Williams, Roger, 131.

Winkler, Heinrich, 58, 350, 351, 386, 399.
Winsor, Justin, 18.
Woodham, 219.
Worsaae, J. J. A., 153, 158.
Wuttke, Dr., 250, 252.
Wyman, Jeffries, 28.

Ximenez, Francisco, 105, 111, etc.

Zegarra, G. Pacheco, 426.
Zeisberger, D., 187, 189.
Zetina, Lic. ,164, 172, 175.

INDEX OF SUBJECTS.

Abañeenga, language, 381.
Abipones, language of, 336.
Abundance, the house of, 145.
Acheron, the river of Hades, 141.
Acolhuacan, 86.
Acozpa, hieroglyph of, 224.
Adjectives, absence of, 405.
Adjidjiatig, or grave posts of Chipeways, 228.
Age of Iron, Bronze, and Stone, 49.
Agglutination in language, 340, 361.
Ahau katuns of Mayas, 264, 268, 269.
Ahkul Chel, a Maya priest, 248.
Ahpu, magicians, 118.
Ah-raxa-lak, a sacred name, 117.
Ah-raxa-sel, a sacred name, 117.
Ahuitzotzin, Emperor of Mexico, 281-3.
Akahal tribe, 423.
Algonkin grammar, remarks on, 190, 364, 366.
Algonkin language, extension of, 35; radicals of, 36, 332, 400; "love words" in, 413.
Algonkins, hero-god of, 130-134.
Algonkin stock, area of, 311.
Algonkin tribes, their "grandfather," 184; as mound-builders, 70; legendary origin of, 24.

Alliteration, rare in primitive poetry, 285.
Allibamons, 71.
Alphabet, of Cherokees, 199; of Valades, 200; in early speech, 393; of Landa, 199, 240-245; of Chinese, etc., 214.
Alternating consonants, 398.
Amenti, the Egyptian Hades, 137.
American languages, tenacity of, 35; diversity of, 35; traits of, 36; study of, 37, 308 *sq.*
American Indians, origin of, 17.
Anahuac, 84.
Analtes, sacred books of Itzas, 239, 247.
Andover, a rebus of, 223.
Animals, transformation into, 114, 170, 171.
Animate and inanimate conjugations, 406.
Animism, doctrine of, 117.
Anthropoid apes, not found in America, 43.
Anthropology, classification in, 349.
Apaches, language of, 35, 394.
Apalacha, fabulous description of, 76.
Apap, god of evil, in Egypt, 137.
Araucanian language, 398.
Araucanians, skulls of, 39.

INDEX OF SUBJECTS.

Arawacks, tribe, 40; language, 430.
Argillite implements, 41.
Arithmetic of Mayas, 268.
Arizona, ruins in, 25.
Arrhenic gender, 406.
Arrow, in Lenape, 183.
Arrow heads, ancient forms of, 31.
Arrow-release, the American, 60.
Arsut, a song of 290.
Art, American, wholly indigenous, 60.
Arthur, King, story of, 130, 142.
Artificial shell-heaps, age of 27.
Aryan languages, the, 312, 323, 344, 358; dialects, alleged, in America, 59; nations, mythology of, 141.
Assumptive arms, in heraldry, 219.
Astrology, native Yucatecan, 259.
Astronomic cycles of Mexicans and Mayas, 23.
Asymmetry, intentional, 448.
Athapascan language, the, 21, 58, 394; extension of the, 35; elements of, 36.
Atecpanamochco, 86.
Atlantis, the fabled, 43.
Atoyac, the river, 86.
Auroral gods, 111, 113.
Autochthony of American culture, 60.
Avalon, the Isle of, 142.
Aymarian depression in American skulls, 62.
Azteca *or* Aztecs, 85, 87, 367.
Aztec calendar explained, 276-9; codices, 221; love songs, 295-7; war songs, 298; year cycles of, 159, *see* Nahuatl, Mexican.
Aztlan, derivation of, 88.

Bacab, Maya deities, 173.
Baffin's Land, natives of, 286.
Balam, meaning of, 128, 258; the Maya prophet, 248.
Balams, Maya deities, 172-176.
Ball play in Mexico, 89.
Banana, not an American plant, 33, 34.
Basque language, the, 316, 351.
Bát, as a totemic animal, 114.
Baures, language of, 397.
Beard in American Indians, 39.
Being and Not-Being, in language, 401.
Biceitas, tribe, 375.
Bilderschrift, 207.
Birds as winds, 123, 175; symbolism of, 169, 179.
Bi-sexual divinities, 96, 109.
Blackfeet, myths of, 131.
Black-tail, a fabulous snake, 178.
Blood, in myths, 114, 124.
Blowpipe, use of, 109.
Blue, as sacred color, 95, 118.
Boat of the Sun, 138; of Charon, 141.
Bokol k'otoch, a Maya imp, 178.
Bones, collection of, 78.
Book, Maya word for, 247.
Books of Chilan Balam, 255 *sqq*.
Books of Mayas described, 232, 235, 237.
Bolivia, tribes of, 397, 405.
Boruca language, the, 375 *sq*.
Botocudos, traits of, 38, 39, 40, 65.
Bow-and-arrow, modern use of, 31, 183.
Brachycephalism in America, 63.
Brazil, designs of pottery from, 157, 159; mound-builders from, 67; ethnology of, 38, 40; lan-

INDEX OF SUBJECTS. 477

guages of, 380 *sq.*, 428 *sq.*; shell heaps in, 28.
Bri-bri language, the, 374 *sq.*
Bronka *or* Brunka language, 375 *sq.*
Bronze, Age of, 49, 50.
Brush-net, use of, 184.
Buenos Ayres, archæology of, 31, 40.
Buffalo, Lenâpé name for, 184.
Burial customs, 75, 77, 78, 119.
Burial mounds in Florida, 75.

Cabecar language, the, 375 *sq.*
Cabrakan, god of earthquakes, 121, 122.
Cachis, tribe, 375.
Cahokia, pyramid at, 81.
Cakchiquels, totemic animals, 114; language, 35, 104, 106, 107, 345, 347, 370, 423; lineal measures of, 433, 439; writing of, 228.
Cakulha-Hurakan, a Quiche god, 120, 121.
Calaveras skull, the, 40.
Calculiform writing explained, 243, 253.
Calendar, mystic relations of, 99, 129; of Mexicans, 276-8; the Quiche-Cakchiquel, 129; of the Taensas, 469.
California, languages of, 386; auriferous gravels of, 31; remains from, 40.
Campeachy, Bay of, 233.
Canals, ancient, in Florida, 73.
Canek, chief of Itzas, 239.
Cannibalism, unknown in Yucatan, 235.
Canoes, manufacture of, 185.
Cantico, meaning of, 187.
Canting arms, in heraldry, 218.

Capaha, the village of, 73.
Caracaracol, a Haytian divinity, 116.
Cardinal points, sacred characters, 154, 161, 166, 167, 172, 175; signs for in Maya, 203.
Carib language, 331, 337.
Caribs, mythology of, 123.
Carvara, the dog, 141.
Catarrhine monkeys not found in America, 43.
Ceh Pech, a province of Yucatan, 233.
Central America, poetry of, 288.
Centzon Huitznahua, the, 94.
Cerberus, the dog, 141, 146.
Chiapas, dialects of, 420.
Cincalco, in Aztec myth, 145.
Civilization, centers of, 61.
Chac, Maya deities, 173.
Chahta-Muskokee family, the, 71, 79.
Chahta tribes, the, 80, 81; *see* Choctaws.
Chan Pal, a Maya imp, 177.
Chapallan, Lake, 88.
Chapanec language, 398.
Charon, the ferryman, 141.
Chelles, objects from, 32.
Cherokees, wars with Iroquois, 69; as mound-builders, 71, 82; alphabet, 198.
Che Vinic, a Maya ogre, 176.
Chibcha language, 400.
Chicagua, a village, 73.
Chichen Itza, 254, 302.
Chichimecs, tribe, 90, 298.
Chicomoztoc, land of, 23.
Chikasaws, 71.
Chilan, signification of, 258, 260, 272; prophecy of, 303.

INDEX OF SUBJECTS.

Chilan Balam, books of, 255.
Chile, languages of, 398.
Chimalman, the virgin, 96.
Chinese, alphabet of, 214, 215; language, the, 323, 336; supposed presence in America, 59; philosophy and symbolism, 150, 151.
Chipi-cakulha, a Quiche god, 120.
Chipeways, build mounds, 70; myths of, 131.
Chipeway pronouns, 324; pictography, 228.
Chipeways, their "grandfather," 188.
Chipeway love song, 294; love words, 418.
Chipped Stone, period of, 50.
Chiquita language, 405.
Chirakan Xmucane, a Quiche goddess, 122.
Choctaws, 24, 71, 77, 461; *see* Chahta.
Choctaw language, the, 364.
Chronological system of Mayas, 263.
Chumayel, book of, 248, 257, 291.
"Chunk yards" of the Creeks, 76.
Clark's Works, mounds at, 81.
Classification of languages, 339.
Coatepetl, the, 86, 89.
Coatlan Tonan, an Aztec goddess, 94.
Codices, the existing Maya, 250.
Coatlicue, an Aztec goddess, 94, 95.
Colhua, Colhuacan, 85.
Color of American Indians, 39, 61.
Colors in races of men, 38; phonetic value in hieroglyphs, 223; symbolism of, 166, 167.
Columbian gravel, relics found in, 53.

Communal burial, 78.
Communal dwellings, 185, 445.
Conjunctions, in American languages, 345, 404.
Connecticut, Indian names in, 309.
Consonants, alternating, 398; significance of, 394.
Copan, calendar stone from, 155, 254.
Coptic, ancient, 215, 402.
Cordova, Hernandez de, his expedition, 232.
Cortes, H., his conquest, 280, 282.
Costa Rica, age of shell-heaps in, 28, 31; languages of, 374 *sq.*
Counter-sense in language, 401.
Courous, tribe, 77.
Coyote, as sacred animal, 112.
Cozumel, island of, 232.
Cranial characteristics of red race, 62, 63.
Craniologic data from the mounds, 82.
Cranioscopic formulas of American Indians, 40.
Cree, language, 21, 363, 383, 395, 401, 403; love words in, 413.
Crees, myths of, 131.
Creeks, 24, 71, 76.
Criteria of languages, 336.
Cross, as a sacred symbol, 148 *sqq.*
Cubit, as a measure, 441.
Cukulkan, 84.
Culcalkin, a Maya ogre, 177.
Culture-heroes, American, 130.
Cycles, of Aztecs and Mayas, 159, 264.

Dakotas, 79; winter counts of, 159; dialects, 407.
Dawn, master of the, 113.

INDEX OF SUBJECTS.

Day-maker, the, 111, 129.
Days, signs of, in Maya MSS., 270.
Death, prognostics of, 169; lord of, 170; primitive notion of, 143; river of, 147.
Deer, as totemic animal, 114, 128.
Delaware, State, discoveries in, 32, 53.
Delaware river, relics from, 41, 53.
Delaware Indians, *see* Lenâpé.
Déuè Dindjié, tribe, 21; language, 395.
Dependent clauses, 404.
Determinatives, their use in writing, 216.
Devil, words for, 126.
Diluvial epoch, human remains in, 29.
Divination, by beans, 118; by thorns, 94; by stones, 165.
Diviners, of Mayas, 165.
Dogs, as sacred animals, 140, 141, 144, 146.
Dresden, the Maya MS. at, 250.
Dwarfs, fabulous, of Mayas, 177.
Dyes used by the Mayas, 246.

Earth, the heart of the, 126.
Ego, phonetic element of, 396.
Egyptian theory of the soul, 136–140; hieroglyphic origin of, 216; alphabet, 217.
Eight, as sacred number, 140, 146.
Ekoneil, a fabulous snake, 179.
Elephant, the American, 32.
Elysium, fields of, 141.
Epicanthus, in America, 64.
English language, the, 336.
Epochs of the Palæolithic Period, 51.
Escamela, inscribed stone at, 274.

Eskimo, skulls of, 63; physical traits of, 65; songs of, 286–290; language, 58, 538, 340.
Etowah valley, mound in, 80.
Eye, oblique or Mongolian, in America, 63, 64.

Fac-simile of Landa's MS., 242.
Father, the great, 175.
Feathers, as symbolic ornaments, 116.
Female line, hereditary, 189.
Fire, earliest knowledge of, 391; festival of, among Mayas, 168.
Fish, the, in Aztec calendar, 283.
Fishing, ancient methods of, 184.
Fleur-de-lys, origin of, 220.
Flores, island, capture of, 239.
Florida, ancient mounds in, 73, 75, 77; shell heaps in, 28, 31; limonite skeletons from, 41.
Folk-lore of Yucatan, 163; of Lenâpé, 181.
Food-plants of native Americans, 33.
Foot, as measure of length, 434 *sq.*, 444.
Four, as sacred number, 140, 146, 157.
Four Ages of World, 161.
Four hundred, meaning of, 94.
Friendship, native words for, 420, 428.
Fuegians, appearance of, 39; language, 338.

Games, of Lenâpé, 186.
Generation, gods of, 120.
Georgia, antiquities in, 80.
Ghosts, superstitions about, 127.
Giant bison, the American, 41, note.

Giant Grab, 176; Stone of the, 274 sq.
Glacial age in North America, date of, 41, 44, 54; in South America, 42, 55.
Gluskap the Liar, a Micmac hero 130.
Grammatic forms, origin of, 331.
Grammatical categories, the, 405.
Graphic systems, phonetic elements of, 195 sq.
Graphic system of Mayas, 245.
Greek language, the, 344, 348.
Green, as a color symbol, 118.
Greenland, poetry from, 287–290.
Grijalva, Juan de, his expedition, 232.
Guadalajara, University of, 326.
Guarani, language, 35, 380 sq., 398, 399, 400; love words in, 428.
Guarayos, bearded Indians, 39, note.
Guatemala, dialects in, 104; tribes of, 105, 420.
Gucumatz, derivation of, 116; transformations of, 171.
Gucumatz Catuha, a king, 114.
Guiana, shell-heaps in, 31; ethnology of, 39, 40.
Gulf States, antiquities of, 72–80.

Hades, derivation of, 141; descent to, 125-6.
Hair, of American Indians, 62; of the Sun-god, 99, 140, 146; long, as symbol, 146, 280.
Hare, the Great, 132.
Harmachis, Egyptian divinity, 138.
Hatchet, burying the, 71.
Hayti, mythology of, 116, 121.

"Heart of the Lake," a sacred name, 116.
Heart, as a symbol, 117.
Hell, words for, 126, 127; descent to, 123–130.
Hemenway Exploring Expedition, 25.
Heraldry, methods of, 218, 219.
Hermapolis, eight gods of, 140.
Hesperides, garden of the, 142.
Hidatsa language, 407.
Hieroglyphs, Maya, 201, 265-7.
Hog, the, as a god, 113.
Holophrasis, explained, 322, 354 sq.
Homo alalus, the, 390–392.
Homophones in languages, 198, 215, 216.
Hooks, used in fishing, 184.
Horus, the Egyptian, 138.
Horse, Delaware word for, 321; fossil, in America, 31, 32, 42.
Houses, of beams, 97; communal, 185.
Huasteca language, the, 221, 331, 343; love words in, 422.
Hueman, an Aztec hero-god, 96.
Huguenots, settlement of, 74.
Huitzilopochtli, an Aztec god, 85, 88; derivation of, 95; birth of, 96; temple of, 25.
Huitznahua, Aztec divinities, 94, 95.
Human species, divisions of, 38.
Humor, among native Americans, 288.
Hun-ahpu, birth of. 125.
Hun-ahpu-utiu, derivation, 112.
Hun-ahpu-vuch, derivation of, 109.
Hun-came, a Quiche god, 124.
Hunhun-ahpu, a Quiche god, 124.

INDEX OF SUBJECTS.

Hunting, ancient methods of, 184.
Hunyecil, meaning of, 237.
Hurakan, god of the storm, 120–123.
Hurons, burial customs, 69.
Hurricane, derivation of, 121, 122; lord of, 167.

Ichcanziho, ancient name of Merida, 233.
Ideograms in phonetic writing, 197; of Mayas, 248.
Idols of Lenâpé, 187; of Itzas, 240; priest of, 248.
Idols, superstitions concerning, 177.
Ikonographic writing, 213.
Ikonomatic method of phonetic writing, 86, 89, 207, 211, 213–229, 281.
Illinois, archæology of, 40, 81.
Implements, simple and compound, 30, 51, 52.
Inca bone, the, 62.
Incas of Peru, false lists of, 23.
Incorporative character of American languages, 36.
Incorporation, explained, 321, 340, 341, 352–357, 403.
Indo-Aryans, myths of, 146.
Industrial art in ancient America, 29.
Ioskeha, Iroquois hero-god, 130.
Iron, Age of, 49, 50.
Iroquois, 24, 68, 69; Lenâpé name for, 184.
Itza, town in Yucatan, 302.
Itzamul, temples of, 236.
Itzamna, hero-god of Mayas, 238.
Itzas, the tribe of, 239.
Iztimquilpan, hieroglyph of, 223.

Jaguar, as sacred animal, 128.
Japanese writing, 231.
Jesuits, settlement near Savannah, 76.
Jew, Book of the, 273.
Jonaz language, the, 368.

Katun, lord of the, 249; of Mayas, 260.
Katuns, of Mayas, 159.
Kaua, Book of Chilan Balam of, 268.
Kentucky, archæology of, 82.
Khetsua language, *see* Qquichua.
Kiches, *see* Quiches.
Kichigouai, Algonkin divinities, 111.
Kin Ich, a Maya deity, 170.
Kinich-ahau, hero-god of Mayas, 238.
Kioways, songs of, 293.
Klamath language, the, 321, 398.
Koonak, Mt., poem about, 290.
Kitchen-middens, in America, 27.

Labrador, natives of, 311.
Lacandon, province of, 239.
Lagoa Santa, skulls from, 40.
La Naulette, jaw from, 390.
Language, ethnologic value of, 193; origin of, 390.
Languages discussed: *See tribal names.*
Laws of Thought, 402.
Lead, known to Mexicans, 450.
Leif Erikson, his voyage, 22.
Left hand, as stronger, 95.
Legends, value in savage tribes, 24.
Lenâpé, Folk-lore of the, 181; derivation of, 183.

Lenâpé dialect, pronunciation of, 189; grammar of, 190, 191, 313.
Letters, single, significant, 394.
Life, the Tree of, 161.
Light, the mother of, 119; divinity of, 112, 129.
Lightning, as a deity, 121, 133, 174.
Lingoa Geral, of Brazil, 380.
Limonite skeletons from Florida, 41.
Lineal measures, American, 433 *sq.*
Linguistic stocks, number of in America, 34; origin of, 392.
Lithuanian dialect, the, 316.
Lorelei, an American, 178.
Love, songs of, 293-7; conceptions of in American languages, 410 *sq.*, definition of, 432.
Lulé language, the, 331, 342.

Mbaya language, the, 331, 342, 343.
Mackenzie River, tribes of, 35.
Madrid, Maya MSS. at, 253.
Maguey, the, a sacred plant. 88; paper, 253.
Maize, origin and extension of, 33.
Maiayan race, the, 349.
Malinalxochitl, an Aztec goddess, 88.
Mammoth, remains of, 32.
Manabozho, a Chipeway hero, 131, 133.
Man, not developed in America, 43; oldest remains of, in America, 53; a singing animal, 284; subdivisions of, 348.
Manco Capac, his date, 22.
Mandioca, a native food-plant, 33.

Manhattan, derivation of, 183.
Mani, the Book of Chilan of, 264.
Manuscripts in Maya characters, 250.
Mapachtepec, hieroglyph of, 222.
Maps of Mayas, 438.
Markets, Mexican, 449.
Marriage song, 460.
Masks, used in rites, 114, 187.
Mass, the field, 165.
Maya language, the, 181, 345; love words in, 420; civilization, 84; witch story, 171; year-counts, 159; phonetic characters, 199, hieroglyphic system, 227, 228;
Mayas, ancient, writings and records of, 230-254; earliest ancestors of, 24; the, traditions of, 22; conversion of, 164; folk-lore of, 162; burial customs of, 119; lineal measures of, 434; maps of, 438.
Mayacimil, meaning of, 237.
Mayapan, ancient city of, 239.
Maya-Qniche linguistic stock, 104.
Mazahna language, the, 368, 372 *sq.*
Meco language, the, 368.
Meconetzin, a name of Quetzalcoatl, 88.
Meday magic, figures in, 157.
Meda sticks of Chipeways, 228.
Medical practice among Delawares, 187.
Medicines of the Mayas, 272.
Medicine-songs, native, 292.
Mengwe, name of Iroquois, meaning of, 184.
Merida, ancient ruins at, 26, 233.
Messier Mound, the, 80.
Messianic hope, among natives, 183.

Messou, *see* Michabo.
Meta river, tribes of, 329.
Metrical standards, native, 446-8.
Mexcalla, an island, 88.
Mexi *or* Mexica, 85, 87.
Mexican phonetic writing, 205.
Mexitl, an Aztec chief, 88.
Mexico, ancient, 23, 84, 88, 282; human remains in, 42.
Mexican grammar, 324, 341, 344, 346. *See* Aztec, Nahuatl.
Mexico-Tenochtitlan, 85.
Micmacs, mythology of, 130.
Michabo, a Chipeway deity, 131, 132-4.
Michoacan, 88.
Mictlan, the Aztec Hades, 143.
Mictlantecutli, the Aztec Pluto, 145.
Migration, lines of in America, 44, 45.
Minsi tribe, 181; derivation of, 189.
Mississippi, the, 74, 77.
Mitla, ruins of, 448.
Mixteca language, the, 331, 345.
Mongolian affinities, alleged, of the American race, 56.
Mongolian eye, the, in America, 63.
Mongoloid traits in Americans, 38, 39, 56.
Monosyllabism in languages, 215.
Montejo, Francisco de, 233.
Montezuma, his hieroglyphs, 208, 209, 282; his forebodings, 302.
Montezuma, Rio de, 86.
Months, hieroglyphs of, of Mayas, 265-7.
Moon, origin of, 125.
Moraines, the line of, in North America, 54.

Moteuczomatzin, 283.
Mound-Builders, their nationality, 67; their metrical standard, 447.
Mounds in Ohio and Mississippi valleys, age of, 27.
Mural paintings, of Mayas, 254.
Muskokees, 71, 75.
Mutsun language, 386 *sq.*
Mythology, interpretations of, 101.

Nabula, the book of, 259.
Nagualism, in Central America, 170.
Nahua ollin, the, 161.
Nahuatl hieroglyphs, dictionary of, 210; geographic names, 210; lineal measures, 444.
Nahuatl language, 23, 59, 205, 363, 366, 399; love words in, 417.
Nahuas, tribes of, 22, 85, 418. *See* Aztecs, Mexicans.
Names, bestowal of, 114.
Nanabojoo, a Chipeway hero, 131.
Nanahuatl, an Aztec divinity, 116.
Nanih Waiya, the Sloping Hill, 80.
Nanticokes, native name of, 189.
Napiw, a Blackfoot hero, 131.
Nasal index in American Indians, 39, 64.
Natchez, 71, 77, 78, 463.
Navaho language, 394.
Nebraska, ancient lake-beds of, 31.
Nenaboj, a Chipeway hero, 131.
Neolithic period, the, 30, 51.
New England Indians, 131.
Newfoundland, natives of, 311.
New Granada, tribes of, 330; languages, 400.
New Jersey, archæology of, 32, 53.
New Mexico, ruins in, 25.

INDEX OF SUBJECTS.

New York State, earth-works in, 69.
Nezahualcoyotl, a chief, 445.
Nicaragua, ancient human footprints in, 42.
Night, master of the, 113.
Nim-ak, meaning of, 113.
Nine Waters, river of, 143.
Nith songs of Eskimo, 287.
Norsemen, myths of, 142.
North Pacific coast, tribes of, 65.
Northmen, voyages of, 22, note.
Nova Scotia, discovered by Northmen, 22.
Nun, the celestial river, 137, 139.
Numbers, sacred or mystic, 99. *See* Four, Seven, Twelve, etc.
Numerals, deficiency of, 326.
Numeration, Maya signs of, 268; words for, 406.

Oblique eye as racial trait, 39, 63, 64.
Obsidian found in Ohio, 32.
Occipital bone in American skulls, 62.
Ocelotl, *or* jaguar, in myths, 128.
Ocnakuchil, meaning of 237.
Ogier the Dane, 142.
Ohio, mounds in, 27, 67-81; obsidian in, 32.
Ojibway picture writing, 153, 154.
Offogoula, tribe, 77.
Ollanta, drama of, 300.
Omagua language, 405.
Oriental symbols in America, 148 *sqq.*
Origin of language, 317.
Orinoco, tribes of, 405.
Orizaba, inscribed stone at, 274.
Orosi, natives at, 375.

Os Incæ, the, in Americans, 62.
Osiris, the Egyptian god, 137-140.
Otchipwe language, the, 364.
Otherness, how expressed, 396.
Otomis, *or* Othomis, the tribe, 117: war songs, 298.
Otomi language, the, 59, 366 *sq.*
Ouspie, tribe, 77.
Owl, superstitions concerning, 114, 169.

Pacaha, a province, 74.
Paducas, tribe of, 291.
Pah ah tun, Maya deities, 166, 173.
Palœoliths, American and other, 48.
Palæolithic period, the, 30, 51, 390.
Palæolithic man, his habitat, 54; language, 390 *sq.*
Palenque, the ruins of, 26, 84, 126, 254, 448.
Palpan, a place name, 87.
Pame language, the, 368, 373.
Pampas, lacustrine deposits of, 31; skulls from, 40.
Papa, name of Quetzalcoatl, 99.
Paper of Maya MSS., 253.
Paradise, the Aztec, 144.
Patagonians, height of, 39.
Patine, as a sign of age, 51.
Pavant Indians, the, 321.
Pawnees, poetry of, 291-2.
Pech, a Maya priest, 302.
Pennsylvania, ancient works in, 70; Indian names in, 309; relics found in, 53.
Penobscots, mythology of, 130.
Personality, idea of in language, 320.
Peru, ruined cities of, 26.

INDEX OF SUBJECTS. 485

Peruvians, language of, 397; songs of, 300.
Peten, Lake, conquest of, 239.
Petroglyph, near Orizaba, 274.
Philosophy of language, 328.
Phonetic elements, origin of, 393.
Phonetics of Mexican and Maya writing, 195.
Phoneticism in writing, origin of, 216.
Picture writing, 213, 231; Ojibways, 153, 154, 228; of Mexicans, 221 *sq.*
Pirinda language, the, 368, 372.
Pisote, the white, 113.
Pleasure, physiological principle of, 285.
Pleistocene epoch, human remains in, 29.
Plumed serpents, house of, 97.
Plummet, unknown in America, 442, 450.
Pluto, the Greek god, 141.
Poetry, native American, 284 *sq.*
Pokonchi dialect, the, 104, 112.
Polished stone, period of, 50.
Polychromatic hieroglyphs, 223.
Polynesians, alleged migrations of, 18, 43.
Polysynthesis, explained, 36, 321, 351 *sq.*
Pontemelo, ancient skull from, 40.
Pop, name of a Maya month, 249.
Popol vuh, the, 105 *sq.*
Potato, the, its extension, 33.
Pottery, designs on, 157, 159; of Lenâpé, 185.
Pound-the-stones, Miss, 179.
Prehistoric archæology, 392.
Prepositions, in American languages, 345.

Pronominal languages, 320.
Pronouns, in American languages, 396-8.
Proper names, in early times, 218.
Prophecies of Mexicans and Mayas, 302.
Pueblo Indians, 25, 87.
Pulque, liquor made from, 254.

Quetzalcoatl, 24, 84 *sq.*; baths of, 86; absent, 145.
Quiches, myths of, 104 *sq.*, 124, 171; dialect of the, 104, 423; king of, 114; lineal measures of, 433; writing of, 228; sacred book of, 105 *sq.*, 171.
Qquichua language, the, 346, 365, 425; traditions, 22; love-words in, 425 *sq.*
Qux cah, a sacred name, 116.
Qux cho, a sacred name, 116, 120.
Qux palo, a sacred name, 116.

Ra, the sun-god, 137, 140.
Rabbit myths, 112, 132, 179, 276.
Races of men, 348.
Rain, the gods of, 175.
"Rakan," meaning of, 122.
Rattlesnake bites, cure for, 188.
"Rax," in Quiche, meaning of, 118.
Raxa-cakulha, a Quiche god, 120.
Rebus, method of writing by, 211, 215, 219.
Red, as sacred color, 144, 166, 176.
Refref, serpent in Egyptian myth, 137.
Relative pronouns, in American languages, 346.
Religious sentiment, the, 432.
Remedies, native, 272.

INDEX OF SUBJECTS.

Repetition, in poetry, 285.
Reproductive principle, worship of, 119.
Rhyme, unknown in native poetry, 285.
Ring-cross, the, 158.
Rio de Montezuma, 86.
Rio de Tula, 86.
Ritual of the dead, in Egypt, 139.
Rituals of Mayas, 247.
River, the celestial and infernal, 137–145.
Rock Bluff, skulls from, 40.
Rosetta stone, the, 218.

St. Augustine, Florida, 74, 75, 77.
St. John River, 74.
St. Louis, "big mound" at, 81.
San Isidro, stone relics from, 391.
Sacred book of the Quiches, 105, 107.
Saliva, in myths, 124.
Salonge, an ogre, 176.
Salt, magic power of, 171.
Sanscrit language, the, 340, 344, 415; alleged affinity with Nahuatl, 57.
Sambaquis, shell heaps in Brazil, 28, 29.
Sarbacane, the, 109.
Sauteux, language of, 400.
Savacon, a Carib deity, 123.
Schipka cave, bones from, 390.
Sciences of the Mayas, 245.
Seminoles, 71, 77.
Semitic traditions, supposed in America, 21.
Serpent, as sacred animal, 116, 132, 133.
Serpent mount, the, 86.
Serpent, fabulous, of Mayas, 179.

Seven, as sacred number, 124, 129, 171, 439.
Seven Caves, land of the, 23.
Sex distinctions in grammar, 406.
Shell-heaps, the age of, 27; in Florida, Tennessee, Costa Rica, Brazil, 28; in Gulf States, 72.
Shooting stars, in myths, 174.
Shoshonian family, languages of, 23.
Signatures of natives, 234.
Skin, color of, in American Indians, 39.
Skull, shape of, in Americans, 63.
Skulls, types of, in Brazil, 29.
Sky, soul of the, 120.
Snake-Hill, the, 86.
Sodomy, not found in Yucatan, 235.
Sonora, languages of, 23.
Soto, Hernando de, his expedition, 72, 74.
Soul, seat of, 117; food of the, 168; Journey of the, 135–145.
Sound-writing, 213, 230.
Span, as measure, 441.
Speech, earliest form of, 390 *sq.*
Speechless man, 390–392.
Spiral, development of the, 159, note.
Spittle, as genetic fluid, 124.
Squaw, word for, 181.
Stars, origin of, 125.
Stature of American Indians, 39.
Stone, age of, its subdivisions, 50; survivals of, 183.
Stone and brick edifices, 25.
Stone of the Giants, 274 *sq.*
Stone implements, oldest specimens, 391.
Stone, the clear, divination by, 165.

INDEX OF SUBJECTS. 487

Stones, adoration of, 40; column of, 70.
Storm, Quiche gods of, 120.
Straw bird, the, 179.
Sun-god, Aztec myth of, 116; in Yucatan, 167.
Sun, origin of, 125; worship in Egypt, 137–140; in America, 146; in picture writing, 156–8.
Sun worship in Apalacha, 76; "brother of," 77, 78; the mother of, 119; four motions of, 157, 161; worship, 170; place of the, 93; creation of, 95; rays of in symbolism, 146, 280.
Svastika, the, as a symbol, 148 *sqq.*
Sweat lodge, of Lenâpé, 187.
Syllabic writing, 231.
Symbols, phonetic, 197; the sacred, in America, 149 *sqq.*
Symbolic writing, 213.
Syncope in American languages, 371.
Syphilis, sacred associations of, 115, 116, 144.

Taensa language, the hoax of, 452 *sq.*
Ta Ki, a Chinese symbol, 148 *sqq.*
Tales, Indian, 182.
Tamanaca language, the, 331.
Tamaulipas, Sierra of, 295.
Tampa Bay, mound at, 75.
Tamuch, a Huasteca town, 221.
Tarascas, a tribe, 228.
Tat Acmo, a Maya deity, 175.
Tata Polin, a Maya sprite, 170.
Tat Ich, a Maya sprite, 170.
Tennessee River, shell heaps on, 28.
Tenochtitlan, 25, 85, 100.

Tenochtitlan, state of, 23, 283.
Teotihuacan, ruins of, 446.
Tepeu, sacred name, meaning of, 115.
Terminos, Bahia de, 232.
Terraba language, the, 375 *sq.*
Tertiary, human remains in, 43.
Tezcatlipoca, 85, 90; the black and white, 96; contests of, 98.
Tezcuco, State of, 23, 25, 86, 445.
Tezcucans, the, 367; philosophy of, 154.
Thirteen, as sacred number, 161, 167.
T'Ho, native name of Merida, 26.
Thought-writing, 213, 230.
Three-legged figures, 149.
Thunder, in mythology, 174.
Tiahuanaco, ruins near, 26.
Tiger, as totemic animal, 114, 128.
Time, idea of, absent, 404.
Time-wheel, Mexican, 160, 161.
Timuquana tribe, 75.
Tin, use of, 86.
Tinné language, 35, 394, 400.
Tiribi language, the, 375 *sq.*
Titicaca, Lake, ruins near, 26.
Tlacopan, State of, 23, 299.
Tlalocan, the Aztec Paradise, 144.
Tlalocs, Aztec rain-gods, 144.
Tlamapa, hieroglyph of, 225.
Tlapallan, the place of colors, 87.
Tlapan, hieroglyph of, 224.
Tobacco, its origin and extension, 33.
Tollan, 93.
Tollanatl, the, 86, 96.
Toltecs, supposed mound-builders, 67; their fabulous history, 24, 83–100; their mythical home, 145.

INDEX OF SUBJECTS.

Tomahawk, word for, 183.
Tomaka, a town, 77.
Tonacatecutli, an Aztec god, 96.
Tonalan, the sunny place, 93.
Topiltzin, king of Tula, 84.
Totem marks, as autographs, 234.
Totemic deities, 88, 113, 114; divisions of Lenâpé, 189.
Tradition, permanence of, in savages, 22.
Transitions in verbs, 370.
Tree of Life, in Maya and Mexican art, 161.
Trenton gravels, objects discovered in, 32, 53.
Trepanned skulls from Peru, 188.
Trephining, among the Lenâpé, 188.
Tribute rolls of ancient Mexicans, 231.
Triplicate constitution of things, 154.
Triple division of the human race, 57.
Triquetrum, as a symbol, 149 *sqq.*
Triskeles, a sacred symbol, 149 *sqq.*
Tucurrique, tribes at, 375.
Tula, the story of, 83–100; derivation, 93.
Tupi, the language, 323, 343, 380 *sq.*, 400; love words in, 428.
Turanian languages, 58.
Turtle totem of Lenâpé, 189.
Twins, the divine, 125.
Twelve, as sacred number, 187.
Tzendal dialect, 126.
Tzontemoc, Aztec deity, 146.
Tzontemoc mictlan tecutli, 278–9.
Tzutuhil dialect, the, 104, 434.

Ua ua pach, a Maya god, 176.
Ucita, a town in Florida, 75.
Underworld, the, in Quiche myth, 125; in other tribes, 128.
Uniter, the Great, 150.
Unwritten languages, study of, 305.
Ural-Altaic languages, 58.
Ursua, General, expedition of, 239.
Usumasinta, river, 126.
Ute language, the, 323.
Utlatlan, a Quiche city, 124.

Vaku, a Quiche god, 123.
Valladolid, in Yucatan, 236.
Vancouver's Island, tribes on, 22; black slate from, 32.
Vara, Spanish, length of, 436, 446.
Verb, the American, 347, 405.
Verb, in Algonkin grammar, 190.
Vineland, its position, 22, note.
Virginia, antiquities of, 70.
Virginia, West, Cherokees in, 82.
Virgin-mother, the myths of, 95, 96, 124, 125.
Visuaires, primitive men were, 408.
Vizeitas, tribe, 375.
Vowels, permutable, 398; significance of, 394.
Vuch, the opossum, etc., 111.
Vukub-came, a Quiche god, 124.
Vukub-hun-ahpu, a Quiche god, 124.

Wampum, use among Lenapé, 188.
Warraus, height of, 39.
War clubs, 183.
War Songs of Aztecs, 299 *sq.*
War-whoop, name for, 184.
Way cot, a Maya imp, 178.

Weighing, unknown in America, 434, 449.
West, as abode of souls, 141-144.
West Indies, no palaeoliths in, 42, 55; native tribes of, 310.
Wetncks, a hero-god, 131.
Wheels, of Mayas, for computing time, 264.
Wheel-cross, the, 158.
White, as sacred color, 113, 132, 166, 186, 188.
Wigwams of Lenâpé, 185.
Winds, the gods of, 123, 175.
Winter-counts, of Dakotas, 139.
Wisakketjak, a Cree hero, 131, 132.
Wives, buying, 424.
Wooden utensils of Lenâpé, 185.
Woods, the Man of the, 176.
Words, number of in American tongues, 325.
Writing, different methods of, 213, 230.

Xbalanque, the Quiche hero-god, 123-129.
Xbolonthoroch, a Maya imp, 178.
Xkanleox, a Maya goddess, 166.
Xibalba, the Quiche Hades, 84, 123-129.
Xipacoyan, a river, 86.

Xmucane, a Quiche goddess, 118, 119, 122, 124.
Xocotitlan, a place name, 93.
Xochicalco, hieroglyph of, 282.
Xpiyacoc, a Quiche deity, 118, 119, 124.
Xquiq, the Virgin mother, 124.
Xtabai, a Maya sprite, 178.
Xthol Chaltun, a Maya sprite, 178.

Yancopek, a Maya imp, 178.
Yasons, tribe, 77.
Ycasqui, a province, 74.
Year counts, of natives, 159, 160.
Yellow, symbolism of, 166, 167.
Yin and Yang, 151.
Yucatan, ancient, 302; folk-lore of, 163; dialects in, 104; civilization of, 84; ruins in, 26; legendary peopling of, 24.
Yum cimil, a Maya divinity, 169.
Yurari, the language, 329.

Zaki-nim-ak, name of a god, 113.
Zaki-nami-tzyiz, 113.
Zapote, superstition concerning, 169.
Zapotecs, a Mexican tribe, 228.
Zaztun, the, of Mayas, 165.
Zohol chich, a phantom bird, 179.
Zuñis, the, 108.

Milton Keynes UK
Ingram Content Group UK Ltd.
UKHW020610050324
438776UK00006B/815